Architectural Drawing
Using Pencil Sketches
and AutoCAD®

Architectural Drawing

Using Pencil Sketches and AutoCAD®

JAMES M. KIRKPATRICK
Eastfield College

Prentice
Hall

Upper Saddle River, New Jersey
Columbus, Ohio

Library of Congress Cataloging-in-Publication Data

Kirkpatrick, James M.
   Architectural drawing using pencil sketches and AutoCAD /
James M. Kirkpatrick.
     p. cm.
   Includes index.
   ISBN 0-13-094072-0
   1. Architectural drawing--Data processing. 2. Architecture--Computer-aided design. 3.
AutoCAD. I. Title

NA2728 .K575 2002
720′.28′402855369--dc21

2001036666

Editor in Chief: Stephen Helba
Executive Editor: Debbie Yarnell
Media Development Editor: Michelle Churma
Production Editor: Louise N. Sette
Editorial Assistant: Sam Goffinet
Production Supervision: Lisa Garboski, bookworks
Design Coordinator: Diane Ernsberger
Cover Designer: Jason Moore
Cover art: Jason Moore
Production Manager: Brian Fox
Marketing Manager: Jimmy Stephens

This book was set in Times Roman by STELLARViSIONs and was printed and bound by
Courier Kendallville, Inc. The cover was printed by Phoenix Color Corp.

Pearson Education Ltd., *London*
Pearson Education Australia Pty. Limited, *Sydney*
Pearson Education Singapore Pte. Ltd.
Pearson Education North Asia Ltd., *Hong Kong*
Pearson Education Canada, Ltd., *Toronto*
Pearson Educación de Mexico, S. A. de C.V.
Pearson Education—Japan, *Tokyo*
Pearson Education Malaysia Pte. Ltd.
Pearson Education, *Upper Saddle River, New Jersey*

10 9 8 7 6 5 4 3 2 1
ISBN: 0-13-094072-0

Preface

The purpose of this textbook is to teach the fundamentals of architectural drawing through the use of sketches on gridded paper done with triangles, a circle template, and a minimum of other tools and supplies. In addition, the student is introduced to the Auto-CAD program as partially drawn AutoCAD drawings that are the same as or similar to the pencil sketches are completed. These drawings are included in the textbook on a disk and are compatible with any version of AutoCAD or AutoCAD LT from AutoCAD R14 to the present. Tutorials are not tied to any specific version of AutoCAD, as commands are typed from the keyboard.

This approach allows the instructor to cover more subject matter without concentrating on the rigors of manual instrument drawing and mastering skills and purchasing expensive instruments that have little application in today's construction industries. After the student completes sketches on a topic, one or more tutorials on the AutoCAD program are presented so that the student will be comfortable with AutoCAD when the course is completed. A variety of exercises are provided in each chapter to challenge students on many levels.

Contents

Architectural Drawing
Using Pencil Sketches
and AutoCAD®

1 Introduction

OBJECTIVES

After completing this chapter, you will be able to

☐ Describe why drawing fundamentals are important in architecture.
☐ List seven personal characteristics needed to become successful in architectural drawing.
☐ Describe the purpose of this book.
☐ Describe how to use this book.
☐ Identify the types of drawings to be assigned.
☐ Identify the hardware and software necessary to complete the computer-aided tutorials in this book.

DRAWING FUNDAMENTALS

Drawing fundamentals make up a language that is used in architecture for communicating ideas and instructions. These fundamentals are used by designers, engineers, and architects to design products, to communicate, and to sell ideas. After these products have been approved for construction they are refined and built by people who must understand the same language of graphic communication. Without this means of communication, building construction would be greatly hampered, if not impossible.

NECESSARY PERSONAL CHARACTERISTICS

Although there are people of many different personality types in the business of architectural graphics, they usually possess the following common traits:

They work closely and for long periods with details.
They tolerate repeated, daily contact with the same people.
They accept changes and corrections to their work.
They sit in the same place for long periods. This can be a health problem for people who do not get enough of the right kind of exercise. If you decide to make a career of this type of work, develop a good exercise program and stay with it.
They visualize objects in two and three dimensions, as shown in Figure 1–1.
They check their own work systematically and carefully. This is difficult for beginners, but it is extremely important. Most companies are very understanding with beginners who are slow, but they are not so patient with employees who are consistently inaccurate. The extra time it takes to check your work carefully and correct it before you turn it in is well worth it. Checking your own work and knowing it is right encourages you to develop the final personal trait.
They take pride in their work. Students who do not develop strong graphics skills will quickly become discouraged when a deadline approaches. It is impossible to

FIGURE 1–1
Drawings in Two and Three
Dimensions

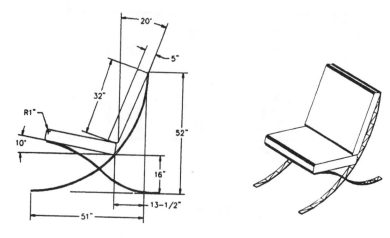

do good work in a reasonable time with poor skills. This situation can be corrected only by spending the time necessary to develop good skills and the resulting pride in your work.

Many students in beginning architectural drawing classes either do not have the time or will not spend the time necessary to develop good drawing and visualizing skills. They believe that some mysterious trait was left out of their set of abilities. In most cases this is not true. Drawing fundamentals come more easily at first for some people, but those who have to work at it often develop better skills than those who have an extremely easy time of it.

The technical graphic language is foreign to many beginners. Learning to read and draw with this new language is exciting and well worth the time necessary to learn it. Whether or not you make a career of this type of work, the graphic language of drawing provides a set of skills that will allow you to understand and communicate many things in your life that you would not be able to otherwise.

PURPOSE OF THIS BOOK

The purpose of this textbook is to teach the fundamentals of drawing through the use of sketches on grid paper done with triangles, a circle template, and a minimum of other tools and supplies. If the instructor wishes, only a pencil and eraser is absolutely necessary. In addition, the student will be introduced to the AutoCAD or AutoCAD LT programs as partially drawn AutoCAD drawings that are the same as or similar to the pencil sketches are completed. These drawings are included in the textbook on a floppy disk and are compatible with any version of AutoCAD or AutoCAD LT from Release 2002 to the present. Tutorials are not tied to any specific version of AutoCAD, as commands will be typed from the keyboard.

This approach allows the instructor to cover more subject matter without concentrating on the rigors of manual instrument drawing and mastering skills and purchasing expensive instruments that have little application in today's industries. After the student completes sketches on a topic, one or more tutorials on the AutoCAD program are presented so that the student will also be comfortable with AutoCAD when the course is completed. A variety of exercises are provided in each chapter to challenge students on many levels.

HOW TO USE THIS BOOK

Using Sketches to Learn Drawing Fundamentals

Step 1. Read the assigned chapter.
Step 2. Remove the sketch assignment page from your book.
Step 3. Read the assignment carefully.

Step 4. Make the sketch using pencils, erasers, triangles, scales, and circle template, or use only pencils and erasers, per your instructor.

Step 5. Complete the title block using a good architectural lettering style of a consistent height and slant.

Step 6. Check your drawing and make any necessary corrections.

Step 7. Give the drawing to your instructor for grading.

Using the AutoCAD or AutoCAD LT Tutorials

All the tutorials require you to type commands. Because the many versions of AutoCAD and AutoCAD LT have commands located on toolbars or menus that are labeled differently, typing is the only common means of operating these software packages. If you wish to click commands from the menus or toolbars, you will have to study their locations and find them when you want to use them.

In many cases typing is absolutely the fastest way to operate AutoCAD software. The specifics of how the tutorials are constructed are listed next.

Drives

This book assumes that the hard drive of your computer is labeled drive C. It also assumes there is a floppy disk drive labeled A and a Zip drive labeled B. If you have a compact disk drive, this text assumes it is labeled D.

Prompt-and-Response Columns

Throughout the exercises in this text, Prompt-and-Response columns provide step-by-step instructions for starting and completing a command. The Prompt column text repeats the AutoCAD or AutoCAD LT prompt that appears in the Command: prompt area of the display screen. The text in the Response column shows your response to the prompt and appears as follows:

1. All responses are shown in bold type.
2. The response **<enter>** is used to indicate that the command is to be entered, either by pressing a button on the pointing device or a key on the keyboard. On keyboards this key is marked <enter>, Enter, or Return.
3. A response that is to be typed and entered from the keyboard is preceded by the word *Type*: and is followed by **<enter>** (for example, Type: **L<enter>**).
4. Function keys are the keys marked F1 through F10 on the keyboard (F11 and F12 are available on many keyboards). If the response is to use a function key, the key name will be preceded by the word *Press*: (for example, Press: **F7**).
5. When you are required to use the click button on your digitizer (the left button on your mouse) to select an object or to specify a location, the word *Click*: is used followed by a description (for example, Click: **D1**).
6. Helpful notes such as (F1 is the flip-screen function key for DOS; F2 is the flip-screen function key for Windows) are provided in parentheses.

Margin Notes

Helpful notes, tips, and warnings are included in the margin.

Steps in Using the Tutorials

Step 1. Copy all drawings from the floppy disk included in your book to a folder on the hard drive of your computer. If you are using a computer in a school laboratory, be sure to get your instructor's permission before taking this step.

Step 2. Open the assigned drawing.

Step 3. Follow the steps in your book to make the assigned drawing.

Step 4. Carefully check your drawing on the screen and make any necessary corrections.

Step 5. Save your drawing in at least two places.

Step 6. Print or plot your drawing as instructed.

Step 7. Check the hard copy of your drawing, make corrections, and reprint if necessary.

Step 8. Give the drawing to your instructor for grading.

TYPES OF DRAWINGS TO BE COVERED IN THIS BOOK

Line Weights and Drawing Constructions

Figure 1–2 is an example of the types of drawing constructions for sketching and Auto-CAD. These exercises are provided to teach some of the basic skills you will need to make the other drawings in this book.

Orthographic Drawings

Two-dimensional (2D) drawings are called *orthographic drawings* in architectural drawing. These drawings are the universal language of technical drawing. Only two dimensions are seen in any one view. Those dimensions may be height and width, height and depth, or width and depth. Figure 1–3 shows some examples of orthographic drawings.

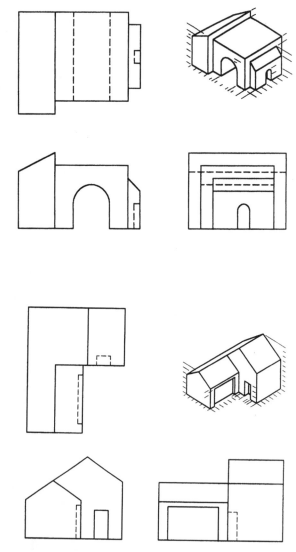

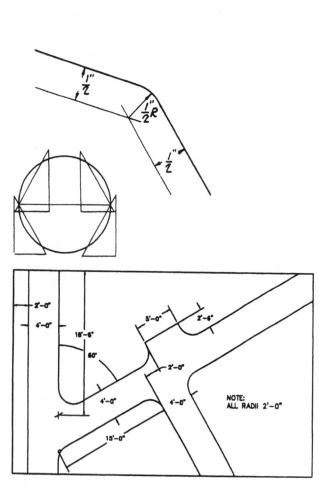

FIGURE 1–2
Drawing Constructions

FIGURE 1–3
Orthographic Drawings from an Isometric Sketch

Sectional Drawings

Sectional drawings are used in many different industries to clarify internal or hidden external construction. Figure 1–4 shows two sectional drawings: one sketch and one made using AutoCAD. This type of drawing can be done with more consistent lines and with much less effort using AutoCAD than by drawing it manually. Shading lines are often drawn with a thinner line by using a layer command. Layers are used to separate linetypes or other features that allow the drawing to be used more efficiently.

Isometric Drawings

Isometric drawings are often used to show pictorial views of objects. Although isometric drawing is not three-dimensional, it is a two-dimensional drawing form that shows what a part looks like in three dimensions. Figure 1–5 shows examples of isometric drawings.

Dimensioned Drawings

A dimensioned drawing is a type of orthographic drawing that gives the size and location of features. AutoCAD is very useful in dimensioning because it can become almost automatic when drawings are made full size. Figure 1–6 shows two drawings: a sketch and one done with AutoCAD.

Floor Plans

Floor plans show the walls, doors, windows, and other details of a building as if the roof were removed and you were looking down on the top view of it, such as the one shown in Figure 1–7.

FIGURE 1–4
Sectional Drawings

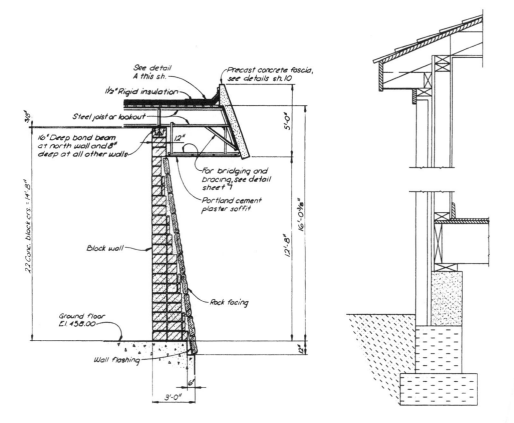

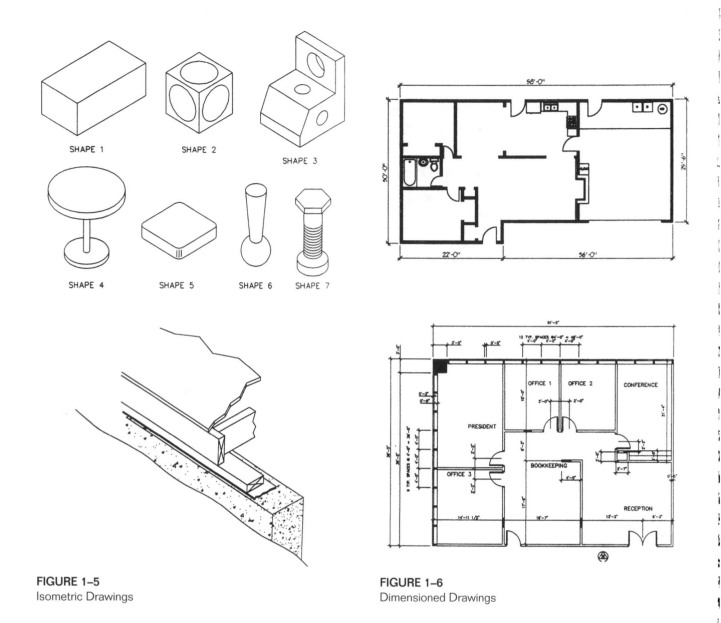

FIGURE 1–5
Isometric Drawings

FIGURE 1–6
Dimensioned Drawings

Elevations

Elevations are the views you see when you look directly at the front, rear, and sides of an object or building. The drawings in Figure 1–8 show the exterior elevations of a building.

Electrical Plans

Electrical plans show where electrical parts are installed and how they are connected, as shown in Figure 1–9.

THE HARDWARE AND SOFTWARE NECESSARY TO COMPLETE THE COMPUTER-AIDED TUTORIALS IN THIS BOOK

Hardware

The parts of a typical personal computer system (Figure 1–10) on which AutoCAD or AutoCAD LT software can be used are as follows:

FIGURE 1–7
Floor Plans

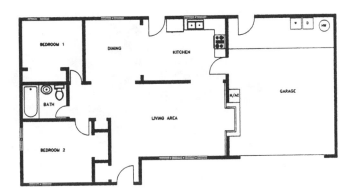

Computer
Floppy disk drive
Hard disk drive
Compact disk drive
Video monitor
Keyboard
Printer
Plotter

Computer

The computer should be of sufficient capacity to run AutoCAD or AutoCAD LT easily. In general, a minimum of 64 megabytes (MB) (64,000 bytes) of RAM on a Pentium computer is necessary. The computer should also have a graphics card (a printed circuit board that allows a high-quality display of graphic data) and other features that will allow the display (the screen) to be easily read and quickly generated. Most computers manufactured in recent times are adequate.

Floppy Disk Drive, Zip, or Read/Write Compact Disk Drive

At least one floppy disk drive, Zip drive, or a read/write compact disk drive is needed to move large blocks of information into and out of the computer. Floppy disks are inserted into a floppy disk drive. AutoCAD and AutoCAD LT drawings can be stored on floppy disks. Floppy disk drives are identified by a one-letter name followed by a colon (for example, A:).

FIGURE 1–8
Exterior Elevations

The 3½″ high-density disk drive uses a 3½″ floppy diskette. This diskette stores approximately 1.44 MB to 2 MB of information.

Zip and compact disks store up to hundreds of megabytes of information

Compact Disk Drive

Compact disk drives are available in a variety of speeds. The faster they are, the higher the price. Some models allow you to write files (such as drawings) to compact disks. Because much of the new software is available on compact disks, and as a result is more convenient and faster to load, a compact disk drive is a necessity.

Hard Disk Drive

A hard disk drive, also called a hard drive or hard disk, is usually permanently installed inside the computer. It can store much more information than the removable floppy disks and is used to store the AutoCAD or AutoCAD LT program. AutoCAD drawings may also be stored on the hard disk drive. The hard disk drive is commonly called drive C (C:). A hard drive with adequate storage capacity for your situation is necessary; 2 gigabyte (GB) (2,000,000,000 bytes) to 60 GB hard drives are commonly used.

Video Monitor

A video monitor is similar to a television screen. A color video monitor is a necessity for most drawings. The physical size of the screen is not as important as the resolution. The resolution of the video is stated in *pixels*, which is the number of dots arranged in rows and columns to produce the visual display on the screen. The finer the resolution, the better. AutoCAD and AutoCAD LT require a video screen of reasonably high resolution.

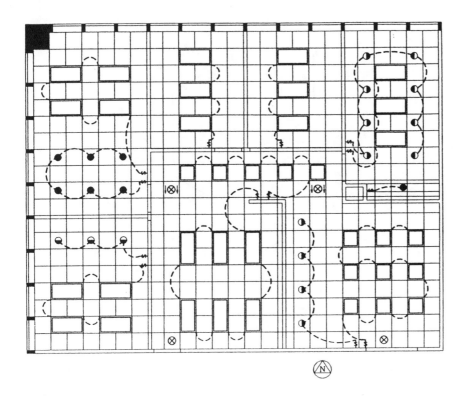

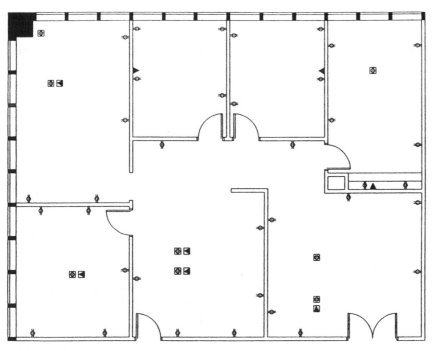

ELECTRICAL LEGEND

SYMBOL	DESCRIPTION
⊕	Duplex Receptacle
⊞	Floor Duplex Receptacle

TELEPHONE LEGEND

SYMBOL	DESCRIPTION
◀	Telephone
◪	Floor Telephone

FIGURE 1–9
Electrical Plans

Keyboard

The keyboard has three parts:

Alphanumeric keys Located in the center of the keyboard, these are used to type the lettering and numbers that will appear on your drawings and occasionally to type commands. The number keys can also be used as a calculator with an AutoCAD LT command.

FIGURE 1–10
Parts of a CAD System

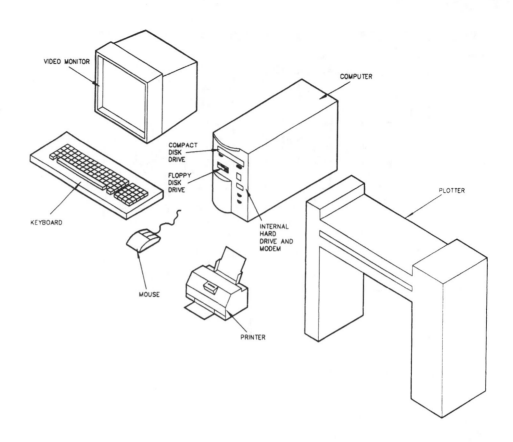

Function keys Keys labeled F1–F12, often located to the left or above the alphanumeric keys of many keyboards. These keys are used to perform special functions such as turning a grid on or off. These keys are used and their functions are explained in later chapters.

Numeric keys Often located to the right of the alphanumeric keys, these keys can be used to type numbers that will appear on your drawings and can also be used as a calculator in combination with an AutoCAD or AutoCAD LT command. The directional arrows, which can be toggled on or off, may be used to move the location of the pointer, although moving the pointer with a mouse is usually much faster.

Mouse

A mouse is used to select commands from the AutoCAD or AutoCAD LT toolbars or menus that appear on the right edge or top of the AutoCAD LT screen video. The mouse allows the eyes of the operator to remain on the screen at all times. It is also used to enter points of a drawing, such as where a line starts or where a circle is located. The mouse is moved across a tabletop or pad, and its action is described on the video screen by the movement of crosshairs. The crosshairs are positioned to highlight a command or to locate a point. The click button (usually the far-left button) on the mouse is pushed to select a command or to enter a point on the drawing. The extra buttons on a mouse can be assigned to perform different tasks. Most commonly one extra button is assigned the return <enter> function.

Printer

Laser printers are available that produce hard copies of excellent quality in black and white. Many of the newer color printers are relatively inexpensive and produce high-quality hard copies. The low-cost color printers are slow, however, so take the speed factor into account if you buy one.

Plotter

To make high-quality, usable drawings (hard copies), a plotter is a necessity. One type of plotter commonly available uses pens similar to technical drawing pens for manual inking. Felt markers are also available for this type of plotter. Both types of pens can be used for multicolor drawings. A good plotter makes drawings with smooth curves, dense lines, and crisp connections. Pen plotters may have one pen or multiple pens. A plotter may accept only $8\frac{1}{2}'' \times 11''$ paper, or it may accept larger sizes and rolls of paper. Color electrostatic and ink-jet plotters are also available and are rapidly replacing the earlier pen plotters.

Software

Any release of AutoCAD or AutoCAD LT from Release 2000 to the current version can be used to make the drawings in this book. The drawings contained on the included disk are Release 2002 drawings. These drawings can be opened in any of the releases just described above. If, however, you work on one of the drawings in a later release of AutoCAD or AutoCAD LT, that drawing becomes the later release file and cannot be used in earlier versions unless you save it as a Release 2000 (or earlier) drawing.

REVIEW QUESTIONS

Circle the best answer.

1. Checking your own work is unnecessary because someone else can check it better.
   a. True
   b. False
2. Which of the following is not used to make pencil sketches in this book?
   a. Triangles
   b. Circle template
   c. Compass
   d. Eraser
   e. Scales
3. When the words Click: **D1** are shown in the Response column which button on your mouse do you press?
   a. The left button
   b. The right button
   c. The middle button
4. Which of the following is the flip-screen function key for Windows?
   a. F2
   b. F3
   c. F5
   d. F7
   e. F9
5. Orthographic drawings show how many dimensions in any one view?
   a. One
   b. Two
   c. Three
   d. Four
   e. None
6. Dimensioning in AutoCAD can be almost automatic.
   a. True
   b. False
7. An exterior elevation shows which switches turn on which lights.
   a. True
   b. False
8. Sectional drawings are used to
   a. Make 3D drawings
   b. Show where to place dimensions
   c. Introduce 3D commands
   d. Introduce 2D commands
   e. Clarify internal details
9. Isometric drawing is not the same thing as a 3D model.
   a. True
   b. False

10. This book assumes that the hard drive of your computer is labeled
    a. A
    b. B
    c. C
    d. D
    e. This book does not assume anything about your hard drive.

Complete.

11. List five personal characteristics necessary to become successful in technical graphics.

    _____

    _____

    _____

    _____

    _____

12. What must be done to use a later-release drawing in Release 2000 of AutoCAD?

    _____

13. What must be done to use a Release 2000 drawing in a later release?

    _____

14. List two items that a video monitor must have to display most of the drawings in AutoCAD.

    _____

15. Which releases of AutoCAD are required to complete the AutoCAD tutorials in this book?

    _____

2

Sketching Tools, Supplies, and Their Uses

OBJECTIVES

After completing this chapter, you will be able to

☐ Correctly identify the tools used for sketching.
☐ Describe how these tools are used.
☐ Read architectural scales accurately.
☐ Draw lines to scale.

SKETCHING

Sketching well can be very useful for people who are designing and drawing any product. Sketching can be done with nothing more than a pencil, an eraser, and a piece of paper. Sketching can also be done with triangles, a circle template, pencils, eraser, scales, drawing powder, and paper. Sketching can even be done on the computer using AutoCAD software. This book is designed for you to use as elaborate a sketching system as you want.

If you choose not to use triangles and a circle template for manual sketches, be aware that architectural sketches such as the ones that will be assigned in this course must be accurate, neat, and legible. This book will show you how to make manual sketches with or without the aid of triangles and circle templates. It also introduces you to the Auto-CAD program by using commands that are common to any version of the program within recent years.

SKETCHING TOOLS

The tools for sketching include pencils, erasers, scales, grid paper, and if desired, triangles, a circle template, and drawing powder. This chapter describes these tools, how to use them, and how to keep them in good working condition.

Pencils

Both thin-lead mechanical pencils and wooden pencils work well for technical sketching.

Mechanical Pencils

Lead for mechanical pencils (Figure 2–1) is made in several degrees of hardness and several widths. Those most commonly used for technical sketching are:

.5-mm diameter, 2H or H hardness: used for thinner lines
.7-mm diameter, 2H or H hardness: used for thicker lines

You should hold mechanical pencils perpendicular to the paper when using them with triangles or templates so you draw with the full diameter of the lead and avoid breaking the lead (Figure 2–2).

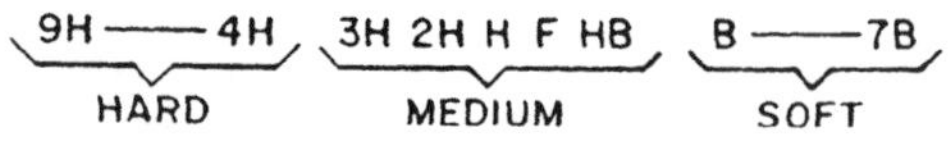

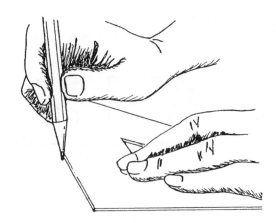

FIGURE 2–2
Holding a Mechanical Pencil

9H ——— 4H , 3H 2H H F HB , B ——— 7B
HARD   MEDIUM   SOFT

FIGURE 2–1
Lead Hardnesses

Wooden Pencils and Lead Holders

Wooden drawing pencils are made in several degrees of hardness, from 9H to 7B. 9H is the hardest; 7B is the softest. H, HB, or 2H is a good hardness for sketching. A standard No. 2 yellow pencil with a soft red eraser on the end of it is fine for most sketches. Keep wooden pencils fairly sharp. Crush the end of a finely sharpened pencil or lead holder a little so sketch lines will not be too fine (Figure 2–3).

When using wooden pencils and lead holders with triangles or templates, hold the pencil or lead holder at about a 60° angle to the paper and roll it slightly between the fingers to make lines of uniform width (Figure 2–4).

Erasers

A Pink Pearl eraser is best for erasing on bond or vellum papers. You will find this type of eraser on the end of a No. 2 yellow pencil as well as in a round or rectangular form (Figure 2–5).

Grid Paper

Your book contains pages with grids that will aid you in sketching. This paper is also available at most stores that sell architectural, engineering, or drawing supplies. Grids at $\frac{1}{10}$", $\frac{1}{4}$", or isometric angles are available at these locations.

Triangles

Both 30-60° and 45° triangles (Figure 2–6) are used for technical drawing. Inexpensive triangles are fine.

SHARP POINT
FOR CONSTRUCTION,
AND GUIDELINES

CRUSH SMALL
END FOR CENTER
LINES, DIMENSIONS, ETC.

CRUSH LARGER
END FOR OBJECT
LINES

FIGURE 2–3
Preparing a Sharpened Pencil

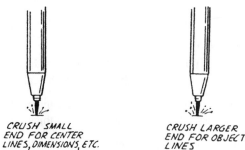

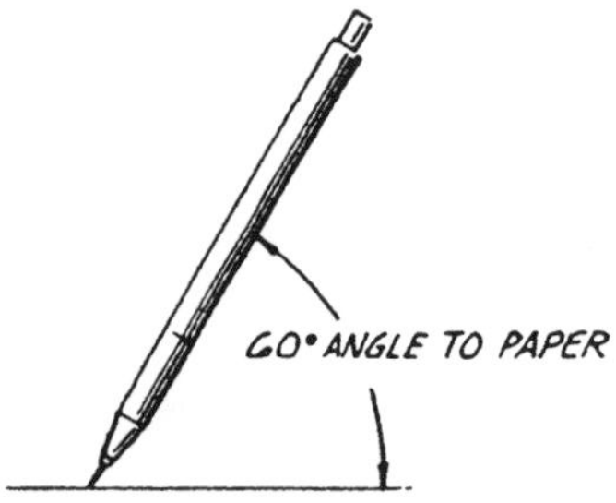

60° ANGLE TO PAPER

FIGURE 2–4
Holding a Wooden Pencil
or Lead Holder

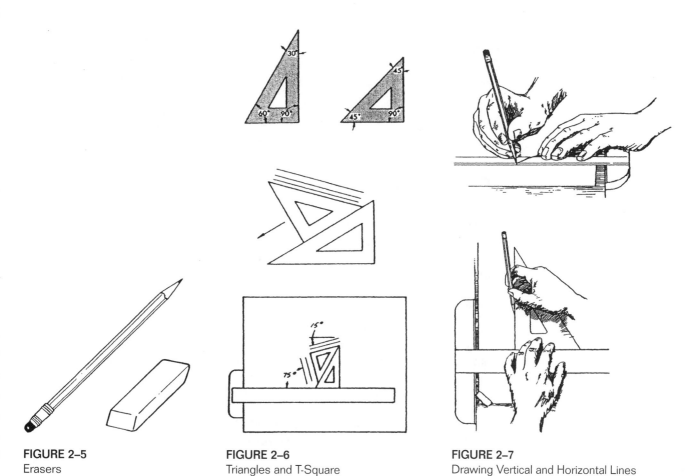

FIGURE 2–5
Erasers

FIGURE 2–6
Triangles and T-Square

FIGURE 2–7
Drawing Vertical and Horizontal Lines

To draw vertical lines, place the triangle on a grid line or on a straightedge such as a T-square and hold the triangle firmly with one hand as you draw upward with the other hand.

You will soon learn to return downward over a line to improve its density. Notice that the pencil is slanted in the direction of the line (Figure 2–7) but is not tilted in relation to the edge of the triangle.

Circle Template

Circle templates can be used to draw most of the circles in the assignments in this book. The template should contain circles from $\frac{1}{8}''$ to $1\frac{1}{2}''$ in diameter. To use the circle template align the crosshairs of the template on the centerlines of where the circle will be drawn. Draw the circle with the pencil held perpendicular to the paper (Figure 2–8).

FIGURE 2–8
Drawing with a Circle Template

FIGURE 2-9
Drawing Powder

Drawing Powder

An excellent aid for keeping drawings clean is the drawing powder bag or can. The bag is made of a coarsely woven material so that the coarse powder falls out of it when the bag is kneaded (Figure 2–9). The powder is sprinkled over the drawing before a drawing is started. When the drawing is completed, the powder is rubbed over the drawing very lightly to pick up the excess graphite. The powder is then brushed off the drawing.

Scales

Scales are made in a variety of styles. All scales are designed to be used by selecting the correct scale for the situation and measuring with it. No arithmetic is involved. You do not have to multiply, divide, add, or subtract to use a scale; you just read it. For example, the 5 mark on a scale can be only .5, 5, 50, 500 or some other number with a 5 and more zeros or a decimal point with zeros and then a 5 (.005). It cannot be read as 10, 200, or any other number.

Although there are many different types of scales, only the architect's scale is used in most of the exercises in this book. The civil engineer's scale is introduced in this chapter so you have an idea of how that scale is used in maps, plats, and other land drawings relating to architecture.

Architect's Scale

The architect's scale is designed to be used to draw architectural structures and is therefore divided into sections for feet and inches. The six-sided triangular architect's scale has a total of 11 different scales marked on its edges.

Using the Architect's Scale to Represent Feet and Inches

Figure 2–10 shows the edge of the architect's scale that contains the 1/4 scale on the right end and the 1/8 scale on the left end. Notice that the 1/8 scale uses the smaller divisions marked on the shorter lines and is read from the left 0 on the scale. The 1/4 scale uses the larger divisions marked on the longer lines and is read from the right 0 on the scale.

The section to the left of the left 0 shows a foot on the 1/8 scale divided into inches. There are six spaces in this section, and since there are 12 inches in a foot, each mark represents 2 inches. The section to the right of the right 0 shows a foot on the 1/4 scale divided into inches. There are 12 spaces in this section, so each space represents 1 inch.

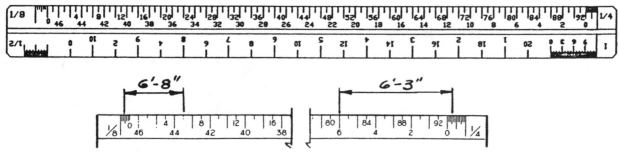

FIGURE 2–10
Architect's Scale

Notice the labeled measurement on the 1/8 scale. The measurement showing 6'-8" starts at the right of the 0 on the 6' mark (two marks to the right of 4) and stops at the fourth space to the left of the 0. These 4 spaces represent 8 inches, since each mark to the left of 0 represents 2 inches.

Study the labeled measurements on the 1/4 and 1/8 scales until you are satisfied you know how to read these two scales. After you know how to read these scales, you know how to read all scales on the architect's scale.

Using the Architect's Scale to Represent Inches and Fractions of an Inch

The architect's scale can also be used to represent inches, with the section to the right or left of 0 representing fractions of an inch. Figure 2–11 shows the 3/4 scale representing inches and fractions of an inch. The labeled measurement closest to the 3/4 scale shows the right end of the measurement stopping on the 3" mark and the left end stopping on 0. The next line up shows the right end on the 4" mark and the left end one quarter of the distance across the section that in this case shows fractions of an inch. The top line shows the left end 3 marks short of the full inch. Since there are 24 spaces in this inch scale, 3 marks is $\frac{1}{8}$ ($\frac{8}{8} - \frac{1}{8} = \frac{7}{8}$).

Civil Engineer's Scale

The civil engineer's scale divides the inch into a certain number of units. On the scale shown in Figure 2–12 the inch is divided into 20 units on one edge and 40 units on the

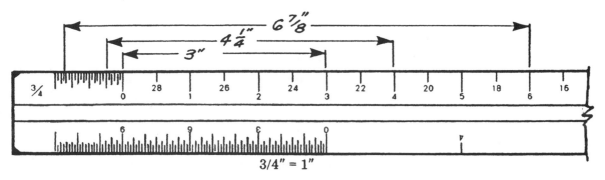

FIGURE 2–11
Using the Architect's Scale for a Scale of $\frac{3}{4}$"=1" (inches, not feet)

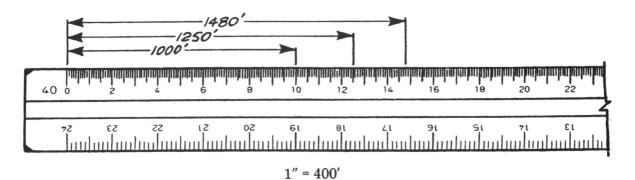

1" = 400'

FIGURE 2–12
Civil Engineer's Scale

Sketching Tools, Supplies, and Their Uses

other edge. The lower part of Figure 2–12 is an enlarged view of the 40 scale. If you needed to draw something to a scale of 1″=400′, you would use the 40 scale, and each of the smallest spaces on the scale would represent 10 feet. On the 40 scale in Figure 2–12, there is a 0, then four small marks, then a longer mark. The longer mark makes it easier to locate measurements on the scale (every 5th mark is long). Notice that the 200th mark is identified with the number 2, the 400th with the number 4, and so on. If you use those numbers, adding zeros after them to represent the correct scale, you will find this scale simple to use.

On a drawing with a scale of 1″=400 miles, for example, you would select the 40 scale and add two zeros after each number on the scale; each of the smallest spaces on the scale would then represent 10 miles.

To draw at a scale of 1″=20′, you should select the 20 scale and add one zero to each of the numbers on the scale; on a scale of 1″=60′, select the 60 scale and add one zero; on a scale of 1″=5000 miles, select the 50 scale and add three zeros to each of the numbers on the scale.

As with other scales, to use the civil engineer's scale you simply select the correct scale and measure with it. **No arithmetic is necessary.**

EXERCISE 2–1:
Drawing Lines to Scale

Remove the sheet labeled Exercise 2–1 from your book and use the following instructions to draw lines to scale.

Use the Architect's Scale to Draw Lines to Scale

Step 1. **Use the 3/4 scale to represent $^3/_4''=1'$ and draw a line 4′-3″ long (Figure 2–13).**

    1. Determine which scale is required to fit the drawing on the sheet size you are sketching. In this case use the 3/4 scale.

    2. Align the 3″ mark (6 of the small spaces to the left of 0) with the start point of the measurement and make a small mark or dot at that point with your pencil on one of the grid lines of your gridded paper.

    3. Locate the 4′ mark and make a small mark or dot at that point with your pencil.

    4. Use a triangle to draw a line between the marks.

Step 2. **On your own:**

    1. Use the 3/4 scale to represent $^3/_4''=1'$ to draw a line 6′-2″ long.

    2. Use the 1/8 scale to represent $^1/_8''=1'$ to draw a line 15′-6″ long.

    3. Use the 1/2 scale to represent $^1/_2''=1'$ to draw a line 7′-10″ long.

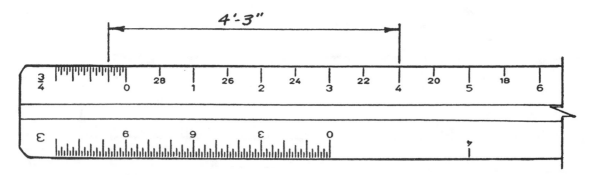

FIGURE 2–13
4′-3″ at a Scale of $^3/_4''$=1′-0″

Chapter 2

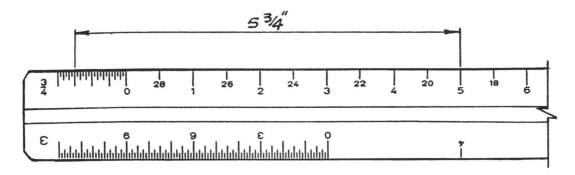

FIGURE 2–14
5¾″ at a Scale of ¾″=1″ (inches not feet)

Step 3. **Use the 3/4 scale to represent ¾″=1″. Draw a line 5¾″ long (Figure 2–14).**

1. Determine which scale is required to fit the drawing on the sheet size you are sketching. In this case use the 3/4 scale.

2. Align the ¾″ mark to the left of the 0 with the start point of the measurement and make a small mark or dot at that point with your pencil.

3. Locate the 5″ mark to the right of 0 and make a small mark or dot at that point with your pencil.

4. Use a triangle to draw a line between the marks.

Step 4. **On your own:**

1. Use the 3/4 scale to represent ¾″=1″ to draw a line 6¾″ long.

2. Use the 1/8 scale to represent ⅛″=1″ to draw a line 20½″ long.

3. Use the 1/2 scale to represent ½″=1″ to draw a line 8¼″ long.

Use the Civil Engineers' Scale to Draw Lines to Scale

Step 5. **Use the 20 scale to represent 1″=20′ to draw a line 84′ long (Figure 2–15).**

1. Determine which scale is required to fit the drawing on the sheet size you are sketching. In this case use the 20 scale. To read this scale place a 0 after each of the numbers on the scale so that 1 becomes 10, 2 becomes 20, 10 becomes 100, and so on.

2. Align the 0 on the scale with the start point of the measurement and make a small mark or dot at that point with your pencil on one of the grid lines of your gridded paper.

3. Locate the mark numbered 8 and move two of the small marks to the right (8 represents 80, and each of the small spaces is 2 because there are 10

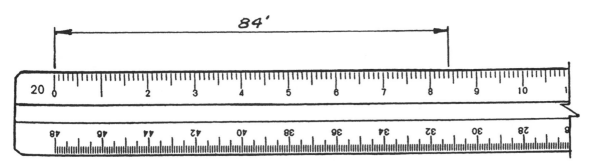

FIGURE 2–15
84′ at a Scale of 1″=20′

Sketching Tools, Supplies, and Their Uses   19

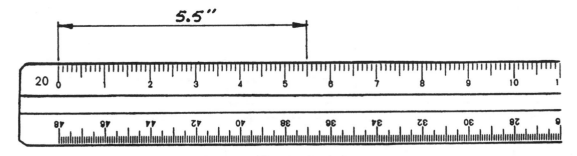

FIGURE 2–16
5.5″ at a Scale of ½″=1″

spaces between each pair of the larger numbered marks) and make a small mark or dot at that point with your pencil.

4. Use a triangle to draw a line between the marks.

Step 6. **On your own:**

1. Use the 20 scale to represent 1″=20′ to draw a line 68′ long.

2. Use the 40 scale to represent 1″=400′ to draw a line 1650′ long.

3. Use the 50 scale to represent 1″=50 miles to draw a line 214 miles long.

Step 7. **Use the 20 scale to represent ½″=1″. Draw a line 5.5″ long (Figure 2–16).**

1. Determine which scale is required to fit the drawing on the sheet size you are sketching. In this case use the 20 scale.

2. Align the 0 on the scale with the start point of the measurement and make a small mark or dot at that point with your pencil on one of the grid lines of your gridded paper.

3. Locate the mark numbered 5 to the right of 0 and move 5 small marks to the right (each of the small marks is .1 because there are 10 spaces between each pair of the larger numbered marks) and make a small mark or dot at that point with your pencil.

4. Use a triangle to draw a line between the marks.

Step 8. **On your own:**

1. Use the 20 scale to represent ½″=1″ to draw a line 6.2″ long.

2. Use the 40 scale to represent ¼″=1″ to draw a line 17.5″ long.

3. Use the 40 scale to represent ¼″=1″ to draw a line 11.4″ long.

4. Use a triangle to draw a line between the marks.

EXERCISES

EXERCISE 2–1. Complete Exercise 2–1 using steps 1 through 8 described in this chapter. Fill in the title block with your best lettering. Title the drawing SCALES. If you do not have a civil engineer's scale, use the architect's scale for those measurements.

EXERCISE 2–2. Complete Exercise sheet 2–2 by drawing lines parallel to the printed lines. Your final drawing should look like Figure 2–17. Use the following steps:

Step 1. Make sure lines are parallel by using your 30-60° and 45° triangles in the manner shown in Figure 2–7. Refer to Chapter 5 if necessary for a description of this procedure.

Step 2. Concentrate on making your pencil lines the same thickness and density as the printed lines.

Step 3. The lower left quarter of the drawing will require you to use a 30-60° triangle to construct a line perpendicular to the two existing ones.

Draw construction lines perpendicular to the angular lines, and make tick marks or dots ½″ apart so all lines will be the same dis-

FIGURE 2–17
Exercise 2–2 Complete

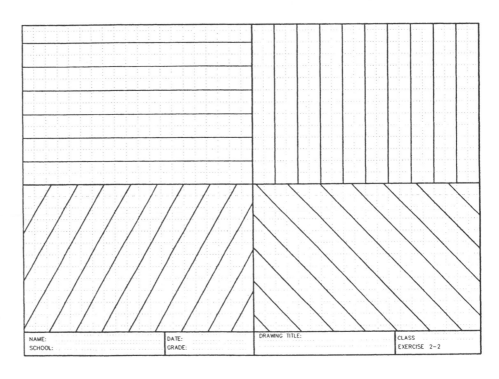

tance apart. Refer to Chapter 5 if necessary for a description of this procedure.

Step 4. Use a procedure similar to step 3 to draw the lower right quarter using a 45° triangle.

Step 5. Use your best lettering to fill in the title block with the required information using all capital letters. Title the drawing LINES. You will learn the preferred methods of lettering for technical drawing in Chapter 4.

EXERCISE 2–3.   Complete Exercise sheet 2–3 by drawing the floor plan described in Figure 2–18 at a scale of $\frac{1}{4}''=1'$ Your final drawing should look like Figure 2–18 without dimensions. Use the following steps:

FIGURE 2–18
Exercise 2–3 Complete (Do not show dimensions.)

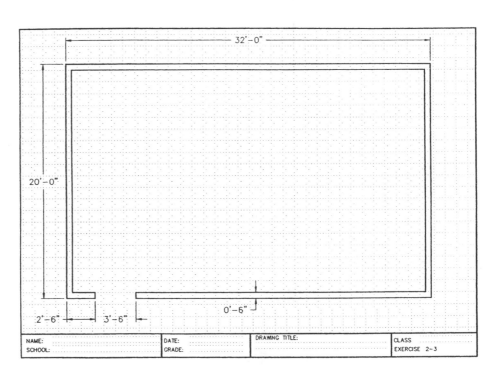

Step 1. Draw construction lines parallel to the grid lines for the vertical lines so you will know where to stop the horizontal lines.

Step 2. Draw all horizontal lines dark making sure they are parallel by using your 30-60° 45° triangles to draw lines on the grid lines or parallel to them if the measurement falls between grid lines.

Step 3. Concentrate on making your pencil lines the same thickness and density as the printed lines.

Step 4. Draw the vertical lines solid to complete the drawing.

Step 5. Use your best lettering to fill in the title block with the required information using all capital letters. Title the drawing FLOOR PLAN. You will learn the preferred methods of lettering for technical drawing in Chapter 4.

EXERCISE 2–4.   Complete Exercise sheet 2–4 by drawing the site plan described in Figure 2–19 at a scale of $\frac{1}{4}''=1'$. Your final drawing should look like Figure 2–19 without dimensions. Use the following steps:

Step 1. Draw construction lines by extending two of the angular lines to the right edge of the border.

Step 2. Draw a construction line parallel to the other angular line 4′ from it using a scale of $\frac{1}{4}''=1'$.

Step 3. Draw all radii in their final form. Concentrate on making your pencil lines the same thickness and density as the printed lines.

Step 4. Draw the remaining vertical line solid and darken all lines necessary to complete the drawing.

Step 5. Use your best lettering to fill in the title block with the required information using all capital letters. Title the drawing FLOOR PLAN. You will learn the preferred methods of lettering for technical drawing in Chapter 4.

FIGURE 2–19
Exercise 2–4 Complete (Do not show dimensions.)

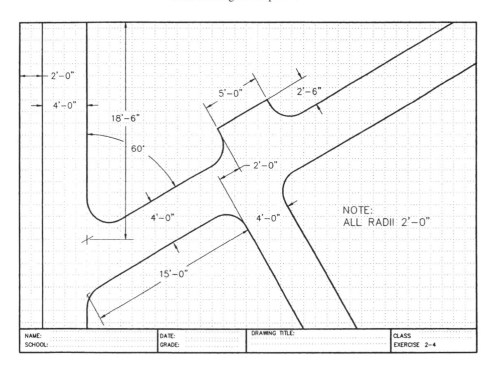

REVIEW QUESTIONS

Circle the best answer.

1. Which of the following is not a technical sketching tool?
   a. Pencil
   b. Eraser
   c. Compass
   d. Scale
   e. Triangle

2. Which of the following diameter leads should be used for sketching thin lines?
   a. .3 mm
   b. .5 mm
   c. .7 mm
   d. .9 mm
   e. Any of the above is OK for thin lines.

3. Which hardness of lead should be used for technical sketching?
   a. 7B
   b. 2B
   c. H
   d. 4H
   e. 9H

4. At what angle should a mechanical pencil be held to make a line that reflects the full diameter of the lead?
   a. 30°
   b. 45°
   c. 60°
   d. 90°
   e. Any angle will do.

5. Which of the following erasers is best for technical sketching?
   a. Pink Pearl
   b. Art gum
   c. Gray ink
   d. White
   e. Red ink

6. Which of the following diameter circles is found on common circle templates?
   a. $\frac{1}{32}'$
   b. $\frac{1}{8}'$
   c. $\frac{1}{64}$
   d. $.2\frac{1}{16}''$
   e. $3''$

7. Which of the following is found on the same edge of the architect's scale as the 1/4 scale?
   a. 1/16
   b. 1/8
   c. 3/8
   d. 1/2
   e. 3/4

8. When the architect's scale is used to represent $\frac{1}{8}''=1'$, each of the small spaces in the area to the left of 0 on the 1/8 scale represents:
   a. 1 foot
   b. 1 inch
   c. 2 feet
   d. 2 inches
   e. 3 inches

Sketching Tools, Supplies, and Their Uses

9. When the civil engineer's scale is used to draw at a scale of $1'' = 2000'$, which of the following scales should be selected?
   a. 10
   b. 20
   c. 30
   d. 40
   e. Use the 60 scale and divide by 3.
10. When the civil engineer's scale is used to draw at a scale of $1'' = 40$ miles, which of the following scales should be selected?
    a. 10
    b. 20
    c. 30
    d. 40
    e. The civil engineer's scale cannot be used to measure miles.

    Complete.
11. List all the tools you will be using for sketching in this course.

    _____

    _____

    _____

    _____

12. List six of the scales on an architect's scale.

    _____   _____   _____

    _____   _____   _____

    _____   _____   _____

13. List four of the scales on a civil engineer's scale.

    _____   _____

    _____   _____

14. Describe how to hold a wooden pencil to draw a vertical line with a triangle.

    _____

    _____

15. Describe how to hold a triangle to draw a vertical line.

    _____

    _____

3

AutoCAD Fundamentals

OBJECTIVES

After completing this chapter, you will be able to

☐ Make settings for an AutoCAD or AutoCAD LT drawing to include Units, Limits, Grid, and Snap.
☐ Create layers and assign a color and linetype to each layer.
☐ Use function keys F1 and F2 (flip screen), F7 (grid), and F9 (snap) to control the display screen, grid, and snap as required.
☐ Use the commands Save, Save As, and Quit to save work and exit AutoCAD or Auto-CAD LT.

INTRODUCTION

Important: If you type a command and a dialog box appears that is confusing, Press: the Esc key until the command prompt reappears, then retype the command with a minus sign before it. The dialog box will not appear if the minus sign preceeds the command.

Note: Some of the prompts you will see may vary slightly from the ones shown in the book. All your responses will be as descibed in the book, however.

When a project that is to be manually drawn is started, decisions are made about the number of drawings required, the appropriate sheet size, scale, and so on. Similar decisions are made when preparing to draw with AutoCAD or AutoCAD LT. This chapter describes the settings that must be made before drawing can begin and some common means of making sure work is saved. The drawings contained on the disk that came with your book already have these settings made, but knowing how to make these settings is important to your understanding of the AutoCAD program. Knowing how to save your work is not just important, it is absolutely necessary for you to continue from one step to the next.

Although you can make all the settings described in this chapter using toolbars or menus, you can also make them by typing from the keyboard. This book is designed to be used with any version of AutoCAD or AutoCAD LT, and the only common means of activating these commands is by typing the command; therefore, typing is the method used throughout this book.

The following is a hands-on, step-by-step procedure to make the setup for your first drawing. Each step is followed by an explanation of the command used. To begin, turn on the computer and start AutoCAD or AutoCAD LT.

MAKE THE SETUP FOR THE FIRST DRAWING EXERCISE

EXERCISE 3–1:
Start a New Drawing

Step 1.   Name the new drawing.

Click: **Start from Scratch** and **OK**. Or English units (AutoCAD 2002 Click: Create Drawings tab, then Click: **Start from Scratch,** then Click: **English (feet and inches)**).

Make Settings

Step 2.   Select Units.

Prompt	Response
Command:	Type: **UNITS<enter>**

Units

Any of the units may be used. The decimal selection can be used for any units (commonly inches or millimeters). The architectural selection (4) allows feet and inches to be used. Architectural units will be used in this book.

Type: 4<enter>, or Select: Architectural from the list of units. The Precision: button allows you to set the number of digits to the right of the decimal point or the lowest fraction to be displayed. The remaining settings are for measuring angles. There is no reason to change these settings. By clicking OK, AutoCAD's default values, which measure angles using decimal degrees in the counterclockwise direction, are accepted.

If you get a series of options allowing you to select values:

Press: **<enter>** after each option to accept the default value until you return to the Command: prompt. Then Press: **F2** to return to the graphics screen.

Step 3.   Set the Drawing Limits.

Prompt	Response
Command:	Type: **LIMITS<enter>**
Specify Lower left corner or [ON/OFF/] <0'-0",0'0">:	**<enter>**
Specify Upper right corner <1'-0", 0'-9">:	**Type: 8-1/2,11<enter>**

Limits

Think of drawing limits as the sheet size or sheet boundaries. Here 8-1/2,11 was set as the drawing limits. In AutoCAD and AutoCAD LT that value is entered as $8\frac{1}{2}$,11 using a comma with no spaces to separate the X and Y axes. AutoCAD defaults to inches (or any other basic unit of measure), so the inch symbol is not required. The X axis is entered first ($8\frac{1}{2}$) and measures drawing limits from left to right. The Y axis is entered second and measures drawing limits from bottom to top. You will be drawing in a vertical 8-1/2,11 area similar to a standard sheet of typing paper.

The lower left corner of the drawing boundaries is 0,0. The upper right corner is 8-1/2,11 (Figure 3–1). These are the limits for this exercise. To turn the 8-1/2",11" area horizontally, enter the limits as 11,8-1/2.

FIGURE 3–1
Drawing Limits

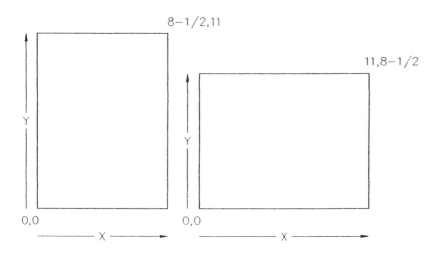

You can also respond to the Limits: prompt "Specify Lower left corner or [ON/OFF/]<0'-0",0'-0">:" by selecting ON or OFF on the menu. The ON mode, when activated, helps you avoid drawing outside the drawing limits by responding in the prompt line with "** Outside limits" if a point is selected outside the limits. Some drawing elements, such as a circle, may be started inside the limits and completed outside the limits without the appearance of this prompt. The OFF mode, when activated, allows you to draw outside the drawing limits.

If you need to change the drawing limits, you may do so at any time by entering new limits to the "Upper right corner>:" prompt. Changing the drawing limits will automatically change the grid pattern to the new limits.

Step 4.   Set the Grid and Snap spacing.

Prompt	Response
Command:	Type: **GRID<enter>**
Specify grid spacing (X) or [ON/OFF/ Snap/Aspect] <0'-0 1/2">	Type: **1/2<enter>** (or **.5<enter>**)
Command:	Type: **SNAP<enter>**
Specify snap spacing or [ON/OFF/Aspect/ Rotate/Style/Type] <0'-0 1/2">:	Type: **1/8<enter>** (or. **125<enter>**)

Grid

You have just set $\frac{1}{2}$ as the grid spacing. The grid is the visible pattern of dots on the display screen. With a setting of $\frac{1}{2}$, each grid dot is spaced $\frac{1}{2}$ vertically and horizontally. The grid is not part of the drawing, but it helps in getting a sense of the size and relationship of the drawing elements. The grid is never plotted.

Function key F7 turns the grid ON or OFF. The grid can also be turned ON or OFF by selecting either option in response to the prompt "Specify grid spacing(X) or [ON/OFF/Snap/Aspect] <0'-0 $\frac{1}{2}$">" or by clicking **GRID** at the bottom of the screen if you are in Windows.

Snap

You have set $\frac{1}{8}$ as the snap spacing. Snap is an invisible pattern of dots on the display screen. As you move the digitizer across the screen, the crosshairs will snap, or lock, to an invisible snap grid when SNAP is ON. With a setting of $\frac{1}{8}$, each snap point is spaced $\frac{1}{8}$ horizontally and vertically.

Function key F9 turns the snap ON or OFF. The snap can also be turned ON or OFF by selecting either option in response to the prompt "Specify snap spacing or[ON/OFF/Aspect/Rotate/Style/Type] <0'-0 $\frac{1}{2}$">:" or by clicking **SNAP** at the bottom of the screen. Rotate and Style options are used in later chapters.

It is helpful to set the snap spacing the same as the grid spacing or as a fraction of the grid spacing so the crosshairs snap to every grid point or to every grid point and in between. The snap can be set to snap several times in between the grid points.

Some drawings or parts of drawings should never be drawn with snap off. Snap is a very important tool for quickly locating or aligning elements of your drawing. You may need to turn snap off and on while drawing, but remember that a drawing entity drawn on snap is easily moved, copied, or otherwise edited.

Drawing Aids Dialog Box and Components of All Dialog Boxes

You can also set snap and grid by using the Drawing Aids or Drafting Settings dialog box.

To locate the Drawing Aids or Drafting Settings dialog box, move the pointer across the top of the display screen and highlight each menu on the menu bar until you see the label Drawing Aids or Drafting Settings. When you Click: **Drawing Aids,** the Drawing Aids dialog box appears on your screen.

There are some basic components that are common to all dialog boxes. The following is a description of the Snap and Grid components that appear in the Drawing Aids dialog box and also other dialog boxes if you choose to use them:

1. **Cursor**: Changes to an arrow.

2. **OK button:** Digitize this button to complete the command, leave the dialog box, and return to the drawing. If any changes have been made, they will remain as changes. Pressing **<enter>** has the same effect.

3. **Cancel button**: Digitize this button to cancel the command, leave the dialog box, and return to the drawing. If any changes have been made, they will be canceled and the original settings will return. Pressing the **Esc** key has the same effect.

4. **Input buttons:** An input button has two parts, its name and the area where changes can be made by typing new input. Digitize the second part of the input button **X Spacing** under SNAP and experiment with the text cursor that is attached to the point of the arrow. As you move the digitizer and click a new spot the text cursor moves also. The following editing keys can be used to edit the text in input buttons.
   Backspace key: Deletes characters to the left of the text cursor one at a time as it is pressed.
   Delete key: Deletes characters to the right of the text cursor one at a time as it is pressed.
   Left arrow: Moves the text cursor to the left without changing the existing text.
   Right arrow: Moves the text cursor to the right without changing the existing text.
   Character keys: After existing settings are deleted, new settings can be typed.
   Snap X spacing input button: Enter the X spacing in this input button and the Y spacing is automatically set to the same spacing.
   Grid X spacing input button: Enter the X spacing in this input button and the Y spacing is automatically set to the same spacing.
   Snap angle, X base, and Y base input buttons: These buttons relate to the Rotate option and are discussed in later chapters.

5. **Check buttons:** A check button has two parts, its mode name and the area that can be digitized to toggle the check mark and mode on and off. A check mark in the box indicates the mode is on.

While in the Drawing Aids dialog box, experiment with the different editing keys to become familiar with their functions. The dialog box is a handy tool to use for setting the snap and grid spacing, but if you are a fair typist, typing these commands from the keyboard is faster. After experimenting, be sure to return the grid spacing to 1/2 and the snap to 1/8 to have the correct settings for this exercise.

Create Layers

Layers

The layer concept in AutoCAD is similar to the transparent overlays used with a manually drafted project. Different parts of the project can be placed on separate layers. The building shell may be on one layer, the interior walls on another, the electrical on a third layer, the furniture on a fourth layer, and so on. There is no limit to the number of layers you may use in a drawing. Each is perfectly aligned with all the others. Each layer may be viewed on the display screen separately, one layer may be viewed in combination with one or more of the other layers, or all layers may be viewed together. Each layer may also be plotted separately or in combination with other layers, or all layers may be plotted at the same time. The layer name may be from 1 to 255 characters in length.

Step 5.   Create layers using the keyboard.

The LAYER prompt "?/Make/Set/New/ON/OFF/Color/Ltype/LWeight/Plot/Freeze/Thaw:" allows you to select 10 options.

To use the options Make and Color:

Prompt	Response
Command:	Type: **-LA<enter>**

Enter an option [?/Make/Set/New/ON/ OFF/Color/Ltype/LWeight/Plot/Freeze/ Thaw/LOck/Unlock]:	Type: **M\<enter\>**
Enter name for new layer (becomes the current layer) \<0\>:	Type: **R\<enter\>**
Enter an option [?/Make/Set/New/ON/ OFF/Color/Ltype/LWeight/Plot/Freeze/ Thaw/LOck/Unlock]:	Type: **C\<enter\>**
Enter color name or number (1-255):	Type: **R\<enter\>**
Enter name for new layer (becomes the current layer) \<R\>:	Type: **\<enter\>** (If the default name shown is not R, Type: **R\<enter\>**)
Enter an option [?/Make/Set/New/ON/ OFF/Color/Ltype/LWeight/Plot/Freeze/ Thaw/LOck/Unlock]:	**\<enter\>** (to exit from the Layer command.)

Make and Color

With the option "Make" from the LAYER: prompt, you have just created a layer named "R." Upper- or lowercase letters may be entered for the name; AutoCAD converts all layer names to uppercase. The name may be as long as 255 characters, including numbers and letters. It may include only letters, numbers, and three special characters: $ (dollar sign), - (hyphen), and ___ (underscore).

Note that the prompt is for "New current layer \<0\>." By using the option "Make," you may create one new layer *and* it is automatically set as the current layer on which you will draw. The new layer name appears in the status line on the display screen as the current layer on which you will be working.

Using the option "Color" from the LAYER: prompt allows you to choose a color from seven standard colors and assign it to a layer in response to the prompt "Layer name(s) for color 1 (red) \<R\>." R is the *default*, so the enter key is used. If the option "Color" is not used, the layer will default to the color white.

The option "Ltype" was not used, so the linetype for layer R will default to a "continuous" linetype. Continuous is a solid line.

The option "Ltype" from the LAYER: prompt allows you to choose a linetype from nine standard linetypes and assign it to a layer. A linetype was not assigned to layer G, so it will default to a continuous linetype. Later versions of AutoCAD have three sizes for each linetype, for example, HIDDEN (the standard size), HIDDEN2 (half the standard size), and HIDDENX2 (twice the standard size).

ON or OFF—FREEZE or THAW

The options ON and OFF pertain to the visibility of layers. When a layer is turned OFF, it is still part of the drawing, but it is not visible on the screen, nor can it be plotted. For instance, the building shell layer, interior walls layer, and furniture layer can be turned ON and all other layers turned OFF to view, edit, or plot a furniture plan. One or more layers can be turned OFF and ON as required to get the combination of layers needed.

The options FREEZE and THAW also pertain to the visibility of layers. The difference between ON or OFF and FREEZE or THAW is a matter of how quickly the drawing *regenerates* on the display screen. If a layer is frozen, it is not visible, it cannot be plotted, and AutoCAD does not spend any time regenerating it. A layer that is turned OFF is not visible and cannot be plotted, but AutoCAD does regenerate it.

Regeneration of a layer takes time. If you are switching between layers and doing some editing on each layer, it is best to use ON and OFF. If, while editing layers, there are layers that you do not need to edit or see, it is best to FREEZE those layers to avoid their regeneration.

When a layer is created, it is automatically turned ON and is thawed.

Note: Layer 0, color white, with a continuous linetype, is created automatically by AutoCAD. It has some special properties that will be used in later chapters. Layer 0 cannot be deleted.

The Layer Dialog Box

When you Type: **LA\<enter>** or Click: **the Layer icon in the upper left of your screen**, the Layer Manager dialog box appears. It is very easy to create new layers and assign colors and linetypes to them with the dialog box.

The Layer List

After you have created new layers and assigned colors and linetypes, a Layer List box appears in the upper left of your screen (on the object properties toolbar). You can turn layers on and off, freeze and thaw, and set a layer current using the Layer List. On and off requires you to Click: **the light bulb**, freeze and thaw requires you to Click: **the sun** or **the snowflake**, and set requires you to Click: **on the desired current layer** to close the Layer List.

Save the Drawing and Exit AutoCAD

Step 8. **Save the settings and layers for Exercise 3–1 on the hard drive. The drawing name will be EX3–1(your initials).**

Prompt	Response
Command:	Type: **SAVEAS\<enter>**
The Save Drawing As dialog box appears with File Name: highlighted:	Type: **EX3–1(your initials)** (Because File Name: was highlighted you were able to type in that place. If you had used any other part of the dialog box first, you would have had to click to the left of Drawing1, hold down the click button, and drag the cursor across the name to highlight it and then begin typing.) The drawing name may be from 1 to 255 characters in length. Keep the name to 8 characters or less for now.
	Click: **OK**

Be sure to make note of the drive and folder where the drawing is being saved so you can retrieve it easily when you need it.

Step 9. **Save the same drawing to a floppy disk in the A: drive. |**
(Substitute B: for A: if your computer is so labeled.) Insert a formatted diskette into the A: drive.

Prompt	Response
Command:	**\<enter>** (to repeat the previous command)
The Save Drawing As dialog box appears:	Click: **the down arrow in the Drives: button, highlight the a: drive, and** Click: **a:** or Click: **the Up LArrow and locate "3-1/2 Floppy Drive [A:]" and click it**
	Click: **OK**

The light should brighten on the A: drive indicating that the drawing is being saved.

Because the drawing was named when you saved it on the hard drive, you did not have to type the name again to save it with that name on the floppy disk. You could have chosen to give the drawing another name when you saved it on the floppy disk, in which case you would have to type the new name in the File Name: input button.

Save Drawing As Dialog Box

The parts and functions of the Save Drawing As dialog box are as follows:

File Name: input button The drawing file name that will be saved appears here. Beneath the File Name: button is an alphabetized list of all files of the type defined by the Save File as Type: button in the drive and directory specified in the Directories: and Drives: buttons. If you want to use one of the names in this list, Click: it and that name will replace the one in the File Name: button. You will need to use the scroll bar if the list of files is longer than the area shown.

Save as Type: button Clicking the down arrow reveals a list of file types under which the drawing may be saved. All have the extension .dwg except the Drawing Template Type, which has the extension .dwt. Some of these file types can be used interchangeably, but others require that a specific file type be used. In this book you will use only the AutoCAD File Type .dwg for drawings.

Save in: button The Drive and folder where the file will be saved is listed in the area. The area beneath this lists the drive and folders existing on that drive. The list indicates that the folder is open and that it contains other folders. The list of files in this area shows the files with the .dwg extension that exist in the folder. If you double-click the folder labeled c:\, a list of the other folders on the c: drive appears.

Drives: button When you click the down arrow here a list of the drives existing on your computer appears. Clicking any one of them allows you to move from drive to drive as needed.

OK button When clicked, this button executes the Save As command.

Cancel button When clicked, this button cancels the command or closes any open button on the dialog box. The Esc key has the same effect.

Step 10.   Exit AutoCAD or AutoCAD LT

Prompt	Response
Command:	Type: **QUIT<enter>** (to exit)

Exiting AutoCAD or AutoCAD LT

Three commands, Save, Save As, and Exit (or Quit), and their uses must be understood to save your work in the desired drive and directory and to exit AutoCAD after you have saved your work.

Save

When the command Save is clicked and the drawing has been named, the drawing is saved automatically to the drive and directory in which you are working, and a backup file is created with the same name but with the extension .bak. If the drawing has not been named, Save behaves in the same manner as Save As.

Save As

Save As activates the Save Drawing As dialog box whether or not the drawing has been named and allows you to save your drawing to any drive or directory you choose.

Some additional features of the Save As command are as follows:

1. A drawing file can be saved and you may continue to work because with the Save As command the drawing editor is not exited.

2. If the default drive is used (the drive on which you are working), and the drawing has been opened from that drive, .dwg and .bak files are created.

3. If a different drive is specified (a floppy disk in the floppy drive), only a .dwg file is created.

4. To change the name of the drawing, you may save it under a new name by typing a new name in the File Name: button.

5. If the drawing was previously saved or if a drawing file already exists with the drawing file name you typed, AutoCAD gives you the message **"This file already exists. Do you want to replace it?"**

When a drawing file is updated, the old .dwg file is replaced with the new drawing, so the answer is to Click: **Yes**. If an error has been made and you do not want to replace the file, Click: **No**.

6. A drawing may be saved to as many floppy disks or to as many directories on the hard disk as you wish. You should save your drawing on two different floppy disks as insurance against catastrophe.

Exit

If you have not made any changes to the drawing since you last saved it, the Exit command takes you out of the AutoCAD or AutoCAD LT program. If you have made changes to the drawing and have not saved these changes, AutoCAD will give you the message "Save changes to EX3–1MK?" (or whatever the drawing name is). This is a safety feature because the Exit command, by itself, *does not update or save a drawing*. You have three options: Yes, save the changes; No, do not save changes; or Cancel the Exit command.

If you have just entered a drawing, have made a lot of mistakes, and just want to get rid of everything, respond with No to the Save changes question. If you opened an existing drawing and use the Exit command without making any changes, the stored .dwg file and .bak files are preserved unchanged.

While you are making a new drawing AutoCAD is creating a .dwg (drawing) file of your drawing. There is no .bak (drawing file backup) file for a new drawing.

Each time an existing drawing file is opened for editing, the original drawing file (.dwg) becomes the drawing file backup (.bak). The new edited version of the drawing becomes the .dwg file. Thus, there is a copy of the original drawing file (.bak) and a copy of the new edited version (.dwg).

TIPS FOR BEGINNING AUTOCAD AND AUTOCAD LT USERS

If you make a mistake and want to back up one or more steps:

Prompt	Response
Command:	Type: **U<enter>**
	Continue pressing **<enter>** to repeat the UNDO command until you back up to the desired point.

If you UNDO too much:

Prompt	Response
Command:	Type: **REDO<enter>** to redo one undo. REDO undoes only one undo.
If you have drawn a wrong line and want to back up one or more lines but still stay in the line command:	Type: **U<enter>** until you are back to the desired point.
If you want to cancel a command:	Press: the **Esc** key

If you are having trouble selecting items, Zoom a window around the items to enlarge the view, then Zoom back out to complete the command.

If you Zoom-All and your drawing is very small in one corner of the display, look for a stray piece of the drawing on an opposite side of the display and erase it. You may have to pan the display to select the problem piece. After you find it and erase, Zoom-All again.

If you still have the same problem, thaw and turn on all layers and Zoom-All again to locate and move or erase the problem. To thaw all layers: Type: **-LA<enter>**), then

T\<enter> for Thaw, then ***\<enter>** for all layers. To turn on all layers: Type: **-LA\<enter>** , then **ON\<enter>**, then ***\<enter>** for all layers.

EXERCISES

EXERCISE 3–1.   Complete Exercise 3–1 using steps 1 through 10 described in this chapter.

REVIEW QUESTIONS

Circle the best answer.

1. Which of the following is *not* on the list of units?
   a. Scientific
   b. Metric
   c. Decimal
   d. Fractional
   e. Architectural
2. The default lower left corner of the drawing limits is 8-1/2,11.
   a. True
   b. False
3. The function key F7, described in this chapter, does which of the following?
   a. Provides a check list of the layers created
   b. Turns Snap ON or OFF
   c. Flips the screen from the text display to the graphics display
   d. Turns Grid ON or OFF
   e. Turns Ortho ON or OFF
4. Which of the following function keys is used to turn Snap ON or OFF?
   a. F1
   b. F2
   c. F7
   d. F8
   e. F9
5. If you want to correct a mistake made by the previous command, which of the following is the correct response?
   a. Type: U\<enter>
   b. Press: Esc
   c. Press: Ctrl-C
   d. Type: REDO\<enter>
   e. Press: F7
6. To make sure you have all layers thawed, which of the following should you type to select all layers?
   a. #
   b. @
   c. *
   d. <
   e. F9
7. A frozen layer may be turned ON before it is thawed.
   a. True
   b. False
8. How many layers may be set current at the same time?
   a. 1
   b. 2
   c. 3
   d. 16
   e. An unlimited number
9. When a layer is OFF, it will regenerate but is not visible.
   a. True
   b. False

10. Later versions of AutoCAD provide you with how many sizes of each standard linetype (except continuous)?
    a. 1
    b. 2
    c. 3
    d. 4
    e. As many as you want

Complete.

11. Describe the effect of using the Esc key or Ctrl-C while in a command.

    _____

12. An invisible grid to which the crosshairs will lock is called

    _____

13. What is the maximum number of characters that may be used in a layer name?

    _____

14. How many layers may be used in a drawing?

    _____

15. What is the maximum number of characters that may be used in a drawing name?

    _____

16. Explain what .dwg and .bak files are.

    .dwg _____

    .bak _____

17. Describe how the Layer dialog box can be used to make a new layer and assign a color to it.

    _____

18. List three functions the Layer List can perform.

    _____

    _____

    _____

19. What does the QUIT command do when used by itself?

    _____

20. Describe how Save differs from Save As when the drawing has been named.

    _____

Warning:
Remember, do not use the Exit command without first saving your work. If you answer yes to the Exit question without first saving a drawing, you will lose all your work.
Note:
The number of units to the right of the decimal has no bearing on how accurately AutoCAD LT draws. It controls the display of dimensions and other values displayed on the screen such as coordinates and defaults. No matter what the decimal places setting, AutoCAD draws with extreme accuracy.

4 Lettering for Pencil Sketches

OBJECTIVE

After completing this chapter, you will be able to:

☐ Develop a legible, uniform lettering style that is pleasing in appearance.

INTRODUCTION

The sketches you draw in this book must not only have correct construction, good line quality, good arrangement in the field of the drawing (the field of the drawing is that area inside the border where the drawing is placed), they must also have lettering that is uniform, legible, and pleasing in appearance. A good lettering style is a result of careful planning and a controlled lettering style. The following alphabet is a good model for a legible, uniform lettering style that you can develop with a little careful practice.

THE SKETCHING ALPHABET

The letters used in the **sketching alphabet** are made with single strokes and are as simple as possible. This alphabet is very similar to the Simplex font, which is one of the fonts available to you in AutoCAD and AutoCAD LT. There are no serifs on the letters, and all strokes are the same width (Figure 4–1). Most companies use all capital (uppercase) letters because lowercase letters are more likely to become illegible when they are copied in a reduced size.

Uppercase Letters

The sequence of strokes for each letter in the vertical alphabet is shown in Figure 4–2. Study each character until you know what it should look like. It may take a while for you to form the letters well. After you have drawn a letter, compare it with the form in Figure 4–2. If your letter does not look as good as or better than that in the figure, stop, analyze what is wrong, and correct it. *Go slowly at first and do it right*. You can pick up speed later.

Fractions

It is important that fractions be large enough to be reproduced at a reduced size and still be legible. Fractions should be twice the height of whole numbers if they are vertical (Figure 4–3A). Each number of the fraction should be almost the same size as the whole numbers if the fraction must be horizontal to fit a given space (Figure 4–3B). The vertical

FIGURE 4–1
The Sketching Alphabet Style

SINGLE STROKE · SERIFS (NOT THIS) · SANS (NO) SERIF THIS · GOTHIC (ALL STROKES SAME WIDTH) · ROMAN

FIGURE 4–2
The Vertical Alphabet

FIGURE 4–3
Fractions

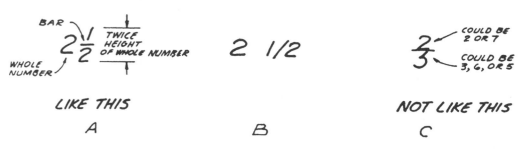

fraction is preferred. Do not let fraction numbers touch the horizontal bar, because that can make the fraction illegible (Figure 4–3C).

Slant

Letters may be vertical or inclined; either style is usually acceptable. Which one you use usually depends on your natural ability. The important characteristics of a good lettering style are that all letters are the same height and slant and that they are bold enough to reproduce well. Figure 4–4 shows the inclined alphabet.

Guidelines

Use guidelines, ruled paper, or a lettering aid like that shown in Figure 4–5 for all letters and numbers. The lettering aid shown in Figure 4–6 is easy to use. Just letter inside a slot and make all letters "bounce off" the top and bottom of the slot so that they are all the same height. Guidelines must be very thin and light—so light that they are barely visible. All lettering should be very dark and thin enough to be easily read.

FIGURE 4–4
The Inclined Alphabet

ABCDEFGHIJKLMN
OPQRSTUVWXYZ
1234567890

70°
APPROXIMATE
SLANT

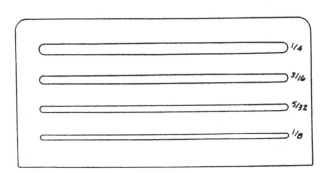

FIGURE 4–5
A Lettering Guide

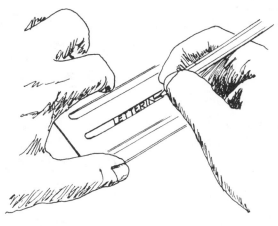

FIGURE 4–6
Using a Lettering Guide

DEVELOPING A GOOD LETTERING STYLE

The most important characteristic of lettering is legibility. Lettering must be consistent and neat, but above all it must be easily read so that numbers and values cannot be mistaken. The alphabets shown in Figures 4–2 and 4–4 can be drawn legibly with a little practice. The rules for developing a good lettering style are as follows:

1. Make sure the form of the letter is right. Do not mix uppercase and lowercase letters. Use all uppercase letters unless your instructor tells you otherwise.

2. Use guidelines, a lettering aid, or ruled paper. When drawing guidelines, make sure they are very light and thin.

3. Keep the slant of the letters the same. Use either a vertical or slanted stroke, but keep the stroke consistent.

4. Put all the letters in words as close to each other as you can while still making them look good.

5. Concentrate on keeping the characters open and easily read.

6. Do not make letters too tall for the thickness of your stroke. With a slightly blunted pencil point, letters $\frac{1}{8}''$ to $\frac{3}{16}''$ high look good.

7. Make the space between words approximately big enough for the letter *I*. The space between lines of lettering should be half to two-thirds the height of the letter (Figure 4–7).

8. Do not allow letters or numbers to touch any object line, border, or fraction bar. Leave a clear space all around letters and numbers (sides, top, and bottom).

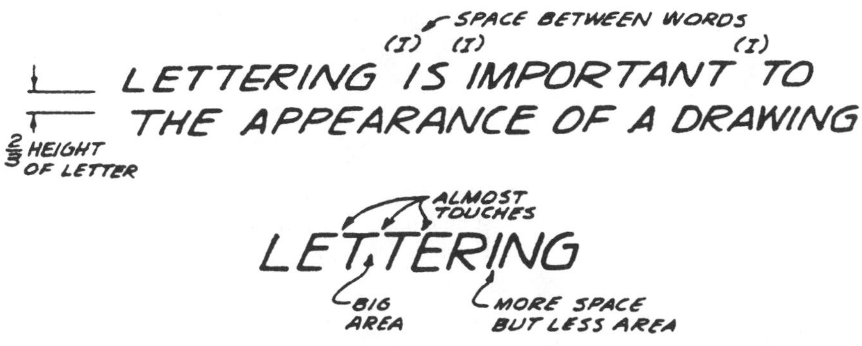

FIGURE 4–7
Spacing between Words and Lines

SPACE BETWEEN WORDS
(I)   (I)   (I)
LETTERING IS IMPORTANT TO
THE APPEARANCE OF A DRAWING
$\frac{2}{3}$ HEIGHT OF LETTER

ALMOST TOUCHES
LET,TERING
BIG AREA   MORE SPACE BUT LESS AREA

FIGURE 4–8
Vertical Architectural Alphabet

A B C D E F G H I J K L M
N O P Q R S T U V W X Y Z
1 2 3 4 5 6 7 8 9 0

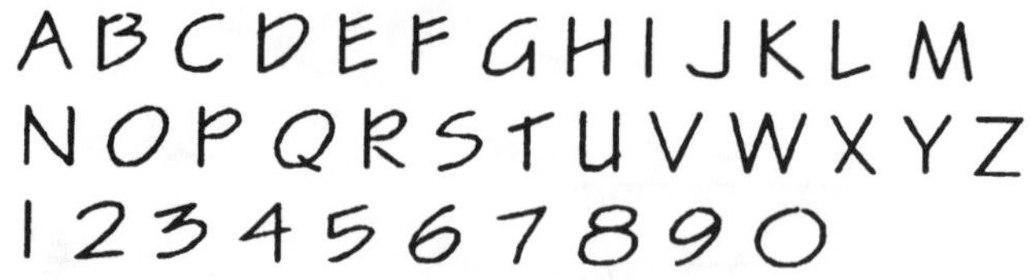

FIGURE 4–9
Inclined Architectural Alphabet

A B C D E F G H I J K L M
N O P Q R S T U V W X Y Z
1 2 3 4 5 6 7 8 9 0

9. Begin by drawing letters and numbers. *Take your time.*

10. Make all letters very dark. If you must repeat a stroke to improve its density, do so. A No. 2 pencil or an H-grade lead is right for most people.

11. Work to improve your speed as soon as you have the form, density, and slant correct.

The two architectural alphabets you will use in this book are shown in Figures 4–8 and 4–9.

EXERCISES

EXERCISE 4–1. Using the vertical style of lettering, repeat each of the letters, numbers, fractions, words, and sentences in Figure 4–8 (on the sheet in the back of this book labeled Exercise 4–1) the stated number of times.

EXERCISE 4–2. Using the inclined style of lettering, repeat each of the letters, numbers, fractions, words, and sentences in Figure 4–9 (on the sheet in the back of this book labeled Exercise 4–2) the stated number of times.

REVIEW QUESTIONS

Circle the best answer.

1. The sketching alphabet described in this chapter is similar to which of the following AutoCAD fonts?
   a. Simplex
   b. Standard
   c. Txt
   d. Italic
   e. Freehand
2. Guidelines for lettering should be drawn
   a. Thin and dark
   b. Thin and light
   c. Thick and dark
   d. Thick and light
   e. Guidelines should not be used.
3. Vertical fractions should be
   a. Twice the height of whole numbers
   b. The same height as whole numbers
   c. About one and a half times the height of whole numbers
   d. A little smaller than whole numbers
   e. Height is not important.

4. The most important quality of good lettering is
   a. Consistent height
   b. Consistent slant
   c. Consistent darkness
   d. Legibility
   e. Good appearance
5. Either vertical or inclined lettering is acceptable in most companies.
   a. True
   b. False
6. The space between words should be approximately
   a. The spacing for the letter *W*
   b. The spacing for the letter *O*
   c. The spacing for the letter *I*
   d. Twice the height of the letters
   e. Approximately two-thirds the height of the letters
7. The space between lines of lettering should be
   a. Approximately two-thirds the height of the letters
   b. Approximately twice the height of the letters
   c. Invisible (lines of lettering should touch)
   d. Approximately one and a half times the height of the letters
   e. Approximately one-fourth the height of the letters
8. A good lead grade for lettering is
   a. H
   b. 4H
   c. F
   d. 6H
   e. B
9. It is OK for letters to touch the lines forming the title block of a drawing.
   a. True
   b. False
10. When you practice lettering, you should letter as fast as you can in the beginning.
   a. True
   b. False

5

Sketching Line Weights and Drawing Constructions

OBJECTIVES

After completing this chapter, you will be able to

□ Draw dense, uniform, dark lines of the correct thickness for object, cutting plane, center, dimension, and extension lines.
□ Draw thin, light lines for drawing construction and lettering guidelines for stated problems.
□ Divide lines, angles, and arcs.
□ Construct polygons.
□ Draw tangents to circles, lines, and arcs.

LINES USED IN TECHNICAL DRAWINGS

Line quality is one of the most important elements of a good drawing. Many different types of lines are commonly used. All lines except construction lines for drawing and guidelines for lettering must be sharp and dark. Some are thicker than others, but all lines must be black and uniformly dark. Lettering guidelines and construction lines must be very thin and light—just barely dark enough to be followed for drawing the final lines.

The alphabet of lines is shown in Figure 5–1. AutoCAD calls these different lines, *linetypes*. These linetypes are the same as the ones that you will use to sketch the exercises in this book.

FIGURE 5–1
Alphabet of Lines

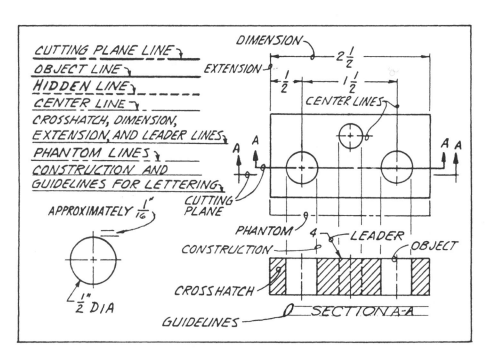

They are described as follows:

Cutting plane lines are the thickest lines. They consist of a long dash and two short dashes. Another form of the cutting plane line, also shown in Figure 5–1, is used in making sectional views, which will be covered in Chapters 9 and 10.

Object lines are approximately half as thick as cutting plane lines and are continuous (no breaks).

Hidden lines, a series of short dashes, are the same thickness or slightly thinner than object lines. Dashes are approximately $\frac{1}{8}''$ long and are separated by $\frac{1}{16}''$ spaces.

Hatch, dimension, extension, and leader lines are continuous and are approximately half as thick as object lines but are just as dark.

Center lines are the same width as dimension lines and consist of a long dash and one short dash. The long dash is approximately 5/8" long; the short dash is approximately 1/16" long, and the space between dashes is approximately 1/16". The center line should extend approximately 1/16" past the feature it is describing. Center lines describe circular features and the centers of some objects.

Phantom lines are used to show some alternative position or feature that differs from the main drawing. They are similar to center lines with a long dash and two short dashes instead of one.

Construction lines and guidelines for lettering are continuous and are thin and very light.

SKETCHING GOOD LINES

Using a Wooden Pencil or a Lead Holder

Drawing good lines with a wooden pencil or lead holder requires that the pencil be sharpened often. When drawing thin lines, such as center lines and dimension lines, you must sharpen the lead to a point, as shown in Figure 5–2. In drawing object, hidden, and cutting plane lines, use a blunter point (Figure 5–2). To draw the line, hold the pencil about 1″ from the end, at approximately a 60° angle to the paper (Figure 5–3). Roll the pencil in your hand as you draw the line from left to right. Apply enough pressure to get a solid, dark line. Go back over the lines from right to left if necessary. Use a No. 2 pencil and H or 2H lead for these lines.

Using a Mechanical Pencil

The mechanical pencil has a lead of uniform thickness and as a result must be held perpendicular to the paper. To draw object and hidden lines, use a .7-mm lead of H or 2H softness. To draw thin lines, such as dimension lines, center lines, and extension lines, use a .5-mm lead of H or 2H softness. Use a firm, even pressure to get a solid line and to

SHARP POINT
FOR CONSTRUCTION
AND GUIDELINES

CRUSH SMALL
END FOR CENTER
LINES, DIMENSIONS, ETC.

CRUSH LARGER
END FOR OBJECT
LINES

60° ANGLE TO PAPER

FIGURE 5–2
Preparing the Pencil Point

FIGURE 5–3
Drawing Angle

avoid breaking the lead. Go back over lines if necessary to get a solid, dark line. Construction lines and lettering guidelines can be drawn with a .3-mm lead of 2H or 4H softness.

CONSTRUCTION TERMS

Many drawing constructions are done repeatedly in technical drawings. Because many of the terms used to describe these constructions are not familiar to everyone, the most common terms are defined as follows:

Radius   The distance from the center of a circle or arc to the outside edge or circumference (Figure 5–4). It is the distance halfway across a circle template.

Diameter   The distance all the way across a circle, though the center (Figure 5–5). It is the size marked on circles on a circle template.

Circumference   The distance around the outside of a circle.

Intersection   Where two or more lines, circles, or arcs cross (Figure 5–6).

Parallel   Two lines or curves that are the same distance apart along all parts of the lines or curves (Figure 5–7).

Perpendicular   Lines at 90° angles to each other (Figure 5–8).

Tangent   Lines or arcs that touch at only one point. When lines or arcs are tangent, they lie exactly on top of each other at one point (Figure 5–9).

Bisected   Divided in half (Figure 5–10).

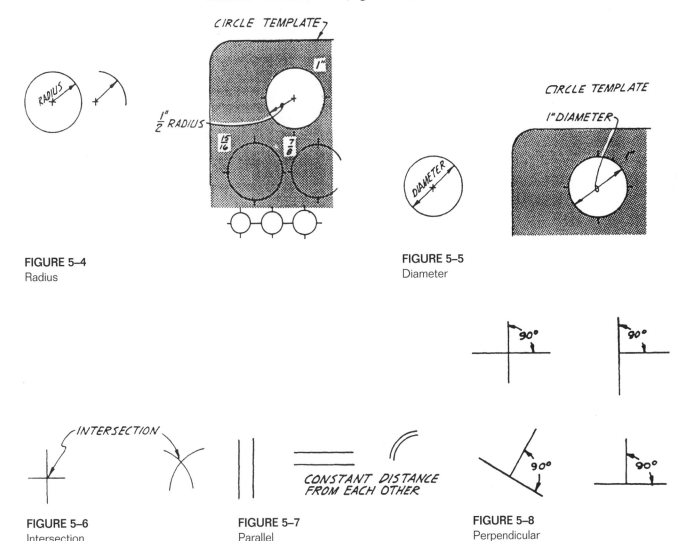

FIGURE 5–4
Radius

FIGURE 5–5
Diameter

FIGURE 5–6
Intersection

FIGURE 5–7
Parallel

FIGURE 5–8
Perpendicular

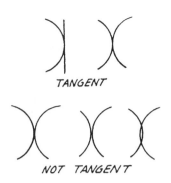

TANGENT

NOT TANGENT

FIGURE 5–9
Tangent

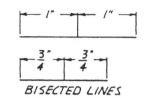

BISECTED LINES

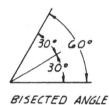

BISECTED ANGLE

FIGURE 5–10
Bisected

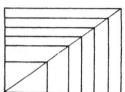

ALL THESE RECTANGLES ARE PROPORTIONAL TO ONE ANOTHER

FIGURE 5–11
Proportional

Proportional   In the same ratio or proportions (Figure 5–11).

Across corners   A measurement made across corners through the center of a feature (Figure 5–12).

Across flats   A measurement made across the parallel sides of a feature (Figure 5–13). The measurement is made perpendicular to the sides.

Right angle   A 90° angle (Figure 5–14).

Acute angle   An angle of less than 90° (Figure 5–15).

Obtuse angle   An angle of greater than 90° (Figure 5–16).

Fillet   An inside radius (Figure 5–17).

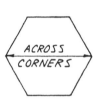

ACROSS CORNERS

FIGURE 5–12
Across Corners

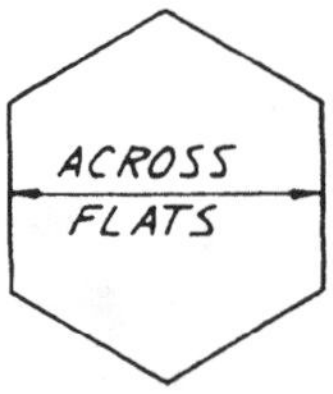

ACROSS FLATS

FIGURE 5–13
Across Flats

90°

A RIGHT ANGLE

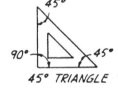

45°   90°   45°

45° TRIANGLE

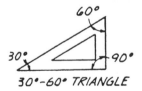

60°   30°   90°

30°-60° TRIANGLE

FIGURE 5–14
Right Angles

80°

60°

45°

30°

FIGURE 5–15
Acute Angles

Chapter 5

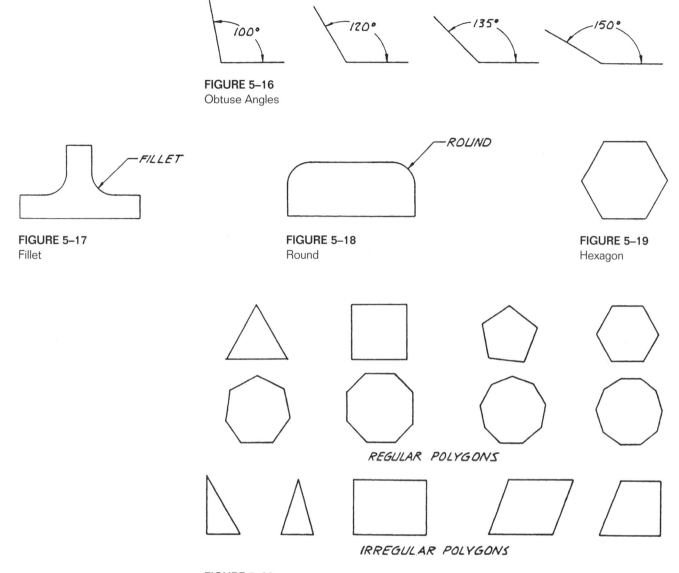

FIGURE 5–16
Obtuse Angles

FIGURE 5–17
Fillet

FIGURE 5–18
Round

FIGURE 5–19
Hexagon

FIGURE 5–20
Polygons

Round   An outside radius (Figure 5–18).
Hexagon   A feature with six equal sides and angles (Figure 5–19).
Polygon   A feature enclosed with straight lines (Figure 5–20). Regular polygons have equal sides and angles. Irregular polygons have unequal sides and/or angles.

DRAWING CONSTRUCTIONS

Now that we have defined the construction terms, we shall describe the most common drawing constructions.

Sketching Parallel Lines

There are several methods for drawing parallel lines. The grid paper in your book allows you to use the grid for sketching parallel vertical and horizontal lines. Figure 5–21 shows the use of a drafting machine or T-square and triangles to sketch parallel lines. This book is designed for you to use triangles to sketch parallel lines. AutoCAD has a command

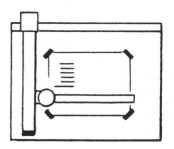

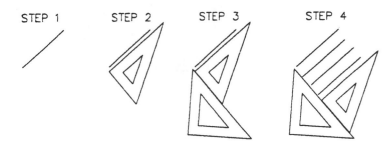

called **Offset** that is used to draw parallel lines. To sketch parallel lines on an angle follow these steps:

Step 1. Sketch one line at the desired angle.

Step 2. Align one edge of a triangle on the newly drawn line.

Step 3. Place one edge of another triangle at the base of the first triangle as shown in Figure 5–21.

Step 4. Either tape the second triangle in place or hold it firmly as you slide the first triangle along its edge and sketch the parallel lines.

Figure 5–22 shows the steps in sketching parallel lines a given distance apart (in this case $^3/_4''$) by drawing a construction line perpendicular to the first line sketched. The perpendicular ensures that the lines are spaced exactly the distance marked. The steps are as follows:

Step 1. Sketch one line at the desired angle.

Step 2. Construct a perpendicular construction line by aligning one triangle on the line and placing another triangle containing a 90° angle on it as shown in Figure 5–22. Make sure your construction line is very thin and light.

Step 3. Using either a dot or a small light line, mark $^3/_4''$ spaces on the perpendicular line.

Step 4. Using the two-triangle method described in Figure 5–21, sketch lines through the points.

FIGURE 5–22
Sketching Parallel Lines Using
Two Triangles

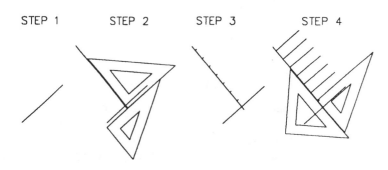

FIGURE 5–23
Sketching Perpendicular Lines

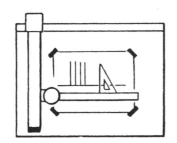
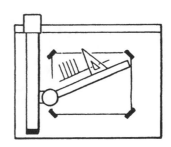

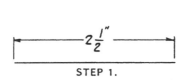

STEP 1.

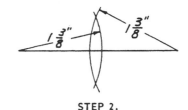

STEP 2.

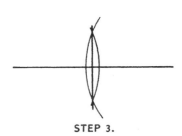

STEP 3.

Sketching Perpendicular Lines

In addition to the method for sketching perpendicular lines described in Figure 5–22, two methods are shown in Figure 5–23. The first method involves the use of a straight edge and a triangle. The straight edge can be a drafting machine, a T-square, or another triangle. The second method has the following steps:

Step 1.   Start with a line of a specified length (in this case 2½″).
Step 2.   Using a radius greater than half the length of the line, draw arcs from each end of the line.
Step 3.   Connect the intersections of the arcs to form a perpendicular.

AutoCAD uses a command called **Osnap-Perpendicular** to draw lines perpendicular to other lines.

Sketching Tangents

Figures 5–24 through 5–30 show several instances where tangents are used and the methods for sketching them. AutoCAD uses a combination of **Osnap-Tangent** and arc and circle commands that use the **Tangent-Tangent-Radius** option to draw tangents. The **Fillet** command is also used to draw arcs of a specified radius tangent to two lines.

Sketching a line tangent to two circles (Figure 5–24):

Step 1.   Lay a triangle so that it rests just below the outside edges of both circles. This small space allows your pencil lead to pass exactly through both circles, making the line tangent to them.
Step 2.   Draw the line tangent to both circles.
Step 3.   Repeat step 1, positioning the triangle differently to draw another tangent.

FIGURE 5–24
Sketching a Line Tangent to Two
Circles

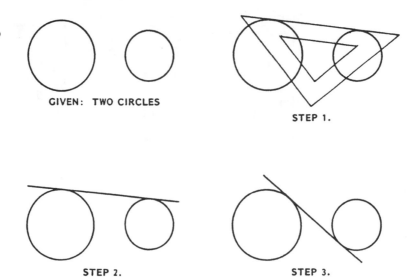

Sketching an inside arc tangent to two circles (Figure 5–25):

Although you will not use method 1 in your sketching exercises because it often requires a compass, it is important that you study this method so you will know how it is done. You will find it to be useful in understanding constructions in both sketching and AutoCAD.

FIGURE 5–25
Sketching an Inside Arc Tangent
to Two Circles

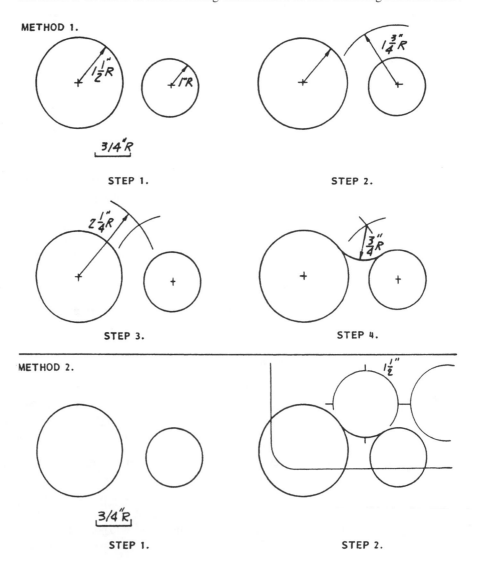

Chapter 5

Method 1

Step 1. Start with two given circles and a given radius (in the example, a larger circle with a $1\frac{1}{2}''$ radius, a smaller circle with a $1''$ radius, and a $\frac{3}{4}''$ radius for the arc to be sketched tangent. The circles must be close enough together to allow the arc to touch.

Step 2. From the center of the $1''$ radius circle, sketch an arc with a radius that is $1''$ (the small circle radius) plus $\frac{3}{4}''$ (the radius of the arc to be sketched).

Step 3. From the center of the $1\frac{1}{2}''$ radius circle, sketch an arc with a radius that is $1\frac{1}{2}''$ (large circle radius) plus $\frac{3}{4}''$ (radius of the arc to be sketched).

Step 4. From the intersection of the two arcs, sketch an arc with a radius of 3/4". This arc will be exactly tangent to both circles.

Method 2

Step 1. Start with the same given circles and radius used in Method 1.

Step 2. Using a circle template, place a circle hole with a $\frac{3}{4}''$ radius ($1\frac{1}{2}''$ diameter) tangent to both circles and draw the radius (be sure you allow for the width of the pencil lead).

Sketching an outside arc tangent to two circles (Figure 5–26):

Although you will not use this technique in your sketching exercises because it requires a compass, it is important that you study this method so you will know how it is done. You will find it to be useful in understanding constructions in both sketching and AutoCAD.

Step 1. Start with two given circles and a given radius (in the example, a larger circle with a $1\frac{1}{2}''$ radius, a smaller circle with a $1''$ radius, and a $4''$ radius for the arc to be sketched tangent. The radius must be large enough to touch the outside edges of both circles.

Step 2. From the center of the $1\frac{1}{2}''$ radius circle, sketch an arc with a radius that is $2\frac{1}{2}''$ (the $4''$ radius minus the radius of the $1\frac{1}{2}''$ radius circle).

FIGURE 5–26
Sketching an Outside Arc Tangent to Two Circles

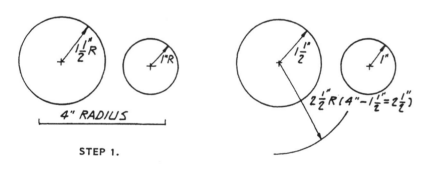

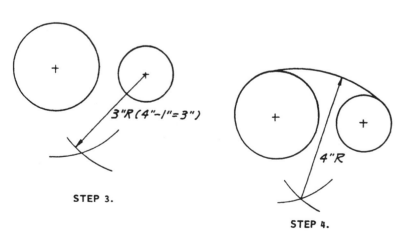

Step 3. From the center of the 1″ radius circle, sketch an arc with a radius of 3″ (the 4″ radius minus the radius of the 1″ radius circle).

Step 4. From the intersection of the two arcs, sketch an arc with a radius of 4″. This arc will be exactly tangent to both circles.

Sketching an arc (fillet) tangent to lines at right angles (Figure 5–27):

Method 1

Step 1. Start with given lines *AB* and *CD* at right angles and a given radius ($\frac{1}{2}$″ in the example).

Step 2. Draw construction lines parallel to lines *AB* and *CD* $\frac{1}{2}$″ from the lines.

Step 3. From the intersection of the construction lines, draw a $\frac{1}{2}$″ radius arc, which will form the fillet.

Method 2

Step 1. Start with the same given lines and the radius used in Method 1.

Step 2. Using a circle template, place a circle with a $\frac{1}{2}$″ radius (1″ diameter) in the correct position and draw the radius tangent to lines *AB* and *CD*.

Sketching an arc (fillet) tangent to lines at any angle (Figure 5–28):

Method 1

Step 1. Start with given lines *AB* and *CD* that will intersect if extended and a given radius ($\frac{1}{2}$″ in the example).

FIGURE 5–27
Sketching a Fillet Tangent to Two
Lines at Right Angles

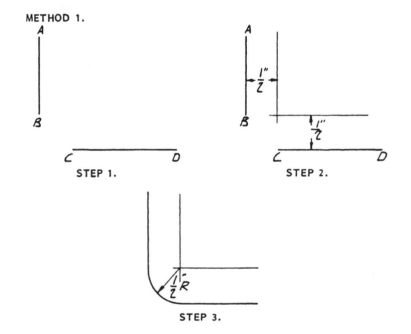

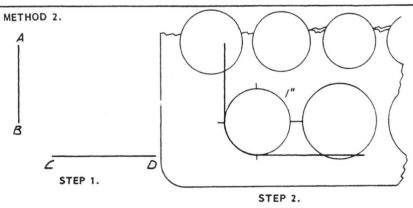

Chapter 5

FIGURE 5–28
Sketching a Fillet Tangent to
Lines at Any Angle

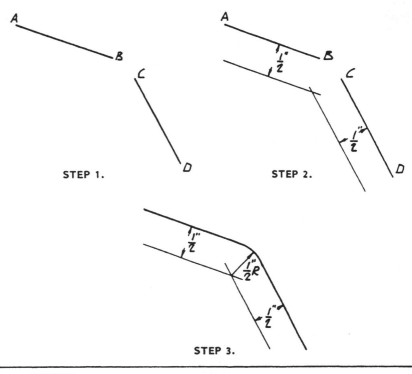

METHOD 1.

STEP 1.

STEP 2.

STEP 3.

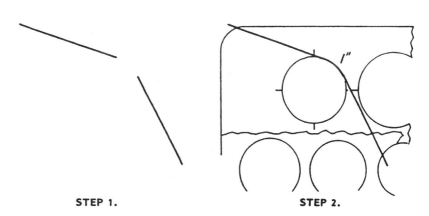

METHOD 2.

STEP 1.

STEP 2.

Step 2. Draw construction lines parallel to lines *AB* and *CD* ½″ from the lines.

Step 3. From the intersection of the construction lines, draw a ½″ radius arc, which will form the fillet.

Method 2

Step 1. Start with the same given lines and the radius used in Method 1.

Step 2. Using a circle template, place a circle with a 1/2″ radius (1″ diameter) in the correct position and draw the radius tangent to lines *AB* and *CD*.

Sketching an arc of a given radius tangent to a straight line and a circle (Figure 5–29):

Method 1

Step 1. Start with a given circle (1½″ radius in the example), a straight line, and a given radius (³⁄₄″ in the example).

Step 2. From the center of the circle, draw an arc that has a radius of 1½″ (the radius of the circle) plus ³⁄₄″ (the radius of the arc to be drawn).

FIGURE 5–29
Sketching an Arc of a Given
Radius Tangent to a Circle and a
Straight Line

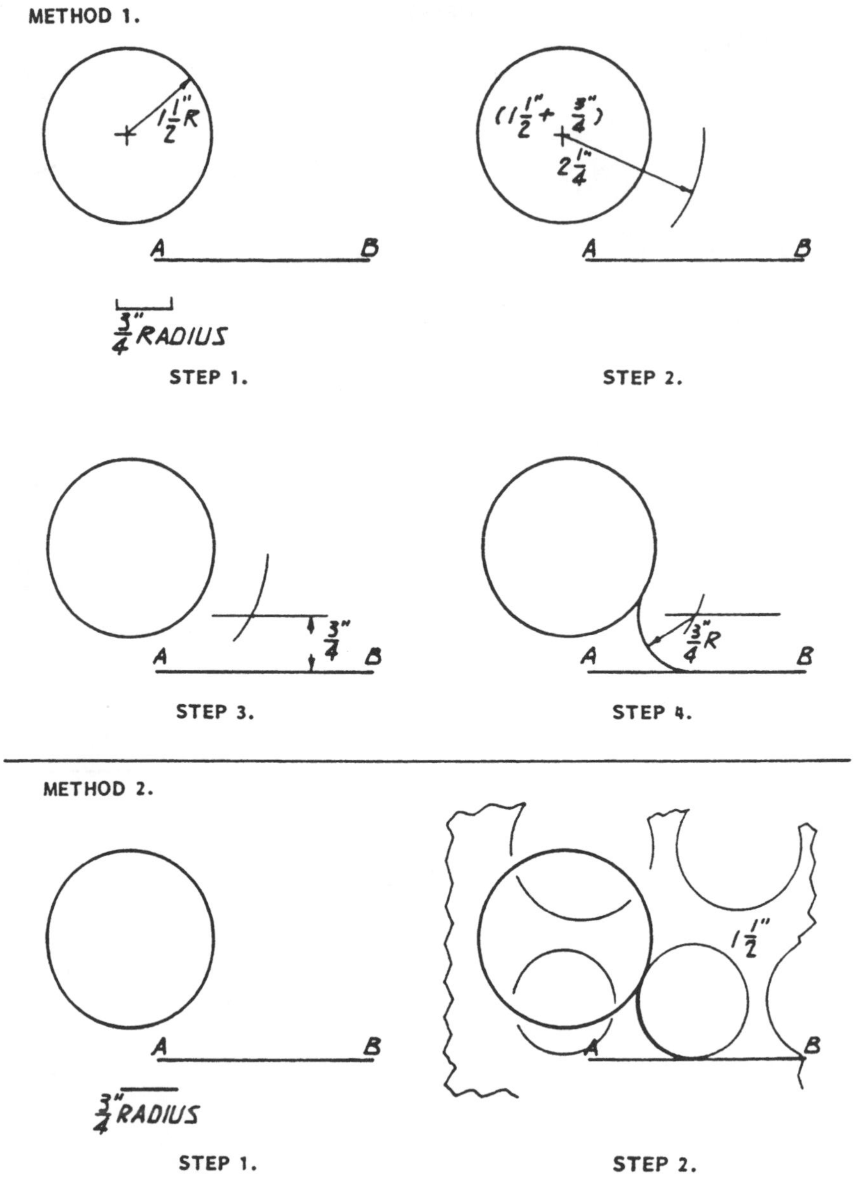

METHOD 1.

METHOD 2.

Step 3.   Draw a line parallel to line AB $^3/_4''$ away from it to intersect the arc.

Step 4.   From the intersection, draw the $^3/_4''$ radius tangent to the line and the circle.

Method 2

Step 1.   Start with the same given circle, line, and radius used in Method 1.

Step 2.   With a circle template, place a circle with a $^3/_4''$ radius ($1^1/_2''$ diameter) tangent to the circle and the line, and draw the $^3/_4''$ radius.

Sketching an arc tangent to two parallel lines (Figure 5–30):

Method 1

Step 1.   Start with two given parallel lines ($2^1/_2''$ apart in the example).

Step 2.   Draw a perpendicular that crosses both lines.

Step 3.   From each intersection, draw an arc with a radius greater than half the distance between the two lines.

Step 4.   Draw a line through the intersection of the two arcs. Then, using the distance AB as a radius and point A as the center, draw the arc tangent to the two parallel lines.

FIGURE 5–30
Sketching an Arc Tangent to Two
Parallel Lines

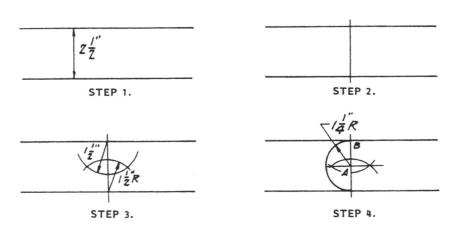

METHOD 1.

STEP 1.   STEP 2.

STEP 3.   STEP 4.

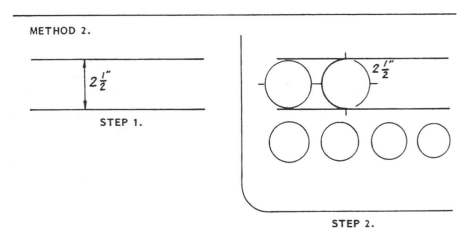

METHOD 2.

STEP 1.

STEP 2.

Method 2

Step 1. Start with the same given parallel lines used in Method 1.

Step 2. With a circle template, place a circle with a $2\frac{1}{2}''$ diameter between the lines, and draw the arc tangent to the two lines.

Dividing Lines and Angles

When you are sketching it is sometimes necessary to divide a line into a specified number of parts or to bisect an angle. AutoCAD makes this very easy with the Divide command, but when you are sketching you can use the following methods.

Dividing a line into any number of equal parts (Figure 5–31):

Method 1

Step 1. Start with a line of any length, *AB*.

Step 2. Draw a line perpendicular to one end of line *AB*.

Step 3. On a scale, select any convenient length that has equal units (six in the example) and place it so that one end is at point *A* and the other end lies on the perpendicular line. Make marks on the paper at the six unit points.

Step 4. Draw perpendicular lines through the six marks to intersect line *AB* and divide it into six equal parts.

FIGURE 5–31
Dividing a Line into Any Number
of Equal Parts

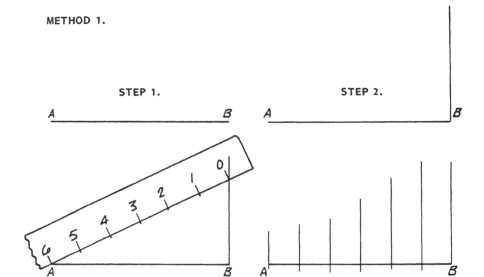

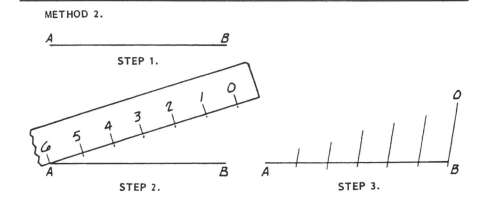

Method 2

Step 1.	Start with a line of any length, *AB*.
Step 2.	Place a scale with six equal units on it at a convenient angle to point *A*. Make marks on the paper at the six unit points.
Step 3.	Connect the last unit (0 in the example) with point *B* and draw lines parallel to line *OB* to divide line *AB* into six equal parts.

Dividing a line into proportional parts (Figure 5–32):

Step 1.	Start with a line of any length, *AB*.
Step 2.	Place a scale with six equal units on it at a convenient angle to point *A*. Make marks on the paper at the specified unit points (5 units, 3 units, 2 units, and 1 unit in the example).
Step 3.	Connect the last unit (0 in the example) with point *B* and draw lines parallel to line *OB* to divide line *AB* into parts proportional to 5, 3, 2, and 1.

Bisecting an angle (Figure 5–33):

Step 1.	Start with a given angle (52° in the example).
Step 2.	Draw a radius from the start point of the angle (*A*) to intersect the sides of the angle.
Step 3.	Using the intersections *B* and *C* as centers, draw arcs of equal radius.

FIGURE 5–32
Dividing a Line into Proportional Parts

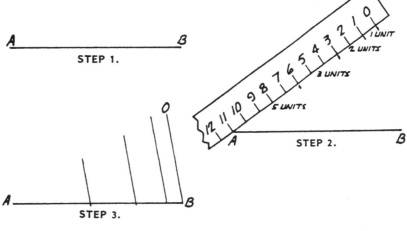

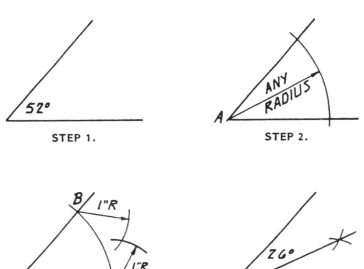

FIGURE 5–33
Bisecting an Angle

Step 4. Draw a line from the intersection of the arcs to point *A* to bisect the angle.

Sketching Polygons

Sketching polygons requires considerable construction. AutoCAD has a **Polygon** command that makes drawing polygons very easy. The sketching technique is described next.

Inscribing a hexagon in a circle (Figure 5–34);
(Inscribing means drawing the hexagon inside the circle.)

Step 1. Start with a given circle.
Step 2. Draw a horizontal line through the center of the circle to the outside edge.
Step 3. Using a 30-60° triangle as shown, draw lines from the points at which the horizontal line intersects the circle.
Step 4. Complete the hexagon by drawing horizontal lines at the top and bottom.

Circumscribing a hexagon around a circle (Figure 5–35):
(Circumscribing means drawing the hexagon outside the circle and tangent to it.)

Step 1. Start with a given circle.

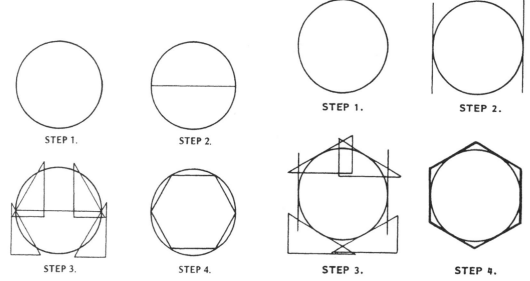

FIGURE 5–34
Inscribing a Hexagon in a Circle

FIGURE 5–35
Circumscribing a Hexagon around a Circle

Step 2.   Draw vertical lines tangent to the circle.
Step 3.   Using a 30-60° triangle as shown, draw lines tangent to the circle.
Step 4.   Darken the lines to complete the hexagon.

Inscribing an octagon in a circle (Figure 5–36):

Step 1.   Start with a given circle and draw perpendicular construction lines through the center for reference.
Step 2.   Draw a $22\frac{1}{2}°$ line through the center (bisect a 45° angle).
Step 3.   Where the $22\frac{1}{2}°$ line intersects the circle, draw 90° and 45° angles. (Use 45° triangles as shown.)
Step 4.   Draw horizontal lines at the top and bottom to complete the octagon.

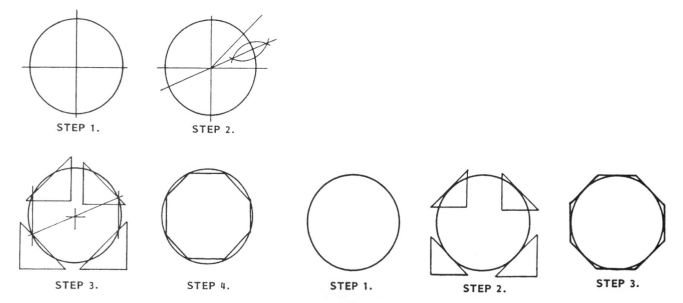

FIGURE 5–36
Inscribing an Octagon in a Circle

FIGURE 5–37
Circumscribing an Octagon around a Circle

Circumscribing an octagon around a circle (Figure 5–37):

Step 1. Start with a given circle.

Step 2. Use a 45° triangle in the position shown to draw 45° and 90° angles tangent to the circle.

Step 3. Draw horizontal lines at the top and bottom to complete the octagon.

EXERCISES

EXERCISE 5–1. Draw Exercise 5–1 on the sheet in your book labeled EXERCISE 5–1 using the dimensions shown in Figure 5–38. Make sure that your lines are the cor-

FIGURE 5–38
Dimensions for Exercise 5–1

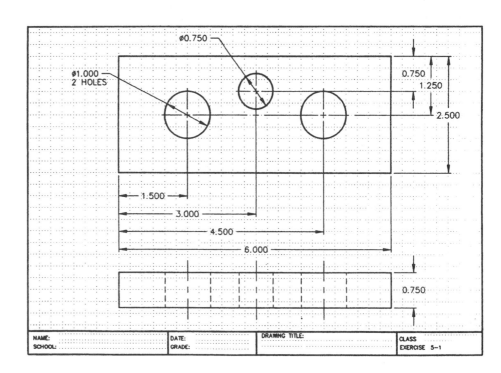

FIGURE 5–39
Instructions for Exercise 5–2

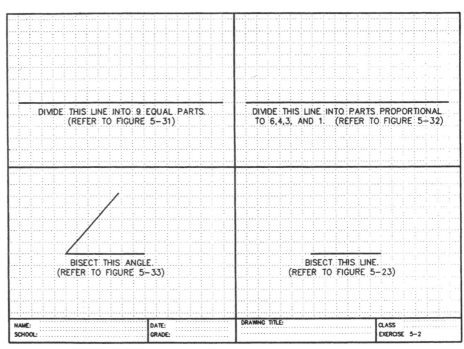

rect weight and are of even width and darkness. Use guidelines for lettering, and make your lettering the best you can. Draw and letter everything that is shown in Figure 5–38. Refer to Figure 5–1 for correct line weights.

EXERCISE 5–2.   Use the sheet in your book labeled EXERCISE 5–2 for this exercise. Divide the drawing area into four equal parts as shown in Figure 5–39 and make the required constructions. Center your construction in the areas. Darken the object lines and the division marks. Leave very light construction lines. Fill in the title block information. Title the drawing LINES.

EXERCISE 5–3.   Use the sheet in your book labeled EXERCISE 5–3 for this exercise. Divide the drawing area into four equal parts as shown in Figure 5–40 and draw the polygons described in that figure. Center your construction in the areas.

FIGURE 5–40
Instructions for Exercise 5–3

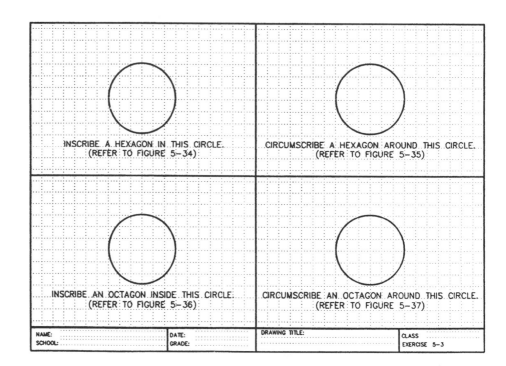

FIGURE 5–41
Dimensions for Exercise 5–4

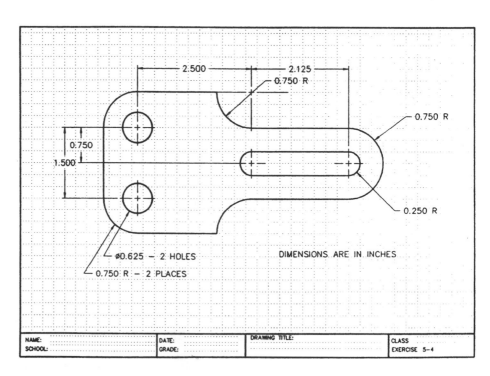

Darken the object lines and leave very light construction lines. Fill in the title block information. Title the drawing POLYGONS.

EXERCISE 5–4. Draw Exercise 5–4 on the sheet in your book labeled EXERCISE 5–4 using the dimensions shown in Figure 5–41. Make sure that your lines are the correct weight and are of even width and darkness. Do not show any dimensions or other lettering on the drawing itself. Fill in the title block using your best lettering. Title the drawing PLATE. Use construction methods shown in Figures 5–24 through 5–30.

EXERCISE 5–5. Draw Exercise 5–5 on the sheet in your book labeled EXERCISE 5–5 using half scale of the dimensions shown in Figure 5-42. Make sure that your lines are the correct weight and are of even width and darkness. Do not show any dimensions or other lettering on the drawing itself. Fill in the title block using your best lettering. Title the drawing GASKET. Use construction methods shown in Figures 5–24 through 5–30.

FIGURE 5–42
Dimensions for Exercise 5–5

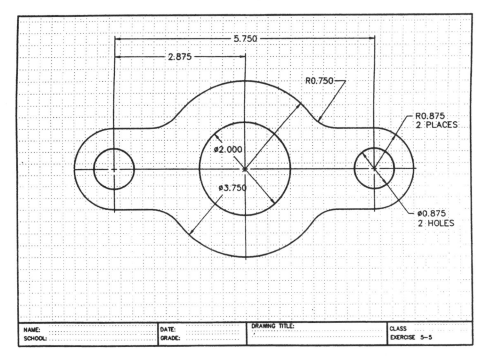

Figure 5–43
Dimensions for Exercise 5–6

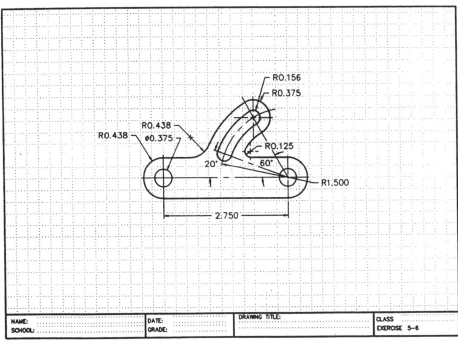

Sketching Line Weights and Drawing Constructions

EXERCISE 5–6.   Draw Exercise 5–6 on the sheet labeled EXERCISE 5–6 in your book using the dimensions shown in Figure 5–43. Make sure that your lines are the correct weight and are of even width and darkness. Do not show any dimensions or other lettering on the drawing itself. There are four large arcs that you will have to sketch without using a circle template. Use your scale and make several dots along the path of the arc to aid you in sketching. Fill in the title block using your best lettering. Title the drawing STOP. Use construction methods shown in Figures 5–24 through 5–30.

REVIEW QUESTIONS

Circle the best answer.
  1. Construction lines and guidelines for lettering should be
     a. Thin and very dark
     b. Thick and very dark
     c. Thin and very light
     d. Thick and very light
     e. Any of the above is OK.
  2. Hidden lines are shown with
     a. A series of short dashes
     b. A long dash followed by a short dash
     c. Solid lines
     d. Two short dashes and a long dash
     e. Hidden lines are not shown.
  3. Center lines, hatch lines, extension lines, and dimension lines are drawn thin and very dark.
     a. True
     b. False
  4. A cutting plane line is drawn
     a. Thin and very dark
     b. Very thick and very dark
     c. Thin and very light
     d. Very thick and very light
     e. Any of the above is OK.
  5. A good lead softness to use for object lines is
     a. H
     b. B
     c. 4H
     d. 6H
     e. Any of the above is OK.
  6. A good lead thickness for object lines is
     a. .25 mm
     b. .35 mm
     c. .5 mm
     d. .7 mm
     e. 1.0 mm
  7. The distance from the center of a circle to the outside edge is called
     a. A diameter
     b. A radius
     c. A circumference
     d. An arc
     e. A tangent
  8. The circles on a circle template are measured in
     a. diameters
     b. radii

9. Lines that are the same distance apart along all parts of the lines are
    a. Parallel
    b. Perpendicular
    c. Tangent
    d. Proportional
    e. Intersecting

10. Lines that are at 90° to each other are
    a. Parallel
    b. Perpendicular
    c. Tangent
    d. Proportional
    e. Intersecting

11. Lines that are tangent
    a. Lie very close to each other
    b. Just touch at the edges
    c. Lie exactly on top of each other at one point
    d. Do not touch
    e. Are perpendicular

12. A 90° angle that is bisected will result in
    a. Two angles greater than 90°
    b. Two 45° angles
    c. No angle at all
    d. Two 90° angles
    e. Two 30° angles

13. A right angle is
    a. 90°
    b. Greater than 90°
    c. Less than 90°
    d. Any angle correctly drawn
    e. Either a 45° or a 30° angle

14. An obtuse angle is
    a. 90°
    b. Greater than 90°
    c. Less than 90°
    d. Any angle correctly drawn
    e. Either a 45° or a 30° angle

15. An acute angle is
    a. 90°
    b. Greater than 90°
    c. Less than 90°
    d. Any angle correctly drawn
    e. Either a 45° or a 30° angle

16. A circumference is
    a. The distance across a circle
    b. The distance from the center of a circle to the outside edge
    c. The distance around the outside of a circle
    d. The form of an arc
    e. The area of a circle

17. A fillet is
    a. Another name for diameter
    b. An arc forming the corner of two lines
    c. An intersection
    d. A complete circle
    e. A form of polygon

18. A hexagon has
    a. Four sides
    b. Five sides
    c. Six sides
    d. Eight sides
    e. Any number of sides greater than three
19. An octagon has
    a. Four sides
    b. Five sides
    c. Six sides
    d. Eight sides
    e. Any number of sides greater than three
20. Which AutoCAD command will divide a line into equal parts?
    a. Divide
    b. Proportional
    c. Edit
    d. Line
    e. Offset

6   Linetypes and Drawing Constructions Using AutoCAD

OBJECTIVES

After completing this chapter, you will be able to

☐ Make drawings using continuous, hidden, and center linetypes.
☐ Correctly answer questions regarding linetypes and drawing constructions in Auto-CAD.
☐ Use the following commands to produce drawings:
   Line
   Osnap
   Circle
   Zoom
   Trim
   Offset
   Fillet
   Chamfer
☐ Answer questions regarding the preceding commands.

LINETYPES

Chapter 3 describes the concept of layers and how to assign colors and linetypes to them. This chapter shows you how to use AutoCAD commands to make drawings containing different linetypes.

    The drawings on the disk that came with your book already have layers created and linetypes assigned. When you need to draw lines with, for example, the HIDDEN linetype, you will change the current layer to one that has the HIDDEN linetype assigned to it.

    AutoCAD has many standard linetypes and a means of creating custom linetypes if needed. You will not need any custom linetypes to complete the drawings in this book.

DRAWING CONSTRUCTIONS

There are many ways to use AutoCAD to make drawings. The commands described here are not the only ones that can be used to make the drawings in this chapter, but they are the ones commonly used. Every feature of each command is not described in detail. The purpose of these exercises is to introduce you to the AutoCAD program while you learn drawing fundamentals.

    The commands you will use in this chapter are described next.

Line and Pline (Polyline)

The **Line** and **Pline** commands can be used to draw lines very accurately. Lines drawn with the Line command are separate lines, so that if you pick any one of them to move, erase, or otherwise modify, only the line picked is modified. Lines drawn with the Pline command are all connected, so that if any one of them is picked, all of them are selected to be modified. There are four common ways to do draw lines with either of these commands. There is a fifth method called Direct Distance Entry which will be discussed in a later chapter.

Drawing Lines Using the Grid Marks

Lines can be drawn by snapping to the grid marks visible on the screen.

While in the Line command, if you decide you do not like the last line segment drawn, Type: **U<enter>** to erase it and continue with the "Specify next point:" prompt. Picking more than one undo will backtrack through the line segments in the reverse order in which they were drawn.

The Line command has a very handy feature. If you respond to the prompt "Specify next point:" by pressing the enter key or the space bar, the line will start at the end of the most recently drawn line. The "continue" feature of the Line command will do the same.

Drawing Lines Using Absolute Coordinates

Remember, 0,0 is the lower left corner of the page. When absolute coordinates are used to draw, the X axis coordinate is entered first and identifies a location on the horizontal axis. The Y axis coordinate is entered second and identifies a location on the vertical axis. An absolute coordinate of 1,2 commands the line to move to a location that is 1″ in the X direction and 2″ in the Y direction from the lower left corner of the page.

Drawing Lines Using Relative Coordinates

Relative coordinates are taken from a point entered. (Relative to what? Relative to the point just entered.) After picking a point on the drawing, enter relative coordinates by typing @, followed by the X,Y coordinates. For example after entering a point to start a line, typing and entering **@1,0** will draw the line 1″ in the X direction, 0″ in the Y direction.

A minus sign (−) is used for negative line location with relative coordinates. Negative is to the left for the X axis, or down for the Y axis.

Drawing Lines Using Polar Coordinates

Absolute and relative coordinates are extremely useful in some situations; however, for many design applications polar coordinates are used. Be sure you understand how to use all three types of coordinates.

Polar coordinates also are relative to the last point entered. They are typed starting with an @, followed by a distance and an angle of direction. Figure 6–1 shows the polar coordinate angle directions. The angle direction is preceded by a < sign.

A polar coordinate of @4<0 commands the line to move 4″ to the right of the previous point. A polar coordinate of @4<270 commands the line to move 4″ downward from the previous point.

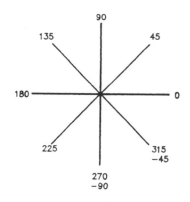

FIGURE 6–1
AutoCAD Polar Directions

ID

ID identifies a location from which relative or polar coordinates may be given. If, for example, you need to draw a circle that is 1.05″ in the X direction and 2.12″ in the Y direction from the intersection of two lines, you can specify that location by, first, identifying to AutoCAD the intersection by using the ID command and, second, typing the coordinates as **@1.05,2.12** when AutoCAD asks for the location of the circle center.

OSNAP

It is very important to become familiar with and use Object Snap modes while drawing. If an existing drawing entity is not drawn on a snap point, it is nearly impossible to snap a line or other drawing entity exactly to it. You may try, and think that the two points are connected, but a close examination will reveal they are not. Object Snap modes such as ENDpoint, MIDpoint, and CENter can be used to snap exactly to specific points of existing objects in a drawing. Object Snap modes need to be used constantly for complete accuracy while drawing. The exercises in this book direct you to use OSNAP modes whenever they are needed.

You can type the first three letters of any OSNAP mode to activate it, or you can select OSNAP modes from one of the menus in AutoCAD or AutoCAD LT.

Running OSNAP Modes

You may also set a "running" OSNAP mode to be constantly in effect while drawing, until it is disabled. A running OSNAP mode may include one or more modes. When you right-click **OSNAP** from the STATUS bar at the bottom of the screen and Click: Settings, the Drafting Settings dialog box appears, with the Object Snap tab active. Any number of OSNAP modes may be checked to be active. For instance if INTersection, MIDpoint, and ENDpoint are all checked, all of them will be in effect. When one or more modes are entered this way, they become the running object snap modes. The running mode can be disabled by clicking OSNAP at the bottom of the screen so all running OSNAP modes are disabled. You can also override the running mode for a single point by selecting another mode or typing the first three letters (followed by <enter>) of another mode not included in the running mode. The running mode returns after the single override.

Circle

The **Circle** command allows you to draw circles with extreme accuracy. There are several options to the Circle command that you will use in the exercises in this book. AutoCAD asks you first, to locate the center of the circle; second, to specify the radius. If you do not want to divide the diameter of the circle to be specified by 2 to obtain the radius, you can Type: **D <enter>** to tell AutoCAD you want to specify the diameter of the circle. Other options of the Circle command will be explained as they are used in the exercises.

Trim

The **Trim** command is one that is very useful. It allows you to trim many objects to one or more cutting edges. AutoCAD asks you first, to select cutting edges; second, to press <enter> to move to the next phase of the command; third, to select objects to trim.

Watch the TRIM prompts carefully. Not until all cutting edges have been selected and the prompt "<Select object to trim>:" appears can you pick the objects to trim. When you have many lines to trim, use the TRIM, Crossing, or All options to select the cutting edges. If you are unable to trim an entity because it does not intersect a cutting edge, use the Erase command.

Offset

The **Offset** command allows you to copy and enlarge or shrink a shape through a point or at a specified distance. AutoCAD asks you first, to specify a distance or select the through default; second, to pick the object to be offset; third, to pick on which side of the selected object you want the shape to appear. You will use the Offset command often in the exercises.

Mirror

The **Mirror** command is used to produce a mirror image of one or more selected objects. AutoCAD asks you first, to select the object(s) to be mirrored; second, to define a line that acts as the edge about which the object will be flopped; third, do you want to delete old (or source) objects? (the ones you originally selected). You will find the Mirror command to be very useful.

Fillet

The **Fillet** command is used to connect two lines, arcs, or circles with an arc of a specified radius. The specified radius must be smaller than the selected lines. The Polyline option of the Fillet command allows you to fillet all the intersections of a polyline at the same time. The Polyline command will be used in later chapters.

Erase

You will have occasion to erase something you have done. You can activate the **Erase** command by typing **E** and pressing <enter>. AutoCAD then asks you to select objects to be erased. You may select each individual object or you may use a window or crossing window to select objects to be erased. If you select one or more objects that you do not want to erase, you can hold down the Shift key and remove objects from those selected to be erased by picking them individually or using a window.

Zoom

The different **Zoom** commands (Realtime, All, Center, Extents, Previous, Window, Dynamic, and Scale) control how you view the drawing area on the display screen. Only three of these Zoom commands—Window, All, and Previous—are described because they are the most commonly used.

Zoom-Window

The **Zoom-Window** command allows you to pick two opposite corners of a rectangular window on the screen. The crosshairs of the pointer change to form a rubber band that shows the size of the window on the screen. The size of the window is controlled by the movement of the pointer. The part of the drawing inside the windowed area is magnified to fill the screen when the second corner of the window is picked.

Zoom-All

Zoom-All provides a view of the entire drawing area.

Zoom-Previous

Zoom-Previous is a very convenient feature. AutoCAD and AutoCAD LT remember up to 10 previous views. This is especially helpful and timesaving if you are working on a complicated drawing.

Now that you have read some descriptions of several commands, you will complete three exercises that use these commands.

EXERCISE 6–1:
Making a Drawing Using Continuous, Hidden, and Center Linetypes

Your final drawing will look like the drawing in Figure 6–2 without dimensions.

Step 1. **To begin Exercise 6–1, turn on the computer and start AutoCAD or AutoCAD LT.**

Step 2. **Open drawing EX6–1 supplied on the disk that came with your book.**

Step 3. **Use Zoom-All to view the entire drawing area.**

Prompt	Response
Command:	Type: **Z** <enter>
Specify corner of window, enter a scale factor (nX or nXP), or [All/Center/Dynamic/Extents/ Previous/Scale/Window] <real time>:	Type: **A<enter>**

Step 4. **Use the Line command to draw the object lines in the top and front views.**

Prompt	Response
Command:	Type: **L<enter>**
Specify first point:	
Specify next point or [Undo]:	Type:**END<enter>**

FIGURE 6–2
Dimensions for Exercise 6–1

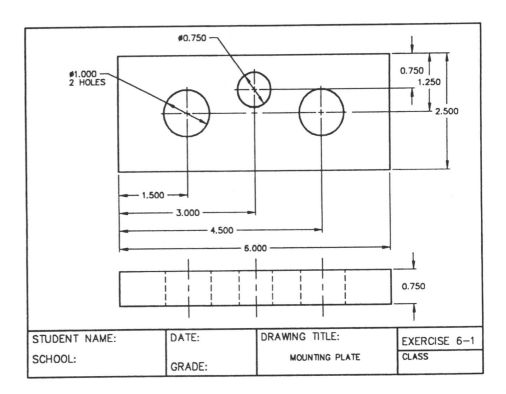

STUDENT NAME:	DATE:	DRAWING TITLE:	EXERCISE 6–1
		MOUNTING PLATE	CLASS
SCHOOL:	GRADE:		

Prompt	Response
of	Pick: **the top end of the long vertical line**
Specify next point or [Undo]:	Type: **@6<180<enter>**
Specify next point or [Undo]:	Type: **@2.5<270<enter>**
Specify next point or [Close/Undo]:	Type: **END<enter>**
of	Pick: **the bottom end of the longer vertical line**
Specify next point or [Close/Undo]:	**<enter>**
Command:	**<enter>**
Specify first point:	Type: **END<enter>**
of	Pick: **the top end of the short vertical line**
Specify next point or [Undo]:	Type: **@6<180<enter>**
Specify next point or [Undo]:	Type: **@.75<270<enter>**
Specify next point or [Close/Undo]:	Type: **END<enter>**
of	Pick: **the bottom end of the short vertical line**
Specify next point or [Close/Undo]:	**<enter>**

Step 5. Use the ID and Circle commands to draw holes in the top view.

Prompt	Response
Command:	Type: **ID<enter>**
Specify point:	Type: **END<enter>**
of	Pick: **D1 (Figure 6–3)**
Command:	Type: **C<enter>**

FIGURE 6–3
Use the ID and Circle Commands
to Draw Holes in the Top View

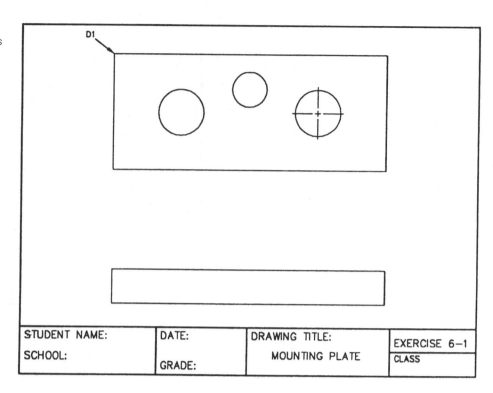

| STUDENT NAME: | DATE: | DRAWING TITLE: | EXERCISE 6–1 |
| SCHOOL: | GRADE: | MOUNTING PLATE | CLASS |

Prompt	Response
Specify center point for circle or [3P/2P/Ttr (tan tan radius)]:	Type: **@1.5,-1.25<enter>**
Specify radius of circle or [Diameter]:	Type: **.5<enter>**
Command:	Type: **ID<enter>**
Specify point:	Type: **END<enter>**
of	Pick: **D1 (again)**
Command:	Type: **C<enter>**
Specify center point for circle or [3P/2P/Ttr (tan tan radius)]:	Type: **@4.5,-1.25<enter>**
Specify radius of circle or [Diameter] <1.0000>:	**<enter>**
Command:	Type: **ID<enter>**
Specify point:	Type: **END<enter>**
of	Pick: **D1 (again)**
Command:	Type: **C<enter>**
Specify center point for circle or [3P/2P/Ttr (tan tan radius)]:	Type: **@3,-.75<enter>**
Specify radius of circle or [Diameter] <1.0000>:	Type: **D<enter>**
Diameter <1.000>:	Type: **.75<enter>**

Important: Make sure Snap and Ortho are ON (press function keys F8 and F9 once or twice and test that they are) so you can accurately line up hidden lines with the circle quadrants.

Note: You can set any layer current by clicking it from the Layer list at the top of your screen and ignoring the –LA response.

Step 6.   Set the HID layer current and draw hidden lines in the front view.

Prompt	Response
Command:	Type: **-LA<enter>**
[?/Make/Set/New/ON/OFF/Color/ Ltype/LWeight/Plot/Freeze/Thaw/ Lock/Unlock/stAte]:	Type: **S<enter>**
New current layer <OBJECT>:	Type: **HID<enter>**

[?/Make/Set/New/ON/OFF Specify next point or [Close/Undo]/Color/Ltype/LWeight/ Plot/Freeze/Thaw/Lock/Unlock/stAte]:	<enter>
Command:	Type: **L<enter>**
Specify first point:	Pick: **D1 (Figure 6–4)**
Specify next point or [Undo]:	Pick: **D2**
Specify next point or [Undo]:	<enter>
Command:	<enter>
Specify first point:	Pick: **D3**
Specify next point or [Undo]:	Pick: **D4**
Specify next point or [Undo]:	<enter>
Command:	<enter>
Specify first point:	Pick: **D5**
Specify next point or [Undo]:	Pick: **D6**
Specify next point or [Undo]:	<enter>
Command:	<enter>
Specify first point:	Pick: **D7**
Specify next point or [Undo]:	Pick: **D8**
Specify next point or [Undo]:	<enter>
Command:	<enter>
Specify first point:	Pick: **D9**
Specify next point or [Undo]:	Pick: **D10**
Specify next point or [Undo]:	<enter>
Command:	<enter>
Specify first point:	Pick: **D11**
Specify next point or [Undo]:	Pick: **D12**
Specify next point or [Undo]:	<enter>

FIGURE 6–4
Draw Hidden Lines in the Front
View

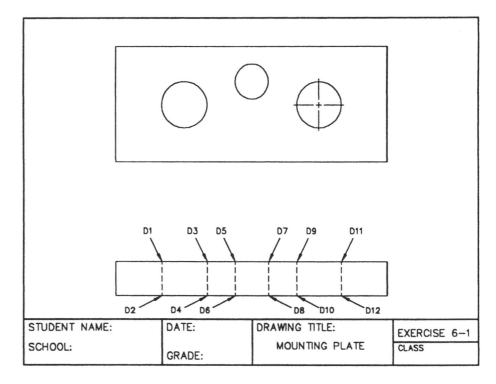

Step 7. Set the CEN layer current and draw center lines to complete the drawing.

Prompt	Response
Command:	Type: **-LA<enter>**
[?/Make/Set/New/ON/OFF/Color/Ltype/ LWeight/Plot/Freeze/Thaw/Lock/Unlock/ stAte]:	Type: **S<enter>**
New current layer <HID>:	Type: **CEN<enter>**
[?/Make/Set/New/ON/OFF/Color/Ltype/ LWeight/Plot/Freeze/Thaw/Lock/Unlock/ stAte]:	**<enter>**
Command:	Type: **DIM<enter>**
Dim:	Type: **CEN<enter>**
Select arc or circle:	Pick: **D1 (Figure 6–5)**
Dim:	**<enter>**
Select arc or circle:	Pick: **D2**
Dim:	Type: **E<enter>**
Command:	Type: **L<enter>**
Specify first point:	Pick: **D3 (Figure 6–5)**
Specify next point or [Undo]:	Pick: **D4**
Specify next point or [Undo]:	**<enter>**
Command:	**<enter>**
Specify first point:	Pick: **D5**
Specify next point or [Undo]:	Pick: **D6**
Specify next point or [Undo]:	**<enter>**
Command:	**<enter>**
Specify first point:	Pick: **D7**
Specify next point or [Undo]:	Pick: **D8**
Specify next point or [Undo]:	**<enter>**

Important: Be sure Snap is ON before you draw the following center lines.

FIGURE 6–5
Draw Center Lines

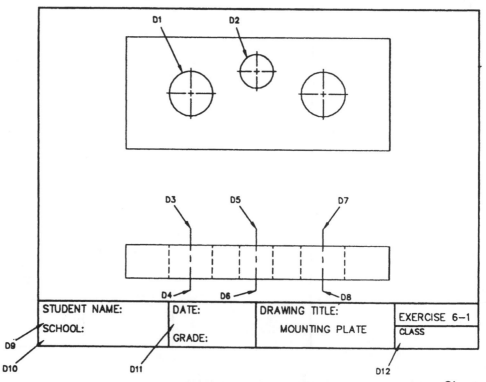

Step 8. Use the Dtext command to complete the title block.
On your own: **set Layer OBJECT current.**

Prompt	Response
Command:	Type: **DT<enter> or DTEXT<enter>**

Current text style: "Standard"
   Text height: 0.2000
    Specify start point of text or
    [Justify/Style]:
	Pick: **D9 (Figure 6–5)**

Specify height <0.2000>:	Type: **.12<enter>** (or just **<enter>** if the default is .12)
Specify rotation angle of text <0>:	**<enter>**
Enter text:	Type: **YOUR FIRST INITIAL AND YOUR LAST NAME<enter>** (Make sure all lettering in the title block is all capital letters.)
Enter text:	Pick: **D10 (Figure 6–5) and Type: YOUR SCHOOL NAME<enter>**
Enter text:	Pick: **D11 and Type: TODAY'S DATE<enter>**
Enter text:	Pick: **D12 and Type: YOUR CLASS NAME OR NUMBER<enter>**
Enter text:	**<enter>**

Step 9. Use the SAVEAS command to save your drawing as EX6–1 (your initials) on a floppy disk and again on the hard drive of your computer.

Step 10. Plot or print your drawing full size on an 11" x 8½" sheet.

EXERCISE 6–2:
Making a Drawing Containing Several Circles, Fillets, and Parallel Lines

Your final drawing will look like the drawing in Figure 6–6 without dimensions.

FIGURE 6–6
Dimensions for Exercise 6–2

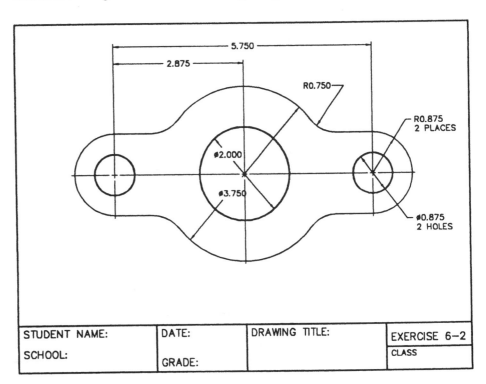

Step 1. To begin Exercise 6–2, turn on the computer and start AutoCAD or Auto-CAD LT.

Step 2. Open drawing EX6–2 supplied on the disk that came with your book.

Step 3. Use Zoom-All to view the entire drawing area:

Prompt	Response
Command:	Type: **Z<enter>**
Specify corner of window, enter a scale factor (nX or nXP), or [All/Center/ Dynamic/Extents/Previous/Scale/ Window] <real time>:	Type: **A<enter>**

Step 4. Use the Circle and ID commands to draw circles on the right and in the center of the part.

Prompt	Response
Command:	Type: **C<enter>**
Specify center point for circle or [3P/2P/Ttr (tan tan radius)]:	Type: **CEN<enter>**
of	Pick: **D1 (Figure 6–7)**
Specify radius of circle or [Diameter]:	Type: **.875<enter>**
Command:	Type: **ID<enter>**
Specify point:	Type: **CEN<enter>**
of	Pick: **D1 (again)**
Command:	Type: **C<enter>**
Specify center point for circle or [3P/2P/Ttr (tan tan radius)]:	Type: **@-2.875,0<enter>**
Specify radius of circle or [Diameter] <0.8750>:	Type: **D<enter>**
Specify diameter of circle <1.7500>:	Type: **3.75<enter>**

FIGURE 6–7
Use the Circle and ID Commands
to Draw Circles

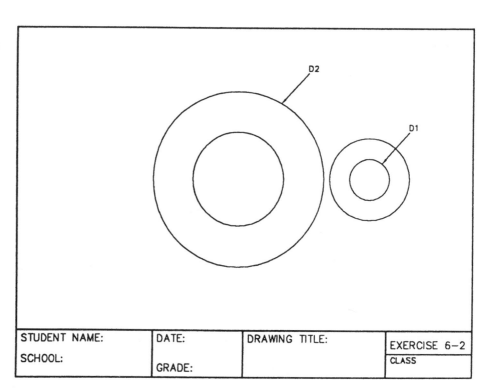

STUDENT NAME:	DATE:	DRAWING TITLE:	EXERCISE 6–2
SCHOOL:	GRADE:		CLASS

Command:	<enter>
Specify center point for circle or [3P/2P/Ttr (tan tan radius)]:	Type: **CEN<enter>**
of	Pick: **D2 (Figure 6–7)**
Specify radius of circle or [Diameter] |<1.875>:	Type: **1<enter>**

Step 5.   Use the Line and Offset commands to draw parallel lines.

Prompt	Response
Command:	Type: **L<enter>**
Specify first point:	Type: **QUA<enter>**
of	Pick: **D1 (Figure 6–8)**
Specify next point or [Undo]:	Type: **@1.25<180<enter>**
Specify next point or [Undo]:	<enter>
Command:	Type: **O<enter>** (for OFFSET)
Specify offset distance or [Through]:	<enter> (or Type: **T<enter> if Through is not the default**)
Select object to offset or <exit>:	Pick: **D2 (Figure 6–8)**
Specify through point:	Type: **QUA<enter>**
of	Pick: **D3**
Select object to offset or <exit>:	<enter>

Step 6.   Use the Trim command to remove circle excesses.

Prompt	Response
Command:	Type: **TR<enter>** (for TRIM)
Current settings: Projection=UCS Edge=None	
Select cutting edges ...	
Select objects:	Pick: **D1 and D2 (Figure 6–9)**

FIGURE 6–8
Use the Line and Offset Commands to Draw Parallel Lines

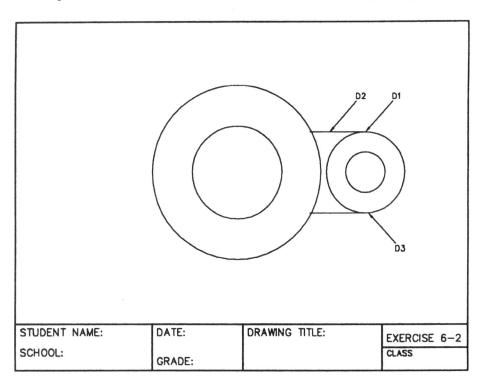

FIGURE 6–9
Use the Trim Command to
Remove Circle Excess

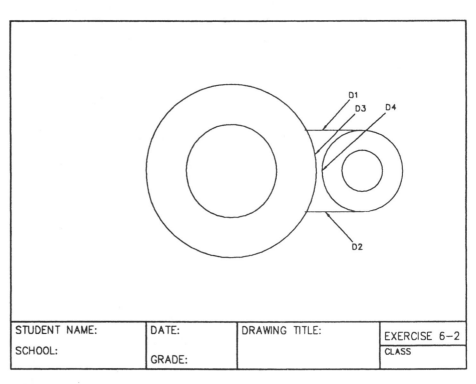

| STUDENT NAME: | DATE: | DRAWING TITLE: | EXERCISE 6–2 |
| SCHOOL: | GRADE: | | CLASS |

Select objects:	<enter>
Select object to trim or shift-select to extend or [Project/Edge/Undo]:	**Pick: D3 and D4**
Select object to trim or shift-select to extend or [Project/Edge/Undo]:	<enter>

Step 7.   Use the Mirror command to draw the left side of the figure.

Prompt	Response
Command:	Type: **MI<enter>** (for MIRROR)
Select objects:	Pick: **D1 (Figure 6–10)**
Specify opposite corner:	Pick: **D2**
Select objects:	<enter>
Specify first point of mirror line:	Type: **CEN<enter>**
of	Pick: **D3**
Specify second point of mirror line:	**Make sure Ortho is ON and** Pick: **D4** (any point directly above or below the center)
Delete source objects? [Yes/No] <N>:	<enter>

Step 8.   Use the Trim command to remove circle excess on the left side of the figure.

Prompt	Response
Command:	Type: **TR<enter>**
Select cutting edges:	
Select objects:	Pick: **D1 and D2 (Figure 6–11)**
Select objects:	<enter>
Select object to trim or shift-select to extend or [Project/Edge/Undo]:	Pick: **D3**
Select object to trim or shift-select to extend or [Project/Edge/Undo]:	<enter>

FIGURE 6–10
Use the Mirror Command to
Draw the Left Side

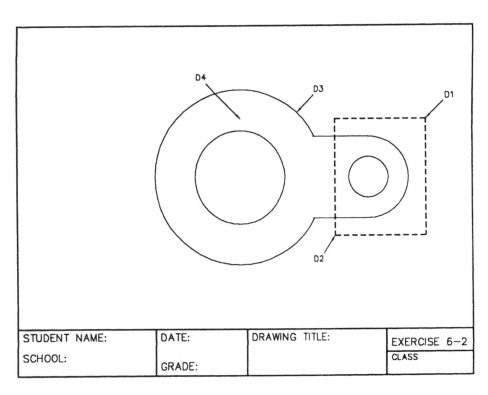

FIGURE 6–11
Use Trim Again

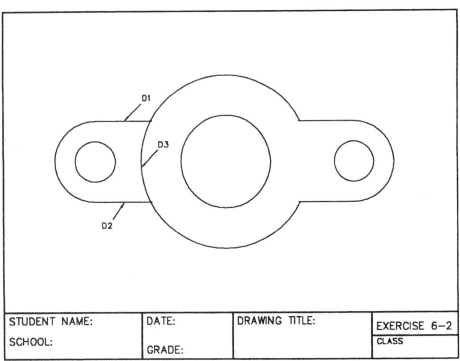

Step 9. **Use the Fillet command to complete the figure.**

Prompt	Response
Command:	Type: **F<enter>** (for FILLET)
Current settings: Mode = TRIM, Radius = 0′-0 1/2″ Select first object or	
[Polyline/Radius/Trim]:	Type: **R<enter>**
Specify fillet radius <0′-0 1/2″>:	Type: **.75<enter>**

FIGURE 6–12
Use the Fillet Command to
Complete the Drawing

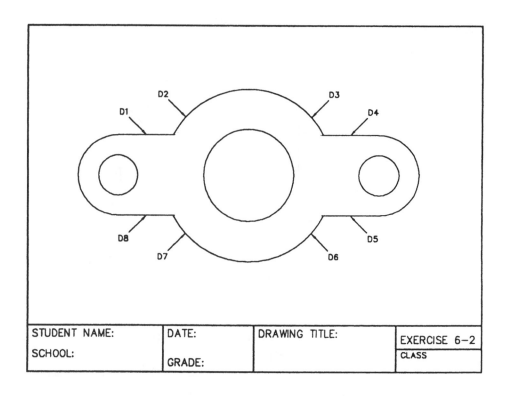

STUDENT NAME:	DATE:	DRAWING TITLE:	EXERCISE 6–2
SCHOOL:			CLASS
	GRADE:		

Current settings: Mode = TRIM, Radius = 0′-0 3/4″ Select first object or [Polyline/Radius/Trim]:	Pick: **D1 (Figure 6–12)**
Select second object:	Pick: **D2**
Command:	**\<enter\>**
Current settings: Mode = TRIM, Radius = 0′-0 3/4″ Select first object or [Polyline/Radius/Trim]:	Pick: **D3 (Figure 6–12)**
Select second object:	Pick: **D4**
Command:	**\<enter\>**
Current settings: Mode = TRIM, Radius = 0′-0 3/4″ Select first object or [Polyline/Radius/Trim]:	Pick: **D5**
Select second object:	Pick: **D6**
Command:	**\<enter\>**
Current settings: Mode = TRIM, Radius = 0′-0 3/4″ Select first object or [Polyline/Radius/Trim]:	Pick: **D7**
Select second object:	Pick: **D8**

Step 10. Use the Dtext command to complete the title block as you did for EX6–1. Title the drawing, GASKET.

Step 11. Use the SAVEAS command to save your drawing as EX6–2 (your initials) on a floppy disk and again on the hard drive of your computer.

Step 12. Plot or print your drawing full size on an 11″ x 8½″ sheet.

EXERCISE 6–3:
Drawing a Complex Shape Containing a Curved Slot

Your final drawing will look similar to the drawing in Figure 6–13 without dimensions.

Step 1. **To begin Exercise 6–3 , turn on the computer and start AutoCAD or Auto-CAD LT.**

Step 2. **Open drawing EX6–3 supplied on the disk that came with your book.**

Step 3. **Use Zoom-All to view the entire drawing area.**

Prompt	Response
Command:	Type: **Z<enter>**
Specify corner of window, enter a scale factor (nX or nXP), or [All/Center/Dynamic/Extents/	
Previous/Scale/Window] <real time>:	Type: **A<enter>**

Step 4. **Use the Line command to draw the 2.75 line forming the bottom of the shape.**

Prompt	Response
Command:	Type: **L<enter>**
Specify first point:	Type: **END<enter>**
of	Pick: **D1 (Figure 6–14)**
Specify next point or [Undo]:	Type: **@2.75<180<enter>**
Specify next point or [Undo]:	Type: **<enter>**

FIGURE 6–13
Dimensions for Exercise 6–3

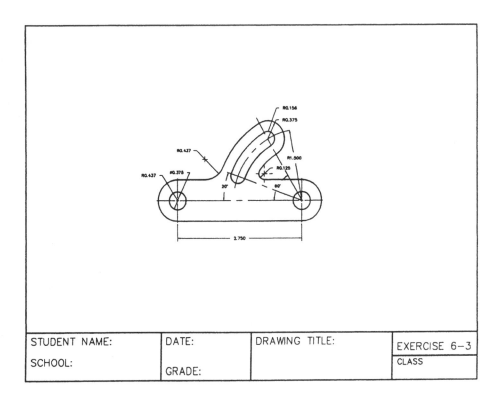

Linetypes and Drawing Constructions Using AutoCAD

FIGURE 6-14
Use the Line and Mirror Commands to Draw the Left Side

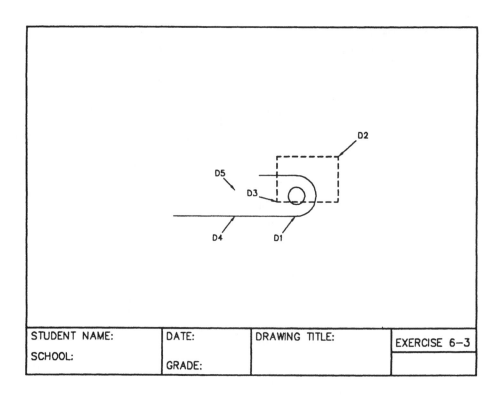

STUDENT NAME:	DATE:	DRAWING TITLE:	EXERCISE 6-3
SCHOOL:	GRADE:		

Step 5.   Use the Mirror command to draw circles on the left side of the part.

Prompt	Response
Command:	Type: **MI<enter>**
Select objects:	Pick: **D2 (Figure 6–14)**
Specify opposite corner:	Pick: **D3**
Select objects:	**<enter>**
Specify first point of mirror line:	Type: **MID<enter>**
of	Pick: **D4**
Specify second point of mirror line:	**Make sure Ortho is ON and** Pick: **D5** (any point directly above or below D4)
Delete source objects? <N>	**<enter>**

Step 6.   Use the ID and Circle commands to draw circles at the top and bottom of the curved slot.

Prompt	Response
Command:	Type: ID<enter>
Specify point:	Type: **CEN<enter>**
of	Pick: **D1 (Figure 6–15)**
Command:	Type: **C<enter>**
Specify center point for circle or [3P/2P/Ttr (tan tan radius)]:	Type: **@1.5<120<enter>**
Specify radius of circle or [Diameter]:	Type: **.375<enter>**
Command:	**<enter>**
Specify center point for circle or [3P/2P/Ttr (tan tan radius)]:	Type: **CEN<enter>**
of	Pick: **D2 (Figure 6–15)**
Specify radius of circle or [Diameter]:	Type: **.156<enter>**

FIGURE 6–15
Use the ID and Circle Commands

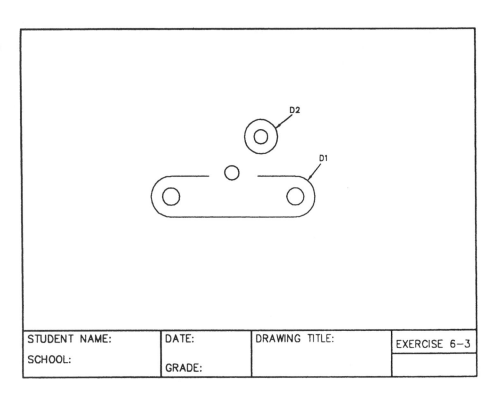

STUDENT NAME:	DATE:	DRAWING TITLE:	EXERCISE 6–3
SCHOOL:	GRADE:		

Command:	Type: **ID<enter>**
Specify point:	Type: **CEN<enter>**
of	Pick: **D1 (again)**
Command:	Type: **C<enter>**
Specify center point for circle or [3P/2P/Ttr (tan tan radius)]:	Type: **@1.5<160<enter>**
Specify radius of circle or [Diameter]:	Type: **.156<enter>**
Command:	**<enter>**

Because the drawing we are using to make our CAD drawing has several dimensions on it, the easiest way to make the CAD drawing is to use those dimensions without adding and subtracting. Therefore, if you make a circle through the center of the slot, you can use the Offset command and the radii shown to make the other circles.

Step 7.   Use the Circle and Offset commands to draw circles for the slot.

Prompt	Response
Command:	Type: **C<enter>**
Specify center point for circle or [3P/2P/Ttr (tan tan radius)]:	Type: **CEN<enter>**
of	Pick: **D1 (Figure 6–16)**
Specify radius of circle or [Diameter]:	Type: **1.5<enter>**
Command:	Type: **O<enter>**
Specify offset distance or [Through]:	Type: **.156<enter>**
Select object to offset or <exit>:	Pick: **D2 (Figure 6–16)**
Specify point on side to offset:	Pick: **D3**
Select object to offset or <exit>:	Pick: **D2 (again)**
Specify point on side to offset:	Pick: **D4**

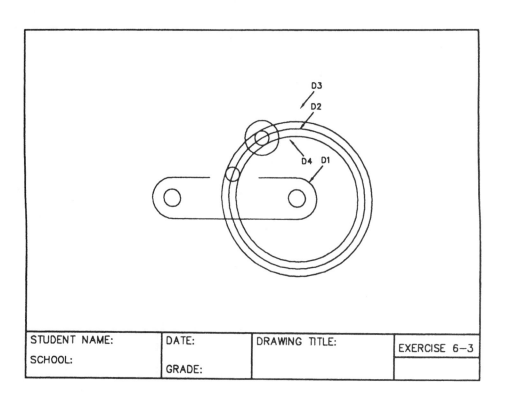

Step 8.   Use the Trim command to remove the circle excess.

Prompt	Response
Command:	Type: **TR<enter>**
Select cutting edges:	
Select objects:	Pick: **D1 (Figure 6–17)**
Select objects:	Pick: **D2**
Select objects:	Pick: **D3**

FIGURE 6–17
Use Trim to Remove Circle Excess

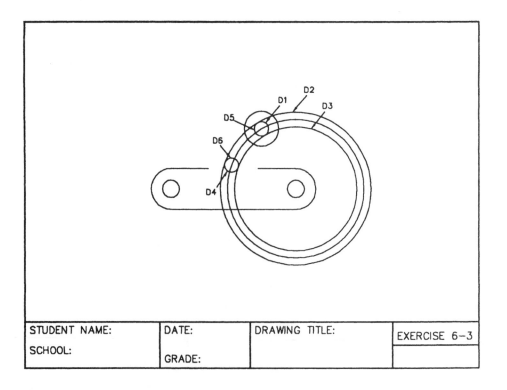

Select objects:	Pick: **D4**
Select objects:	**<enter>**
Select object to trim or shift-select to extend or [Project/Edge/Undo]:	Pick: **D2 (again)**
Select object to trim or shift-select to extend or [Project/Edge/Undo]:	Pick: **D3 (again)**
Select object to trim or shift-select to extend or [Project/Edge/Undo]:	Pick: **D5**
Select object to trim or shift-select to extend or [Project/Edge/Undo]:	Pick: **D6**
Select object to trim or shift-select to extend or [Project/Edge/Undo]:	**<enter>**

Step 9.   Use the Offset command to draw the remaining circles.

Prompt	Response
Command:	Type: **<enter>**
Specify offset distance or [Through]:	Type: **.375<enter>**
Select object to offset or <exit>:	Pick: **D1 (Figure 6–18)**
Specify point on side to offset:	Pick: **D2**
Select object to offset or <exit>:	Pick: **D1 (again)**
Specify point on side to offset:	Pick: **D3**

Step 10.   Use the Fillet command to draw fillets on each side of the curve.

Prompt	Response
Command:	Type: **F<enter>**
Current settings: Mode = TRIM, Radius = 0'-0 1/2'	
Select first object or [Polyline/Radius/Trim]:	Type: **R<enter>**
Specify fillet radius <0'-0 1/2">:	Type: **.437<enter>**

FIGURE 6–18
Use Offset to Draw the Remaining Circles

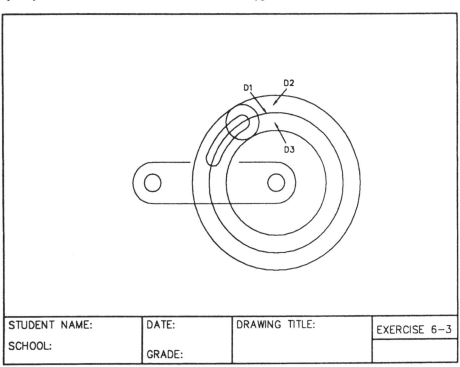

STUDENT NAME: DATE: DRAWING TITLE: EXERCISE 6–3

SCHOOL: GRADE:

FIGURE 6–19
Use the Fillet Command to Draw
Fillets on Each Side of the Curve

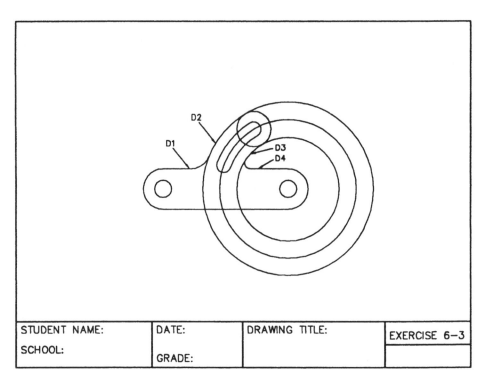

STUDENT NAME:	DATE:	DRAWING TITLE:	EXERCISE 6–3
SCHOOL:	GRADE:		

Command:	**<enter>**
Select first object or [Polyline/Radius/Trim]:	Pick: **D1 (Figure 6–19)**
Select second object:	Pick: **D2**
Command:	**<enter>**
Current settings: Mode = TRIM, Radius = 0'-0 1/2'	
Select first object or [Polyline/Radius/Trim]:	Type: **R<enter>**
Specify fillet radius <0'-0 7/16">:	Type: **.125<enter>**
Command:	**<enter>**
Select first object or [Polyline/Radius/Trim]:	Pick: **D3 (Figure 6–19)**
Select second object:	Pick: **D4**

Step 11. **Use the Trim and Erase commands to remove the circle excess and complete the drawing.**

Prompt	Response
Command:	Type: **TR<enter>**
Select cutting edges:	
Select objects:	Pick: **D1 (Figure 6–20)**
Select objects:	Pick: **D2**
Select objects:	Pick: **D3**
Select objects:	Pick: **D4**
Select objects:	Pick: **D5**
Select objects:	**<enter>**
Select object to trim or shift-select to extend or [Project/Edge/Undo]:	Pick: **D2 (again)**
Select object to trim or shift-select to extend or [Project/Edge/Undo]:	Pick: **D4 (again)**
Select object to trim or shift-select to extend or [Project/Edge/Undo]:	Pick: **D6**

FIGURE 6–20
Use the Trim and Erase Commands to Complete the Drawing

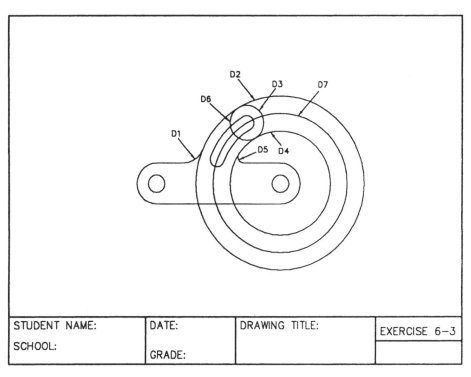

STUDENT NAME:	DATE:	DRAWING TITLE:	EXERCISE 6–3
SCHOOL:			
	GRADE:		

Select object to trim or shift-select to extend or [Project/Edge/Undo]:	Pick: **\<enter>**
Command:	Type: **E\<enter>**
Select objects:	Pick: **D7 (Figure 6–20)**
Select objects:	**\<enter>**

Step 12. Use the Dtext command to complete the title block as you did for EX6–1. Title the drawing, **SWIVEL PLATE**.

Step 13. Use the SAVEAS command to save your drawing as EX6–3(your initials) on a floppy disk and again on the hard drive of your computer.

Step 14. Plot or print your drawing full size on an 11″ x 8½″ sheet.

EXERCISES

EXERCISE 6–1.   Complete Exercise 6–1 using steps 1 through 10 described in this chapter.
EXERCISE 6–2.   Complete Exercise 6–2 using steps 1 through 12 described in this chapter.
EXERCISE 6–3.   Complete Exercise 6–3 using steps 1 through 14 described in this chapter.

REVIEW QUESTIONS

Circle the best answer.

1. Which of the following will produce a line 3½″ long downward from a point?
    a. 3.5 X 90
    b. @3.5<90
    c. @0<3.5
    d. @3.5<-90
    e. 90<3.5

2. Which of the following is used to identify a point that may be used for one command?
    a. Status
    b. Point
    c. ID
    d. Line
    e. Dist

3. A rounded corner may be obtained most easily with which of the following commands?
   a. Chamfer
   b. Fillet
   c. Draw
   d. Offset
   e. Break

4. Which of the following circles is produced if 1/2 is entered in response to the circle prompt "Specify radius of circle or [Diameter]:"?
   a. $\frac{1}{2}''$ diameter
   b. $\frac{1}{2}''$ radius
   c. $1''$ radius
   d. $2''$ diameter
   e. $\frac{1}{4}''$ diameter

5. Which command is used to trim lines between cutting edges?
   a. Edit
   b. Trim
   c. Erase
   d. Copy
   e. Extend

6. From the Line prompt "Specify next point or [Undo]:" which is the correct response to draw a horizontal line $4\frac{1}{2}''$ to the right of the starting point?
   a. 4-1/2<180
   b. 4-1/2<0
   c. <180<4-1/2
   d. @4-1/2<0
   e. <0<4-1/2

7. To draw a line parallel to another line, which of the following commands should be used?
   a. Line parallel
   b. Parallel
   c. Offset
   d. Offset parallel
   e. LP

8. To draw a line perpendicular to another line, which of the following options should be used?
   a. Square
   b. Rt Angle
   c. 90 Angle
   d. Osnap-PERpendicular
   e. @90

9. If you have just drawn a line at the wrong angle and you want to return to the starting point of the line, what should you enter?
   a. Redo
   b. R
   c. U
   d. Ctrl-C
   e. Erase

10. To produce a circle with a diameter of $\frac{1}{2}$, what is the correct response to the prompt "Specify radius of circle or [Diameter]"?
    a. D, then 1/2
    b. R, then 1/2
    c. 1/2
    d. Circle-diameter
    e. 1/2''

Complete.
11. Describe the differences among absolute, relative, and polar coordinates.

_____

_____

_____

12. Write a sequence of "Line responses" to the "Specify next point or [Undo]:" prompt that will produce a $4\frac{1}{2}''$ x 3" rectangle using polar coordinates. Make the first line $4\frac{1}{2}''$ to the right and the second line 3" up.

_____

_____

_____

13. Describe the function of the ID command.

_____

14. Describe what is meant by a running OSNAP mode.

_____

15. The following coordinates are an example of _____ coordinates:
    2,1

16. The following coordinates are an example of _____ coordinates:
    @2,1

17. The following coordinates are an example of _____ coordinates:
    @2<0

18. List the command that asks you to select objects and then specify a line about which the selected objects are to be copied as a mirror image.

_____

19. Which key must you hold down to remove an object from a set of objects selected to be erased?

_____

20. AutoCAD stores up to _____ views for the Zoom-Previous command.

Reading and Sketching Orthographic Views

OBJECTIVES

After completing this chapter, you will be able to

☐ Correctly identify surfaces in two-dimensional views from given three-dimensional views.

☐ Correctly sketch two-dimensional views from given three-dimensional views.

☐ Correctly answer questions regarding the orthographic projection method of drawing.

ORTHOGRAPHIC PROJECTION

Orthographic projection is a system of drawing that is used throughout the world. Orthographic views are two-dimensional or flat views of objects. One of the reasons orthographic drawing is used instead of pictorial drawing is that it is easy to place dimensions on these drawings; therefore, confusion about measurements is avoided (Figure 7–1).

Two forms of orthographic projection are commonly used: first-angle and third-angle (Figure 7–2). Third-angle projection is used in the United States and many other countries, whereas first-angle projection is used in several countries in Europe.

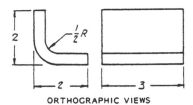

NO CONFUSION EXISTS REGARDING WHERE MEASUREMENTS ARE MADE.

ORTHOGRAPHIC VIEWS

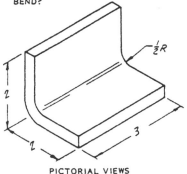

NOTE: SOME CONFUSION EXISTS. WHERE ARE THE 2" DIMENSIONS MEASURED FROM--THE BEGINNING OF THE BEND, THE INSIDE OF THE BEND, OR THE OUTSIDE OF THE BEND?

PICTORIAL VIEWS

FIGURE 7–1
Orthographic and Pictorial Views

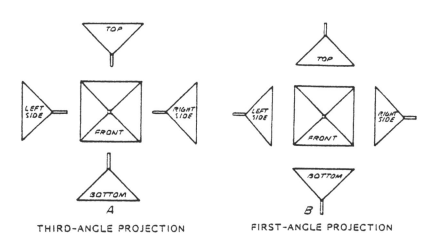

THIRD-ANGLE PROJECTION

FIRST-ANGLE PROJECTION

FIGURE 7–2
Third- and First-Angle Orthographic Projection

This chapter presents third-angle orthographic projection in detail but first describes the differences between first- and third-angle projection.

Differences Between First-Angle and Third-Angle Orthographic Projection

In the third-angle projection shown in Figure 7–2, think of the pyramid shape as being attached in the center and swinging to all four sides to give right-side, left-side, top, and bottom views. In first-angle projection think of the object as tipped to its sides to give the four views. Third-angle orthographic projection is used in the rest of this book, and no further reference will be made to first-angle projection.

Third-Angle Projection Theory

One of the best ways to explain third-angle projection is with the transparent box model (Figure 7–3), in which an imaginary cube is placed around the object. The surfaces you would see if you looked into each side of the cube are registered on the cube. When the cube is unfolded, the views are arranged as shown in Figure 7–4. This arrangement of views is understood throughout the world. Your drawings must follow the same arrangement, with two exceptions, as shown in Figure 7–5.

Views

The transparent box model shows that every object has six possible views: front, back, top, bottom, left side, and right side. Often, an object can be fully described using three of these views, or sometimes fewer. Many objects such as screws and other fasteners need only one view to completely describe them. Other complex objects require all six views and several auxiliary, section, and detail views for a complete description. These other types of views will be presented in later chapters.

Height, Width, and Depth Dimensions

Each view of the object contains only two of its three dimensions: top and bottom views show width and depth; right- and left-side views show height and depth; and front and back views show width and height (Figure 7–6). The most commonly used combination of views is the top, front, and right-side views, and the next most commonly used combi-

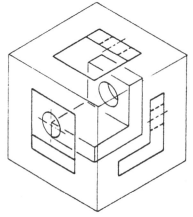

FIGURE 7–3
Transparent Box Model

FIGURE 7–4
Standard View Arrangement

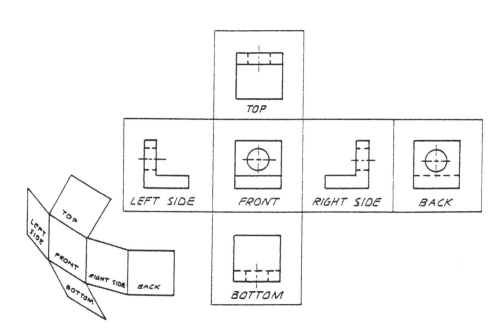

FIGURE 7–5
Exceptions to Standard View
Arrangement

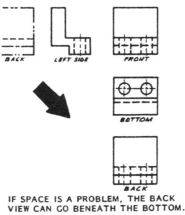

IF SPACE IS A PROBLEM, THE BACK
VIEW CAN GO BENEATH THE BOTTOM.

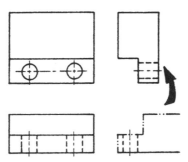

IF SPACE IS A PROBLEM, THE RIGHT
SIDE CAN GO TO THE
RIGHT OF THE TOP VIEW (BUT AVOID
ANY EXCEPTIONAL ARRANGEMENT).

FIGURE 7–6
Each View Shows Only Two
Dimensions

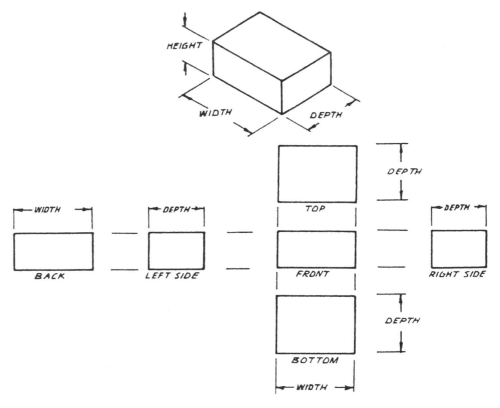

nation is top, front, and left side (Figure 7–7). Usually, the front view is drawn first, and then either the top or side view is drawn. Height and width dimensions are easily projected into the adjacent view, but depth dimensions must be either transferred using a scale or a piece of paper or projected through a 45° angle (Figure 7–8).

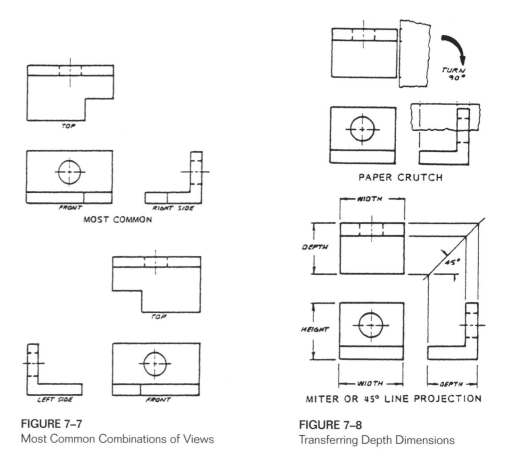

FIGURE 7–7
Most Common Combinations of Views

FIGURE 7–8
Transferring Depth Dimensions

IDENTIFYING SURFACES AND FEATURES

To make two-dimensional drawings from three-dimensional drawings or an actual part you must learn to identify surfaces, edges, and other features. The following discussion and exercises will give you practice in doing that.

Normal Surfaces

The easiest surfaces to read are the flat, unslanted surfaces. These are called *normal* (normal means perpendicular) surfaces because they are perpendicular to your line of sight when you look at the object. Figure 7–9 shows an object that has all normal surfaces. Exercise 7–1 will test your skill in identifying normal surfaces from a three-dimensional drawing.

FIGURE 7–9
Normal Surfaces

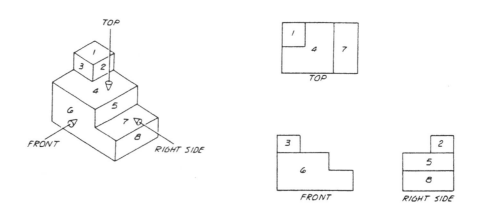

FIGURE 7–10
Inclined Surfaces

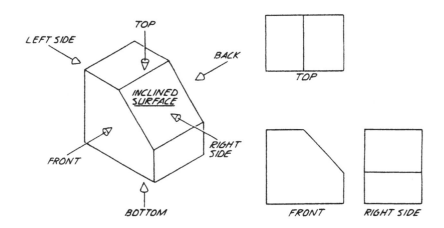

EXERCISE 7–1:
Identifying Normal Surfaces

Step 1. Remove the sheet labeled EXERCISE 7–1 from your book.

Step 2. Identify the numbered surfaces in the normal views in the spaces provided. Use the numbers from the pictorial view. Use your best lettering with guidelines top and bottom.

Step 3. Fill in the title block with your best lettering. Title the drawing NORMAL SURFACES.

Inclined or Slanted Surfaces

An inclined or slanted surface is perpendicular to two of the normal surfaces but at an angle other than 90° to the other four normal surfaces. The slanted surface in Figure 7–10 is perpendicular to the front and back surfaces but inclined to the top, bottom, right side, and left side. The surface is said to be *foreshortened* when its true length is not shown. When you view this inclined surface, you see it slanted in only the front view. (You could see it slanted in the back view, but since it would appear exactly as it does in the front view, only the front is shown.)

Complete Exercise 7–2 now to see how well you can identify inclined and normal surfaces.

EXERCISE 7–2:
Identifying Inclined Surfaces

Step 1. Remove the sheet labeled EXERCISE 7–2 from your book.

Step 2. Identify the numbered surfaces in the normal views in the spaces provided. Use the numbers from the pictorial view. Use your best lettering with guidelines top and bottom.

Step 3. Fill in the title block with your best lettering. Title the drawing INCLINED SURFACES.

Oblique Surfaces

Slanted surfaces that are inclined to all the normal surfaces are called *oblique surfaces* (Figure 7–11). Notice that the oblique surface appears in all three views and that only one line of the surface is the true length in each view. Try Exercise 7–3 to identify oblique and normal surfaces.

FIGURE 7–11
Oblique Surfaces

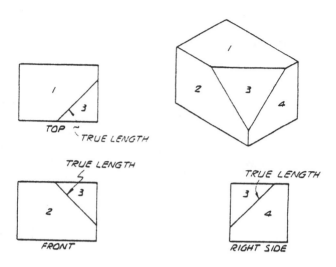

EXERCISE 7–3:
Identifying Oblique Surfaces

Step 1. Remove the sheet labeled EXERCISE 7–3 from your book.

Step 2. Identify the numbered surfaces in the normal views in the spaces provided. Use the numbers from the pictorial view. Use your best lettering with guidelines top and bottom.

Step 3. Fill in the title block with your best lettering. Title the drawing OBLIQUE SURFACES.

Identifying Edges

In reading two-dimensional drawings, it is often helpful to identify surfaces where they appear as an edge. As shown in Figure 7–12, when you look at a very thin sheet of metal from the front you see the true shape of its front surface. When you view it from its right side, you see it as an edge. Then when you flip it over, you see the true shape of its back surface.

If the metal is thicker, as in Figure 7–13, the edges are farther apart, and the side view takes on a shape. In Figure 7–14 notice that edges in one view line up with edges in the view adjacent to it. Surfaces 2, 5, 7, and 10 in the top view, for example, line up with the

FIGURE 7–12
Edges on a Thin Sheet

FIGURE 7–13
Edges on a Thicker Part

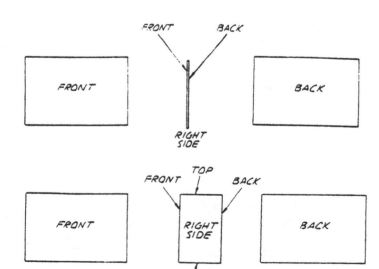

FIGURE 7–14
Identifying Edges

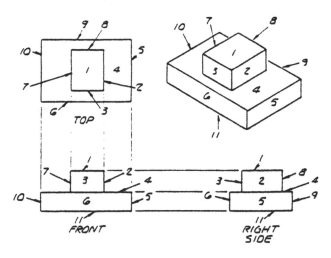

same surfaces in the front view. Surfaces 1, 4, and 11 line up with the same surfaces in the right-side view.

Study Figure 7–14 for a few minutes until you feel certain that you understand these views and can number edges correctly. After you feel confident about Figure 7–14, complete Exercise 7–4.

EXERCISE 7–4:
Identifying Edges

Step 1. Remove the sheet labeled EXERCISE 7–4 from your book.

Step 2. Identify the numbered surfaces as edges in the normal views in the spaces provided. Use the numbers from the pictorial view. Use your best lettering with guidelines top and bottom.

Step 3. Fill in the title block with your best lettering. Title the drawing EDGES.

Cut Cylinders

When cylinders are cut at right angles, their shapes in adjacent views do not change (Figure 7–15). When they are cut at an angle their shapes appear as ellipses in one of the adjacent views (Figure 7–16).

Runouts

A *runout* is a surface that blends into another surface without forming an edge at the point where the runout ends. Figure 7–17 shows a runout on a casting. Castings and other

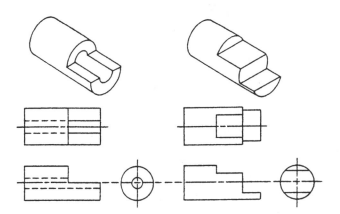

FIGURE 7–15
Cylinders Cut at Right Angles

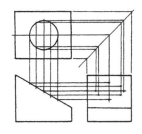

FIGURE 7–16
Cylinders Cut at an Angle

Reading and Sketching Orthographic Views

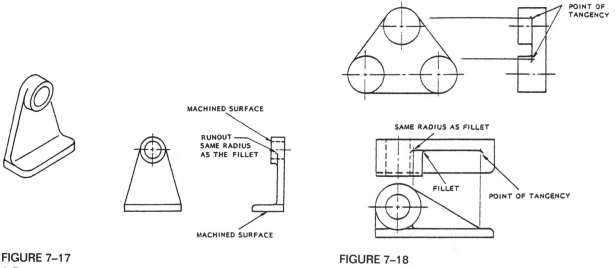

FIGURE 7–17
A Runout

FIGURE 7–18
Two Shapes for Runouts

molded parts often have runouts. Castings also often have rounded edges because of the way they are manufactured. The only sharp edges on most castings are surfaces that have been machined to allow a part to fit or function better. Some rounds of the cast parts are usually found connected to the runout. Figure 7–18 shows two shapes with runouts. Runouts are drawn just as you see them in this figure. The edge-view line ends with the radius of the fillet drawn at the end. The point of tangency, where the flat surface meets the cylindrical surface, is where the runout ends.

Different Shapes that Look the Same in One or More Views

In reading two-dimensional views, it is easy to make a mistake about the shape of an object if you look at only two views. Figure 7–19 shows several objects that have the same appearance in two views. Only the right-side view shows the true shape of each object.

Hidden Features

To describe many objects fully, hidden surfaces must often be shown. These surfaces are shown with hidden lines (Figure 7–20). Notice that the right-side view would not be complete if the hidden surface were not shown with a hidden line.

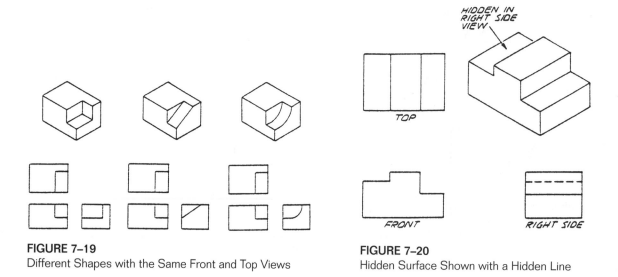

FIGURE 7–19
Different Shapes with the Same Front and Top Views

FIGURE 7–20
Hidden Surface Shown with a Hidden Line

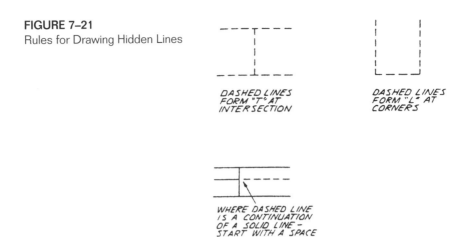

FIGURE 7–21
Rules for Drawing Hidden Lines

DASHED LINES FORM "T" AT INTERSECTION

DASHED LINES FORM "L" AT CORNERS

WHERE DASHED LINE IS A CONTINUATION OF A SOLID LINE – START WITH A SPACE

When hidden lines are drawn at a corner, they should form an L shape (Figure 7–21). When they intersect, they should form a T or a cross if one line crosses over the other. If they are a continuation of a solid line, there should be a break between the solid line and the first dash of a hidden line. The dashes should be about $\frac{1}{8}$″ long, with $\frac{1}{16}$″ between dashes. They can be longer on larger drawings.

Figures 7–22 and 7–23 show several hidden lines. In Figure 7–23 notice that the solid line in the top view takes precedence over the hidden line that shows the hidden slot. On complex objects, the number of hidden lines often can be very confusing, so it is generally understood that only one layer of hidden lines is shown (Figure 7–24).

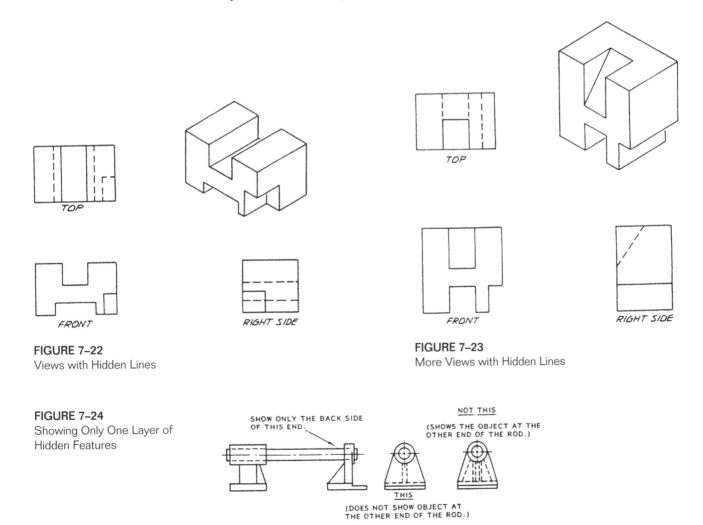

FIGURE 7–22
Views with Hidden Lines

FIGURE 7–23
More Views with Hidden Lines

FIGURE 7–24
Showing Only One Layer of
Hidden Features

SHOW ONLY THE BACK SIDE OF THIS END.

NOT THIS
(SHOWS THE OBJECT AT THE OTHER END OF THE ROD.)

THIS
(DOES NOT SHOW OBJECT AT THE OTHER END OF THE ROD.)

Reading and Sketching Orthographic Views

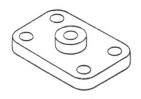

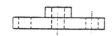

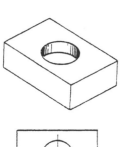

FIGURE 7–25
Normal Cylinders

Normal Cylinders

Cylinders that are perpendicular to the normal surfaces of an object are called *normal cylinders*. These cylinders may be round holes or round rods. Figure 7–25 shows how normal cylinders look in two-dimensional views. Notice that the edges of the holes are shown with hidden lines in the view where they are hidden. The hidden lines in the front view that show the holes in front exactly cover the hidden lines that show the holes in the back.

When holes do not go all the way through an object, the bottom of the hole is shown with a hidden line, as in Figure 7–26. Notice that the hole in Figure 7–26B is slanted, so that the circle at the bottom of the hole is smaller than the circle at the top of the hole.

Countersinks and Counterbores

Figure 7–27 shows a countersink and a counterbore. The countersink feature is used to allow a flathead screw that has the same shape as the countersunk hole to fit below the surface of the part. A hole is drilled in the part first, and then the countersink is added. The counterbore comprises two holes, one larger than the other. The smaller hole is drilled first, and then the counterbore is added. Notice that the bottom of the larger hole that does not go through the part is shown with a hidden line. A counterbore is used to allow parts to fit deeper into the material. A variation of the counterbore, called a spotface, is a shallow counterbore that makes the surface smoother so that the head of a screw or bolt fits better.

Now, use your hidden-line skills to fill in the hidden lines on the views in Exercise 7–5.

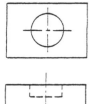

A

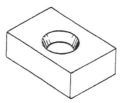

B

FIGURE 7–26
Holes that Do Not Go Through

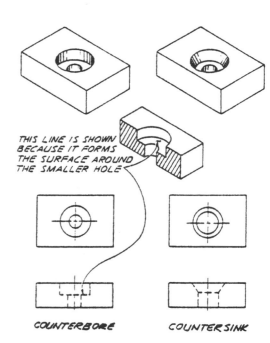

THIS LINE IS SHOWN BECAUSE IT FORMS THE SURFACE AROUND THE SMALLER HOLE

COUNTERBORE

COUNTERSINK

FIGURE 7–27
Counterbore and Countersink

EXERCISE 7–5:
Sketching Hidden Lines

Step 1. Remove the sheets labeled EXERCISE 7–5, Sheets 1 and 2, from your book.

Step 2. Add missing object lines and the missing hidden lines in the top and front view of sheet 1, and in the front and right-side views of sheet 2. Make the dashes about $\frac{1}{8}''$ long with a $\frac{1}{16}''$ space between dashes. Make sure the hidden lines are aligned with features in the adjacent views and that your hidden lines follow the rules described in Figure 7–21. Use the pictorial drawing as a guide.

Step 3. Fill in the title blocks with your best lettering. Title the drawings HIDDEN SURFACES.

SKETCHING ORTHOGRAPHIC VIEWS

Although you have already begun sketching in the previous chapters, we need to review some of the common practices in technical sketching and add some other information that will make your sketches professional quality.

Materials

The materials you will need have already been listed in a previous chapter: paper (the exercises in this book), pencils, triangle, eraser, and a circle template. If you are making sketches on your own, you may prefer gridded paper for some objects, but you will find that plain paper is just as easy to use for some drawings. Be sure the eraser you use makes a clean erasure because you will make some mistakes, and erasing not only is OK, it is encouraged.

Lines

You have already begun using lines in your sketches. If you are not certain about how they should appear, review Chapter 5 before completing the remaining exercises in this chapter.

Circles

Some of the circles you will sketch will be bigger than the largest circle on your circle template. These circles will not look as good as the ones you draw with the circle template, but they should be as accurate as you can make them. Figure 7–28 shows an easy method for drawing circles.

Step 1. Determine the diameter of the circle you want to sketch.

Step 2. Using light lines, draw a square the size of the diameter of the circle.

Step 3. Find the center of the circle by drawing diagonals across the corners of the square.

Step 4. Using the center as a guide, estimate the midpoint of each side and mark it.

Step 5. Along the diagonals, mark the radius of the circle from its center.

Step 6. Connect the construction points using a dark sketch line.

FIGURE 7–28
Sketching a Circle

FIGURE 7–29
Another Method for Sketching a Circle

Figure 7–29 shows another method for drawing circles.

Step 1. Determine the diameter of the circle you want to sketch.
Step 2. Draw horizontal, vertical, and 45° construction lines through a center point.
Step 3. Mark the radius of the circle on the construction lines.
Step 4. Connect the construction points using a dark sketch line.

Arcs

Arcs larger than your circle template are sketched in a similar manner to circles. To draw an arc using the method shown in Figure 7–30, follow these steps:

Step 1. Sketch a square the size of the radius of the arc.
Step 2. Draw a construction line across a diagonal of the square.
Step 3. Mark the radius on the diagonal.
Step 4. Sketch the radius using a dark sketch line from one corner of the square through the mark on the diagonal to the other corner.

Aligning Views

As noted earlier, all features of an object in one view must line up with those same features in another view. When you make your sketches, drawing will be much easier if you make sure to keep all the views lined up with one another. Often, one view will have a feature that must be completed before it can be projected into the adjacent view, as shown in Figure 7–31. The 45° miter-line method shown in Figure 7–32 can be used to project depth dimensions from the top view to the right-side view.

View Selection

Selecting the views that best describe the object completely using the fewest number of views is very important. The views that show the fewest number of hidden lines and fully describe all contours of all surfaces should be selected. Figure 7–33 shows several objects and the correct view selection for them.

FIGURE 7–30
Sketching an Arc

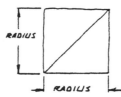

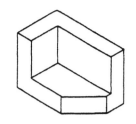

FIGURE 7–31
Aligning Features in Adjacent Views

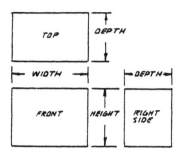

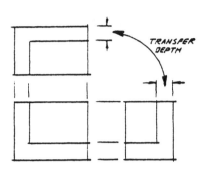

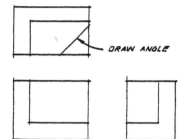

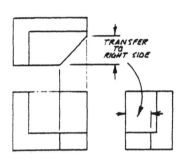

FIGURE 7–32
Miter-Line Method for Projecting
Depth

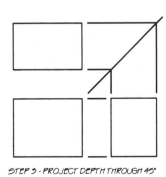

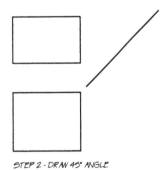

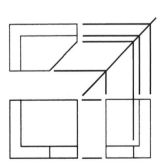

Reading and Sketching Orthographic Views

FIGURE 7-33
View Selection

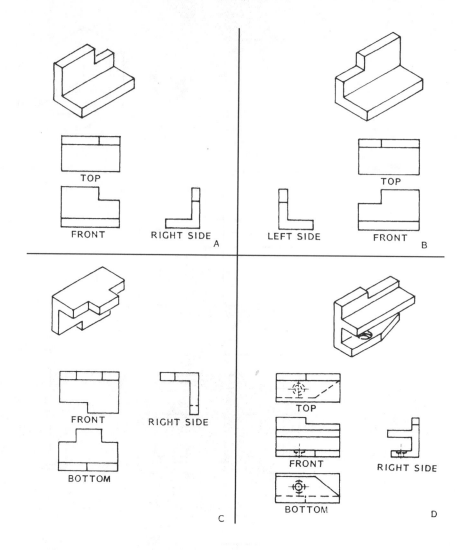

In Figure 7–33A, top, front, and right-side views show no hidden surfaces. Any other view selection would have shown hidden lines and would not have been as clear. The top view is necessary to show the shape of the surface, which could have had rounded corners, for example.

The same description as for 7–33A applies to the objects in 7–33B and C.

The objects in 7–33D, E, and F are more complex, so additional views are necessary to describe fully the features that appear only as hidden lines in all other views.

The object in 7–33G is an example of a flat object that can be described with only one view by placing a note on the drawing giving the thickness of the object.

The object in 7–33H is an example of a round object that can be described with either two views or one view by showing the diameter on that view. The notation DIA (or ∅) means that the only shape the object can have is round.

Front View Selection

The front view is usually the starting point for all orthographic drawings. There are three factors to consider when you are deciding which surfaces to use as the front view:

Place the longest side horizontally on the front (Figure 7–34).
Place the most complex feature on the front (Figure 7–35).
Sketch the object in the position in which it is used or most often seen (Figure 7–36).

FIGURE 7–33 (continued)
View Selection

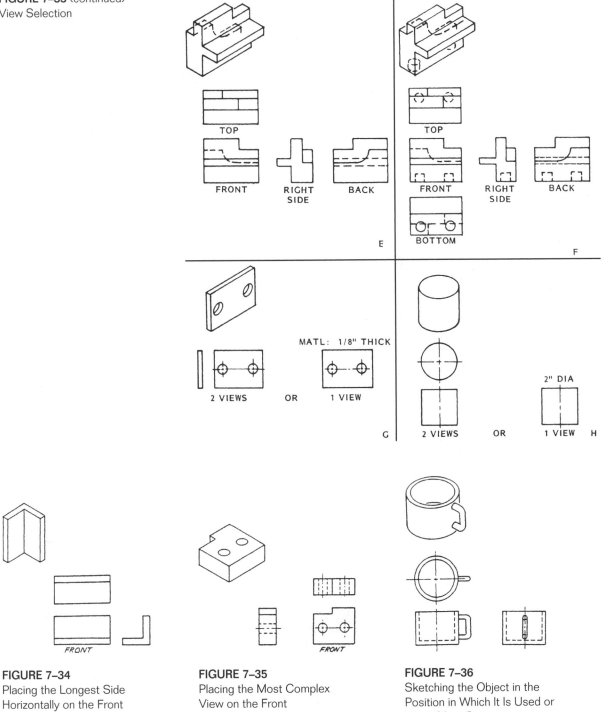

FIGURE 7–34
Placing the Longest Side
Horizontally on the Front

FIGURE 7–35
Placing the Most Complex
View on the Front

FIGURE 7–36
Sketching the Object in the
Position in Which It Is Used or
Most Often Seen

Drawing Circles and Curves on a Slanted Surface

Circular holes that have been cut at other than a 90° angle to their center appear as ellipses. An ellipse has the same major diameter as the circle but a smaller minor diameter. In other words, an ellipse is a circle that has been flattened.

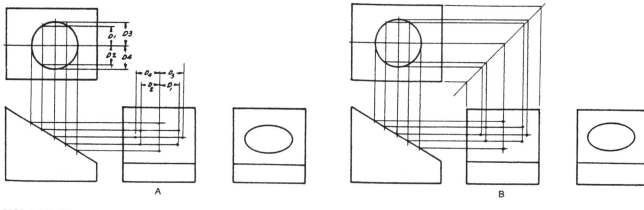

FIGURE 7–37
Sketching Ellipses

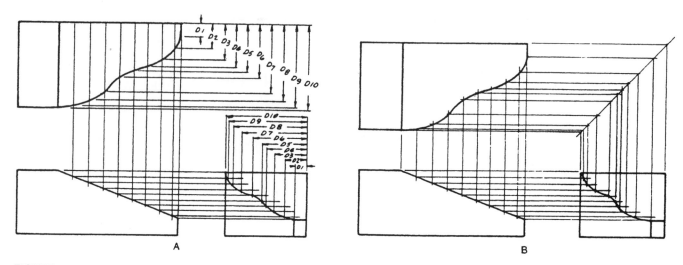

FIGURE 7–38
Sketching Curved Surfaces

Figure 7–37 shows two methods for sketching an ellipse:

> In Figure 7–37A, the circle has been divided into four parts so that points on the circle can be identified. These points are then projected onto the slanted surface in the front view and then into the right-side view. Depth measurements are taken from the center of the circle on the top view and transferred to the right-side view.
>
> In Figure 7–37B, the miter-line method was used to transfer depth dimensions. Ellipses and other curved shapes can be sketched more accurately by dividing the circle or other shape into a greater number of parts.

Figure 7–38 shows a curved surface that has been drawn using the same methods as those shown in Figure 7–37. The only difference is that depth dimensions in 7–38A were taken from the back surface.

Placement of Views on the Drawing

Placement of the views on the page is important to the appearance of the drawing. At first, you should center the views in the drawing. Later, notes, dimensions, revisions, and parts lists will require a different arrangement, but first you have to know how to center the drawing before you can use the other arrangements.

As an example of centering, assume that the drawing will contain top, front, and right-side views of the object shown in Figure 7–39.

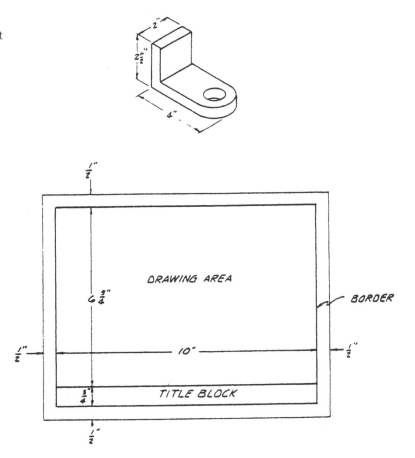

FIGURE 7–39
The Object and the Drawing Format

Step 1. Calculate the area called the *field of the drawing* that will contain the complete drawing. The drawing will be placed on an 11″ x 8½″ sheet. The border is ½″ on all sides, and the title block measures ¾″ deep. The drawing area is 10″ x 6¾″.

Step 2. Calculate where to start the left side of the front and top views (Figure 7–40). Add the width and depth dimensions (4″ + 2″ = 6″). Subtract this total from 10″, the width of the drawing field (10″ - 6″ = 4″). Divide this number by 4

FIGURE 7–40
Centering Views in the Field of the Drawing

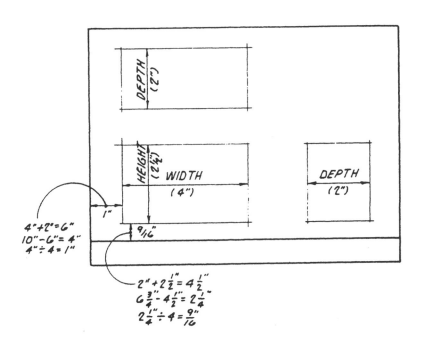

$(4''/4 = 1'')$. Place one quarter of the space $(1'')$ on the left, one quarter on the right $(1'')$, and half the available space between the views $(2'')$. The $1''$ dimension is not critical. You can make it a little more or less if you choose.

Step 3. Calculate where to start the bottom of the front and right-side views. Add the height and depth dimensions $(2\frac{1}{2}'' + 2'' = 4\frac{1}{2}'')$. Subtract this total from $6\frac{3}{4}''$, the height of the drawing field $(6\frac{3}{4}'' - 4\frac{1}{2}'' = 2\frac{1}{4}'')$. Divide this number by 4 $(2\frac{1}{4}''/4 = \frac{9}{16}'')$. Place one quarter of the space above the top view, one quarter below the front view, and half of the available space between views. The $\frac{9}{16}''$ dimension is not critical. You can make the top and bottom spaces $\frac{1}{2}''$, $\frac{5}{8}''$, or $\frac{3}{4}''$ if you choose.

Be aware that views must be moved farther apart when dimensions and notes are added. The preceding example is a guide only. Many other methods will work just as well.

Order of Sketching

The order of sketching is important to maintain accurate sizes and to improve speed (Figure 7–41).

Step 1. Block in the overall dimensions of all views using very light construction lines.

Step 2. Locate and mark the center lines of all circles and arcs using light construction lines.

Step 3. Darken all circles and arcs.

Step 4. Darken all other object lines.

Step 5. Add hidden lines by projecting the surfaces from views where the features are visible.

Step 6. Darken the border and title block if the form is not preprinted, and letter the title block using guidelines and your best lettering.

Now, use what you have learned about sketching to complete Exercises 7–6 through 7–10.

FIGURE 7–41
Order of Drawing

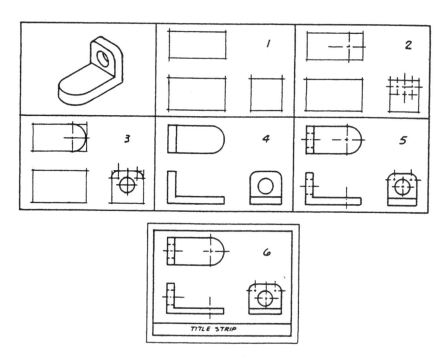

EXERCISES

EXERCISE 7–1.   Complete Exercise 7–1 using steps 1 through 3 described in this chapter. Fill in the title block with your best lettering. Title the drawing NORMAL SURFACES.

EXERCISE 7–2.   Complete Exercise 7–2 using steps 1 through 3 described in this chapter. Fill in the title block with your best lettering. Title the drawing INCLINED SURFACES.

EXERCISE 7–3.   Complete Exercise 7–3 using steps 1 through 3 described in this chapter. Fill in the title block with your best lettering. Title the drawing OBLIQUE SURFACES.

EXERCISE 7–4.   Complete Exercise 7–4 using steps 1 through 3 described in this chapter. Fill in the title block with your best lettering. Title the drawing EDGES.

EXERCISE 7–5.   Complete Exercise 7–5 using steps 1 through 3 described in this chapter. Fill in the title block with your best lettering. Title the drawing HIDDEN SURFACES.

EXERCISE 7–6.   Complete Exercise 7–6 using the following steps:

Step 1.   Remove the sheet labeled Exercise 7–6 from your book.

Step 2.   Complete the object lines in the front and right-side views of Exercise 7–6.

Use one unit on the three-dimensional drawing to equal one unit on the two-dimensional sketch.

Be sure to line up all features of the object with the adjacent views.

Make sure that your lines are the correct weight and are of even width and darkness. Try to match the thickness and darkness of the existing lines.

Step 3.   Draw hidden lines in the top and right-side views.

Be sure to line up all features of the object with the adjacent views.

Make hidden lines the same width and darkness of the object lines.

Step 4.   Fill in the title block with your best lettering. Title the drawing SKETCH 1.

EXERCISE 7–7.   Complete Exercise 7–7 using the following steps:

Step 1.   Remove the sheet labeled Exercise 7–7 from your book.

Step 2.   Complete the object lines in the top, front, and right-side views of Exercise 7–7.

Use one unit on the three-dimensional drawing to equal one unit on the two-dimensional sketch.

Be sure to line up all features of the object with the adjacent views.

Make sure that your lines are the correct weight and are of even width and darkness. Try to match the thickness and darkness of the existing lines.

Step 3.   Draw hidden lines in the right-side view.

Be sure to line up all features of the object with the adjacent views.

Make hidden lines the same width and darkness of the object lines.

Step 4.   Fill in the title block with your best lettering. Title the drawing SKETCH 2.

EXERCISE 7–8.   Complete Exercise 7–8 using the following steps:

Step 1.   Remove the sheet labeled Exercise 7–8 from your book.

Step 2.   Complete the object lines in the top, front, and right-side views of Exercise 7–8.

Use one unit on the three-dimensional drawing to equal one unit on the two-dimensional sketch.

Be sure to line up all features of the object with the adjacent views.

Make sure that your lines are the correct weight and are of even width and darkness. Try to match the thickness and darkness of the existing lines.

Step 3.   Draw hidden lines in the top view.

Be sure to line up all features of the object with the adjacent views.

Make hidden lines the same width and darkness of the object lines.

Step 4.   Fill in the title block with your best lettering. Title the drawing SKETCH 3.

EXERCISE 7–9.   Complete Exercise 7–9 using the following steps:

Step 1.   Remove the sheet labeled Exercise 7–9 from your book. Use light construction lines to sketch the top, front, and right-side views of step 1 shown on Figure 7–42.

Use one unit on the three-dimensional drawing to equal one unit on the two-dimensional sketch.

Be sure to line up all features of the object with the adjacent views.

Step 2.   Use light construction lines to sketch the L shape in the front view of step 2 shown on Figure 7–42. Project the edges of the L shape into the top and right-side views with light construction lines.

Step 3.   Use light construction lines to draw the notch in the right-side view as shown in step 3. Project the edges of the notch into the top and front views with light construction lines.

FIGURE 7–42
Dimensions for Exercise 7–9

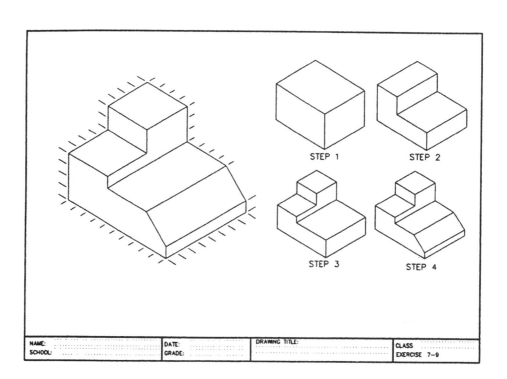

Chapter 7

Step 4. Use light construction lines to draw the slanted surface in the front view of step 4, and project the edges defining the slanted surface into the top and right-side views. (You can draw these lines with dark object lines if you are sure of their locations). Darken all lines as follows:

Sprinkle drafting powder over your drawing before you begin to darken lines.

Darken all other object lines in all views.

Step 5. Fill in the title block with your best lettering. Title the drawing SKETCH 4.

EXERCISE 7–10.   Complete Exercise 7–10 using the following steps:

Step 1. Remove the sheet labeled Exercise 7–10 from your book. Use light construction lines to sketch the top, front, and right-side views of step 1 shown on Figure 7–43.

Use one unit on the three-dimensional drawing to equal one unit on the two-dimensional sketch.

Be sure to line up all features of the object with the adjacent views.

Step 2. Use light construction lines to sketch the L shape in the front view of step 2 shown in Figure 7–43. Project the edges of the L shape into the top and right-side views with light construction lines.

Step 3. Use light construction lines to draw the visible lines of the notch in the upper part of the object in the right-side and top views as shown in step 3. Use light construction lines to draw the notch in the base in the top view. Project the edges of the notch into the front and right-side views.

Step 4. Use light construction lines to draw the hidden lines showing the shape of the slanted surface in the front view of step 4, and project the edges defining the slanted surface into the top and right-side views. (You can draw these lines with dark object lines if you are sure of their locations). Draw the small notch in the bottom of the base in the right-side view using light construction lines. Project

FIGURE 7–43
Dimensions for Exercise 7–10

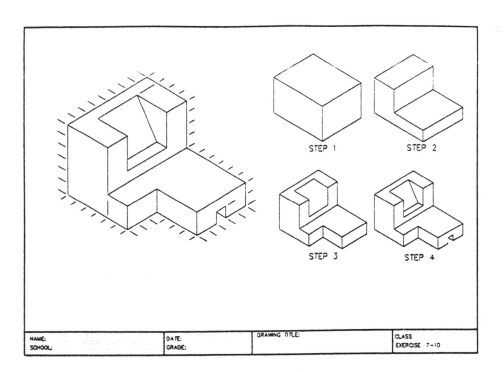

STEP 1   STEP 2   STEP 3   STEP 4

NAME: DATE: DRAWING TITLE: CLASS
SCHOOL: GRADE: EXERCISE 7–10

Reading and Sketching Orthographic Views

the edges of the notch into the front and top views as hidden lines. Darken all lines as follows:

Sprinkle drawing powder over your drawing before you begin to darken lines.

Darken all lines in all views.

Step 5. Fill in the title block with your best lettering. Title the drawing SKETCH 5.

EXERCISE 7–11.   Complete Exercise 7–11 using the following steps:

Step 1. Remove the sheet labeled Exercise 7–11 from your book. Use light construction lines to sketch the top, front, and right-side views of step 1 shown on Figure 7–44.

Use one unit on the three-dimensional drawing to equal one unit on the two-dimensional sketch.

Be sure to line up all features of the object with the adjacent views.

Step 2. Use light construction lines to sketch the L shape in the front view of step 2 shown in Figure 7–44. Project the edges of the L shape into the top and right-side views with light construction lines.

Step 3. Use light construction lines to locate centers for the circles in the top view as shown in step 3. Draw the chamfers in the right-side view using light construction lines, and project these features into the top and right-side views. (You can draw the chamfers with dark object lines if you are sure of their locations).

Step 4. Draw the circles and the radii with dark lines, and darken all other lines as follows:

Sprinkle drafting powder over your drawing before you begin to darken lines.

Darken all other object lines in all views.

Step 5. Draw hidden lines in the top and right-side views.

Be sure to line up all features of the object with the adjacent views.

FIGURE 7–44
Dimensions for Exercise 7–11

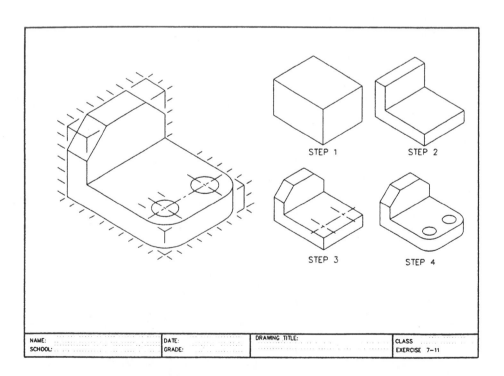

| NAME: | DATE: | DRAWING TITLE: | CLASS |
| SCHOOL: | GRADE: | | EXERCISE 7–11 |

Make hidden lines the same width and darkness as the object lines.

Step 6. Fill in the title block with your best lettering. Title the drawing SKETCH 6.

EXERCISE 7–12.   Complete Exercise 7–12 using the following steps:

Step 1. Remove the sheet labeled Exercise 7–12 from your book. Use light construction lines to sketch the object lines of the top, front, and right-side views of Figure 7–45.

Use one unit on the three-dimensional drawing to equal one unit on the two-dimensional sketch.

Be sure to line up all features of the object with the adjacent views.

Step 2. Use light construction lines to locate centers for the arcs in the front and right-side views.

Step 3. Use light construction lines to draw the top half of the $^3/_4''$ diameter arc in the front view and the $^1/_4''$ arc in the right-side view. Draw all remaining lines and darken all lines as follows:

Sprinkle drawing powder over your drawing before you begin to darken lines.

Darken the arcs.

Draw tangents to the arcs from their left and right corners using dark object lines.

Darken all other object lines in all views.

Step 4. Draw hidden lines in the top, front, and right-side views.

Be sure to line up all features of the object with the adjacent views.

Make hidden lines the same width and darkness as the object lines.

Step 5. Fill in the title block with your best lettering. Title the drawing SKETCH 7.

FIGURE 7–45
Dimensions for Exercise 7–12

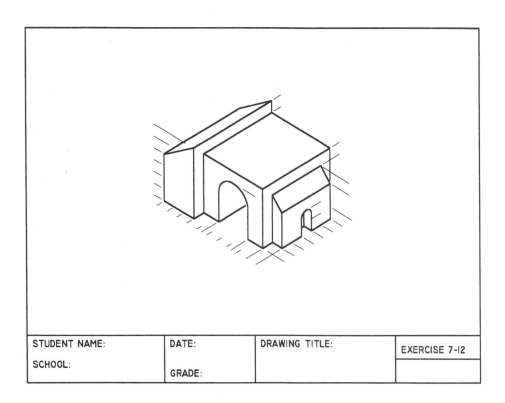

STUDENT NAME:	DATE:	DRAWING TITLE:	EXERCISE 7-12
SCHOOL:	GRADE:		

Reading and Sketching Orthographic Views

FIGURE 7–46
Dimensions for Exercise 7–13

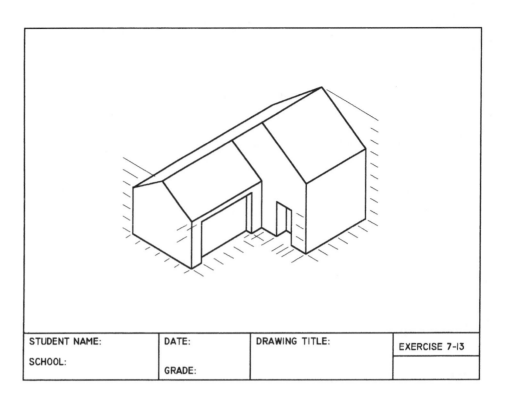

| STUDENT NAME: | DATE: | DRAWING TITLE: | EXERCISE 7-13 |
| SCHOOL: | GRADE: | | |

EXERCISE 7–13.   Complete Exercise 7–13 using the following steps:

Step 1.   Remove the sheet labeled Exercise 7–13 from your book. Use light construction lines to sketch the top, front, and right-side views of Figure 7–46.

Use one unit on the three-dimensional drawing to equal one unit on the two-dimensional sketch.

Be sure to line up all features of the object with the adjacent views.

Step 2.   Use light construction lines to draw the object lines in all three views. Draw all remaining lines and darken all lines as follows:

Sprinkle drawing powder over your drawing before you begin to darken lines.

Darken all object lines in all views.

Step 3.   Draw hidden lines in the top, front, and right-side views.

Be sure to line up all features of the object with the adjacent views.

Make hidden lines the same width and darkness as the object lines.

Step 4.   Fill in the title block with your best lettering. Title the drawing SKETCH 8.

EXERCISE 7–14.   Complete Exercise 7–14 using the following steps:

Step 1.   Remove the sheet labeled Exercise 7–14 from your book.

Step 2.   Fill in the missing information in the views indicated. Use the miter-line method to project depth dimensions. Add missing hidden lines as well as missing object lines. Be sure to line up all features of the object with the adjacent views.

Step 3.   Fill in the title block with your best lettering. Title the drawing MISSING LINES.

REVIEW QUESTIONS

Circle the best answer.

1. The method of technical drawing used in the United States is
   a. First-angle orthographic projection
   b. Second-angle orthographic projection
   c. Third-angle orthographic projection
   d. Fourth-angle orthographic projection
   e. All four are used about the same amount.

2. The top view of an object should be drawn
   a. To the right of the front view
   b. Directly above the front view
   c. To the left of the front view
   d. Anywhere on the same sheet with a label
   e. On a separate sheet

3. Projection theory is known as
   a. The black box model
   b. The transparent box model
   c. The sandbox model
   d. The object box model
   e. Isometric drawing

4. Lines of sight are at what angle to the sides of the projection box?
   a. 30°
   b. 45°
   c. 90° (perpendicular)
   d. 100°
   e. 180°

5. The adjacent sides of the transparent box are at what angles to each other?
   a. 30°
   b. 45°
   c. 90° (perpendicular)
   d. 100°
   e. 180°

6. When the box unfolds, where is the right-side view in relation to the front view?
   a. To the right of the front view
   b. To the left of the front view
   c. Above the front view
   d. Below the front view
   e. Behind the front view

7. Three dimensions are used in referring to the measurements of the object:
   a. Height, width, and length
   b. Height, width, and thickness
   c. Height, width, and depth
   d. Depth, thickness, and length
   e. Width, thickness, and length

8. The total number of possible normal views in orthographic projection is
   a. 1
   b. 2
   c. 4
   d. 6
   e. 9

9. As few as _____ view(s) may be drawn if adequate information is given.
   a. 1
   b. 2
   c. 4
   d. 6
   e. 9

10. A surface seen true size in the top view will appear as a(n) _____ in the front view.
    a. Surface
    b. Edge
    c. Point
    d. Inclined plane
    e. Oblique plane
11. Hidden surfaces are shown with
    a. Shaded areas
    b. Light lines
    c. Colored areas
    d. Short dashed lines
    e. A short dash and a longer dash
12. The first view chosen for most drawings should show
    a. Contour or shape
    b. Length
    c. Height
    d. Width
    e. Depth
13. The first view chosen for most drawings should be used as the
    a. Right-side view
    b. Top view
    c. Left-side view
    d. Back view
    e. Front view
14. A surface that is seen foreshortened in two views and appears as a line in the third view is called
    a. A normal surface
    b. An inclined surface
    c. An oblique surface
    d. A plane surface
    e. Either an inclined or an oblique surface
15. An object line (visible line) should be
    a. Very thick and dark
    b. Thin and dark
    c. Of medium thickness and dark
    d. Thin and light
    e. Of medium thickness and light
16. Dimension lines, extension lines, and center lines should be
    a. Very thick and dark
    b. Thin and dark
    c. Of medium thickness and dark
    d. Thin and light
    e. Of medium thickness and light
17. All lines except construction lines and projection lines should be
    a. Dark
    b. Light
18. Center lines for holes should extend outside the feature
    a. About $1/16''$
    b. About $1/4''$
    c. About $1/2''$
    d. About $1''$
    e. They should be varied to provide interest.
19. If two views of an object give the same information, should both views be drawn?
    a. Yes
    b. No
20. Which of the following is a good rule to follow in deciding how many views to draw of an object?
    a. Draw only the views that seem natural to you.
    b. Draw only the front and top views of any object.
    c. Draw only the front and right-side views of any object.
    d. Draw front, top, and right-side views always.
    e. Draw as many views as are needed to fully describe the object.

8

Making Orthographic Views with AutoCAD

OBJECTIVES

After completing this chapter, you will be able to:

☐ Make orthographic drawings containing one to three views using continuous, hidden, and center linetypes.
☐ Correctly answer questions regarding how to make orthographic drawings in Auto-CAD.
☐ Use the following commands to produce drawings:
   ID
   Mirror
   Dtext
   Offset
   Chamfer
   Fillet
   Copy
   Break
   Circle
   Osnap
   Zoom
   Trim
   Extend
   PLine
☐ Answer questions regarding the preceding commands.

TWO-DIMENSIONAL DRAWINGS IN AUTOCAD

As you learned in the previous chapter, two-dimensional drawings are those showing only two of the three dimensions of an object in any one view. Figure 8–1 illustrates the three most commonly used two-dimensional views. The top view shows width and depth. The front view shows width and height. The right-side view shows height and depth.

AutoCAD and AutoCAD LT have excellent capabilities for drawing in two dimensions. The drawings can be extremely accurate and can be dimensioned in a manner ensuring correct results, as you will learn in a later chapter. In this chapter you will begin with three drawings that have a single view and then make several drawings that have three views.

The first exercise you will draw in this chapter using the AutoCAD program is the floor plan you sketched in Chapter 2.

FIGURE 8–1
Three Most Commonly Used
Orthographic Views

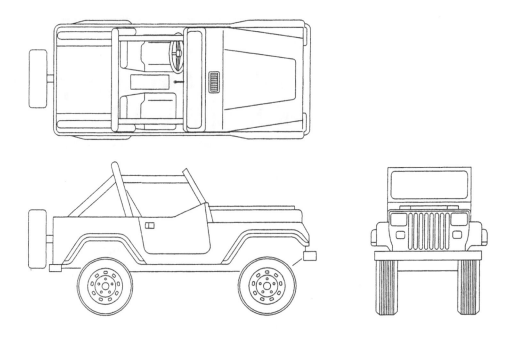

EXERCISE 8–1:
Drawing a Floor Plan Using the Polyline, Offset, Line, and Trim Commands

Your final drawing will look similar to the drawing in Figure 8–2 without dimensions.

Step 1.   **To begin Exercise 8–1, turn on the computer and start AutoCAD or Auto-CAD LT.**

Step 2.   **Open drawing EX8-1 supplied on the disk that came with your book.** Because there are several ways to open a drawing, the laboratory instructor must tell you how to do that on your version of AutoCAD.

Step 3.   **Use Zoom-All to view the entire drawing area.**

FIGURE 8–2
Dimensions for Exercise 8-1

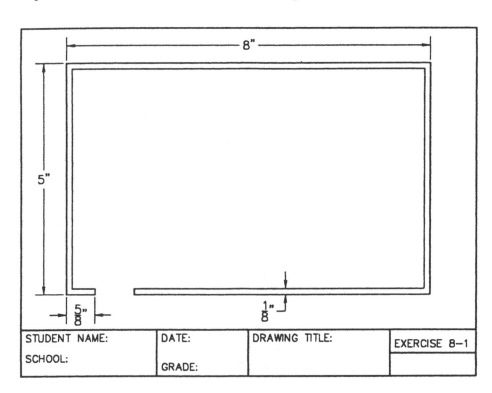

Prompt	Response
Command:	Type: **Z <enter>**
Specify corner of window, enter a scale factor (nX or nXP), or [All/Center/ Dynamic/Extents/Previous/Scale/ Window] <real time>:	Type: **A<enter>**

Step 4. Use the Polyline command to draw the outside edge of the floor plan.

Prompt	Response
Command:	Type: **PL<enter>** (for Polyline)
Specify start point:	Type: **END<enter>**
of	Pick: **the Right End of the lower horizontal line**
Specify next point or [Arc/Close/ Halfwidth/Length/Undo/Width]:	Type: **@5<90<enter>**
Specify next point or [Arc/Close/ Halfwidth/Length/Undo/Width]:	Type: **@8<180<enter>**
Specify next point or [Arc/Close/ Halfwidth/Length/Undo/Width]:	Type: **@5<270<enter>**
Specify next point or [Arc/Close/ Halfwidth/Length/Undo/Width]:	Type: **@5/8<0<enter>**
Specify next point or [Arc/Close/ Halfwidth/Length/Undo/Width]:	Press: **<enter>**

Step 5. Use the Offset command to draw the inside edge of the floor plan.

Prompt	Response
Command:	Type: **O<enter>**
Specify offset distance or [Through]:	Type: **.125<enter>**
Select object to offset or <exit>:	Pick: **the Polyline you just drew**
Specify point on side to offset:	Pick: **any point on the inside of the polyline**
Select object to offset or <exit>:	**<enter>**

Step 6. Use the Pline command to close the left side of the door opening (Figure 8–3).

Prompt	Response
Command:	Type: **PL<enter>**
Specify start point:	Type: **END<enter>**
of	Pick: **D1 (Figure 8–3)**
Specify next point or [Arc/Close/ Halfwidth/Length/Undo/Width]:	Type: **END<enter>**
of	Pick: **D2**
Specify next point or [Arc/Close/ Halfwidth/Length/Undo/Width]:	**<enter>**

Step 7. Use the Trim command to clean up the bottom right corner of the floor plan (Figure 8–4).

Prompt	Response
Command:	Type: **TR<enter>**

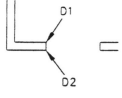

FIGURE 8–3
Draw the End Cap

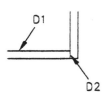

FIGURE 8–4
Trim the Wall

FIGURE 8–5
Filling in the Title Block

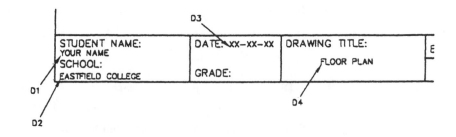

Select cutting edges:

Select objects:	Pick: **D1 (Figure 8–4)**
Select objects:	**<enter>**
Select object to trim or shift-select to extend or [Project/Edge/Undo]:	Pick: **D2**
Select object to trim or shift-select to extend or [Project/Edge/Undo]:	**<enter>**

Step 8.   Use the Dtext command to complete the title block.

Prompt	Response
Command:	Type: **DT<enter>**
Specify start point of text or [Justify/Style]:	Pick: **D1 (Figure 8–5)**
Specify height <0.2000>:	Type: **.12<enter>** (or just **<enter>** if the default is .12)
Specify rotation angle of text <0>:	**<enter>**
Enter text:	Type: **YOUR FIRST INITIAL AND YOUR LAST NAME<enter>** (Make sure all lettering in the title block is in capital letters.)
Enter text:	Pick: **D2 (Figure 8–5)** and Type: **YOUR SCHOOL NAME<enter>**
Enter text:	Pick: **D3** and Type: **TODAY'S DATE<enter>**
Enter text:	Pick: **D4** and Type: **FLOOR PLAN<enter>**
Enter text:	**<enter>**

Step 9.   Use the SAVEAS command to save your drawing as EX8-1(your initials) on a floppy disk and again on the hard drive of your computer.

Step 10.   Print your drawing full size on an 11″ x 8½″ sheet.

The second exercise in this chapter will give you practice in using the Fillet, Offset, Extend, Break, and Copy (also called Duplicate in later versions) commands.

EXERCISE 8–2:
Drawing a Site Plan Using the Fillet, Offset, Extend, Break, and Copy Commands

Your final drawing will look similar to the drawing in Figure 8–6 without dimensions.

FIGURE 8–6
Dimensions for Exercise 8–2

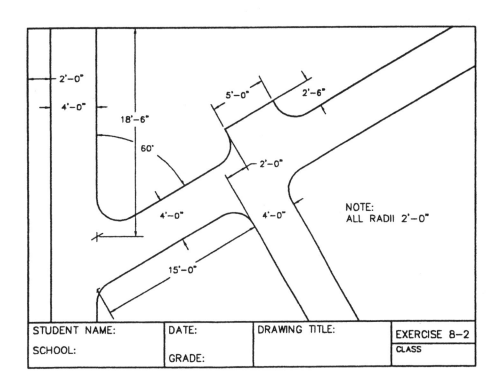

STUDENT NAME: SCHOOL:	DATE: GRADE:	DRAWING TITLE:	EXERCISE 8–2 CLASS

Step 1. To begin Exercise 8–2, turn on the computer and start AutoCAD or Auto-CAD LT.

Step 2. Open drawing EX8-2 supplied on the disk that came with your book.

Step 3. Use Zoom-All to view the entire drawing area.

Prompt	Response
Command:	Type: **Z <enter>**
Specify corner of window, enter a scale factor (nX or nXP), or [All/Center/ Dynamic/Extents/Previous/Scale/ Window] <real time>:	Type: **A<enter>**

Step 4. Use the Fillet command to draw radii on existing lines.

Prompt	Response
Command:	Type: **F<enter>**
Select first object or [Polyline/Radius/Trim]:	Type: **R<enter>**
Specify fillet radius <>:	Type: **.5<enter>**
Select first object or [Polyline/Radius/Trim]:	Pick: **D1 (Figure 8–7)**
Select second object:	Pick: **D2**
Command:	**<enter>**
Select first object or [Polyline/Radius/Trim]:	Pick: **D3**
Select second object:	Pick: **D4**
Command:	**<enter>**
Select first object or [Polyline/Radius/Trim]:	Pick: **D5**
Select second object:	Pick: **D6**

Step 5. Use the Offset command to draw parallel lines.

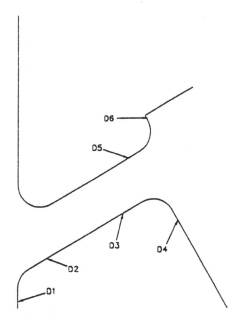

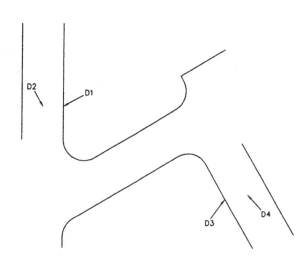

FIGURE 8–7
Use the Fillet Command to Draw Radii
on Existing Lines

FIGURE 8–8
Use the Offset Command to Draw Parallel Lines

Prompt	Response
Command:	Type: **O<enter>**
Specify offset distance or [Through] <>:	Type: **1<enter>**
Select object to offset or <exit>:	Pick: **D1 (Figure 8–8)**
Specify point on side to offset:	Pick: **D2** (any point on the left side of the selected object)
Select object to offset or <exit>:	Pick: **D3**
Specify point on side to offset:	Pick: **D4** (any point on the right side of the selected object)
Select object to offset or <exit>:	**<enter>**

Step 6. **Use the Extend command to extend lines to the borders.**

Prompt	Response
Command:	Type: **EX<enter>**
Select boundary edges ...	
Select objects:	Pick: **D1, D2 (Figure 8–9)**
Select objects:	**<enter>**
Select object to extend or shift-select to trim or [Project/Edge/Undo]:	Pick: **D3, D4, D5, D6 <enter>**

Step 7. **Use the Break command to break diagonal lines into two segments so they can be filleted.**

Prompt	Response
Command:	Type: **BR<enter>**
Select object:	Pick: **D1 (Figure 8–10)**
Specify second break point or [First point]:	Type: **F<enter>**
Specify first break point:	Type: **INT<enter>**

FIGURE 8–9
Use the Extend Command to
Extend Lines to the Border

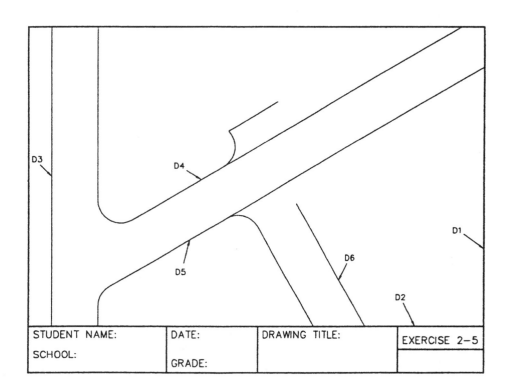

FIGURE 8–10
Use the Break Command to
Break Diagonal Lines So Fillets
Can Be Drawn

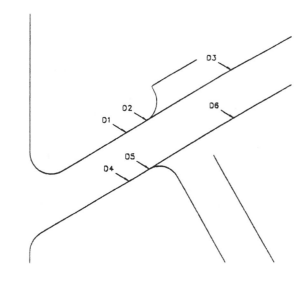

of	Pick: **D2**
Specify second break point:	Pick: **D3** (in the approximate location shown; the exact location is not important.)
Command:	**<enter>**
Select object:	Pick: **D4**
Specify second break point or [First point]:	Type: **F<enter>**
Specify first break point:	Type: **INT<enter>**
of	Pick: **D5**
Specify second break point:	Pick: **D6** (in the approximate location shown; the exact location is not important.)

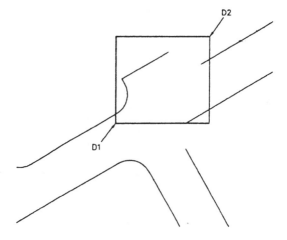

FIGURE 8–11
Zoom In on the Intersection

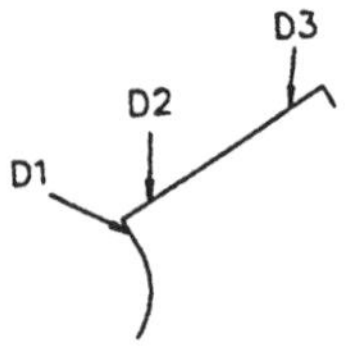

FIGURE 8–12
Use the Copy Command to
Copy the Short Line

Step 8. **Zoom in and use the Copy command to copy the short line on the top of the drawing.**

Prompt	Response
Command:	Type: **Z<enter>**
Specify corner of window, enter a scale factor (nX or nXP), or[All/ Center/Dynamic/Extents/Previous/ Scale/Window] <real time>:	Pick: **D1 (Figure 8–11)**
Specify opposite corner:	Pick: **D2**
Command:	Type: **CP<enter>**(for COPY)
Select objects:	Pick: **D1 (Figure 8–12)**
Select objects:	**<enter>**
Specify base point or displacement, or [Multiple]:	Type: **END<enter>**
of	Pick: **D2**
Specify second point of displacement or <use first point as displacement>:	Type: **END<enter>**
of	Pick: **D3**

Step 9. **Zoom-All and use the Fillet command to complete the drawing.**

Prompt	Response
Command:	Type: **Z<enter>**
Specify corner of window, enter a scale factor (nX or nXP), or[All/ Center/Dynamic/Extents/Previous/ Scale/Window] <real time>:	Type: **A<enter>**
Command:	Type: **F<enter>**
Select first object or [Polyline/Radius/Trim]:	Pick: **D1 (Figure 8–13)**
Select second object:	Pick: **D2**
Command:	**<enter>**
Select first object or [Polyline/Radius/Trim]:	Pick: **D3**
Select second object:	Pick: **D4**

FIGURE 8–13
Use the Fillet Command to Draw
the Remaining Radii

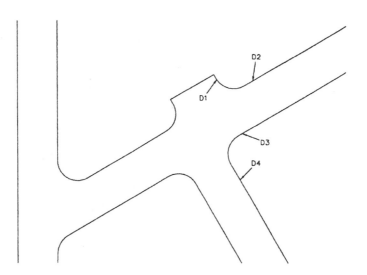

Step 10. Use the Dtext command to complete the title block as you did for EX8-1. Title the drawing SITE PLAN.

Step 11. Use the SAVEAS command to save your drawing as EX8-2(your initials) on a floppy disk and again on the hard drive of your computer.

Because there are several different ways to save drawings using different versions of AutoCAD, consult with the laboratory instructor or your AutoCAD manual on how to do that.

Step 12. Plot or print your drawing full size on an 11″ x 8½″ sheet.

In Exercise 8–3 you will use the Line, Circle, and Mirror commands, and you will make a drawing that contains continuous and center linetypes.

EXERCISE 8–3:
Drawing a Plate Using the Line, Circle, and Mirror Commands

Your final drawing will look similar to the drawing in Figure 8-14 without dimensions.

Step 1. To begin Exercise 8–3, turn on the computer and start AutoCAD or Auto-CAD LT.

Step 2. Open drawing EX8-3 supplied on the disk that came with your book.

Step 3. Use Zoom-All to view the entire drawing area.

Prompt	Response
Command:	Type: **Z <enter>**
Specify corner of window, enter a scale factor (nX or nXP), or[All/ Center/Dynamic/Extents/Previous/ Scale/Window] <real time>:	Type: **A<enter>**

Step 4. Use the Line command to draw lines forming the outside edges of the plate. Notice that you are drawing the plate at half scale.

Prompt	Response
Command:	Type: **L<enter>**
Specify first point:	Type: **END<enter>**
of	**D1 (Figure 8–15)**

FIGURE 8–14
Dimensions for Exercise 8–3

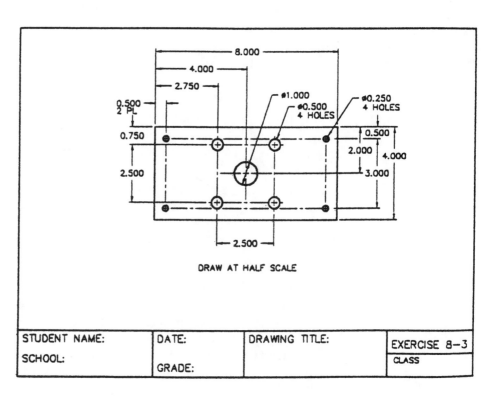

DRAW AT HALF SCALE

STUDENT NAME:	DATE:	DRAWING TITLE:	EXERCISE 8–3
SCHOOL:	GRADE:		CLASS

FIGURE 8–15
Draw the Outside Edges

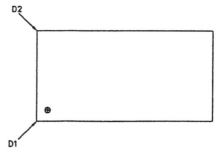

Specify next point or [Undo]:	Type: **@4<0<enter>**
Specify next point or [Undo]:	Type: **@2<90<enter>**
Specify next point or [Close/Undo]:	Type: **END<enter>**
of	Pick: **D2**
Specify next point or [Close/Undo]:	**<enter>**

Step 5. Use the ID command to identify a point from which you may draw circles.

Prompt	Response
Command:	Type: **ID<enter>**
Specify point:	Type: **END<enter>**
of	Pick: **D1 (Figure 8–16)**
Command:	Type: **C<enter>**
Specify center point for circle or [3P/2P/Ttr/(tan tan radius)]:	Type: **@2,-1<enter>**
Specify radius of circle or [Diameter]:	Type: **.25<enter>**
Command:	Type: **ID<enter>**
Specify point:	Type: **END<enter>**
of	Pick: **D1 (Figure 8–16)**

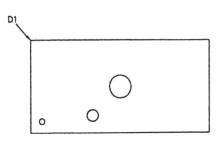

FIGURE 8–16
Use the ID Command to Identify
a Point for a Single Command

Command:	Type: **C<enter>**
Specify center point for circle or [3P/2P/Ttr]:	Type: **@1.375,-1.625<enter>**
Specify radius of circle or [Diameter]:	Type: **.125<enter>**

Step 6.   Use the Mirror command to complete the drawing.

Prompt	Response
Command:	Type: **MI<enter>**
Select objects:	Pick: **the two smaller circles, D1 and D2 (Figure 8–17)**
Select objects:	**<enter>**
Specify first point of mirror line:	Type: **MID<enter>**
of	Pick: **D3**
Specify second point of mirror line:	Type: **MID<enter>**
of	Pick: **D4**
Delete source objects? [Yes/No]<N>:	**<enter>**
Command:	**<enter>**
Select objects:	Pick: **the four smaller circles, D1, D2, D3, D4 (Figure 8–18)**
Select objects:	**<enter>**
Specify first point of mirror line:	Type: **MID<enter>**
of	Pick: **D5**
Specify second point of mirror line:	Type: **MID<enter>**
of	Pick: **D6**
Delete source objects? [Yes/No]<N>:	**<enter>**

Step 7.   Use the Dtext command to complete the title block as you did for EX8-1. Title the drawing MOUNTING PLATE.

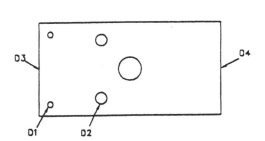

FIGURE 8–17
Use the Mirror Command to Copy
the Two Smaller Holes

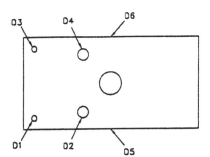

FIGURE 8–18
Use the Mirror Command to
Copy the Four Smaller Holes

Making Orthographic Views with AutoCAD

123

Step 8. Use the SAVEAS command to save your drawing as EX8-3(your initials) on a floppy disk and again on the hard drive of your computer.

Step 9. Plot or print your drawing full size on an 11″ x 8½″ sheet.

In Exercise 8–4 you will use the same commands you used in the earlier exercises in this chapter to make an architectural drawing that has continuous and hidden lines.

EXERCISE 8–4:
Making a Drawing Using Continuous and Hidden Linetypes

Your final drawing will look like the drawing in Figure 8–19 without the pictorial view. Each mark on the pictorial view is ¼″ and your grid is set to ¼″ also.

Step 1. To begin Exercise 8–4, turn on the computer and start AutoCAD or AutoCAD LT.

Step 2. Open drawing EX8-4 supplied on the disk that came with your book.

Step 3. Use Zoom-All to view the entire drawing area.

Prompt	Response
Command:	Type: **Z<enter>**
Specify corner of window, enter a scale factor (nX or nXP), or [All/Center/Dynamic/Extents/Previous/Scale/Window] <real time>:	Type: **A<enter>**

Step 4. Use the **Line, Offset,** and **Fillet** commands to draw object lines in the front view (Figure 8–20).

Command:	Type: **L<enter>**
Specify first point:	Type: **END<enter>**
of	Pick: **D1**

FIGURE 8–19
Dimensions for Exercise 8–4

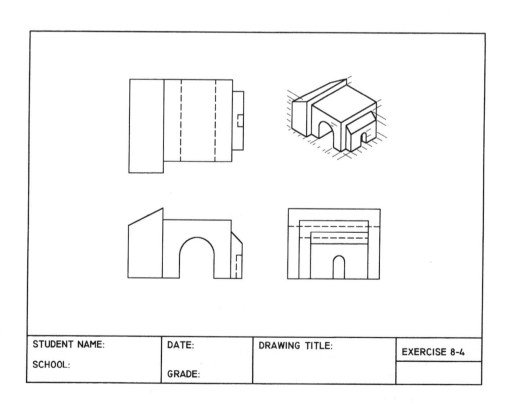

STUDENT NAME:	DATE:	DRAWING TITLE:	EXERCISE 8-4
SCHOOL:	GRADE:		

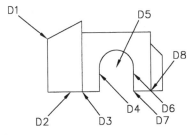

FIGURE 8–20
Draw Object Lines in the
Front View

Prompt	Response
Specify next point or [Undo]:	Type: **@.75,.5<enter>**
Specify next point or [Undo]:	Type: **PER<enter>**
to	Pick: **D2** (anywhere on this line)
Specify next point or [Close/Undo]:	**<enter>**
Command:	Type: **L<enter>**
Specify first point:	Type: **END<enter>**
of	Pick: **D3**
Specify next point or [Undo]:	With ORTHO ON **move your mouse to the right** and Type: **.25<enter>**
Specify next point or [Undo]:	With ORTHO ON **move your mouse up** and Type: **7/8<enter>**
Specify next point or [Undo]:	**<enter>**
Command:	Type: **O<enter>** (for Offset)
Specify offset distance or [Through]:	Type: **.75<enter>**
Select object to offset or <exit>:	Pick: **D4**
Specify point on side to offset:	Pick: **D5**
Select object to offset or <exit>:	**<enter>**
Command:	Type: **F<enter>**
Select first object or [Polyline/Radius/Trim]:	Type: **R<enter>**
Specify fillet radius <0.7500>:	Type: **3/8<enter>**
Select first object or [Polyline/Radius/Trim]:	Pick: **D4**
Select second object:	Pick: **D6**
Command:	Type: **L<enter>**
Specify first point:	Type: **END<enter>**
of	Pick: **D7**
Specify next point or [Undo]:	With ORTHO ON, **move your mouse to the right** and Type: **3/8<enter>**
Specify next point or [Undo]:	With ORTHO ON, **move your mouse up** and Type: **1-1/4<enter**
Specify next point or [Close/Undo]:	With Ortho ON, **move your mouse to the left** and Type: **1-1/2<enter**
Specify next point or [Close/Undo]:	**<enter>**
Command:	Type: **L<enter>**
Specify first point:	Type: **END<enter>**
of	Pick: **D8<enter>**
Specify next point or [Undo]:	With ORTHO ON, **move your mouse to the right** and Type: **1/4<enter>**
Specify next point or [Undo]:	With ORTHO ON, **move your mouse up** and Type: **.75<enter>**
Specify next point or [Close/Undo]:	Type: **@-.25,.25**
Specify next point or [Close/Undo]:	**<enter>**

Step 5. **Use the Line command to draw object lines in the top view (Figure 8–21).**

Prompt	Response
Command:	Type: **L<enter>**
Specify first point:	Type: **END<enter>**

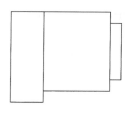

FIGURE 8–21
Draw Object Lines in the
Top View

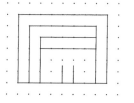

FIGURE 8–22
Draw Object Lines in the
Right-Side View

of	Pick: **the right end of the short horizontal line in the top view**
Specify next point or [Undo]:	With ORTHO ON, **move your mouse to the up** and Type: **2<enter>**
Specify next point or [Undo]:	With ORTHO ON, **move your mouse to the left** and Type: **3/4<enter**
Specify next point or [Undo]:	**<enter>**
Command:	**<enter>**
Specify first point:	Type: **END<enter>**
of	Pick: **the right end of the long horizontal line in the top view**
Specify next point or [Undo]:	With ORTHO ON, **move your mouse up** and Type: **1-3/4<enter>**
Specify next point or [Undo]:	With ORTHO ON, **move your mouse to the left** and Type: **1-1/2<enter**
Specify next point or [Close/Undo]:	**<enter>**
Command:	**<enter>**
Specify first point:	**Turn SNAP ON and move your mouse so the cursor is one grid up from the lower right corner of the top view and Pick: the first point.**
Specify next point or [Undo]:	With ORTHO ON, **move your mouse one grid to the right and Pick: the next point.**
Specify next point or [Undo]:	With ORTHO ON, **move your mouse five grids up and Pick: the next point.**
Specify next point or [Close/Undo]:	With ORTHO ON, **move your mouse one grid to the left and Pick: the final point.**
Specify next point or [Close/Undo]:	**<enter>**

Step 6. **Use the Copy and Line commands to draw object lines in the right-side view (Figure 8–22).**

Prompt	Response
Command:	Type: **CP<enter>**
Select objects:	Pick: **the vertical line in the right-side view**
Select objects:	**<enter>**
Specify base point or displacement, or [Multiple]:	Pick: **any point**
Specify second point of displacement or <use first point as displacement>:	With ORTHO ON **move your mouse to the right** and Type: **2<enter>** (The vertical line is copied 2″ to the right.)
Command:	**<enter>** (to repeat the copy command)
Select objects:	Pick: **the horizontal line in the right side view**
Select objects:	**<enter>**

Specify base point or displacement, or [Multiple]:	Pick: **Any point**
Specify second point of displacement or <use first point as displacement>:	With ORTHO ON **move your mouse up** and Type: **1-1/2<enter>** (The horizontal line is copied 1½″ up.)

On Your Own

With SNAP, GRID, and ORTHO ON (and OSNAP OFF, so you do not pick points that you do not want) use the Line command to draw the remaining lines in the right-side view as shown in Figure 8–22. Notice that the two shortest vertical lines are one and a half grid marks long (³⁄₈″).

Step 7. **Use the Fillet command to draw the arc connecting the two shortest lines in the right-side view.**

Prompt	Response
Command:	Type: **F<enter>**
Current settings: Mode = TRIM, Radius = 0.0000 Select first object or [Polyline/Radius/Trim]:	Type: **R<enter>**
Specify fillet radius <0.0000>:	Type: **.125<enter>**
Select first object or [Polyline/Radius/Trim]:	Pick: **one of the shortest vertical lines**
Select second object:	Pick: **the other shortest vertical line**

Step 8. **Set the HIDDEN layer current and use the Line command to draw hidden lines in all views (Figure 8–23).**

Prompt	Response
Command:	Type: **-LA<enter>**
Enter an option [?/Make/Set/New/ON/OFF/ Color/Ltype/LWeight/Plot/Freeze/Thaw/ LOck/Unlock]:	Type: **S<enter>**
Enter layer name to make current <Layer1>:	Type: **HIDDEN<enter>**
Enter an option [?/Make/Set/New/ON/OFF/ Color/Ltype/LWeight/Plot/Freeze/Thaw/ LOck/Unlock]:	**<enter>**

Note: You can also set a layer current by simply clicking on it from the layer list at the top of your screen.

FIGURE 8–23
Draw Hidden Lines in All Views

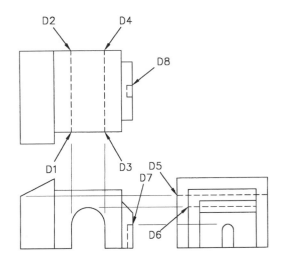

Prompt	Response
Command:	Type: **L<enter>**
Specify first point:	With ORTHO and SNAP ON Pick: **D1** (**Figure 8–23**) (Be sure D1 lines up with the arch in the front view.)
Specify next point or [Undo]:	Pick: **D2**
Specify next point or [Undo]:	**<enter>**
Command:	**<enter>** (to repeat the Line command)
Specify first point:	Pick: **D3**
Specify next point or [Undo]:	Pick: **D4**
Specify next point or [Undo]:	**<enter>**
Command:	**<enter>**
Specify first point:	Pick: **D5** (Be sure D5 lines up with the slanted surface on the left side of the front view.)
Specify next point or [Undo]:	With ORTHO ON **move your mouse to the right** and Type: **2<enter>**
Specify next point or [Undo]:	**<enter>**
Command:	**<enter>**
Specify first point:	Pick: **D6** (Be sure D6 lines up with the top of the arch in the front view.)
Specify next point or [Undo]:	**Move your mouse to the right** and Type: **1-1/2<enter>**
Specify next point or [Undo]:	**<enter>**
Command:	**<enter>**
Specify first point:	Pick: **D7** (Be sure D7 lines up with the top of the small arch in the right-side view.)
Specify next point or [Undo]:	**Move your mouse to the left** and Type: **1/8<enter>**
Specify next point or [Undo]:	Move your mouse down and Type: **1/2<enter>**
Command:	**<enter>**
Specify first point:	Pick: **D8** (Be sure D8 is 2 grids from the top short horizontal line.)
Specify next point or [Undo]:	**Move your mouse to the left** and Type: **1/8<enter>**
Specify next point or [Undo]:	**Move your mouse down** and Type: **1/4<enter>**
Specify next point or [Undo]:	**Move your mouse to the right** and Type: **1/8<enter>**
Command:	**<enter>**

Step 9. Use the Dtext command to complete the title block as you did for EX8-1. Title the drawing ORTHOGRAPHIC VIEWS (Figure 8–24).

Step 10. Use the SAVEAS command to save your drawing as EX8-4(your initials) on a floppy disk and again on the hard drive of your computer.

Step 11. Plot or print your drawing full size on an 11″ x 8½″ sheet.

FIGURE 8–24
Exercise 8–4 Complete

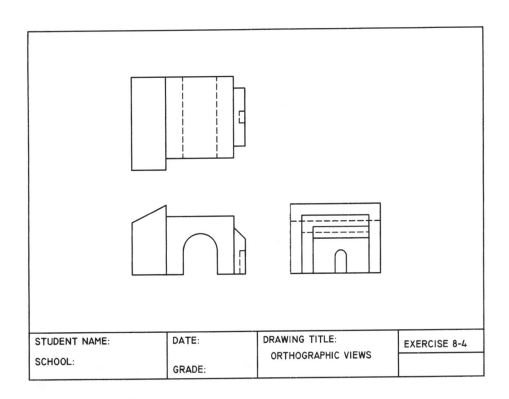

EXERCISE 8–5:
Making a Drawing Containing Top, Front, and Right-Side Views of an Object with Uniform Thickness

Your final drawing will look like Figure 8–25 without the pictorial sketch. Each space on the sketch is 1/4″.

FIGURE 8–25
Quarter-Inch Measurements for
Exercise 8–5

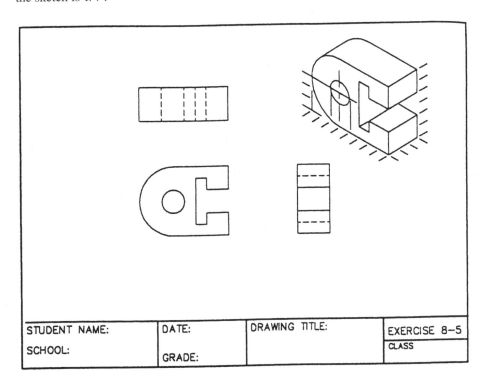

Step 1. To begin Exercise 8–5, turn on the computer and start AutoCAD or AutoCAD LT.

Step 2. Open drawing EX8-5 supplied on the disk that came with your book.

Step 3. Use Zoom-All to view the entire drawing area.

Prompt	Response
Command:	Type: **Z <enter>**
Specify corner of window, enter a scale factor (nX or nXP), or [All/Center/ Dynamic/Extents/Previous/Scale/ Window] <real time>:	Type: **A<enter>**

Step 4. Use the PLine and Arc commands to draw the complete front view.

Prompt	Response
Command:	Type: **PL<enter>**
Specify first point:	Type: **END<enter>**
of	Pick: **D1 (Figure 8–26)**
Specify next point or [Arc/Close/Halfwidth/ Length/Undo/Width]:	Type: **@1/4<0<enter>**
Specify next point or [Arc/Close/Halfwidth/ Length/Undo/Width]:	Type: **@1/4<-90<enter>**
Specify next point or [Arc/Close/Halfwidth/ Length/Undo/Width]:	Type: **@1/2<0<enter>**
Specify next point or [Arc/Close/Halfwidth/ Length/Undo/Width]:	Type: **@1/2<90<enter>**
Specify next point or [Arc/Close/Halfwidth/ Length/Undo/Width]:	Type: **@1-1/4<180<enter>**
Specify next point or [Arc/Close/Halfwidth/ Length/Undo/Width]:	Type: **A<enter>**
Specify endpoint of arc:	Type: **@1-1/2<270<enter>**
Specify endpoint of arc:	Type: **L<enter>**
Specify next point or [Arc/Close/Halfwidth/ Length/Undo/Width]:	Type: **@1-1/4<0<enter>**
Specify next point or [Arc/Close/Halfwidth/ Length/Undo/Width]:	Type: **@1/2<90<enter>**
Specify next point or [Arc/Close/Halfwidth/ Length/Undo/Width]:	Type: **@1/2<180<enter>**
Specify next point or [Arc/Close/Halfwidth/ Length/Undo/Width]:	Type: **@1/4<-90<enter>**

FIGURE 8–26
Use the PLine and Arc Commands to Complete the Front View

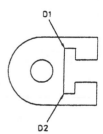

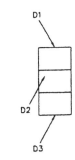

FIGURE 8–27
Use the Offset Command to Draw Object Lines in the Right-Side View

Specify next point or [Arc/Close/Halfwidth/ Length/Undo/Width]:	Type: **END<enter>**
of	Pick: **D2**
Specify next point or [Arc/Close/Halfwidth/ Length/Undo/Width]:	**<enter>**

Step 5.   **Use Offset command to draw object lines in the right-side view.**

Command:	Type: **O<enter>**
Specify offset distance or [Through] <>:	Type: **1/2<enter>**
Select object to offset or <exit>:	Pick: **D1 (Figure 8–27)**
Specify point on side to offset:	Pick: **D2** (any point below D1)
Select object to offset or <exit>:	Pick: **D3**
Specify point on side to offset:	Pick: **D2** (any point above D3)
Select object to offset or <exit>:	**<enter>**

Step 6.   **Set the HIDDEN layer current and use the Line command to draw hidden lines in the top and right-side views.**
(Refer to Step 6 of Exercise 8-4 to set layer HIDDEN current.)

Be sure SNAP and ORTHO are ON so you can line up the hidden lines with the surfaces in the adjacent views.

Prompt	**Response**
Command:	Type: **L<enter>**
Specify first point:	Pick: **D1 (Figure 8–28)**
Specify next point or [Undo]:	Pick: **D2**

FIGURE 8–28
Draw Hidden Lines in the Top and Right-Side Views

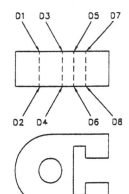

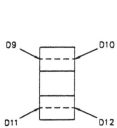

Making Orthographic Views with AutoCAD

Specify next point or [Undo]:	<enter>
Command:	<enter>
Specify first point	Pick: **D3**
Specify next point or [Undo]:	Pick: **D4**
Specify next point or [Undo]:	<enter>
Command:	<enter>
Specify first point:	Pick: **D5**
Specify next point or [Undo]:	Pick: **D6**
Specify next point or [Undo]:	<enter>
Command:	<enter>
Specify first point:	Pick: **D7**
Specify next point or [Undo]:	Pick: **D8**
Specify next point or [Undo]:	<enter>
Command:	<enter>
Specify first point:	Pick: **D9**
Specify next point or [Undo]:	Pick: **D10**
Specify next point or [Undo]:	<enter>
Command:	<enter>
Specify first point:	Pick: **D11**
Specify next point or [Undo]:	Pick: **D12**
Specify next point or [Undo]:	<enter>

Step 7. Use the Dtext command to complete the title block as you have done previously. Title the drawing HANGER.

Step 8. Use the SAVEAS command to save your drawing as EX8-5(your initials) on a floppy disk and again on the hard drive of your computer.

Step 9. Plot or print your drawing full size on an 11″ x 8½″ sheet.

EXERCISE 8–6:
Making a Drawing Containing Top, Front, and Right-Side Views of a Curved Object with Uniform Thickness

Your final drawing will look like Figure 8–29 without the pictorial sketch. Each space on the sketch is 1/4″.

Step 1. To begin Exercise 8–6, turn on the computer and start AutoCAD or AutoCAD LT.

Step 2. Open drawing EX8-6 supplied on the disk that came with your book.

Step 3. Use Zoom-All to view the entire drawing area.

Prompt	Response
Command:	Type: **Z <enter>**
Specify corner of window, enter a scale factor (nX or nXP), or[All/ Center/Dynamic/Extents/Previous/ Scale/Window] <real time>:	Type: **A<enter>**

Step 4. Use the PLine command to draw the outside lines of the front view.

Prompt	Response
Command:	Type: **PL<enter>**

FIGURE 8–29

Quarter-Inch Measurements for
Exercise 8--6

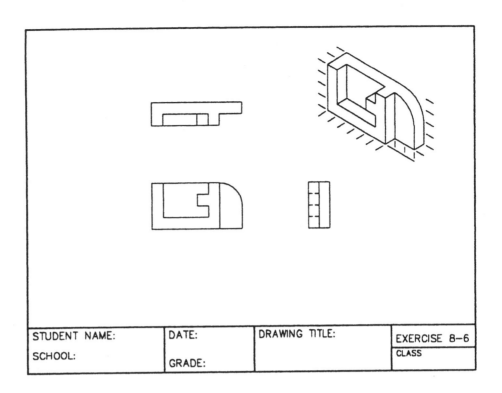

| STUDENT NAME: | DATE: | DRAWING TITLE: | EXERCISE 8–6 |
| SCHOOL: | GRADE: | | CLASS |

FIGURE 8–30

Use the PLine Command to Draw
Outside Lines in the Front View

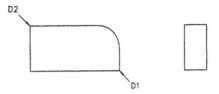

Specify first point:	Type: **END<enter>**
of	Pick: **D1 (Figure 8–30)**
Specify next point or [Arc/Halfwidth/ Length/Undo/Width]:	Type: **@1/2<90<enter>**
Specify next point or [Arc/Close/Halfwidth/ Length/Undo/Width]:	Type: **A<enter>**
Specify endpoint of Arc:	Type: **@-1/2,1/2<enter>**
Specify endpoint of Arc:	Type: **L<enter>**
Specify next point or [Arc/Close/Halfwidth/ Length/Undo/Width]:	Type: **END<enter>**
of	Pick: **D2**

Step 5. **Use the ID and Line commands to draw object lines in the front and top views.**

Prompt	Response
Command:	Type: **ID<enter>**
Specify point:	Type: **END<enter>**
of	Pick: **D1 (Figure 8–31)**
Command:	Type: **L<enter>**
Specify first point:	Type: **@1/4<0<enter>**
Specify next point or [Undo]:	Type: **@3/4<-90<enter>**

Making Orthographic Views with AutoCAD

FIGURE 8–31
Use the ID and Line Commands
to Draw Object Lines in the Front
and Top Views

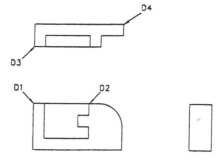

Specify next point or [Undo]:	Type: **@1<0<enter>**
Specify next point or [Close/Undo]:	Type: **@1/4<90<enter>**
Specify next point or [Close/Undo]:	Type: **@1/4<180<enter>**
Specify next point or [Close/Undo]:	Type: **@1/4<90<enter>**
Specify next point or [Close/Undo]:	Type: **@1/4<0<enter>**
Specify next point or [Close/Undo]:	Type: **PER<enter>**
to	Pick: **D2**
Specify next point or [Close/Undo]:	**<enter>**
Command:	**<enter>**
Specify first point:	Type: **END<enter>**
of	Pick: **D3**
Specify next point or [Undo]:	Type: **@1-1/2<0<enter>**
Specify next point or [Undo]:	Type: **@1/4<90<enter>**
Specify next point or [Close/Undo]:	Type: **1/2<0<enter>**
Specify next point or [Close/Undo]:	Type: **END<enter>**
to	Pick: **D4**
Specify next point or [Close/Undo]:	**<enter>**
Command:	Type: **ID<enter>**
Point:	Type: **END<enter>**
of	Pick: **D3 (Figure 8–31)** (again)
Command:	Type: **L<enter>**
Specify first point:	Type: **@1/4<0<enter>**
Specify next point or [Undo]:	Type: **@1/4<90<enter>**
Specify next point or [Undo]:	Type: **@1<0<enter>**
Specify next point or [Close/Undo]:	Type: **@1/4<-90<enter>**
Specify next point or [Close/Undo]:	**<enter>**

Step 6. **Use the Offset command to draw object lines in the front, top, and right-side views.**

Prompt	Response
Command:	Type: **O<enter>**
Specify offset distance or [Through] <>:	Type: **1-1/2<enter>**
Select object to offset or <exit>:	Pick: **D1 (Figure 8–32)**
Specify point on side to offset:	Pick: **D2**
Select object to offset or <exit>:	**<enter>**
Command:	**<enter>**
Offset distance or Through <1.5000>:	Type: **1/4<enter>**

FIGURE 8–32
Use the Offset Command to
Draw Object Lines in the Front,
Top, and Right-Side Views

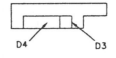

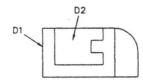

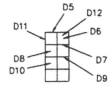

Prompt	Response
Select object to offset or <exit>:	Pick: **D3**
Specify point on side to offset:	Pick: **D4**
ct object to offset or <exit>:	Pick: **D5**
Specify point on side to offset:	Pick: **D6**
Select object to offset or <exit>:	Pick: **D7**
Specify point on side to offset:	Pick: **D8**
Select object to offset or <exit>:	Pick: **D9**
Specify point on side to offset:	Pick: **D10**
Select object to offset or <exit>:	Pick: **D11**
Specify point on side to offset:	Pick: **D12**
Select object to offset or <exit>:	**<enter>**

Step 7.   Use the Chprop (Change properties) command to change the object lines
in the right-side view to hidden lines and trim them to the correct length
using the Trim command.

Prompt	Response
Command:	Type: **CHPROP<enter>**
Select objects:	Pick: **D1 (Figure 8–33)**
Select objects:	Pick: **D2**
Select objects:	Pick: **D3**
Select objects:	**<enter>**
Change what property (Color/Layer/ Ltype/ltScale/Thickness)?	Type: **LA<enter>**
New layer <OBJECT>:	Type: **HIDDEN<enter>**
Change what property (Color/Layer/ Ltype/ltScale/Thickness)?	**<enter>**
Command:	Type: **TR<enter>**
Select cutting edges:	
Select objects:	Pick: **D4 (Figure 8–33)**
Select objects:	**<enter>**

FIGURE 8–33
Use the Chprop and Trim Com-
mands to Change Lines to the
HIDDEN Layer and Trim Them

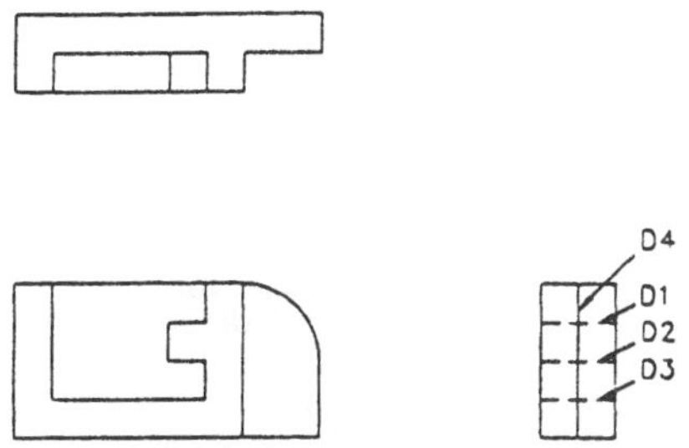

Making Orthographic Views with AutoCAD

135

Select object to trim or shift-select to extend or [Project/Edge/Undo]:	Pick: **D1**
Select object to trim or shift-select to extend or [Project/Edge/Undo]:	Pick: **D2**
Select object to trim or shift-select to extend or [Project/Edge/Undo]:	Pick: **D3**
Select object to trim or shift-select to extend or [Project/Edge/Undo]:	**<enter>**

Step 8. **Use the Dtext command to complete the title block. Title the drawing STOP.**

Step 9. **Use the SAVEAS command to save your drawing as EX8-6(your initials) on a floppy disk and again on the hard drive of your computer.**

Step 10. **Plot or print your drawing full size on an 11″ x 8½″ sheet.**

EXERCISE 8–7:
Making a Drawing Containing Top, Front, and Right-Side Views from an Isometric Sketch

Your final drawing will look like Figure 8–34 without the pictorial sketch. Each space on the sketch is ¼″.

Step 1. **To begin Exercise 8–7, turn on the computer and start AutoCAD or Auto-CAD LT.**

Step 2. **Open drawing EX8-7 supplied on the disk that came with your book.**

Step 3. **Use Zoom-All to view the entire drawing area.**

Prompt	Response
Command:	Type: **Z <enter>**
Specify corner of window, enter a scale factor (nX or nXP), or[All/ Center/Dynamic/Extents/Previous/ Scale/Window] <real time>:	Type: **A<enter>**

FIGURE 8–34

Quarter-Inch Measurements for Exercise 8–7

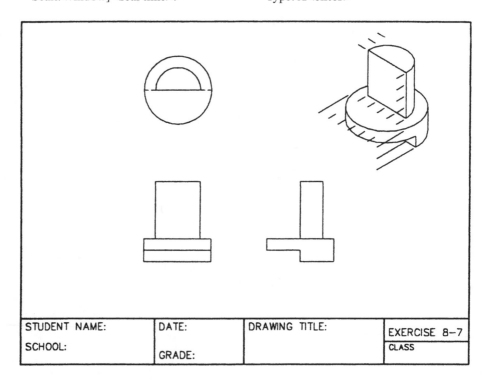

FIGURE 8–35
Use the Line Command to Draw the Outside Lines of the Base in the Front View

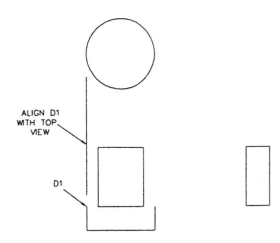

ALIGN D1 WITH TOP VIEW

D1

Important: Make sure SNAP and GRID are ON so you can line up features in adjacent views.

Step 4. **Use the Line command to draw the outside lines of the base in the front view.**

Prompt	Response
Command:	Type: **L<enter>**
Specify first point:	Pick: **D1 (Figure 8–35)**
Specify next point or [Undo]:	Type: **@1/2<-90<enter>**
Specify next point or [Undo]:	Type: **@1-1/2<0<enter>**
Specify next point or [Undo]:	Type: **@1/2<90<enter>**
Specify next point or [Undo]:	**<enter>**

Step 5. **Extend the existing line to both vertical lines.**

Prompt	Response
Command:	Type: **EX<enter>**
Select boundary edges ...	
Select objects:	Pick: **D1 (Figure 8–36)**
Select objects:	Pick: **D2**
Select objects:	**<enter>**
Select object to extend or shift-select to trim or [Project/Edge/Undo]:	Pick: **D3**
Select object to extend or shift-select to trim or [Project/Edge/Undo]:	Pick: **D4**
Select object to extend or shift-select to trim or [Project/Edge/Undo]:	**<enter>**

FIGURE 8–36
Extend an Existing Line to Both Vertical Lines

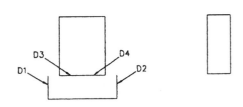

D3 D4
D1 D2

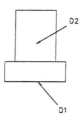

FIGURE 8–37
Use the Offset Command to
Complete the Front View

Step 6. Use the Offset command to complete the front view.

Prompt	Response
Command:	Type: **O<enter>**
Specify offset distance or [Through] <>:	Type: **1/4<enter>**
Select object to offset or <exit>:	Pick: **D1 (Figure 8–37)**
Specify point on side to offset:	Pick: **D2**
Select object to offset or <exit>:	**<enter>**

Step 7. Use the ID and Line commands to draw the base in the right-side view.

Prompt	Response
Command:	Type: **ID<enter>**
Point:	Pick: **D1 (Figure 8–38)**
Command:	Type: **L<enter>**
Specify first point:	Type: **@3/4<180<enter>**
Specify next point or [Undo]:	Type: **@1/4<-90<enter>**
Specify next point or [Undo]:	Type: **@3/4<0<enter>**
Specify next point or [Close/Undo]:	Type: **@1/4<-90<enter>**
Specify next point or [Close/Undo]:	Type: **@3/4<0<enter>**
Specify next point or [Close/Undo]:	Type: **@1/2<90<enter>**
Specify next point or [Close/Undo]:	**<enter>**

Step 8. Extend the existing line in the right side view to both vertical lines.

Prompt	Response
Command:	Type: **EX<enter>)**
Select boundary edges ...	
Select objects:	Pick: **D1 (Figure 8–39)**
Select objects:	Pick: **D2**
Select objects:	**<enter>**
Select object to extend or shift-select to trim or [Project/Edge/Undo]:	Pick: **D3**
Select object to extend or shift-select to trim or [Project/Edge/Undo]:	Pick: **D4**
Select object to extend or shift-select to trim or [Project/Edge/Undo]:	**<enter>**

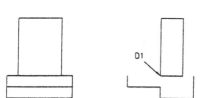

FIGURE 8–38
Use the ID and Line Commands
to Draw the Base in the Right-
Side View

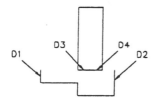

FIGURE 8–39
Extend an Existing Line in the Right-
Side View to Both Vertical Lines

Chapter 8

Step 9. Use the Circle, Line, and Trim commands to draw the semicircular shape in the top view.

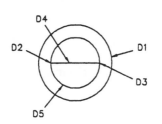

FIGURE 8–40
Use the Circle, Line, and Trim Commands to Draw the Semicircular Shape in the Top View

Prompt	Response
Command:	Type: **C<enter>**
Specify center point for circle or [3P/2P/Ttr]:	Type: **CEN<enter>**
of	Pick: **D1 (Figure 8–40)**
Specify radius of circle or [Diameter]:	Type: **1/2<enter>**
Command:	Type: **L<enter>**
Specify first point:	Type: **QUA<enter>**
of	Pick: **D2**
Specify next point or [Undo]:	Type: **QUA<enter>**
of	Pick: **D3**
Specify next point or [Undo]:	**<enter>**
Command:	Type: **TRIM<enter>**
Select cutting edges:	
Select objects:	Pick: **D4 (Figure 8–40)**
Select objects:	**<enter>**
<Select object to trim or shift-select to extend or [Project/Edge/Undo]:	Pick: **D5**
<Select object to trim or shift-select to extend or [Project/Edge/Undo]:	**<enter>**

Step 10. Set the HIDDEN layer current and draw hidden lines in the top view to complete the drawing. (Be sure SNAP is ON before you start drawing.)

Prompt	Response
Command:	Type: **-LA<enter>**
?/Make/Set/New/ON/OFF/Color/Ltype/ Freeze/Thaw/:	Type: **S<enter>**
New current layer <OBJECT>:	Type: **HIDDEN<enter>**
?/Make/Set/New/ON/OFF/Color/Ltype/ Freeze/Thaw/:	**<enter>**
Command:	Type: **L<enter>**
Specify first point:	Pick: **D1 (Figure 8–41)**

FIGURE 8–41
Draw Hidden Lines in the Top View

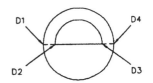

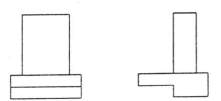

Specify next point or [Undo]:	Pick: **D2**
Specify next point or [Undo]:	Pick: **D3**
Specify next point or [Close/Undo]:	Pick: **D4**
Specify next point or [Close/Undo]:	<enter>

Step 11. Set the **OBJECT** layer current and use the Dtext command to complete the title block. Title the drawing STOP.

Step 12. Use the **SAVEAS** command to save your drawing as EX8-7(your initials) on a floppy disk and again on the hard drive of your computer.

Step 13. Plot or print your drawing full size on an 11″ x 8½″ sheet.

EXERCISE 8–8:
Making a Drawing Containing Top, Front, and Right-Side Views from an Isometric Sketch

Now you will begin to make drawings on your own with suggested commands. The prompt–response format will not be used in this exercise. Refer to previous exercises if you need to remember how to use a suggested command.

Your final drawing will look like Figure 8–42 without the pictorial sketch. Each space on the sketch is ¼″.

Step 1. To begin Exercise 8–8, turn on the computer and start AutoCAD or Auto-CAD LT.

Step 2. Open drawing EX8-8 supplied on the disk that came with your book.

Step 3. Use Zoom-All to view the entire drawing area.

Step 4. Use the Line command starting with D1 (use Osnap mode-Endpoint) (Figure 8–43) as the "Specify first point" to draw the small gable in the front view. You will have one line upward to the right, another downward to the right, and another ending on the existing line with Osnap-PERpendicular, D2. Use relative coordinates to draw these lines:

FIGURE 8–42
Dimensions for Exercise 8–8

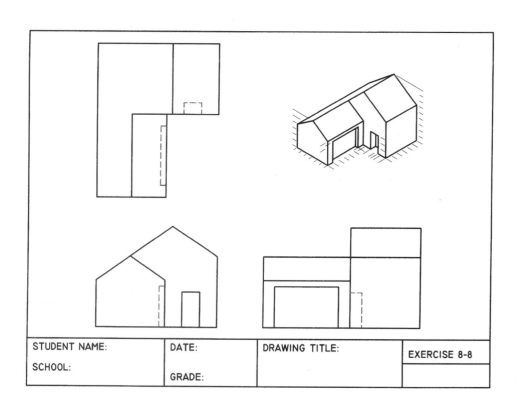

Chapter 8

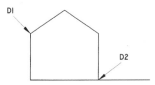

FIGURE 8–43
Draw the Smaller Gable in the Front View

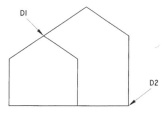

FIGURE 8–44
Draw the Larger Gable in the Front View

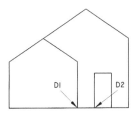

FIGURE 8–45
Draw the Door in the Front View

@3/4,1/2enter>
@3/4,-1/2<enter>
Type: **PER<enter>**, Pick: **D2,** and Press: **<enter>**

Step 5. Use the Line command starting with D1 (use Osnap mode-Endpoint) (Figure 8–44) as the "Select first point" to draw the larger gable in the front view. You will have one line upward to the right, another downward to the right, and another ending on the existing line with Osnap-Endpoint, D2. Use relative coordinates to draw these lines:

@15/16,5/8<enter>
@15/16,-5/8<enter>
Type: **END<enter>**, Pick: **D2,** and Press: **<enter>**

Step 6. Use the ID command to identify the point D1 (use Osnap mode-Endpoint) (Figure 8–45), then use a point $\frac{3}{8}''$ to the right as the "Specify first point" to draw the door in the front view, ending on the existing line with Osnap-PERpendicular, D2. Use relative coordinates to draw these lines:

Type: **ID and** Pick: D1 (Use Osnap-ENDpoint)
Type: **L<enter> at the "Specify first point" prompt:**
@3/8,0<enter>
@0,3/4<enter>
@3/8,0<enter>
Type: **PER<enter>**, Pick: **D2,** and Press: **<enter>**

Step 7. Use the Line and Offset commands to draw the right-side view of the smaller gable (Figure 8–46).

Type: **L<enter>** "Specify first point" Pick: **D1**
With ORTHO ON move your mouse to the right and TYPE: **1-7/8<enter> Press:<enter>**to end the command.
Type: **O<enter>**, then Type: **T<enter>** to offset through a point
Select object to offset: Pick: **the line you just drew**
Through point: Pick: **D2**
Select object to offset: Pick: **the same line**
Through point: Pick: **D3**

Step 8. Use the Rectangle and Extend commands to draw the right-side view of the larger gable (Figure 8–47).

Type: **REC<enter> and** Pick: **D1 (use Osnap-ENDpoint) as the first corner point.** Type: **@1-1/2,2-1/8 for the other corner point.**
Type: **EX<enter> and** Pick: **D2 (Figure 8–47) as the boundary edge;** Press: **<enter>,** then Pick: **the line D3 as the object to extend.**

Step 9. Use the ID and Line commands to draw the garage door in the right-side view (Figure 8–48).

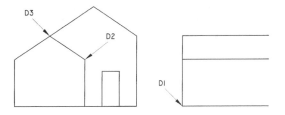

FIGURE 8–46
Draw the Right Side of the Smaller Gable

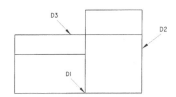

FIGURE 8–47
Use the Rectangle and Extend Commands to Draw the Right-Side View of the Larger Gable

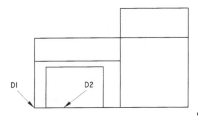

FIGURE 8–48
Draw the Garage Door in the
Right-Side View

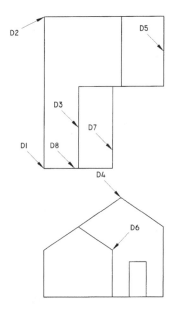

FIGURE 8–49
Draw Object Lines in the Top
View

Type: **ID<enter>** and Pick: **D1** as the point
Type: **L<enter>**
First point: **@1/4<0**
Next point: **@7/8<90**
Next point: **@1-1/4<0**
Next point: Type: **PER<enter>** and Pick: **D2**

Step 10. Use the Line, Offset, and Fillet commands to draw the object lines in the top view (Figure 8–49).

Type: **L<enter>**
First point: **D1**
Next point: **@3/4<0**
Next point: **@1-3/4<90**
Next point: **@1-7/8<0**
Next point: **@1-1/2<90**
Next point: Type: **PER<enter>** and Pick: **D2**
Type: **O<enter>**, then Type: **T<enter>** to offset through a point.
Select object to offset: Pick: **D3**
Through point: Pick: **D4**
Select object to offset: Pick: **D5**
Through point: Pick: **D6**
Type: **F<enter>** (for Fillet)
Set Fillet radius to 0
Pick: **D7** to select first object
Pick: **D8** to select second object

Step 11. Set the HIDDEN layer current and use the Line command to draw hidden lines in the front and right-side views (Figure 8–50).

Click: **HIDDEN** from the Layer List on the Object Properties toolbar (or TYPE: -LA,<enter> then S,<enter> then **HIDDEN<enter>**)

With SNAP and ORTHO ON: **Line up your cursor in the front view with the top of the garage door in the right-side view and** Pick: **D1 (Figure 8–50).**
Move your mouse one snap to the right and Click:
Move your mouse to the bottom line and Click:

With SNAP and ORTHO ON: **Line up your cursor in the right-side view with the top of the front door in the front view and** Pick: **D2 (Figure 8–50).**
Move your mouse two snaps to the right and Click:
Move your mouse to the bottom line and Click:

Step 12. Use the Line command to draw hidden lines in the top view (Figure 8–51).

With SNAP and ORTHO ON: **Line up your cursor in the front view with the right edge of the gable in the front view, move the mouse up two snaps from the lower right corner of the top view and** Pick: **D1 (Figure 8–51).**
Move your mouse one snap to the left and Click:

FIGURE 8–50
Draw Hidden Lines in the Front
and Right-Side Views

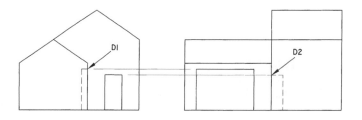

Chapter 8

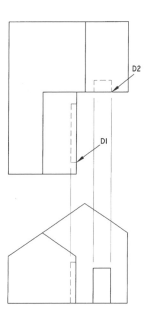

FIGURE 8–51
Draw Hidden Lines in the Top View

Move your mouse five grid marks up and Click:
Move your mouse one snap to the right and Click:

With SNAP and ORTHO ON: **Line up your cursor in the front view with the right edge of the front door in the front view, and** Pick: **D2 (Figure 8–51).**
Move your mouse two snaps up and Click:
Move your mouse three snaps to the left and Click:
Move your mouse two snaps down and Click:

Important: Make sure SNAP and ORTHO are ON so you can line up features in adjacent views.

Step 13. **Set the OBJECT layer current and use the Dtext command to complete the title block. Title the drawing SHAFT SUPPORT.**

Step 14. **Use the SAVEAS command to save your drawing as EX8-8(your initials) on a floppy disk and again on the hard drive of your computer.**

Step 15. **Plot or print your drawing full size on an 11″ x 8½″ sheet.**

EXERCISES

EXERCISE 8–1.   Complete Exercise 8–1 using steps 1 through 10 described in this chapter.
EXERCISE 8–2.   Complete Exercise 8–2 using steps 1 through 12 described in this chapter.
EXERCISE 8–3.   Complete Exercise 8–3 using steps 1 through 9 described in this chapter.
EXERCISE 8–4.   Complete Exercise 8–4 using steps 1 through 11 described in this chapter.
EXERCISE 8–5.   Complete Exercise 8–5 using steps 1 through 9 described in this chapter.
EXERCISE 8–6.   Complete Exercise 8–6 using steps 1 through 10 described in this chapter.
EXERCISE 8–7.   Complete Exercise 8–7 using steps 1 through 13 described in this chapter.
EXERCISE 8–8.   Complete Exercise 8–8 using steps 1 through 15 described in this chapter.

REVIEW QUESTIONS

Circle the best answer.
  1. The top view shows which of the following dimensions?
     a. Height and width
     b. Height and depth
     c. Width and depth
     d. Length and width
     e. Height, width, and depth

2. Which of the following commands draws several lines that are a single entity?
   a. Line
   b. PLine
   c. Offset
   d. Chamfer
   e. Break

3. The polar coordinate @5<180 draws a line
   a. 5″ to the right
   b. 5″ up
   c. 5″ down
   d. 5″ to the left
   e. 5″ at a 120° angle to the right

4. Which of the following commands can be used to produce parallel Plines?
   a. Parallel
   b. Draw
   c. Offset
   d. Change
   e. Osnap

5. A rounded corner can be obtained most easily with which of the following commands?
   a. Chamfer
   b. Fillet
   c. Draw
   d. Ellipse
   e. Offset

6. A 45° angle at a corner may be obtained most easily with the use of which of the following commands?
   a. Chamfer
   b. Fillet
   c. Draw
   d. Ellipse
   e. Offset

7. Which of the following will produce a vertical line $3\frac{1}{2}″$ downward from a point?
   a. 3-1/2 x 90
   b. @3-1/2<0
   c. @3-1/2<270
   d. @3-1/2<90
   e. -90<3-1/2

8. Which of the following is used to identify a point from which you can specify a point for a single command?
   a. Status
   b. Point
   c. ID
   d. Line
   e. Dist

9. Which of the following circles is produced if "1/2" is entered in response to the circle prompt "Specify radius of circle or [Diameter]:"?
   a. $\frac{1}{2}″$ diameter
   b. $\frac{1}{4}″$ radius
   c. 1″ radius
   d. 1″ diameter
   e. $\frac{1}{4}″$ diameter

10. Which command is used to trim lines between cutting edges?
    a. Edit
    b. Trim
    c. Break
    d. Erase
    e. Copy (Duplicate)

Complete.

11. Describe what the Dtext command is used for.

_____

12. Describe how the Extend command is used.

_____

13. If you type F<enter> after you have selected objects to be broken with the Break command, what are you asked to specify next?

_____

14. After you have selected objects to be copied with the Copy command and pressed <enter>, what are you asked to specify next?

_____

15. After you have selected objects to be copied with the Mirror command and pressed <enter>, what are you asked to specify next?

_____

16. Describe what a running OSNAP mode is.

_____

17. Which of the layer options sets a new layer current?

_____

18. Why do you change layers to draw different features?

_____

19. What purpose does the ID command serve?

_____

20. What happens when you type PER<enter> and pick a point on a line in response to the Line prompt "To point"?

_____

9 Sketching Sectional Views

OBJECTIVES

After completing this chapter, you will be able to:

- [ ] Correctly sketch to scale architectural section drawings from unsectioned two-dimensional or three-dimensional drawings.
- [ ] Correctly answer questions regarding sectional drawings.

USES OF SECTIONAL DRAWINGS

It is often necessary to use a drawing technique known as *sectioning*. Sectional drawings are used to show internal construction (Figures 9–1 and 9–2). In many cases, sectional drawings are used to show someone not only how to make a part but also how several parts fit together (Figures 9–3 and 9–4). Sectional views require many conventional practices and symbols, which are described in this chapter.

FIGURE 9–1
Sectional View of Molding

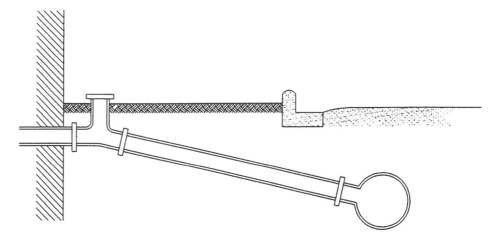

FIGURE 9–2
Plumbing Section

FIGURE 9–3
Sectional View of
Assembled Baluster

147

FIGURE 9–4
Sectional View Showing How a
Wall Is Constructed

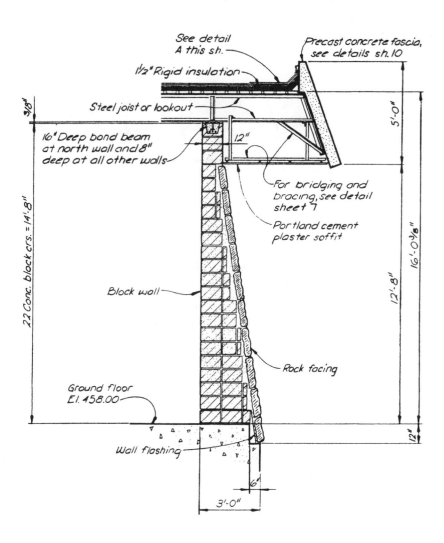

See detail
A this sh.

Precast concrete fascia,
see details sh. 10

1½" Rigid insulation

Steel joist or lookout

16" Deep bond beam
at north wall and 8"
deep at all other walls

12"

For bridging and
bracing, see detail
sheet 7

Portland cement
plaster soffit

22 Conc. block crs. = 14'-8"

Block wall

Rock facing

Ground floor
El. 458.00

Wall flashing

5'-0"

12'-8"

16'-0⅜"

12"

6"

3'-0"

CONSTRUCTING A SECTIONAL VIEW

The object shown in Figure 9–5 is a complex shape. Its features could be misunderstood if only external views were used; therefore, to avoid any misunderstanding, a sectional view is constructed. Sectional views are easy to construct if you follow these steps:

Step 1. **Decide which view will best show the hidden feature**. In your mind, cut off the part that is hiding the feature. The cut, in this case, should be straight and should extend completely across the object.

Step 2. **Throw away the part you cut off, and do not think of it again.** It is easy to be confused about which part to draw. Throwing away the cut part eliminates that confusion.

Step 3. **Look into the part that is left.** Your line of sight should be perpendicular to or straight into the remaining piece.

Step 4. **Draw the shape of what you see.** Draw section or hatch lines on the part that was cut, as if you are drawing saw marks on the part of the object that the saw touched when the cut was made. The parts untouched by the saw are sketched without section lining.

FIGURE 9–5
Constructing a Sectional View

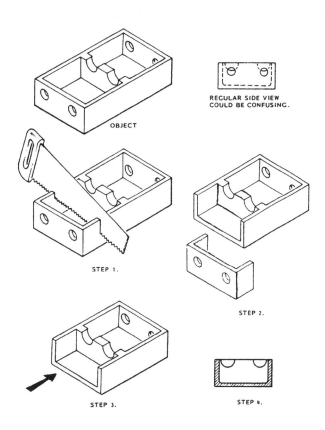

ELEMENTS OF SECTIONAL DRAWINGS

Now that you have read the steps in constructing a sectional view, let's examine the elements of sectional views and start with cutting plane lines.

Cutting Plane Lines

To show exactly where a cut was made, place an extra-heavy line with two dashes in it and arrows on the ends, showing the line of sight (Figure 9–6). This is a cutting plane line. It is about three times as thick as an object line. Another version of the cutting plane line does not extend across the object and is preferred by many companies because it does not hide other lines as often as the complete cutting plane line does. Many architectural drawings show construction features without the use of a cutting plane line.

FIGURE 9–6
Cutting Plane Line

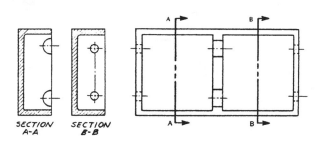

FIGURE 9–7
Patterns for Sectional Views

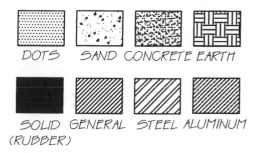

Hatch Lines

Many materials that have been sectioned have standard shadings to identify the feature more easily. Figure 9–7 shows several of the common patterns for some materials. Although these are commonly used, you will find many exceptions in drawings made by different architectural firms.

Draw hatch lines about half as thick as object lines.

Using More Than One Sectional View

If more than one section is used on the same drawing, the sections are identified as details showing construction features throughout the structure.

Standard Architectural Sectional Details

Plan and elevation views show the complete structure, but the sectional drawings and other details show construction features throughout the building. The standard wall section and door jamb details (Figure 9–8) are found on many architectural plans.

FIGURE 9–8
Wall Section and Door Jamb Detail

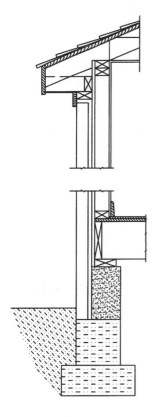

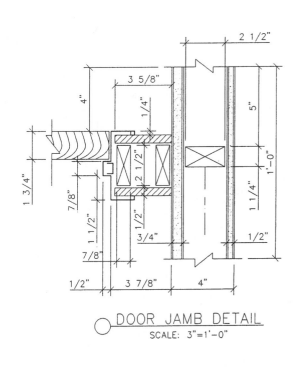

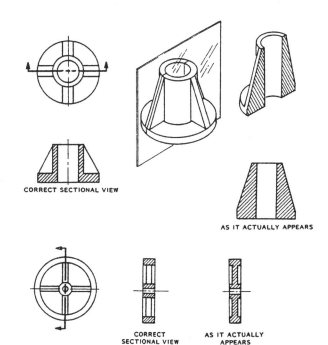

CORRECT SECTIONAL VIEW

AS IT ACTUALLY APPEARS

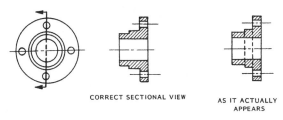

CORRECT SECTIONAL VIEW

AS IT ACTUALLY APPEARS

FIGURE 9–9
Hidden Lines Not Shown on Sectional View

CORRECT SECTIONAL VIEW

AS IT ACTUALLY APPEARS

FIGURE 9–10
Hatch Lines Not Shown on Thin Features

Exceptions to Conventional Drawing Practices

To avoid confusion, it is often necessary to treat some features of parts differently than is customary. The following are common exceptions to standard practices.

Eliminating Hidden Lines in Sectional Views

Sectional views are usually much clearer if hidden lines are not shown. The hidden lines are rarely necessary (Figure 9–9). You should eliminate hidden lines on sectional views unless it is absolutely necessary. In Figure 9–9 the hidden lines not only are unnecessary but would be confusing if they were drawn.

Not Sectioning Thin Features of a Part

To eliminate confusion, it is best not to section thin features such as ribs and spokes (Figure 9–10). Although the cutting plane does cut through the ribs, the object looks like a shortened cone if it is drawn with hatch lines on the ribs.

Sketching hatch patterns on sectional views will make you appreciate the hatching feature of AutoCAD and AutoCAD LT, which is described in the following chapter. Now, sketch some sectional views.

EXERCISES

EXERCISE 9–1.

Complete Exercise 9–1 using the steps described.

Step 1. Remove the sheet labeled EXERCISE 9–1 from your book.

Step 2. Using the sketching and construction techniques you used in Chapter 7, complete the right-side view as a sectional view. The depth dimensions are shown by the horizontal lines at the top and bottom of the vertical line. The smallest circles on the front view are holes that go all the way through the part.

Sprinkle drawing powder over your drawing before you begin to darken lines.

Be sure to line up all features of the object with the adjacent views.

Make sure that your lines are the correct weight and are of even width and darkness. Try to match the thickness and darkness of the existing lines.

Step 3. Draw 45° section lines in the right-side view approximately $\frac{1}{10}''$ apart. Use the lines shown as an example. These lines should be thin and dark.

Step 4. Draw center lines in the right-side view.

Step 5. Fill in the title block with your best lettering. Title the drawing SECTION 1.

EXERCISE 9–2. Complete Exercise 9–2 using the steps described.

Step 1. Remove the sheet labeled EXERCISE 9–2 from your book.

Step 2. Sketch the baluster of Figure 9–11 using the sketching and construction techniques you used in Chapter 7. Complete the view as a sectional view.

Draw the same size as shown.

Sprinkle drawing powder over your drawing before you begin to darken lines.

Make sure that your lines are the correct weight and are of even width and darkness. Try to match the thickness and darkness of the existing lines.

Step 3. Draw 45° section lines approximately $\frac{1}{10}''$ apart. Make the top rail 45° upward to the right. Make the support 45° upward to the left. Use the lines shown in Exercise 9–1 as an example. These lines should be thin and dark.

Step 4. Fill in the title block with your best lettering. Title the drawing BALUSTER.

EXERCISE 9–3. Complete Exercise 9–3 using the steps described.

Step 1. Remove the sheet labeled EXERCISE 9–3 from your book.

Step 2. Sketch the cast stone cap of the mailbox with a flagpole holder in its center as a sectional view (Figure 9–12) using the sketching and construction techniques you used in Chapter 7. Sketch radii with a circle template.

FIGURE 9–11
Sizes for Exercise 9–2

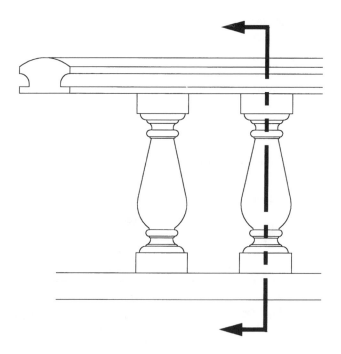

Chapter 9

FIGURE 9–12
Sizes for Exercise 9–3

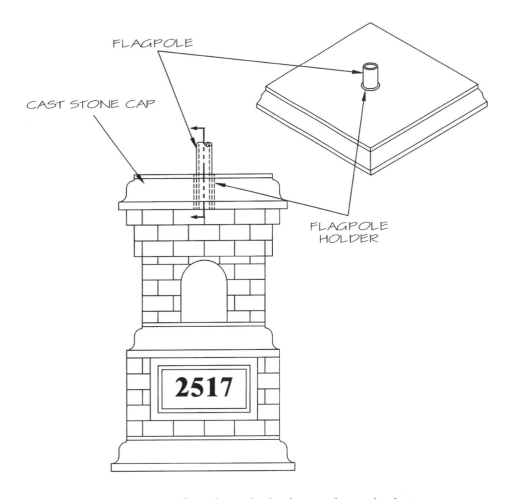

FLAGPOLE

CAST STONE CAP

FLAGPOLE
HOLDER

2517

Draw the cap the size shown on the exercise sheet.

Complete the front view as a sectional view.

Sprinkle drawing powder over your drawing before you begin to darken lines.

Make sure that your lines are the correct weight and are of even width and darkness. Try to match the thickness and darkness of the existing lines.

Step 3. Draw 45° section lines in the front view approximately $\frac{1}{10}''$ apart. Alternate 45° angle lines for the steel pole and the holder. Use a concrete pattern for the cast stone cap. Use the lines shown in Exercise 9–1 as an example. These lines should be thin and dark.

Step 4. Fill in the title block with your best lettering. Title the drawing CAST CAP SECTION.

EXERCISE 9–4. Complete Exercise 9–4 using the steps described.

Step 1. Remove the sheet labeled EXERCISE 9–4 from your book.

Step 2. Sketch the lower half of the wall section (Figure 9–13)(from the break line down) using sketching and construction techniques you used in Chapter 7.

Draw at a scale of $1'' = 1'$. Approximate any dimensions not shown.

Sprinkle drawing powder over your drawing before you begin to darken lines.

Make sure that your lines are the correct weight and are of even width and darkness. Try to match the thickness and darkness of the existing lines.

Do not show dimensions.

FIGURE 9–13
Sizes for Exercise 9–4

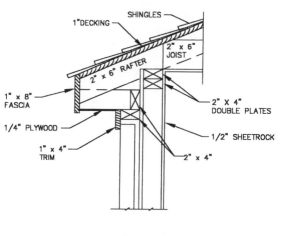

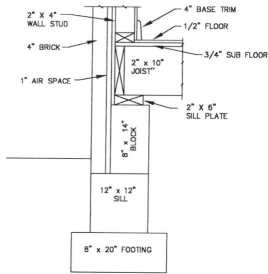

Step 3. Draw section lines as follows:

Sill and Footing—Use the concrete pattern shown in Figure 9–7.

Earth—Use the Earth pattern shown in Figure 9–7.

Block—Use the Sand pattern shown in Figure 9–7.

Brick—Use the Dots pattern shown in Figure 9–7.

Base Trim, Floor, and Subfloor—Use the General pattern shown in Figure 9–7. Draw the Base Trim and the Subfloor at a 45° angle slanting upward to the right. Draw the Floor at a 45° angle slanting upward to the left.

Step 4. Fill in the title block with your best lettering. Title the drawing WALL SECTION.

REVIEW QUESTIONS

Circle the best answer.

1. Why are sectional views needed to describe objects?
   a. To describe surface textures
   b. To show complex interior details
   c. To describe the overall shape of the structure
   d. To show different sides of a building
   e. To complete a top view

2. The object is cut by a _____ to describe the sectional view.
   a. cutting plane
   b. saw
   c. knife
   d. string
   e. blade
3. The solid material cut by the cutting plane is hatched with diagonal lines, usually drawn at a _____ angle.
   a. 20°
   b. 15°
   c. 90°
   d. 0°
   e. 45°
4. The line representing the edge view of the cutting plane is called
   a. The edge view line
   b. The section line
   c. The cut line
   d. The hatch line
   e. The cutting plane line
5. Thin features such as ribs and spokes are often not cut on the sectional view for the following reason:
   a. It saves time.
   b. Ribs and spokes are not drawn at all.
   c. Sectioning of them gives a false impression of how the part is constructed.
   d. It takes up too much space on the drawing.
   e. Labeling of them is difficult.

Complete.
6. Why are hidden lines not usually shown in sectional views?

   _____

7. How are sectional views labeled when there are several sectional views on the same drawing?

   _____

   _____

8. Describe how thick the cutting plane line should be in relation to the object line.

   _____

9. Describe how thick the section lines should be in relation to the object line.

   _____

10. List two standard sectional views often shown on a set of plans.

   _____

   _____

Sketching Sectional Views

10 Making Sectional Views with AutoCAD

OBJECTIVES

After completing this chapter, you will be able to:

- □ Make accurate drawings containing hatch patterns using AutoCAD or AutoCAD LT.
- □ Use the following commands to produce drawings containing hatch patterns:
  - Array
  - Line
  - Osnap
  - Mirror
  - Circle
  - Zoom
  - Trim
  - Offset
  - Fillet
  - Chamfer
  - Hatch
- □ Answer questions regarding the preceding commands.

HATCHING USING AUTOCAD OR AUTOCAD LT

AutoCAD and AutoCAD LT use the **Hatch** command to draw section lines on sectional views. The Hatch command requires that the boundary containing the hatch pattern be selected by picking individual lines or by using a window. The Hatch command also allows you to pick a single point inside the boundary that is to contain the hatch pattern. In this chapter you will use both methods because sometimes picking a single point does not work.

Hatch

The Hatch command contains a number of hatch patterns that may be used to fill areas. Hatch in Exercise 10–1 requires that the boundary selected be complete and that none of the lines extend outside the area to be hatched; therefore, temporary lines are drawn for the boundary and erased after the hatching is complete. Also, the hatch patterns are placed on a layer named HATCH so that the pattern remains on a different layer that is assigned a different color. In Exercise 10–1 you will draw a single view and place a hatch pattern on it. In Exercise 10–2 you will draw a front view that contains a cutting plane line and a right-side view that contains the hatching necessary to make it a sectional view.

EXERCISE 10–1:
Making a Sectional Drawing Using Hatch Patterns

Step 1. To begin Exercise 10–1, turn on the computer and start AutoCAD or AutoCAD LT.

Step 2. Open drawing EX10-1 supplied on the disk that came with your book.

Step 3. Use Zoom-All to view the entire drawing area.

Prompt	Response
Command:	Type: **Z <enter>**
Specify corner of window, enter a scale factor (nX or nXP), or [All/ Center/Dynamic/Extents/Previous/ Scale/Window] <real time>:	Type: **A<enter>**

Step 4. Use the Line command to draw object lines in the right-side view.

Prompt	Response
Command:	Type: **L<enter>**
Specify first point:	Type: **END<enter>**
of	Pick: **D1 (Figure 10–1)**
Specify next point or [Undo]:	Type: **@4-1/2<90<enter>**
Specify next point or [Undo]:	Type: **@3/4<180<enter>**
Specify next point or [Close/Undo]:	Type: **@2-1/2<270<enter>**
Specify next point or [Close/Undo]:	Type: **@3/4<180<enter>**
Specify next point or [Close/Undo]:	Type: **END<enter>**
of	Pick: **D2**
Specify next point or [Close/Undo]:	**<enter>**
Command:	**<enter>**
Specify first point:	Pick: **D3** (Be sure D3 is aligned with the top quadrant of the small upper circle.)
Specify next point or [Undo]:	Pick: **D4**
Specify next point or [Undo]:	**<enter>**
Command:	**<enter>**

Important: Be sure SNAP and ORTHO are ON and OSNAP is OFF so you can align picked points with the circles in the front view.

FIGURE 10–1
Exercise 10–1. Draw Object Lines in the Right-Side View

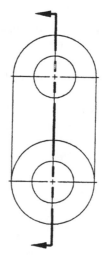
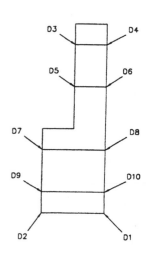

Specifiy first point:	Pick: **D5** (Be sure D5 is aligned with the bottom quadrant of the small upper circle.)
Specify next point or [Undo]:	Pick: **D6**
Specify next point or [Undo]:	**<enter>**
Command:	**<enter>**
Specify first point:	Pick: **D7** (Be sure D7 is aligned with the top quadrant of the small lower circle.)
Specify next point or [Undo]:	Pick: **D8**
Specify next point or [Undo]:	**<enter>**
Command:	<enter>
Specify first point:	Pick: **D9** (Be sure D9 is aligned with the bottom quadrant of the small lower circle.)
Specify next point or [Undo]:	Pick: **D10**
Specify next point or [Undo]:	**<enter>**

Step 5. Because the Selecting Objects with the Hatch command requires a complete boundary with no lines extending outside that boundary, use the Line command to draw boundary lines in the right-side view. Begin by setting a new layer current and a running OSNAP mode of Endpoint so you do not have to type END<enter> for every pick.

Prompt   **Response**

Command:	Click: **Layer 0 from the layer list on the Object Properties toolbar, then** Click: **any point on the drawing to set the 0 layer current**
Command:	**Hold your mouse over OSNAP on the status bar at the bottom of the screen and right-click.** Click: **Settings,** then, **check Endpoint on the Object Snap tab on the Drafting Settings dialog box.** Click: **OK**

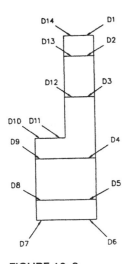

FIGURE 10–2
Draw Boundary Lines in the Right-Side View

Command:	Type: **L<enter>**
Specify first point:	Pick: **D1 (Figure 10–2)**
Specify next point or [Undo]:	Pick: **D2**
Specify next point or [Undo]:	**<enter>**
Command:	**<enter>**
Specify first point:	Pick: **D3**
Specify next point or [Undo]:	Pick: **D4**
Specify next point or [Undo]:	**<enter>**
Command:	**<enter>**
Specify first point:	Pick: **D5**
Specify next point or [Undo]:	Pick: **D6**
Specify next point or [Undo]:	**<enter>**
Command:	**<enter>**
Specify first point:	Pick: **D7**
Specify next point or [Undo]:	Pick: **D8**
Specify next point or [Undo]:	**<enter>**

Command:	\<enter\>
Specify first point:	Pick: **D9**
Specify next point or [Undo]:	Pick: **D10**
Specify next point or [Undo]:	\<enter\>
Command:	\<enter\>
Specify first point:	Pick: **D11**
Specify next point or [Undo]:	Pick: **D12**
Specify next point or [Undo]:	\<enter\>
Command:	\<enter\>
Specify first point:	Pick: **D13**
Specify next point or [Undo]:	Pick: **D14**
Specify next point or [Undo]:	\<enter\>

Step 5. **Turn off the OSNAP mode so you will not be picking endpoints without knowing it.**

Click: **OSNAP** on the status bar at the bottom of the screen so OSNAP is OFF.

Step 6. **Set the layer HATCH current and use the Hatch command to place cross-hatching on the areas where the cutting plane touches.**

Prompt	Response
Command:	Click: **HATCH from the Layer List on the Object Properties toolbar**
Command:	Type: **H\<enter\>**
The Boundary Hatch dialog box appears:	
In the Type: list:	Select: **User defined**
In the Angle list:	Select: **45**
In the Spacing text box:	Type: **.1**
	Click: **Select Objects** in the upper right of the dialog box
Select objects:	Pick: **D1 (Figure 10–3)**
Specify opposite corner:	Pick: **D2**
Select objects:	Pick: **D3**
Specify opposite corner:	Pick: **D4**
Select objects:	Pick: **D5**
Specify opposite corner:	Pick: **D6**
Select objects:	\<enter\>
The Boundary Hatch dialog box appears:	Pick: **OK**

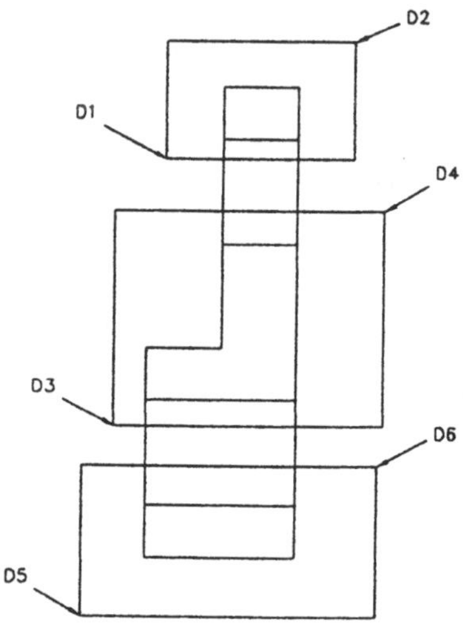

FIGURE 10–3
Hatch Areas Using Selection Windows

Step 7. **Turn off all layers except the 0 layer and erase the boundary lines you drew.**

Prompt	Response
Command:	Click: **the light bulb** in the layer list for all layers so the light bulb is OFF, except Layer 0
Command:	Type: **E\<enter\>**
Select objects:	Pick: **D1 (Figure 10–4)**
Specify opposite corner:	Pick: **D2**
Select objects:	\<enter\>

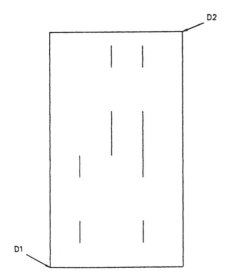

FIGURE 10–4
Erase Boundary Lines

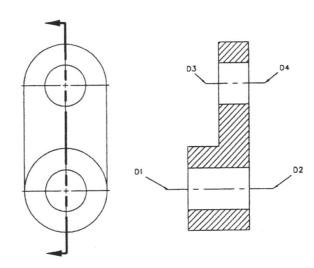

FIGURE 10–5
Draw Center Lines

Important: Be sure SNAP and ORTHO are ON so you can align the center lines with the centers of the circles in the front view. Make the center lines in the right-side view approximately the same length as shown in Figure 10–5.

Step 8. Turn on all layers, set layer CENTER current, and draw center lines in the right-side view.

On your own: Turn on all layers and set layer CENTER current.

Prompt	Response
Command:	Type: **L<enter>**
Specify first point:	Pick: **D1 (Figure 10–5)**
Specify next point or [Undo]:	Pick: **D2**
Specify next point or [Undo]:	**<enter>**
Command:	**<enter>**
Specify first point:	Pick: **D3**
Specify next point or [Undo]:	Pick: **D4**
Specify next point or [Undo]:	**<enter>**

Step 9. Set layer OBJECT current and use the Dtext command to complete the title block as you did for previous exercises. Name the drawing GUIDE.

Step 10. Use the SAVEAS command to save your drawing as EX10-1(your initials) on a floppy disk and again on the hard drive of your computer.

Step 11. Plot or print your drawing full size on an 11″ x 8½″ sheet.

EXERCISE 10–2:
Making a Drawing Containing a Front View with a Cutting Plane, and a Right-Side View in Section from an Isometric Sketch

Step 1. To begin Exercise 10–2, turn on the computer and start AutoCAD or AutoCAD LT.

Step 2. Open drawing EX10-2 supplied on the disk that came with your book.

Step 3. Use Zoom-All to view the entire drawing area.

The sizes for Exercise 10–2 are taken from the sketch shown in Figure 10–6.

FIGURE 10–6
Specifications for Exercise 10–2

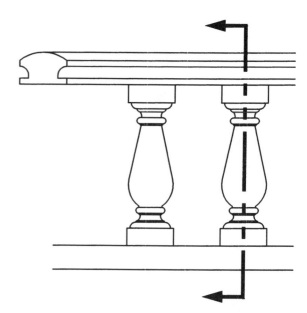

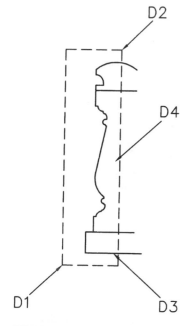

FIGURE 10–7
Use Mirror to Draw the Right
Side of the Figure

Note: If Radius is not 0, Type:
R<enter>, then Type: **0<enter>** and
Press: **<enter>** again before picking D5.

Prompt	Response
Command:	Type: **Z <enter>**
All/Center/Dynamic/Extents/Left/ Previous/Vmax/Window/<Scale(X/XP)>:	Type: **A<enter>**

Step 4.   Use the Mirror and Fillet commands to complete the front view.

The **Mirror** command allows you to copy objects as a mirror image around a mirror line. A vertical mirror line copies the selected items from left to right or from right to left. A horizontal mirror line copies the selected items from top to bottom or from bottom to top. In this case it is important to have ORTHO ON when you pick the mirror line so it is exactly horizontal or vertical.

The **Fillet** command with a radius of 0 allows you to close in a square corner quickly.

Prompt	Response
Command:	Type: **MI<enter>**
Select objects:	Pick: **D1 (Figure 10–7)**
Specify opposite corner:	Pick: **D2**
Select objects:	**<enter>**
Specify first point of mirror line:	Type: **MID<enter>**
of	Pick: **D3**
Specify second point of mirror line:	Pick: **D4** <Ortho on>
Delete source objects? [Yes/No] <N>:	**<enter>**
Command:	Type: **F<enter>**

Current settings: Mode = TRIM,
    Radius = 0'-0" Select first object or
    [Polyline/Radius/Trim]:
	Pick: **D1(Figure 10–8)**

Select second object:	Pick: **D2**

Step 5.   Set layer HATCH current and use the Hatch command to draw section patterns in the front view.

Prompt	Response
Command:	Click: **HATCH from the Layer List on the Object Properties toolbar**
Command:	Type: **H<enter>**

Chapter 10

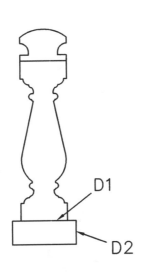

FIGURE 10–8
Use 0 Radius Fillet to Make a
Square Corner

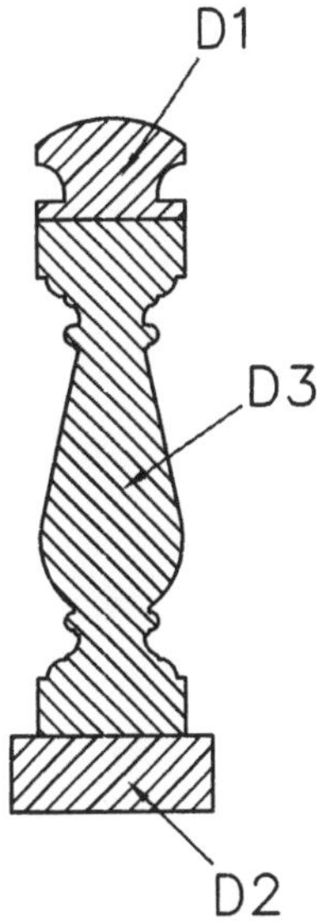

FIGURE 10–9
Use the Hatch Command to Add
Section Lines

The Boundary Hatch dialog box appears:	
In the Type: list:	Select: **User defined**
In the Angle list:	Select: **45**
In the Spacing text box:	Type: **.1**
	Click: **Pick Points** in the upper right of the dialog box
Select internal point:	Pick: **D1 (Figure 10–9)**
Select internal point:	Pick: **D2**
Select internal point:	**<enter>**
The Boundary Hatch dialog box appears:	Pick: **OK**
Command:	**<enter>** (to repeat the Hatch command)
The Boundary Hatch dialog box appears:	
In the Angle text box:	Type: **-45<enter>** (Just put a minus sign in front of the 45.)
	Click: **Pick Points** in the upper right of the dialog box
Select internal point:	Pick: **D3 (Figure 10–9)**
Select internal point:	**<enter>**

Step 6. Use the Dtext command to complete the title block as you have done previously. Title the drawing BALUSTER.

Step 7. Use the SAVEAS command to save your drawing as EX10-2(your initials) on a floppy disk and again on the hard drive of your computer.

Step 8. Plot or print your drawing full size on an 11″ x 8½″ sheet.

EXERCISE 10–3:
Making a Sectional Drawing Containing a Front View of a Three-Part Assembly

Step 1. To begin Exercise 10–3, turn on the computer and start AutoCAD or AutoCAD LT.

FIGURE 10–10
Specifications for Exercise 10–3

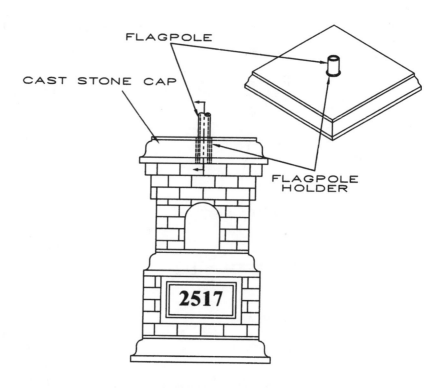

FLAGPOLE

CAST STONE CAP

FLAGPOLE
HOLDER

2517

Step 2.   Open drawing EX10-3 supplied on the disk that came with your book.
Step 3.   Use Zoom-All to view the entire drawing area.

The sizes for Exercise 10–3 are taken from the sketch shown in Figure 10–10.

Step 4. Use the Mirror command to draw the front view of the cast stone cap.

Prompt	Response
Command:	Type: **MI<enter>**
Select objects:	Click: **D1 (Figure 10–11)**
Specify opposite corner:	Click: **D2**
Select objects:	**<enter>**
Specify first point of mirror line:	Type: **MID <enter>**
of	Click: **D3**
Specify second point of mirror line:	Click: **D4(ORTHO ON)**
Delete source objects? [Yes/No] <N>:	**<enter>**

FIGURE 10–11
Use Mirror to Draw the Right
Edge of the Exercise

D4

D2

D3

D1

Step 5. Use the Line and Trim commands to complete the object lines for the front view of the cast stone cap.

Prompt	Response
Command:	Type: **L<enter>**
Specify first point:	Click: **D1<Osnap-Endpoint ON>**
Specify next point or [Undo]:	Click: **D2<Osnap-Endpoint ON>**
Specify next point or [Undo]:	**<enter>**
Command:	Type: **TR<enter>**
Select cutting edges ...	
Select objects:	Click: **D3 (Figure 10–12) (SNAP and OSNAP OFF)**
Specify opposite corner:	Click: **D4**
Select objects:	**<enter>**
Select object to trim or shift-select to extend or [Project/Edge/Undo]:	Click: **D5**
Select object to trim or shift-select to extend or [Project/Edge/Undo]:	**<enter>**

Step 6. Use the Insert command to show the break symbol on the top of the flagpole.

Prompt	Response
Command:	Type: I<enter>
The Insert dialog box appears:	Select: **break** from the Name: list
	Insertion point: Specify On-screen should have a check in it
	Pick: **OK**
Specify insertion point or Scale/X/Y/Z/ Rotate/PScale/PX/PY/PZ/PRotate]:	Click: **D1 (Figure 10-13)**

Step 7. Use the Hatch command to place section lines on the drawing.

Prompt	Response
Command:	Type: **H<enter>**
The Boundary Hatch dialog box appears:	Click: **the three dots in the Pattern list area to display the Hatch Pattern Pallet.** Click: **the Other Predefined tab** and Click: **AR-SAND**
	Click: **OK**

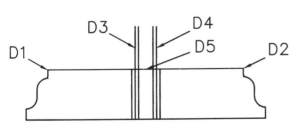

FIGURE 10–12
Use Line and Trim to Complete Object Lines

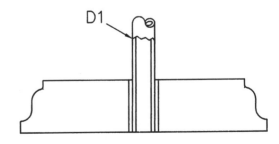

FIGURE 10–13
Use Insert to Insert the Break Symbol

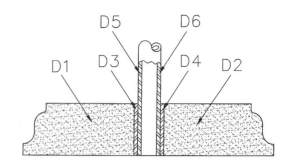

FIGURE 10–14
Use Hatch to Add Patterns

	Type: **.05 in the Scale: box (Delete any other numbers in the Scale: box.)**
	Click: **Pick Points**
Select internal point:	Click: **D1 (Figure 10–14)**
Select internal point:	Click: **D2**
Select internal point:	**<enter>**
The Boundary Hatch dialog box appears:	Click: **OK**
Command:	**<enter>**
The Boundary Hatch dialog box appears:	Click: **the three dots in the Pattern list area to display the Hatch Pattern Pallet**. Click: **the Other Predefined tab** and Click: **STEEL**
	Click: **OK**
	Select: **1.0000 in the Scale: box**
	Click: **Pick Points**
Select internal point:	Click: **D3**
Select internal point:	Click: **D4**
Select internal point:	**<enter>**
The Boundary Hatch dialog box appears:	Click: **OK**
Command:	**<enter>**
The Boundary Hatch dialog box appears:	Select: **90 in the Angle: box**
	Click: **Pick Points**
Select internal point:	Click: **D5**
Select internal point:	Click: **D6**
Select internal point:	**<enter>**
The Boundary Hatch dialog box appears:	Click: **OK**

Step 8. On your own: Explode the "break" drawing (Type: **x<enter>**) and then trim the two lines that extend beyond the break.

Step 9. Use the Dtext command to complete the title block as you have done previously. Title the drawing CAST STONE CAP.

Step 10. Use the SAVEAS command to save your drawing as EX10-3(your initials) on a floppy disk and again on the hard drive of your computer.

Step 11. Plot or print your drawing full size on an 11″ x 8½″ sheet.

EXERCISE 10–4:
Making a Wall Section

Step 1. To begin Exercise 10–4, turn on the computer and start AutoCAD or AutoCAD LT.

Step 2. **Open drawing EX10-4 supplied on the disk that came with your book.**
Step 3. **Use Zoom-All to view the entire drawing area.**

The sizes for Exercise 10–4 are taken from the sketch shown in Figure 10–15.

Step 4. **Draw the wall section (Figures 10–15 and 10–16)**

Draw full scale. Approximate any dimensions not shown.

Do not show dimensions.

Step 5. **Use the Hatch command to draw section lines as follows:**

Sill and Footing—Use the MUDST pattern, Angle 0, Scale 4.

Earth—Use the MUDST pattern, Angle –45, Scale 4.

Block—Use the AR-SAND pattern, Angle 0, Scale .5.

Base Trim, Floor, Subfloor, and other details—Use the LINE pattern. Use a scale of 4 and angles of 45 and –45 (or 315).

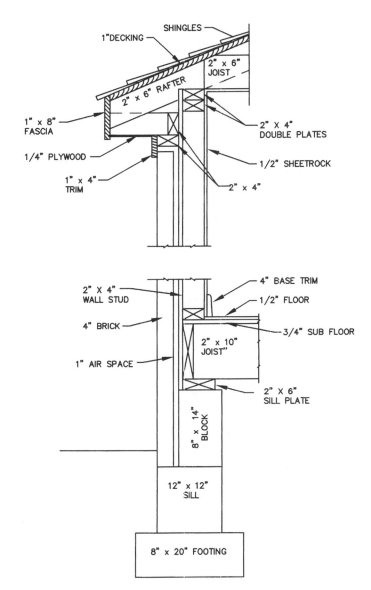

FIGURE 10–15
Sizes for Exercise 10-–4

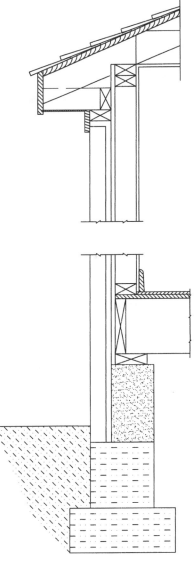

FIGURE 10–16
Exercise 10-–4 Complete

Making Sectional Views with AutoCAD

Step 6. Click: Layout 1 at the bottom of your screen.

Step 7. Use the Dtext command to complete the title block as you have done previously. Use a text height of .1″. Title the drawing **WALL SECTION**.

Step 8. Use the SAVEAS command to save your drawing as EX10-4(your initials) on a floppy disk and again on the hard drive of your computer.

Step 9. Plot or print your drawing at a scale of 1=1, portrait, limits, center the plot, on an 11″ x 8½″ sheet.

EXERCISES

EXERCISE 10–1.   Complete Exercise 10–1 using steps 1 through 11 described in this chapter.
EXERCISE 10–2.   Complete Exercise 10–2 using steps 1 through 8 described in this chapter.
EXERCISE 10–3.   Complete Exercise 10–3 using steps 1 through 11 described in this chapter.
EXERCISE 10–4.   Complete Exercise 10–4 using steps 1 through 9 described in this chapter.

REVIEW QUESTIONS

Circle the best answer.

1. Which of the following will produce a line 3½″ long upward from a point?
   a. 3.5 X 90
   b. @3.5<90
   c. @0<3.5
   d. @3.5<-90
   e. 90<3.5

2. The Select Objects option of the Boundary Hatch dialog box requires
   a. A complete boundary that must be selected
   b. That you pick a single point within the boundary
   c. That at least two lines extend outside the boundary
   d. The use of only the uniform hatch pattern
   e. That only a 45° angle be specified

3. The Pick Points option of the Boundary Hatch dialog box requires
   a. A complete boundary that must be selected
   b. That you pick a single point within the boundary
   c. That at least two lines extend outside the boundary
   d. The use of only the uniform hatch pattern
   e. That only a 45° angle be specified

4. Which of the following patterns produces continuous, evenly spaced lines?
   a. User defined
   b. MUDST
   c. PAT LINE
   d. U-LINE
   e. Concrete

5. Which of the following in the Spacing box of the Boundary Hatch dialog box will produce HATCH lines ¼″ apart?
   a. 1-4
   b. .25
   c. 2.5
   d. 1,4
   e. 25

6. After a hatching command that spaced lines .10 apart has been performed, what is the default response in the Spacing box of the Boundary Hatch dialog box (original default was .08)?
   a. 0
   b. .1
   c. .08
   d. .125
   e. .06

7. What do you type to set the width of a polyline at the prompt "Specify next point or [Arc/Close/Halfwidth/ Length/Undo/Width]"?
   a. A
   b. H
   c. W
   d. The beginning width of the pline
   e. The beginning width and the ending width separated by a comma

8. Which layer used in the exercises in this chapter must be current for hidden lines to be drawn?
   a. HIDDEN
   b. OBJECT
   c. HATCH
   d. DASHED
   e. 0

9. Which layer was used in the exercises in this chapter when hatch lines were drawn?
   a. HIDDEN
   b. OBJECT
   c. HATCH
   d. DASHED
   e. 0

10. If you are using polar array to copy an object four times (total of five objects) what do you type in response to the prompt "Number of items"?
    a. 0
    b. 4
    c. 5
    d. P
    e. N

Complete.

11. Which two functions must be ON when you are aligning items between views that have been drawn with Snap ON?

    _____

    _____

12. How do you turn on all layers?

    _____

13. Describe how to set a layer current.

    _____

14. How can you be sure that only one layer is on?

    _____

15. How do you turn OFF a running OSNAP mode?

    _____

16. Why should you turn off a running OSNAP mode of Endpoint?

_____

17. Why do you Zoom in closer to an area of the drawing?

_____

18. Describe how to use the Offset command to draw parallel lines $\frac{1}{2}''$ apart.

_____

19. Describe how to draw an arrowhead with PLINE.

_____

_____

20. What is the meaning of User defined in the Boundary Hatch dialog box (Type: area)?

_____

11 Sketching Pictorial Views

OBJECTIVES

After completing this chapter, you will be able to:

☐ Arrange correctly the three major forms of pictorial drawings in order of difficulty of drawing and shape distortion.
☐ Correctly sketch oblique figures to scale from orthographic drawings.
☐ Correctly sketch isometric figures to scale from orthographic drawings.
☐ Select shapes that are most effectively illustrated in oblique or isometric drawing methods.

PICTORIAL DRAWING FORMS

There are three major pictorial sketching forms: *oblique, axonometric,* and *perspective* (Figure 11–1). Each of these methods has merits and drawbacks:

Oblique is usually the easiest to draw but is the most distorted.
Axonometric is more difficult to draw but is less distorted.
There are three forms of axonometric drawing: *isometric, dimetric,* and *trimetric*. By far the most commonly used is isometric. Isometric is the only axonometric form that will be covered in this book.
Perspective is the most difficult to draw and is usually the least distorted. The perspective method is not covered in this book.

FIGURE 11–1
Pictorial Drawing Forms

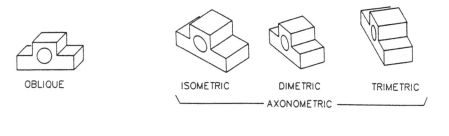

OBLIQUE   ISOMETRIC   DIMETRIC   TRIMETRIC

AXONOMETRIC

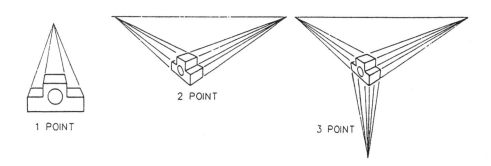

1 POINT   2 POINT   3 POINT

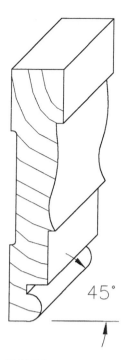

FIGURE 11–2
Object with Uniform Contour

In summary, to give you skills that you can readily use with the least difficulty, only oblique and isometric drawing forms are covered in this book.

Oblique Drawing

The distortions created by oblique drawing can be an advantage in sketching some objects but are unusable for others. A wooden molding that has the same cross-sectional shape along its length, for example, looks fine in oblique (Figure 11–2). An advantage of oblique is that it shows the complete 2D shape of the front view, so there is no possibility of confusion.

Oblique drawing simple involves drawing the front view of an object as an orthographic view and then adding depth to it at an angle, usually 45°. To reduce the distorted appearance, the depth is often drawn half its true size. This technique is called *cabinet oblique*. When the depth dimension is full size, the drawing form is called *cavalier oblique* (Figure 11–3). In Exercise 11-1 you will draw four shapes using the cabinet oblique drawing form.

Figure 11–4 shows a technique for sketching ellipses in oblique. Avoid placing round shapes on the depth planes. Place them on the view where they appear as circles. If you have a shape that has round shapes on depth planes, the oblique method is probably not the one to use.

Isometric Drawing

The isometric drawing form is used a great deal because it is easy to draw and looks good for many objects. If you understand isometric well, the other two axonometric forms, dimetric and trimetric, are easy to learn.

Measurements in isometric are the same in all three dimensions—height, width, and depth. Figure 11–5 shows how to use this method for sketching a simple box, 4″ x 2″ x 2″.

FIGURE 11–3
Cavalier and Cabinet Oblique

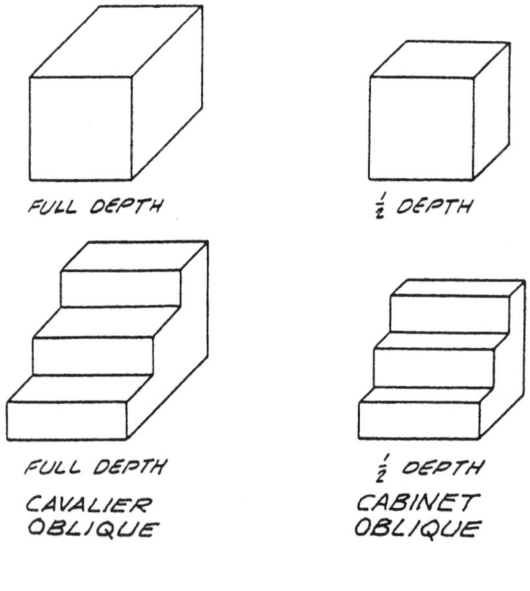

FIGURE 11–4
Sketching Ellipses in Oblique

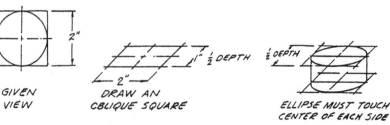

FIGURE 11–5
Measurements in Isometric

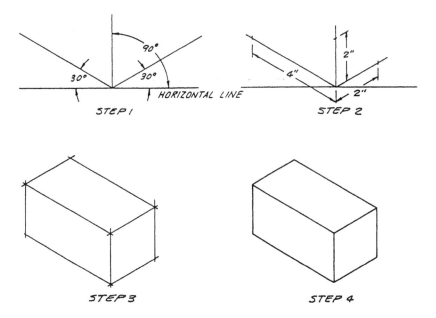

Step 1. Lightly sketch the three isometric axes (or use isometric grid paper): 30° right, 30° left, and 90° to a horizontal line.

Step 2. Measure 4″ along one of the 30° lines, 2″ along the other 30° line, and 2″ on the 90° line.

Step 3. Extend height, width, and depth lines making sure that all lines are parallel, until they meet. Use your 30-60° triangle to sketch the 30° lines if you are not using isometric grid paper.

Step 4. Darken all object lines to complete the drawing.

This simple example provides you with the basics of isometric drawing. There are some details of construction, which will be explained, but if you can draw Figure 11–5, you have a good understanding of the basic principles. The following discussion gives you the details of construction that you will need for complex shapes.

Angles in Isometric Drawing

Without special tools, no measurements can be made on any lines that are not parallel to one of the isometric axes, and angles cannot be measured directly. Each end of the angle must be located and then joined as shown in Figure 11–6.

FIGURE 11–6
Sketching Angles in Isometric

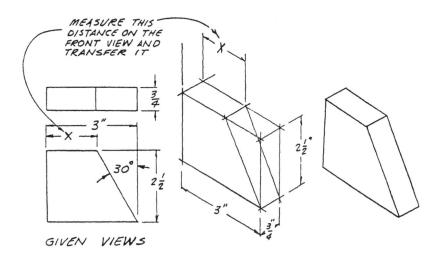

FIGURE 11–7
Positioning Isometric Ellipses

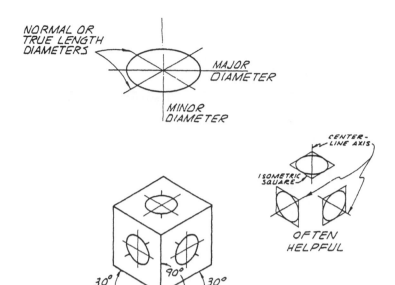

Circles in Isometric Drawing

Circles on the isometric planes appear as ellipses. The angle through which the circle is tilted is 35° 16′. The positions for an ellipse on each face of an isometric cube are shown in Figure 11–7. Notice that the minor diameter of the ellipse is always lined up on a center line that is parallel to one of the isometric axes. Correct positioning of ellipses is very important to the appearance of a drawing and should be carefully studied. It is often helpful for beginners to sketch the center-line axis and the isometric square that the ellipse will fit. The ellipse itself in the past was often drawn with an isometric ellipse template. As you will discover in the next chapter, AutoCAD makes drawing isometric ellipses very easy and almost impossible to turn in the wrong direction. To avoid the use of isometric ellipses, the exercises in this chapter contain very few ellipses, so you can sketch them without the use of a template.

Cylindrical objects must be drawn so that the centers of their ellipses lie on a center line as shown in Figure 11–8. To simplify construction, holes on a curved surface, as hole A in Figure 11–8, are drawn as if they were lying on a flat surface.

Curves in Isometric Drawing

Isometric curves are drawn by locating a number of points (any number that is appropriate for the feature) on the curve in a flat (orthographic) view. Those points are then transferred to the isometric view, using the correct isometric measurements for each point. This process is illustrated in Figure 11–9.

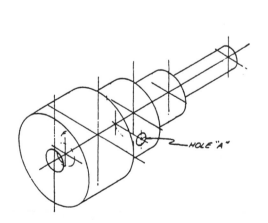

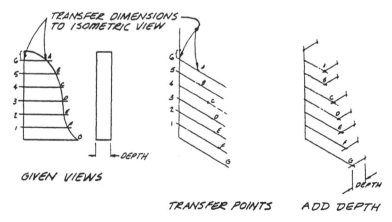

FIGURE 11–8
Sketching Ellipses on a Curved Surface in Isometric

FIGURE 11–9
Sketching Curves in Isometric

FIGURE 11-10
Isometric Spheres

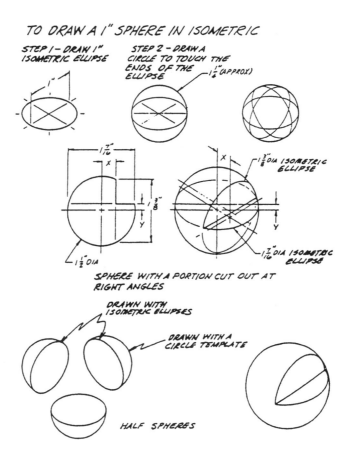

TO DRAW A 1" SPHERE IN ISOMETRIC

STEP 1 - DRAW 1" ISOMETRIC ELLIPSE

STEP 2 - DRAW A CIRCLE TO TOUCH THE ENDS OF THE ELLIPSE — 1¼" (APPROX)

SPHERE WITH A PORTION CUT OUT AT RIGHT ANGLES

1¾" DIA ISOMETRIC ELLIPSE

1⅞" DIA ISOMETRIC ELLIPSE

1 7/16" DIA ISOMETRIC ELLIPSE

1½" DIA

DRAWN WITH ISOMETRIC ELLIPSES

DRAWN WITH A CIRCLE TEMPLATE

HALF SPHERES

Spheres in Isometric Drawing

A sphere using any drawing method is drawn as a circle. If it is necessary to cut pieces out of the sphere, isometric ellipses are helpful. Notice that the ellipses are drawn so that their minor diameters are lined up on one of the isometric axes (Figure 11–10). You cannot measure a sphere directly in isometric; you must take its measurement from the long diameter of an isometric ellipse. To draw a 1″ sphere in isometric, draw a circle that touches the outside edges of the major diameter of a 1″-diameter ellipse. It will measure about $\frac{1}{4}″$ more, or $1\frac{1}{4}″$ in diameter.

General Guidelines for Sketching in Isometric

Some general guidelines for drawing in isometric follow:

For complex shapes it is often helpful to draw a box around the object and measure from the corners of the box to locate features (Figure 11–11).

Locate the centers of all holes and curves and draw those first (Figure 11–12).

FIGURE 11-11
Sketching within a Box

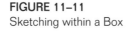
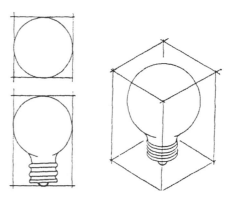

FIGURE 11–12
Locating Centers of Ellipses First

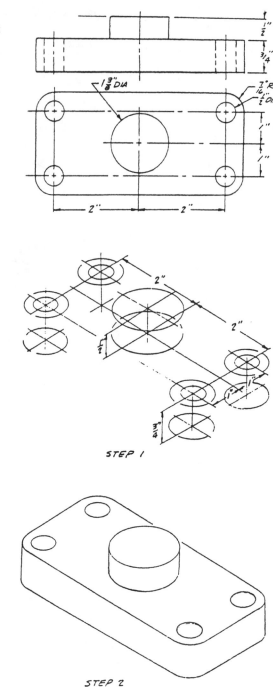

STEP 1

STEP 2

Be sure to locate points and features in all three dimensions: height, width, and depth.

You cannot measure angles in isometric. Locate the ends of the angular line, using height, width, and depth dimensions, as was shown in Figure 11–6.

Be sure to position ellipses correctly, as was shown in Figure 11–7.

For cylindrical objects, work from a center line and locate ellipse centers on that line, as was shown in Figure 11–8.

For curves and irregular shapes, establish some points on the orthographic views and transfer them to the isometric view, as was shown in Figure 11–9.

Simplify the intersections of cylinders and holes, as was shown in Figure 11–8.

Cutaway Drawings

Cutaway drawings are among the most impressive technical drawings. They are used in many different types of publications such as advertising pieces, specification sheets, and repair manuals. Examples of cutaway drawings are shown in Figures 11-13 through 11-15.

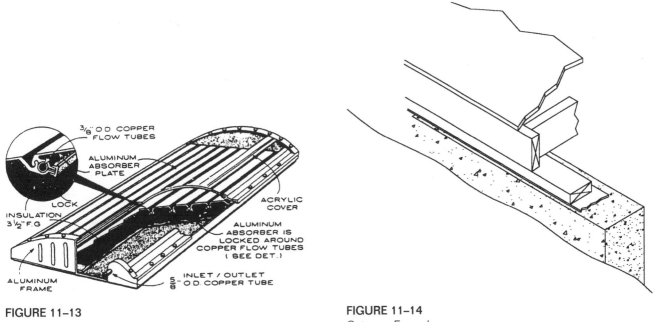

FIGURE 11–13
Cutaway Example

FIGURE 11–14
Cutaway Example

FIGURE 11–15
Cutaway Example

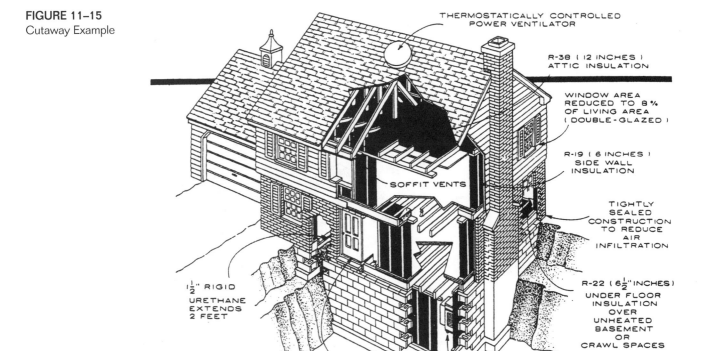

Although cutaways are impressive and can take a great deal of time if the assembly has many parts, they are not difficult to draw. The main things to remember when drawing cutaways are to complete one part at a time and to make sure parts are in the correct position. The drawing shown in Figure 11–15 is an excellent example of a complex cutaway. If you study a few individual parts for a moment, you will quickly see that there is nothing that you have not drawn or could not draw if you knew the shape and size of the part. There are a few rules and details, however, that will help you with drawing cutaways. The following steps, illustrated in Figure 11–16, cover those rules and details.

General Guidelines for Cutaway Drawings

Step 1. Determine the surfaces to be cut
Step 2. Make a rough freehand sketch
Step 3. Draw the cut surfaces
Step 4. Draw the full shapes.
Step 5. Put shading on the cut surfaces.
Step 6. Add callouts.

We shall examine each step in detail.

Determine the surfaces to be cut.   Find out exactly what the drawing is trying to show. When you know the parts to be shown and the position they should be in, you can determine which surfaces should be cut and how deep the cut should be. If the drawing in Figure 11–16 were to be shown as a cutaway, for example, and your instructions were to show how the vacuum switch works, a cut completely across the upper and lower housing through the magnet and the diaphragm should be used. To show less would hide some of the internal parts that reveal how the switch functions.

FIGURE 11–16
Steps in Drawing Cutaways

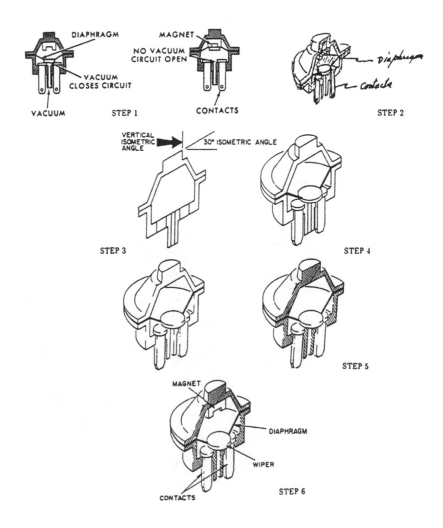

Make a rough freehand sketch. Making a rough freehand sketch allows you to decide which isometric position to use and to make the correct decision about which surfaces to cut. In Figure 11–16 the sketch confirms that a full cut across the part is needed to show both contacts. It also indicates that the vertical isometric axis is a good position for the drawing because it shows how the part functions.

Draw the cut surfaces. It is usually best to draw the cut surfaces first. Sometimes you cannot do this before drawing some of the parts that are not cut. You will discover that as you proceed through the drawing. In Figure 11–16, notice that the cut surfaces are drawn just as they appear on the orthographic views, except that isometric angles have taken the place of horizontal and vertical lines.

Draw the full shapes. Draw the full shapes and complete the uncut parts of the cut surfaces. You must be sure that the parts are shown in their correct positions, which you can determine by measuring. If they are not in the correct positions and still do not show clearly what is intended, do not hesitate to distort dimensions or to make additional cuts, so long as parts do not get too far out of proportion.

Put shading on the cut surfaces. In Figure 11–16, shading lines were used on the cut surfaces. Notice that the shading lines are at steep angles of approximately 60° in opposite directions. It is important to make these lines different from isometric angles, because they can easily be confused with object lines.

Add callouts. Notice that the lettering in the callout is lined up horizontally. The blunt end of the leader points to the center of the line of lettering, and the arrow end breaks the part about $1/16''$. Keep leaders short and with a fan arrangement or with the same angle. Lines of lettering can be centered or arranged flush right and left, whichever is convenient or specified by your customer. Be sure to follow a consistent pattern and be sure that all callouts are clear and easily read.

Further details

If you must cut a flat plane in a cutaway drawing, use obtuse angles for the cut, as shown in Figure 11–17. This allows you to show uniform thickness easily by using the opposite isometric angle and does not distract from the drawing, as extremely jagged cuts do.

Fasteners, shafts, and spheres are shown much more clearly if they are not cut on the drawing. Generally, nothing should be cut in a cutaway that is not necessary to show what is intended.

If you like this kind of drawing, study cutaways in books and magazines to decide what looks good and what does not. Not all the drawings you see printed in books and magazines are good ones.

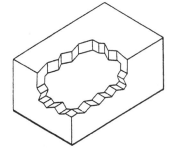

FIGURE 11–17
Use Obtuse Angles for Cut
Surfaces

EXERCISES

EXERCISE 11–1.

Use the following instructions to sketch the final step shown in Figures 11–18, 11–19, 11–20, and 11–21 on the sheet provided, using the cabinet oblique drawing form. Make sure your lines are dense and the same width as object lines. Your drawing will show only the final step in each of these figures.

Remove the sheet labeled EXERCISE 11–1 from your book.

11–1A (Figure 11–18)

Step 1. Sketch the front view of the object using the dimensions shown in the given views. The lower left corner of the front view is in the upper left of the exercise sheet.

Step 2. Extend light construction lines from the front view at a 45° angle to show the depth. Make sure the dimension is half the true depth (in this case, 1/2").

Step 3. Complete the illustration by connecting the points to form the back surface, and darken all object lines.

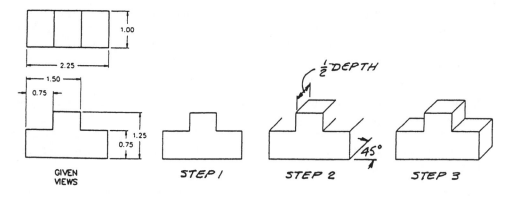

FIGURE 11–18
Exercise 11–1A

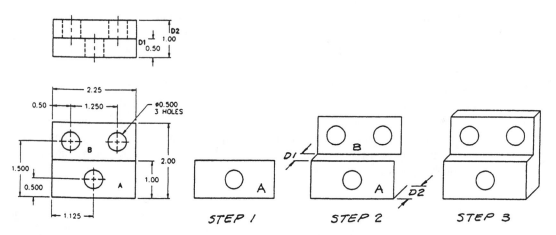

FIGURE 11–19
Exercise 11–1B

11–1B (Figure 11–19)

Step 1. Sketch front surface A using the dimensions shown in the given views. The lower left corner of this drawing is in the upper right of the exercise sheet.

Step 2. Lightly sketch lines D1 and D2 at a 45° angle. Make D1 and D2 half their true length. Sketch front surface B using the dimensions shown in the given views.

Step 3. Darken the other depth lines, and darken all object lines to complete the illustration.

11–1C (Figure 11–20)

Step 1. Look at the given views to decide which circles are on the same center lines.

Step 2. Locate the centers for all circles. Sketch a light 45° construction line from the center of the circle on the exercise sheet. The center of this circle is point A.

Measure half the distance from A to B, and mark point B on the construction line. Do the same for points C and D.

From points C and D sketch light construction lines straight up. Take the distance from C to E on the given views and mark point E on the vertical construction line.

From point E sketch a light 45° construction line to intersect with the vertical line from point D. This locates point F.

FIGURE 11–20
Exercise 11–1C

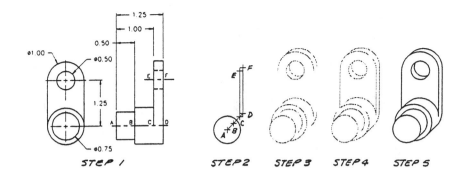

STEP 1   STEP 2   STEP 3   STEP 4   STEP 5

Step 3. Lightly sketch the parts of the circles that will show. You can tell which ones will show by beginning with the circle at point A and working backward.

Step 4. Locate the tangent points by drawing light 45° and vertical construction lines. On this drawing, the tangent points are where straight lines meet the circles. You need to find the tangent points so that your lines have a nice, smooth flow and so that none of the circles are flattened.

Step 5. Darken all lines that show to complete the drawing.

11–1D (Figure 11–21)

On your own: Complete the oblique view on the right side of the figure at half scale. Surface A of this drawing is located in the lower right of the exercise sheet. The angle on surface B can be measured directly $\frac{1}{2}''$ up from its lower right corner. The angle on surface C cannot be measured; you must locate the ends of the line and connect those points to form the angle. Darken all lines after you have completed the construction.

Complete the title block with your best lettering, and name the drawing CABINET OBLIQUE SKETCHES.

EXERCISE 11–2. Use the following instructions to sketch the final step shown in Figures 11–22 and 11–23 on the sheet provided, using the isometric drawing form. Make sure your lines are dense and the same width as object lines. Your drawing will show only the final step in each of these figures.

Remove the sheet labeled EXERCISE 11–2 from your book.

11–2A (Figure 11–22)

Step 1. Mark $\frac{3}{4}''$ from the lower left corner on the 30° axis to the right, $\frac{3}{4}''$ on the vertical axis, and $1\frac{1}{2}''$ on the 30° axis to the left. The lower left corner of this drawing is on the left side of the exercise sheet.

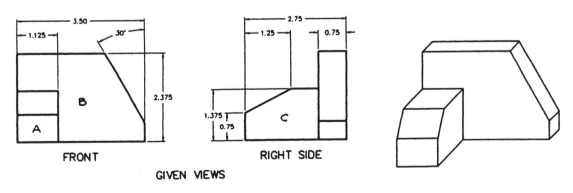

GIVEN VIEWS

FIGURE 11–21
Exercise 11–1D

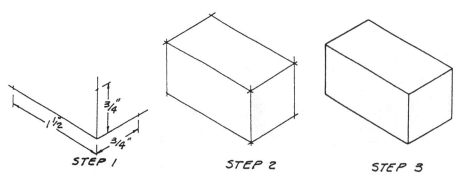

FIGURE 11–22
Exercise 11–2A

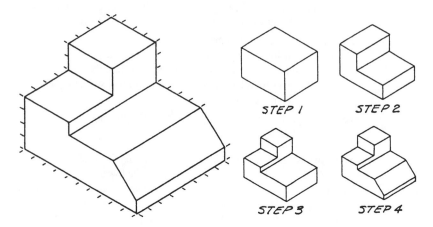

FIGURE 11–23
Exercise 11–2B

Step 2. Using light construction lines, extend height, width, and depth lines until they meet, and sketch parallel lines as needed.

Step 3. Darken the object lines.

11–2B (Figure 11–23)

Step 1. Using light construction lines sketch an isometric box measuring 2″ on the isometric axis to the right, 2½″ on the isometric axis to the left, and 1½″ on the vertical axis. Each mark on the 3D view represents ¼″. The lower right corner of the box is on the right side of the exercise sheet.

Step 2. Use light construction lines to sketch the general shape of the front view as shown.

Step 3. Use light construction lines to sketch the notch in the upper surface shown in the right-side view.

Step 4. Locate the ends of the angular shape and complete the shape as shown. Darken all object lines to complete the illustration.

Complete the title block with your best lettering, and name the drawing ISOMETRIC SKETCHES NO. 1.

EXERCISE 11–3.   Use the following instructions to sketch the final step shown in Figure 11–24 and an isometric sketch of Figure 11–25 on the sheet provided, using the isometric drawing form. Make sure your lines are dense and the same width as object lines. Your drawing will show only the final step in Figure 11–24.

FIGURE 11–24
Exercise 11–3A

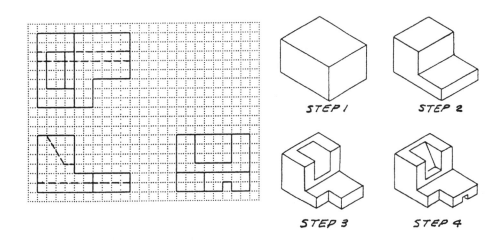

11–3A (Figure 11–24)

Step 1. Using light construction lines sketch an isometric box measuring 2″ on the isometric axis to the right, 2½″ on the isometric axis to the left, and 1½″ on the vertical axis. Each mark on the orthographic views represents ¼″.

Step 2. Use light construction lines to sketch the general shape of the front view as shown.

Step 3. Use light construction lines to sketch the top and right side of the notch in the upper surface. Sketch the notch in the base as shown.

Step 4. Complete the shape of the notch in the upper surface, and sketch the .25 slot in the bottom of the right side of the base as shown. Darken all lines to complete the drawing.

11–3B (Figure 11–25)

On your own: Make an isometric sketch from the top, front, and right-side orthographic views shown in Figure 11–25. You will have to make isometric squares to help you sketch the ellipses forming the holes and the fillets at the corners of the base as shown in Figure 11–7. Use the same method as you used for the other sketches in Exercise 11–2.

Complete the title block with your best lettering and name the drawing ISOMETRIC SKETCHES NO. 2.

EXERCISE 11–4. Make an isometric sketch from the top, front, and right-side orthographic views shown in Figure 11–26 on the sheet provided in your book.

Each mark on the orthographic views represents ¼″. Center the sketch in the sheet by using light construction lines until you are sure the drawing is centered.

Do not show any dimensions.

Complete the title block with your best lettering, and name the drawing BUILDING NO. 1.

FIGURE 11–25
Exercise 11–3B

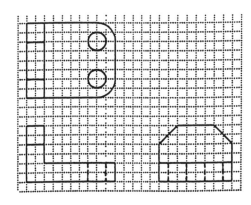

FIGURE 11–26
Exercise 11–4, Grids = $\frac{1}{4}''$

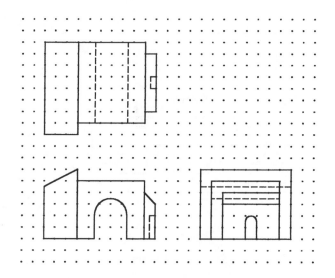

FIGURE 11–27
Exercise 11–5, Grids = $\frac{1}{4}''$

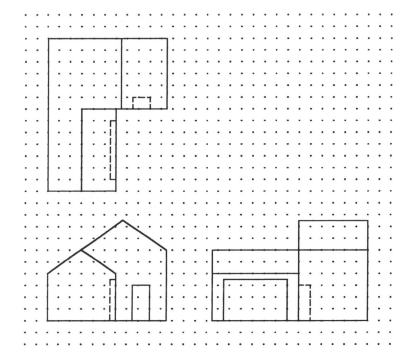

EXERCISE 11–5.   Make an isometric sketch from the top, front, and right-side orthographic views shown in Figure 11–27 on the sheet provided in your book.

Each mark on the orthographic views represents $\frac{1}{4}''$. Center the sketch in the sheet by using light construction lines until you are sure the drawing is centered.

Do not show any dimensions.

Complete the title block with your best lettering, and name the drawing BUILDING NO. 2.

EXERCISE 11–6.   Make an Isometric sketch of Figure 11–28 on the sheet provided in your book.

Draw the figure 3/4 scale using the dimensions shown. Center the drawing in the sheet by using light construction lines until you are sure the drawing is centered.

Do not show any dimensions.

Complete the title block with your best lettering, and name the drawing HOLDER.

FIGURE 11–28
Exercise 11–6, Scale: $^3/_4'' = 1''$

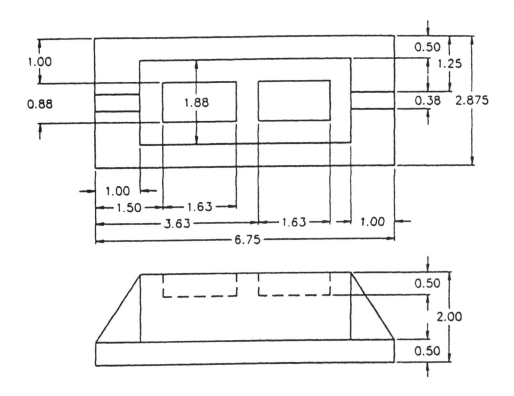

EXERCISE 11–7.   Make an Isometric sketch of Figure 11–29 on the sheet provided in your book.

Draw the figure at a scale of $1''=1'$ using the dimensions shown. Center the drawing in the sheet by using light construction lines until you are sure the drawing is centered. You will have to make isometric squares to help you sketch the ellipses forming the holes, as shown in Figure 11–7.

Do not show any dimensions.

Complete the title block with your best lettering, and name the drawing STOP.

FIGURE 11–29
Exercise 11–7, Scale: $1'' = 1'$

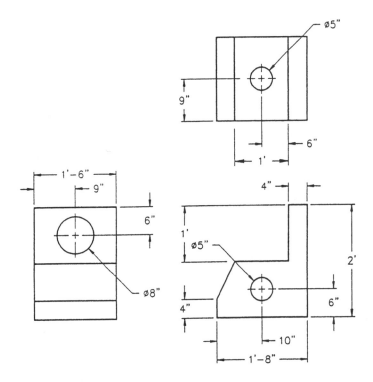

EXERCISE 11–8.　Make an Isometric sketch of Figure 11–30 on the sheet provided in your book.

Draw the figure at a scale of $\frac{3}{8}''=1'$ using the dimensions shown. Center the sketch of the entire reception area furniture in the sheet by using light construction lines until you are sure the drawing is centered.

Do not show any dimensions.

Complete the title block with your best lettering, and name the drawing RECEPTION AREA FURNITURE.

EXERCISE 11–9.　Make an Isometric cutaway sketch of Figure 11–31 on the sheet provided in your book.

Draw the figure full scale using the dimensions shown. Center the drawing in the sheet by using light construction lines until you are sure the drawing is centered.

Make the cut with obtuse angle break lines. Notice that the thickness of all three cut walls is the same.

Do not show any dimensions.

Complete the title block with your best lettering, and name the drawing CUTAWAY.

FIGURE 11–30
Exercise 11–8, Scale: $\frac{3}{8}'' = 1'$

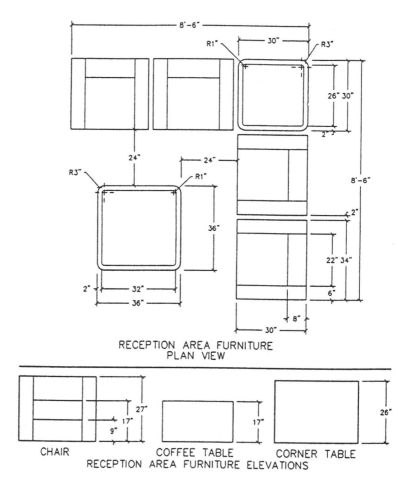

FIGURE 11–31
Exercise 11–9, Full Scale

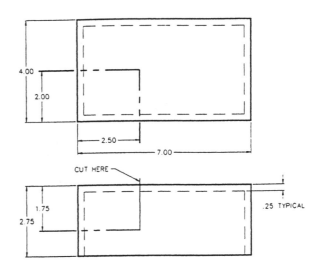

CUT HERE

.25 TYPICAL

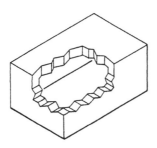

REVIEW QUESTIONS

Circle the best answer.

1. Which of the following is usually the least distorted type of pictorial but the most difficult to draw?
   a. Cabinet oblique
   b. Cavalier oblique
   c. Isometric
   d. Dimetric
   e. Two-point perspective

2. Holes or curves should be placed on receding surfaces in oblique drawing.
   a. True
   b. False

3. The receding oblique surfaces are usually drawn at
   a. 45°
   b. 30°
   c. 60°
   d. 75°
   e. 15°

4. To reduce distortion, receding oblique surfaces are often drawn at half scale.
   a. True
   b. False

5. An isometric gives equal presentations of
   a. Front, top, and right-side views
   b. Front and left-side views
   c. Top and right-side views
   d. Left and right-side views
   e. None of the above
6. On isometric drawings _____ are used.
   a. Isometric measurements
   b. Pictorial measurements
   c. Oblique measurements
   d. True-length measurements
   e. Measurements are not the same on all axes.
7. The three isometric axes are
   a. 30° left, 60° right, and vertical
   b. 30° left, 45° right, and vertical
   c. 30° left, 30° right, and vertical
   d. 60° left, 30° right, and vertical
   e. 45° left, 30° right, and vertical
8. Isometric lines are lines that are parallel to
   a. A level line
   b. The front view
   c. The right-side view
   d. The left-side view
   e. Isometric axes
9. Spheres in isometric drawing appear as
   a. Circles
   b. Ellipses
   c. Straight lines
   d. Irregular curves
   e. It depends on how the sphere is viewed.
10. Cylindrical objects in isometric drawing are best drawn by locating centers on
    a. A box around the surface
    b. An outside surface
    c. A center line or center lines
    d. The edges of preceding ellipses
    e. Their quadrants
11. Angles are measured in isometric drawing by adding the angle of the isometric axis to the angle to be drawn.
    a. True
    b. False
12. An isometric cutaway drawing is best described as
    a. An isometric sectional view
    b. A perspective
    c. An exploded view
    d. An orthographic sectional view
    e. An oblique view
13. Which of the following should be done first in making an isometric cutaway drawing?
    a. Make a freehand sketch.
    b. Shade the cut surfaces.
    c. Draw the cut surfaces in isometric.
    d. Draw the uncut surfaces in isometric.
    e. Place callouts on the drawing.
14. Which of the following is usually cut on a cutaway?
    a. Cylinder walls
    b. Bearings
    c. Shafts
    d. Spheres
    e. Fasteners

Isometric Drawing with AutoCAD

OBJECTIVES

When you have completed this chapter, you will be able to:

☐ Make isometric drawings to scale from two-dimensional drawings.
☐ Correctly use the following commands and settings:

  ELLIPSE-Isocircle
  SNAP-Style Iso

☐ Use the Ctrl-E or F5 keys to change from one isoplane to another.

INTRODUCTION

Isometric drawing is commonly used to show how objects appear in three dimensions. This drawing method is a two-dimensional one (you are drawing on a flat sheet of paper) that is used to give the appearance of three dimensions. It is not a 3D modeling form such as those that are covered in later chapters. In 3D modeling you actually create three-dimensional objects that can be viewed from any angle and can be placed into a perspective mode.

You can make isometric drawings quickly and easily using AutoCAD software. Once you make the proper Grid and Snap settings, the drawing itself proceeds with little difficulty. The three isometric axes are 30° right, 30° left, and vertical.

EXERCISE 12–1:
Fundamentals of Isometric Drawing

Seven isometric shapes are drawn in this exercise to acquaint you with the fundamentals of making isometric drawings using AutoCAD. We will begin with a simple isometric box (Figure 12–1, shape 1) so that you can become familiar with drawing lines on an isometric axis. All seven of these shapes are drawn on the same sheet and plotted on one 8½″ × 11″ sheet. When you have completed Exercise 12–1, your drawing will look similar to Figure 12–1.

Step 1. To begin Exercise 12–1, turn on the computer and start AutoCAD.
Step 2. Open the drawing EX12-1 supplied on the disk that came with your book.
Step 3. Use SAVE AS to save the drawing on the hard drive with the name CH12-EX12-1(your initials).
Step 4. Set Snap as follows.

Set Snap for an isometric grid:

Prompt	Response
Command:	Type: **SN<enter>**
Specify snap spacing or [ON/OFF/Aspect/ Rotate/Style/Type] <0′-0 ½″>:	Type: **S<enter>**

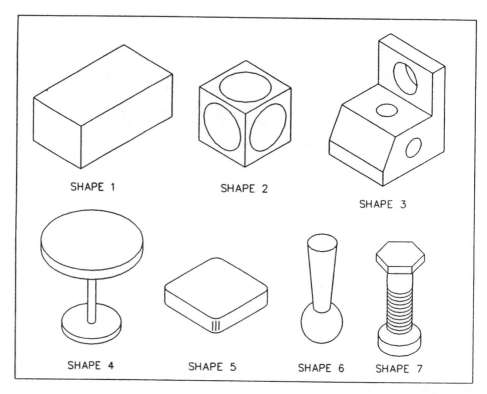

FIGURE 12–1
Exercise 12–1 Complete

Prompt	Response
Enter snap style [Standard/Isometric]<S>:	Type: **I<enter>**
Specify vertical spacing <0'-6">:	Type: **1<enter>** (if 1" is not the default)

When you want to exit the isometric grid, Type: **SN<enter>** and then Type: **S<enter>**, then Type: **S<enter>** again to select the standard grid. Keep the isometric grid for this exercise.

Step 5.   Set Grid: 3".

The following layers have been created in this drawing:

LAYER NAME	COLOR	LINETYPE	LINEWEIGHT
A-furn-iso-r	Red	Continuous	Default
A-furn-iso-g	Green	Continuous	Default

Step 6.   Set Layer A-furn-iso-g current.
Step 7.   Zoom-All.

Shape 1: Drawing the Isometric Rectangle

Drawing shape 1 (Figure 12–2) helps you become familiar with drawing lines using isometric polar coordinates.

Step 1.   Draw the right face of an isometric rectangular box measuring 12″ × 16″ × 30″ using isometric polar coordinates.

Prompt	Response
Command:	Type: **L<enter>**
Specify first point:	**D1** (Figure 12–2) (absolute coordinates 1'7-1/16, 4'11)

FIGURE 12–2
Shape 1: Draw the Isometric
Rectangle

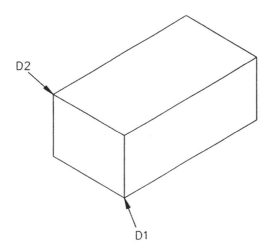

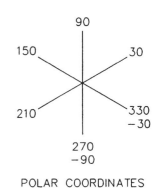

POLAR COORDINATES
FOR ISOMETRIC DRAWING

Specify next point or [Undo]:	Type: **@30<30<enter>**
Specify next point or [Undo]:	Type: **@12<90<enter>**
Specify next point or [Close/Undo]:	Type: **@30<210<enter>**
Specify next point or [Close/Undo]:	Type: **C<enter>**

Step 2. **Draw the left face of the isometric rectangular box.**

Prompt	Response
Command:	**<enter>** (Repeat LINE)
Specify first point:	**D1**
Specify next point or [Undo]:	Type: **@16<150<enter>**
Specify next point or [Undo]:	Type: **@12<90<enter>**
Specify next point or [Close/Undo]:	Type: **@16<330<enter>**
Specify next point or [Close/Undo]:	**<enter>**

Step 3. **Draw the top of the isometric rectangular box.**

Prompt	Response
Command:	**<enter>** (Repeat LINE)
Specify first point:	**D2**
Specify next point or [Undo]:	Type: **@30<30<enter>**
Specify next point or [Undo]:	Type: **@16<-30<enter>**
Specify next point or [Close/Undo]:	**<enter>**

When using polar coordinates to draw lines in isometric, you can ignore Isoplanes. Isoplanes are isometric faces—Top, Right, and Left. Pressing two keys, Ctrl and E, at the same time toggles your drawing to the correct Isoplane—Top, Right, or Left. The function key F5 can also be used to toggle to the correct Isoplane.

Shape 2: Drawing Isometric Ellipses

Shape 2 (Figure 12–3) has a circle in each of the isometric planes of a cube. When drawn in isometric, circles appear as ellipses. You must use the isoplanes when drawing isometric circles using the Ellipse command. The following part of the exercise starts by drawing a 15″ isometric cube.

Step 1. **Draw the right face of a 15″ isometric cube using isometric polar coordinates.**

Prompt	Response
Command:	Type: **L<enter>**

FIGURE 12–3
Shape 2: Draw Isometric
Ellipses

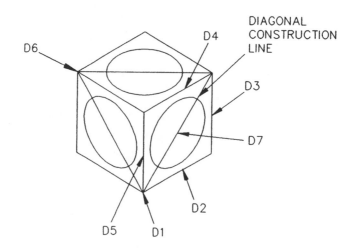

Specify first point:	**D1** (absolute coordinates 5′5-13/16,5′)
Specify next point or [Undo]:	Type: **@15<30<enter>**
Specify next point or [Undo]:	Type: **@15<90<enter>**
Specify next point or [Close/Undo]:	Type: **@15<210<enter>**
Specify next point or [Close/Undo]:	Type: **C<enter>**

Step 2. **Use the Mirror command to draw the left face of the isometric cube.**

Prompt	Response
Command:	Type: **MI<enter>**
Select objects:	**D2,D3,D4<enter>**
Specify first point of mirror line:	**D1** (be sure ORTHO is ON)
Specify second point of mirror line:	**D5** (Press: **F5** to be sure you are in either the right or left isoplane.)
Delete source objects? [Yes/No]<N>:	**<enter>**

Step 3. **Complete the top face of the isometric cube.**

Prompt	Response
Command:	Type: **L<enter>**
Specify first point:	**D6**
Specify next point or [Undo]:	Type: **@15<30<enter>**
Specify next point or [Undo]:	Type: **@15<-30<enter>**
Specify next point or [Close/Undo]:	**<enter>**

On Your Own

Step 4. Draw construction lines, as shown in Figure 12–3, across diagonally opposite corners in each of the visible surfaces. Be sure to turn ORTHO OFF. The construction lines will be used to locate accurately the centers of the ellipses.

Step 5. **Draw an isometric ellipse (6″ radius) that represents a circle in the right isoplane.**

Prompt	Response
Command:	Type: **EL<enter>**
Specify axis endpoint of ellipse or [Arc/Center/Isocircle]:	Type: **I<enter>**
Specify center of isocircle:	**Osnap-Midpoint**

	D7
mid of	
Specify radius of isocircle or [Diameter]:	Press: **the F5 function key until the command line reads <Isoplane Right>**, then Type: **6<enter>**

When you type and enter **D** in response to the prompt "Specify radius of Isocircle or Diameter:", you can enter the diameter of the circle. The default is radius.

On Your Own

Note: If you do not have the isometric snap style active, the Ellipse command will not prompt you with ISO as one of the options for the command.

Note: Select Ellipse-Axis, End if you select from the menu bar. Ellipse-Center or Ellipse-Arc does not allow you to draw an isometric ellipse.

Step 6. **Follow a similar procedure to draw ellipses in the left and top isoplanes.** Be sure to specify Isocircle after you have selected the Ellipse command, and be sure you are in the correct isoplane before you draw the ellipse. Use F5 to toggle to the correct isoplane.

Step 7. **Erase the construction lines.**

When you have completed this part of the exercise, you have the essentials of isometric drawing. Now, apply these essentials to a more complex shape.

Shape 3: Drawing Angles in Isometric and Drawing Ellipses to Show the Thickness of a Material

Shape 3 (Figure 12–4) has an angle and also a hole that shows the thickness of the material that makes up the shape. This part of the isometric exercise describes how to draw an angle and how to draw two ellipses to show the thickness of the material. Begin by drawing the front face of the shape.

Step 1. **Begin to draw the front face of shape 3.**

Prompt	Response
Command:	Type: **L<enter>**
Specify first point:	**D1** (Figure 12–4) (Pick a point in the approximate location shown in Figure 12–1.)
Specify next point or [Undo]:	Type: **@1'8<30<enter>**
Specify next point or [Undo]:	Type: **@2'<90<enter>**
Specify next point or [Close/Undo]:	Type: **@4<210<enter>**
Specify next point or [Close/Undo]:	Type: **@1'<-90<enter>**
Specify next point or [Close/Undo]:	Type: **@1'<210<enter>**
Specify next point or [Close/Undo]:	**<enter>**

Tip: After you become familiar with isometric angles and toggling to isoplanes, use direct distance entry with Ortho ON to draw lines. Just move your mouse in the isometric direction and Type: the number that tells AutoCAD how far you want to go. This is the fastest way to draw lines that are on isometric axes.

Because you do not know the angle for the next line, you must locate the other end of it and connect the two endpoints. This is a common practice in isometric drawing. Any time you encounter an angle in isometric, locate the two endpoints of the angle and connect those points to draw a line that is not one of the isometric axes.

Step 2. **Locate the two endpoints of the angle, and draw the line that is at an angle to complete the front face of shape 3.**

Prompt	Response
Command:	Type: **L<enter>**
Specify first point:	**D1**
Specify next point or [Undo]:	Type: **@4<90<enter>**
Specify next point or [Undo]:	**Osnap-Endpoint**
of	**D2**
Specify next point or [Close/Undo]:	**<enter>**

FIGURE 12–4

Shape 3: Draw Angles in Isometric
and Draw Ellipses to Show Material Thickness

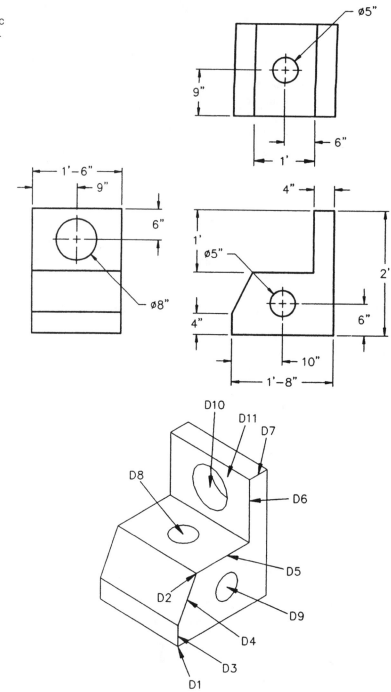

Step 3. Use the Copy command to draw the identical back plane.

Prompt	Response
Command:	Type: **CP<enter>**
Select Objects:	**D3,D4,D5,D6,D7<enter>**
Specify base point or displacement, or [Multiple]:	**D1**
Specify second point of displacement or <use first point as displacement>:	Type: **@1'6<150<enter>**

On Your Own

Step 4. Draw lines connecting the front and back surfaces.

Step 5. Draw an isometric ellipse (5″ diameter) that represents a circle in the top isoplane.

Prompt	Response
Command:	Type: **EL<enter>** (Toggle to the top isoplane using F5.)
Specify axis endpoint of ellipse or [Arc/Center/Isocircle]:	Type: **I<enter>**
Specify center of isocircle:	**D8** (Count the 3″ grid marks (1″ snap) to locate the center of the plane, or draw construction lines from the midpoints of two parallel sides.)
Specify radius of isocircle or [Diameter]:	Type: **D<enter>**
Specify diameter of isocircle:	Type: **5<enter>**

On Your Own

Step 6. Toggle to the right isoplane, and draw a 5″-diameter ellipse in the right isometric plane using D9 as its center.

Step 7. Two ellipses are required in the left isoplane, on the part of the shape that sits on top. One is needed on the front surface, and part of one is needed on the back surface to describe the thickness of the material. To do this:

☐ Toggle to the left isoplane, and draw an 8″-diameter ellipse in the left isometric plane using D10 as its center.
☐ Draw a line from D10 (the center of the first ellipse) to D11 (the center of the second ellipse that is yet to be drawn). Draw this line using @4<30 (4″ is the depth) as the polar coordinates for the second point of the line.
☐ Draw the second 8″-diameter ellipse in the left isoplane using D11 as its center (the endpoint of the 4″ line).
☐ Use the Trim and Erase commands to trim and erase the back part of the second ellipse and center line.

Tip: You can also skip drawing this 4″ center line and simply copy the ellipse using @4<30 as the second point of displacement.

Shape 4: Drawing a Shape That Has a Series of Ellipses Located on the Same Center Line

Shape 4 (Figure 12–5), similar to a round table, will help you become familiar with drawing a shape that has a series of ellipses located on the same center line. Five ellipses must be drawn. The centers of two of them, the extreme top and bottom ellipses, can be located by using Endpoints of the center line. Centers for the other three can be located by using construction lines or the ID command. Construction lines are used for this exercise so that you can see where the centers are.

The following part of the exercise begins by drawing a center line through the entire height of the object.

Step 1. Begin to draw a shape containing several ellipses of different sizes located on the same center line by drawing the center line.

Prompt	Response
Command:	Type: **L<enter>**
Specify first point:	**D1**
Specify next point or [Undo]:	Type: **@24<90<enter>**
Specify next point or [Undo]:	**<enter>**

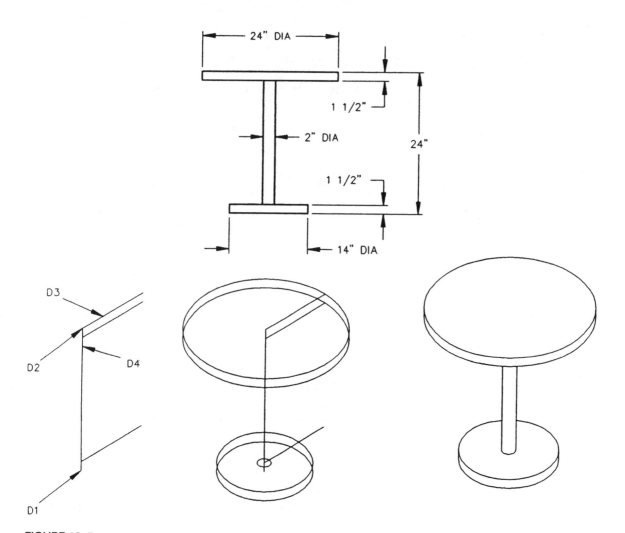

FIGURE 12–5
Shape 4: Draw a Shape That Has a Series of Ellipses Located on the Same Center Line

Step 2.   Draw construction lines used to locate the centers of three ellipses.

Prompt	Response
Command:	Type: **L<enter>**
Specify first point:	**D2**
Specify next point or [Undo]:	Type: **@12<30<enter>**
Specify next point or [Undo]:	**<enter>**
Command:	**Copy** (or Type: **CP<enter>**)
Select objects:	**D3**
Select objects:	**<enter>**
Specify base point or displacement, or [Multiple]:	Type: **M<enter>**
Specify base point:	**Osnap-Endpoint**
of	**D4**
Specify second point of displacement or <use first point as displacement>:	Type: **@1-1/2<270<enter>**
Specify second point of displacement or <use first point as displacement>:	Type: **@22-1/2<270<enter>**
Specify second point of displacement or <use first point as displacement>:	**<enter>**

On Your Own

To draw the five ellipses:

Step 3. Toggle to the top isoplane and use Endpoint to locate the center of the uppermost ellipse on the endpoint of the vertical line. Draw it with a diameter of 24″.

Step 4. Draw a second 24″-diameter ellipse using as its center the Intersection of the construction line that is located 1½″ from the top end of the vertical line, or copy the 24″ ellipse 1½″ down.

Step 5. Draw two isometric ellipses with their centers located at the Intersection of the construction line located 1½″ from the bottom of the vertical line. One ellipse is 2″ in diameter; the other is 14″ in diameter.

Step 6. Draw the 14″-diameter ellipse again using the bottom Endpoint of the vertical line as its center, or copy the 14″ ellipse 1½″ down.

On Your Own

See Figure 12–6.

Note: Although Osnap-Nearest can be used to end an isometric line on another line, the position is not exact. A more exact method is to draw the line beyond where it should end and trim it to the correct length.

Step 7. To draw the 2″ column, toggle to the right or left isoplane (the top isoplane does not allow you to draw vertical lines using a pointing device if Ortho is ON). Turn Ortho (F8) ON. Draw a vertical line from the Quadrant of one side of the 2″-diameter ellipse to just above the first 24″-diameter ellipse. Draw a similar line to form the other side of the column.

Step 8. With Ortho (F8) ON and toggled to the right or left isoplane, draw vertical lines from the Quadrants of the ellipse segments to connect ellipses as shown in Figure 12–6.

Step 9. Use Trim and Erase to remove unneeded lines. The drawing is complete.

Shape 5: Isometric Detail with Rounded Corners

The fifth drawing (Figure 12–7) in this exercise is a shape that has rounded corners. Rounded corners are common in many items. In two-dimensional drawing, the Fillet command allows you to obtain the rounded corners quickly and easily. This is not so in isometric. Drawing shape 5 will help you become familiar with how rounded corners must be constructed with isometric ellipses.

Step 1. Turn on Ortho and Snap, and toggle to the top isoplane. Draw an 18″ × 18″ square shape in the top isoplane.

Prompt	Response
Command:	Type: **L<enter>**
Specify first point:	**D1** (on a grid mark)

FIGURE 12–6
Shape 4: Draw tangents to the Ellipses

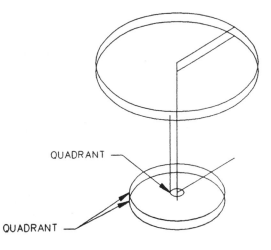

QUADRANT

QUADRANT

FIGURE 12–7
Shape 5: Isometric Detail with
Rounded Corners

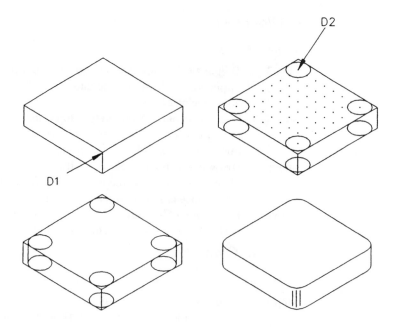

Specify next point or [Undo]:	Type: @**18<30<enter>**
Specify next point or [Undo]:	Type: @**18<150<enter>**
Specify next point or [Close/Undo]:	Type: @**18<210<enter>**
Specify next point or [Close/Undo]:	Type: **C<enter>**

On Your Own

Step 2. **Copy the front two edges of the square to form the bottom of the shape. Copy using @4<270 (4″ is the depth) as the polar coordinates for the second point of displacement.**

Step 3. **Draw lines connecting the top and bottom edges.** (These lines are for reference only. You may skip this step if you choose.)

Step 4. Draw a 2″ radius ellipse in the top isoplane.

Prompt	Response
Command:	Type: **EL<enter>** (Toggle to the top isoplane.)
Specify axis endpoint of ellipse or [Arc/Center/Isocircle]:	Type: **I<enter>**
Specify center of isocircle:	**D2** (Count 2″ from the corner to locate the center of the ellipse.)
Specify radius of isocircle or [Diameter]:	Type: **2<enter>**

On Your Own

To complete shape 5:

Step 5. **Copy the ellipse just drawn to the other four top corners, locating them in a similar manner.**

Step 6. **Copy the front three ellipses 4″ in the 270 direction to form corners in the bottom plane.**

Step 7. **Draw lines connecting the two outside ellipses using Osnap-Quadrant.**

Step 8. **Use the Trim and Erase commands to remove the extra lines.**

Step 9. **Add highlights on the front corner to complete the drawing.**

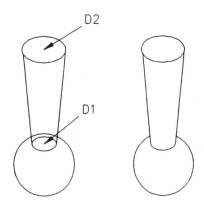

FIGURE 12–8
Shape 6: Isometric Detail—A Rounded Shape Intersecting a Sphere

D2

D1

Shape 6: Isometric Detail—A Rounded Shape Intersecting a Sphere

While drawing in isometric, you may encounter a cylinder intersecting a sphere (Figure 12–8). The cylinder in Figure 12–8 is also tapered.

Step 1.   Draw the sphere.

Prompt	Response
Command:	Type: **C<enter>**
Specify center point for circle or [3P/2P/Ttr (tan tan radius)]:	**Click the center of the circle on a grid mark, in the approximate location shown in Figure 12–1.**
Specify radius of circle or [Diameter]:	Type: **6<enter>**

Step 2.   Draw the bottom ellipse of the tapered cylinder.

Prompt	Response
Command:	Type: **EL<enter>** (Toggle to the top isoplane.
Specify axis endpoint of ellipse or [Arc/Center/Isocircle]:	Type: **I<enter>**
Specify center of isocircle:	**D1** (2″ down from the top quadrant of the circle)
Specify radius of isocircle or [Diameter]:	Type: **2<enter>**

Step 3.   Draw the top ellipse of the tapered cylinder.

Prompt	Response
Command:	**<enter>**
Specify axis endpoint of ellipse or [Arc/Center/Isocircle]:	Type: **I<enter>**
Specify center of isocircle:	**D2** (Click a point 18″ above the center of the first ellipse.)
Specify radius of isocircle or [Diameter]:	Type: **3.5<enter>**

On Your Own

Step 4.   Complete the shape by drawing lines connecting the top and bottom ellipses using Osnap-Quadrant.

Step 5.   Trim the circle and the bottom ellipse to complete the shape. Although the true shape of the intersection between the cylindrical shape and the sphere is a compound curve, it is often simplified in isometric as you have done here. The compound curve is difficult to construct and looks no better than the simplified version.

Shape 7: Isometric Detail—A Polygon and a Threaded Shape

The final shape in this exercise combines several features (Figure 12–9).

Step 1.   Draw the hexagonal head of a threaded spacer (Figure 12–9A).

Prompt	Response
Command:	Type: **POL<enter>**
Enter number of sides <4>:	Type: **6<enter>**
Specify center of polygon or [Edge]:	**Click a point on a grid mark, in the approximate location shown in Figure 12–1 (with Snap ON).**
Enter an option [Inscribed in circle/ Circumscribed about circle] <I>:	Type: **C<enter>**
Specify radius of circle:	Type: **6<enter>**

Now you have a hexagon that cannot be used in isometric drawing. To use it, you must block the hexagon and then insert it with different X and Y values. **Be sure to toggle to the top isoplane when you insert the hexagonal block.**

Step 2.   Block and insert the hexagon (Figure 12–9B).

Prompt	Response
Command:	Type: **B<enter>**
The Block Definition dialog box appears:	Type: **HEX in the Block name: box.** **Make sure Delete is selected.** Click: **Pick point**
Specify insertion base point:	Click: **the center of the hexagon**
The Block Definition dialog box appears:	Click: **Select objects**
Select objects:	Click: **any point on the hexagon**
Select objects:	**<enter>**
The Block Definition dialog box appears:	Click: **OK**
The hexagon disappears:	
Command:	**Insert-Block...** (or Type: **I<enter>**)
The Insert dialog box appears:	Click: **the down arrow in the Name: box** Click: **HEX** Change: **Y: in the Scale area to .58** (This is a very close approximation to the isometric scale factor.) Click: **OK**

FIGURE 12–9
Shape 7: Isometric Detail—A Polygon and a Threaded Shape

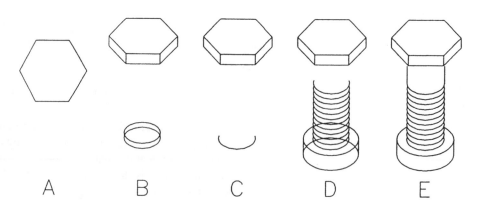

Specify insertion point or [Scale/X/Y/Z/
    Rotate/PScale/PX/PY/PZ/PRotate]:   **Pick the location of the isometric
                                     hexagon as shown in Figure 12–1
                                     (on snap).**

On Your Own

Complete drawing shape 7, and add text to your drawing as follows:

Step 3.   **Draw 2″ vertical lines from each of the visible corners of the hexagon in the 270 direction (Figure 12–9B).**

Step 4.   **Using Osnap-Endpoint, draw lines to form the bottom of the hexagon (Figure 12–9B).**

Step 5.   **At a center point 20″ below the center of the isometric hexagon, draw an isometric ellipse with a 3″ radius in the top isoplane. Copy the ellipse 1″ in the 90 direction (Figure 12–9B).**

Step 6.   **Trim the back of the bottom ellipse using the top ellipse as the cutting edge. Erase the top ellipse (Figure 12–9C).**

Step 7.   **Array the trimmed ellipse using 12 rows, 1 column, and a space between rows of +1″ (Figure 12–9D).**

Step 8.   **Draw a 10″-diameter isometric ellipse using the center of the bottom thread ellipse. Copy the ellipse 3″ in the 270 direction (Figure 12–9D).**

Step 9.   **Draw lines connecting the Quadrants of the two 10″ ellipses (Figure 12–9D).**

Step 10.   **Draw lines from the top thread to just below the lower surface of the hexagon (Figure 12–9E).**

Step 11.   **Trim and Erase as needed to complete the drawing (Figure 12–9E).**

Step 12.   **Set Layer A-furn-iso-r current, and use Single Line Text, 2″H, Simplex font to identify shapes 1 through 7 as shown in Figure 12–1. Place your name in the lower right corner using the Simplex font.**

SAVE

Step 13.   **When you have completed Exercise 12–1, save your work in at least two places.**

PLOT

Step 14.   **Click: Layout1 and plot the drawing on an 8½″ × 11″ sheet of paper.**

EXERCISE 12–2:
Tenant Space Reception Desk in Isometric

The tenant space solid wood reception desk is drawn in isometric in Exercise 12–2. When you have completed Exercise 12–2, your drawing will look similar to Figure 12–10.

Step 1.   **To begin Exercise 12–2, turn on the computer and start AutoCAD.**

Step 2.   **Open the drawing EX12-2 supplied on the disk that came with your book.**

The following layer has been created on this drawing:

LAYER NAME	COLOR	LINETYPE
A-furn-iso-g	Green	Continuous

Step 3.   **Set Layer A-furn-iso-g current.**

Step 4.   **Zoom-All.**

FIGURE 12–10
Exercise 12–2: Reception Desk in
Isometric

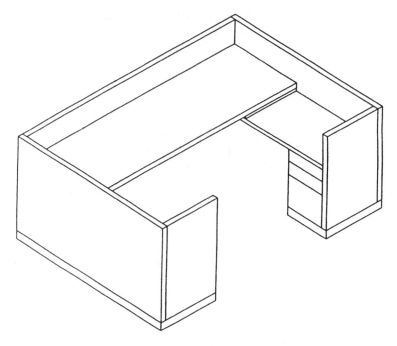

This exercise is a series of straight lines, all of which are on the isometric axes. It is suggested that you follow the step-by-step procedure described next so that you get some ideas about what you can and cannot do when using the isometric drawing method. To draw an isometric view of the reception desk (Figure 12–10) use the dimensions shown in Figure 12–12.

Step 5.   Set SNAP and ORTHO ON. Toggle to the top isometric plane. Draw the top edge of the panels (Figure 12–11).

Prompt	Response
Command:	Type: **L<enter>**
Specify first point:	**D1** (Figure 12–11) (absolute coordinates 8′1,7′4)
Specify next point or [Undo]:	Type: **@24<210<enter>**
Specify next point or [Undo]:	Type: **@66<150<enter>**
Specify next point or [Close/Undo]:	Type: **@96<30<enter>**
Specify next point or [Close/Undo]:	Type: **@66<-30<enter>**
Specify next point or [Close/Undo]:	Type: **@24<210<enter>**

FIGURE 12–11
Drawing the Top Edge of the
Panels

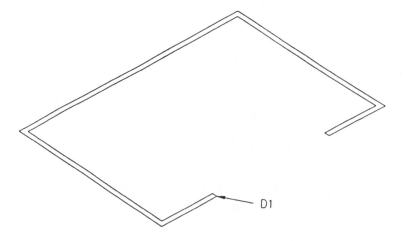

D1

202   Chapter 12

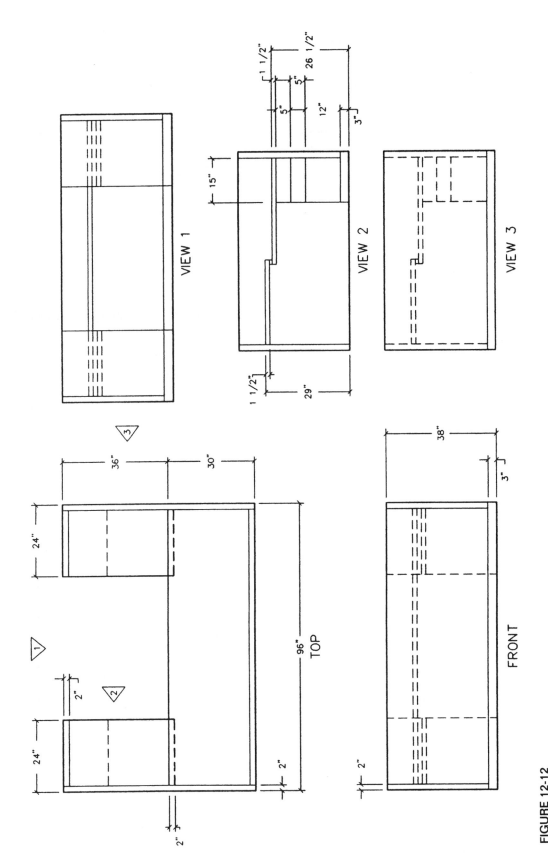

FIGURE 12-12
Dimensions of the Reception Desk (Scale: $^3/_8'' = 1'\text{-}0''$)

VIEW 1

VIEW 2

VIEW 3

TOP

FRONT

Specify next point or [Close/Undo]:	Type: @2<150<enter>
Specify next point or [Close/Undo]:	Type: @22<30<enter>
Specify next point or [Close/Undo]:	Type: @62<150<enter>
Specify next point or [Close/Undo]:	Type: @92<210<enter>
Specify next point or [Close/Undo]:	Type: @62<330<enter>
Specify next point or [Close/Undo]:	Type: @22<30<enter>
Specify next point or [Close/Undo]:	Type: C<enter>

Step 6. **Use the Extend command to extend the inside lines of the panels to form the separate panels (Figure 12–13).**

Prompt	Response
Command:	Type: EX<enter>
Select objects:	D1
Other corner:	D2
Select objects:	<enter>
Select object to extend or shift-select to trim or [Project/Edge/Undo]:	D3,D4,D5,D6<enter>

Step 7. **Copy the top edges of the panels to form the lower kickplate surfaces (Figure 12–14).**

Prompt	Response
Command:	Type: CP<enter>
Select objects:	D1,D2,D3,D4
Select objects:	<enter>
Specify base point or displacement, or [Multiple]:	Type: M<enter>
Specify base point:	D1 (any point is OK)
Specify second point of displacement or <use first point as displacement>:	Type: @35<270<enter>

Tip: You can also use Polar Tracking and direct distance to specify distances when you copy.

FIGURE 12–13
Extend Lines to Form the
Separate Panels

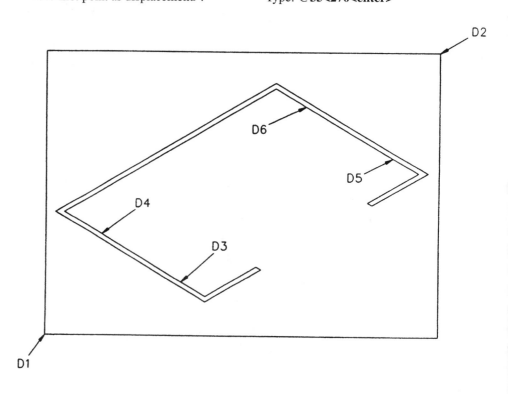

Chapter 12

FIGURE 12-14
Copy the Top Edges to Form the
Lower Kickplate Surfaces and the
Edge of the Main Work Surface

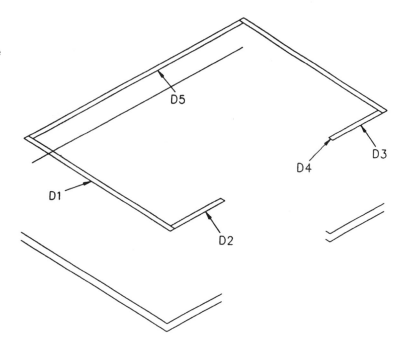

| Specify second point of displacement or <use first point as displacement>: | Type: @38<270<enter> |
| Specify second point of displacement or <use first point as displacement>: | <enter> |

Step 8. **Use the Copy command to draw the edge of the main work surface against the inside of the panel (Figure 12–14).**

Prompt	Response
Command:	Type: **CP<enter>**
Select objects:	**D5**
Select objects:	**<enter>**
Specify base point or displacement, or [Multiple]:	**D5** (any point is OK)
Specify second point of displacement or <use first point as displacement>:	Type: **@9<270<enter>**

On Your Own

See Figure 12–15.

Step 9. **Set a running OSNAP mode of Endpoint and draw vertical lines connecting top and bottom outside lines and the inside corner above the work surface.** Turn the running OSNAP mode OFF when you have completed this part of the exercise. Next, you will draw the work surface.

Step 10. **Draw the work surfaces (Figure 12–15).**

Prompt	Response
Command:	Type: **L<enter>**
Specify first point:	**Osnap-Endpoint, D1**
Specify next point or [Undo]:	Type: **@28<330<enter>**
Specify next point or [Undo]:	**D2** (With ORTHO ON and the top iso-plane active, pick any point beyond the inside of the left partition; you can Trim these later.)

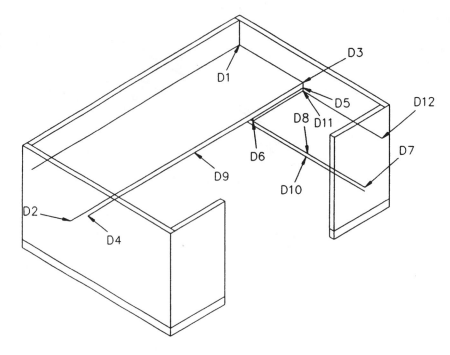

Specify next point or [Close/Undo]:	**<enter>**
Command:	**<enter>** (Repeat LINE)
Specify first point:	**Osnap-Endpoint, D3**
Specify next point or [Undo]:	Type: **@1-1/2<270<enter>**
Specify next point or [Undo]:	**D4** (Pick another point outside the left partition.)
Specify next point or [Close/Undo]:	**<enter>**
Command:	**<enter>** (Repeat LINE)
Specify first point:	**Osnap-Endpoint, D5**
Specify next point or [Undo]:	Type: **@1<270<enter>**
Specify next point or [Undo]:	Type: **@22<210<enter>**
Specify next point or [Close/Undo]:	Type: **@1<90<enter>**
Specify next point or [Close/Undo]:	**<enter>**
Command:	**<enter>** (Repeat LINE)
Specify first point:	**Osnap-Endpoint, D6 (Figure 12–15)**
Specify next point or [Undo]:	**D7** (Pick a point outside the right rear panel.)
Specify next point or [Undo]:	**<enter>**
Command:	**<enter>** (Repeat LINE)
Specify first point:	**Osnap-Endpoint, D11**
Specify next point or [Undo]:	**D12** (Pick a point outside the right rear panel.) **<enter>**
Command:	**Copy** (or Type: **CP<enter>**)
Select objects:	**D8**
Select objects:	**<enter>**
Specify base point or displacement, or [Multiple]:	**D8** (any point is OK)
Specify second point of displacement or <use first point as displacement>:	Type: **@1-1/2<270<enter>**

Command:	Extend (or Type: EX<enter>)
Select objects:	D9<enter>
Select object to extend or shift-select to trim or [Project/Edge/Undo]:	D8, D10<enter>

Step 11. Trim lines that extend outside the panels (Figure 12–16).

Prompt	Response
Command:	Type: TR<enter>
Select objects:	D1,D2,D3<enter>
Select object to trim or shift-select to extend or [Project/Edge/Undo]:	D4,D5,D6,D7,D8,D9<enter>

Step 12. Draw the drawer pedestal.

Prompt	Response
Command:	Type: L<enter>
Specify first point:	Osnap-Endpoint, D10
Specify next point or [Undo]:	Type: @15<150<enter>
Specify next point or [Undo]:	D11 (With ORTHO ON and the left iso-plane active, pick a point above the bottom edge of the desktop.)
Specify next point or [Close/Undo]:	<enter>
Command:	Copy (or Type: CP<enter>)
Select objects:	D12 (Figure 12–16)
Select objects:	<enter>
Specify base point or displacement, or [Multiple]:	Type: M<enter>
Specify base point:	D12 (any point is OK)
Specify second point of displacement, or <use first point as displacement>:	Type: @3<90<enter>
Specify second point of displacement, or <use first point as displacement>:	Type: @15<90<enter>

FIGURE 12–16
Trim Lines and Draw the Drawer
Pedestal

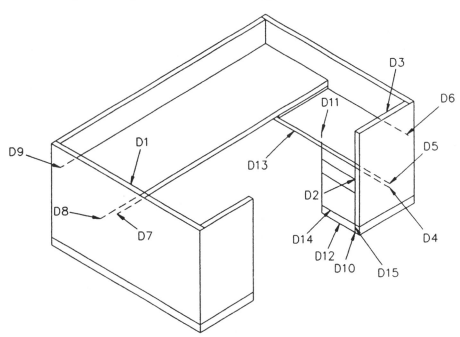

Specify second point of displacement, or	
<use first point as displacement>:	Type: **@20<90<enter>**
Specify second point of displacement, or	
<use first point as displacement>:	**<enter>**

Step 13. Trim the extra lines and add your name.

Prompt	Response
Command:	Type: **TR<enter>**
Select objects:	**D13,D14<enter>**
Select object to trim or shift-select to extend or [Project/Edge/Undo]:	**D15,D11<enter>**

Place your name in the lower right corner using the simplex font.

Save

Step 14. When you have completed Exercise 12–2, save your work in at least two places as EX12-2(your initials).

Plot

Step 15. Click: Layout1 and plot the drawing on an 8½″ × 11″ sheet of paper.

Dimensioning in Isometric

You can resolve the problem of placing dimensions on an isometric drawing by buying a third-party software dimensioning package designed specifically for isometric. Other methods, such as using the aligned option in dimensioning and using an inclined font with the style setting, solve only part of the problem. Arrowheads must be constructed and individually inserted for each isoplane. If you spend a little time blocking the arrowheads and customizing your menu, you can speed up the process significantly.

EXERCISE 12–3:
Tenant Space Reception Seating Area in Isometric

1. Open drawing EX12-3 on the disk that came with your book.
2. Make an isometric drawing, full size, of the chairs, coffee table, and corner table to show the entire reception room seating area. Use the dimensions shown in Figure 12–17. Place your name in the lower right corner. Use the simplex font.
3. Click: **Layout1** and plot the drawing on an 8½″ × 11″ sheet of paper.

EXERCISE 12–4:

1. Make an isometric AutoCAD sketch from the top, front, and right-side orthographic views shown in Figure 12–18 on the sheet provided in your book.
2. Each mark on the orthographic views represents ¼″. Center the sketch in the sheet visually by moving the drawing if necessary until you are sure the drawing is centered.
3. Do not show any dimensions.
4. Complete the title block with the simplex font, and name the drawing BUILDING NO. 1.
5. Plot the drawing to fit on an 8½″ x 11″ sheet.

FIGURE 12–17
Exercise 12–3, Reception Seating
Dimensions (Scale $^3/_8''$=1'-0'')

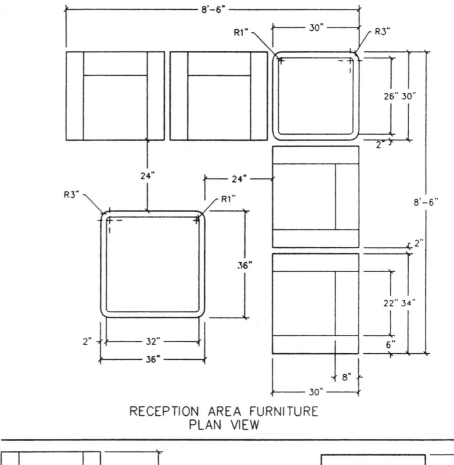

RECEPTION AREA FURNITURE
PLAN VIEW

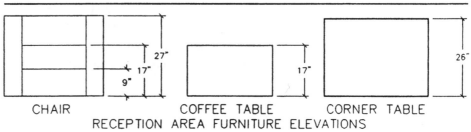

CHAIR   COFFEE TABLE   CORNER TABLE
RECEPTION AREA FURNITURE ELEVATIONS

FIGURE 12–18
Sizes for Exercise 12–4

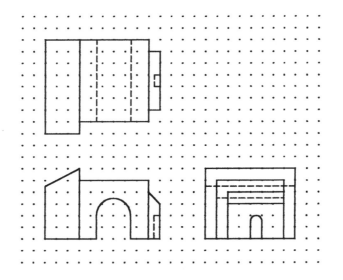

Isometric Drawing with AutoCAD

FIGURE 12–19
Sizes for Exercise 12–5

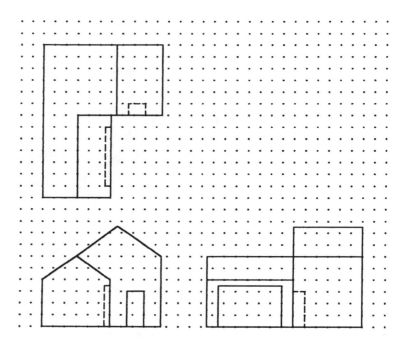

EXERCISE 12–5:

1. Make an isometric AutoCAD sketch from the top, front, and right-side orthographic views shown in Figure 12–19 on the sheet provided in your book.

2. Each mark on the orthographic views represents 1/4". Center the sketch in the sheet visually by moving the drawing if necessary until you are sure the drawing is centered.

3. Do not show any dimensions.

4. Complete the title block with the simplex font, and name the drawing BUILDING NO. 2

5. Plot the drawing to fit on an 8½″ x 11″ sheet.

REVIEW QUESTIONS

Circle the best answer.

1. From which of the following selections on the Tools menu on the menu bar are the isometric snap and grid obtained?
   a. Layer Control...
   b. Drafting Settings…
   c. Set SysVars
   d. Grid On/Off
   e. UCS Control...

2. From which of the Snap options is the isometric Snap obtained?
   a. ON
   b. OFF
   c. Aspect
   d. Rotate
   e. Style

3. Which of the following is not one of the normal isometric axes?
   a. 30
   b. 60
   c. 90
   d. 210
   e. 330

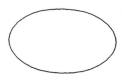

FIGURE 12–20

FIGURE 12–21

FIGURE 12–22

4. From which of the Ellipse prompts is the isometric ellipse obtained?
   a. <Axis endpoint 1>
   b. Center
   c. Isocircle
   d. Axis endpoint 2
   e. Rotation
5. Which isoplane is used to draw the ellipse shown in Figure 12–20?
   a. Top
   b. Left
   c. Right
6. Which isoplane is used to draw the ellipse shown in Figure 12–21?
   a. Top
   b. Left
   c. Right
7. Which isoplane is used to draw the ellipse shown in Figure 12–22?
   a. Top
   b. Left
   c. Right
8. Which key(s) toggle from one isoplane to another?
   a. Ctrl-C
   b. F9
   c. F7
   d. F5
   e. Alt-F1
9. Which of the following is the same as –30°?
   a. 60°
   b. 150°
   c. 180°
   d. 210°
   e. 330°
10. Which of the following isoplanes will not allow vertical lines to be drawn with a mouse when ORTHO is ON?
    a. Top
    b. Left
    c. Right

Complete.
11. Which function key is used to turn the isometric grid ON and OFF?

   _____

12. Write the correct syntax (letters and numbers) to draw a line 5.25″ at a 30° angle upward to the right.

   _____

13. Write the correct sequence of keystrokes, using polar coordinates, to draw the right side of the isometric rectangle shown in Figure 12–23, after the first point (lower left corner) has been picked. Draw to the right and up.

   1. _____   3. _____
   2. _____   4. _____

FIGURE 12–23

14. In Exercise 12–2, why were lines drawn beyond where they should stop and then trimmed to the correct length?

   _____

   _____

15. Which command used in this chapter has a feature labeled "Multiple"?

   _____

16. List the six angles used for polar coordinates in drawing on isometric axes.

_____

17. Describe how to draw an angled line that is not on one of the isometric axes.

_____

_____

18. Describe how to draw a cylindrical object in isometric that has several ellipses of different sizes located on the same center line.

_____

_____

19. Describe two problems that must be solved to place dimensions on an isometric drawing.

_____

_____

20. Describe the difference between isometric drawing and 3D modeling.

_____

_____

13

Sketching Floor Plans

OBJECTIVES

After completing this chapter, you will be able to:

☐ Correctly sketch floor plans to scale from a given set of specifications.
☐ Correctly answer questions regarding floor plan sketches.

INTRODUCTION

Floor plans are created by using the ideas of many people. Clients, architects, city inspectors, builders, salespeople, and others may have input into many final floor plans. The purpose of this chapter is to develop the skills necessary to correctly draw a sketch of a proposed floor plan to scale. The design of the plan has already been developed. You are to draw the sketch as designed from specifications furnished to you.

Steps in Sketching the Proposed Floor Plan (Figure 13–1)

Figure 13–1 shows how your final sketch will appear.

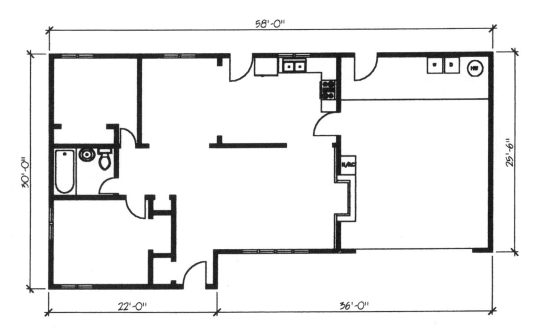

FIGURE 13–1
Exercise 13–1 Complete

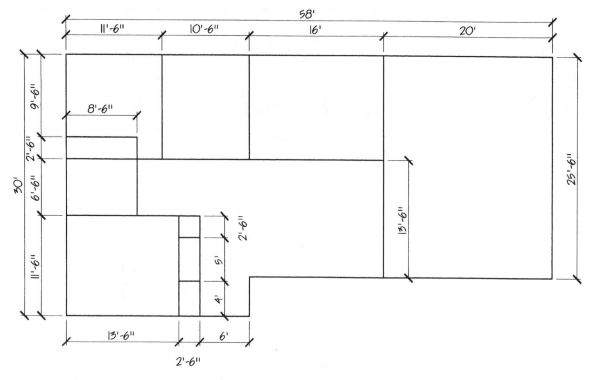

FIGURE 13–2
Sketch Outline Lightly

Step 1. Remove the sheet labeled EXERCISE 13–1 from the back of your book.

Step 2. Draw the outline of the plan very lightly on the paper (Figure 13–2), using the scale of $\frac{1}{8}''=1'-0''$. The outline will be from the outside of outside walls to the center of inside walls.

Step 3. With light lines add thickness to all walls (Figure 13–3). Because the scale is very small, $\frac{1}{8}''$ to $1'$, make all walls approximately $\frac{1}{16}''$ (5″ to 6″).

Step 4. Locate all windows, doors, and the fireplace (Figures 13–4 and 13–5) with light construction lines.

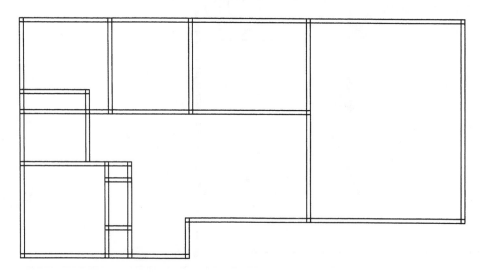

FIGURE 13–3
Add Thickness to All Walls Using Light Construction Lines

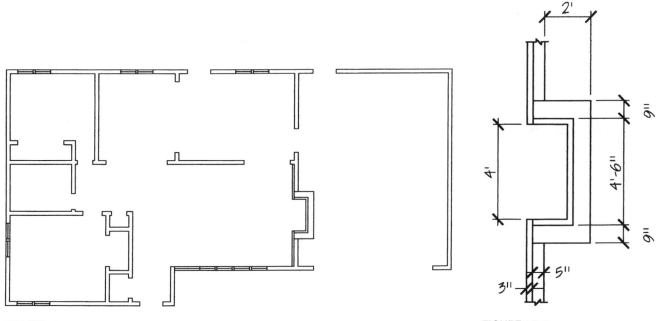

FIGURE 13–4
Locate Windows, Doors, and the Fireplace

FIGURE 13–5
Fireplace Dimensions (Not to Scale)

Step 5. With light construction lines sketch sinks, countertops, cabinets, bathroom fixtures, water heater, washer, dryer, and heating and A/C equipment. Use the sizes shown in Figure 13–6. These symbols are $\frac{1}{8}''=1'$, so draw them the size shown in this figure.

Step 6. Darken all lines (Figure 13–7).

Step 7. Fill in the title block with your best lettering. Title the drawing SINGLE STORY FLOOR PLAN 1 .

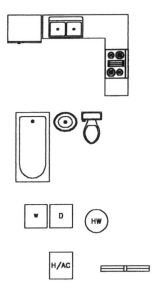

FIGURE 13–6
Symbols for Kitchen, Bath,
Utilities, and Windows at
$\frac{1}{8}''=1'$ Scale

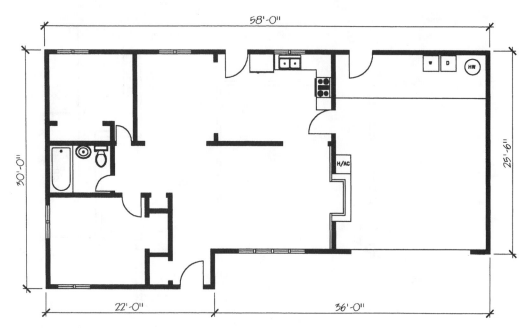

FIGURE 13–7
Exercise 13–1 Complete

EXERCISES

EXERCISE 13–1. Complete Exercise 13–1 using steps 1 through 8 described in this chapter. Fill in the title block with your best lettering. Title the drawing FLOOR PLAN 1.

EXERCISE 13–2. Complete Exercise 13–2 using the specifications described in Figure 13–8. Use the sketching technique described in Exercise 13–1. Locate windows,

FIGURE 13–8
Dimensions for Exercise 13–2

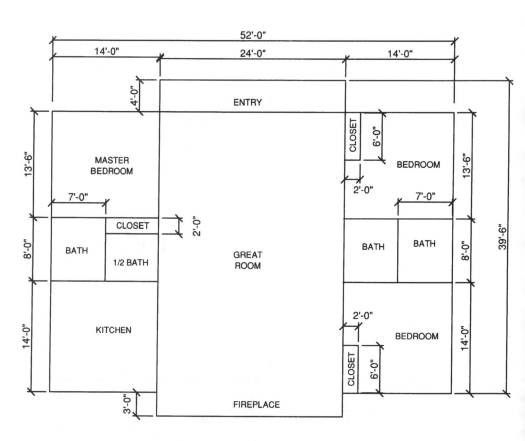

doors, fireplace, kitchen, and all other items shown in Figure 14–6. Use the sizes shown in Figure 13–6. Fill in the title block with your best lettering. Title the drawing FLOOR PLAN 2.

EXERCISE 13–3. Complete Exercise 13–3 using the specifications described in Figure 13–9. Use the sketching technique described in Exercise 13–1. Fill in the title block with your best lettering. Title the drawing TENANT SPACE FLOOR PLAN.

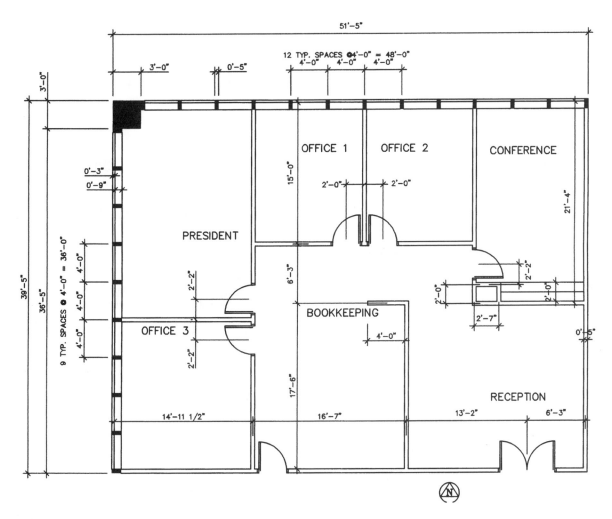

FIGURE 13–9

Dimensions for Exercise 13–3

FIGURE 13–10
Dimensions for Exercise 13–4

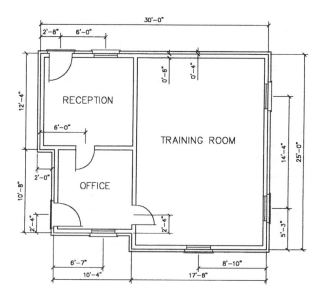

EXERCISE 13–4.   Complete Exercise 13–4 using the specifications described in Figure 13–10. Use the sketching technique described in Exercise 13–1. Fill in the title block with your best lettering. Title the drawing SMALL OFFICE PLAN.

REVIEW QUESTIONS

Circle the best answer.
1. The lines in the preliminary sketch (Figure 13–1) show the inside of the outside walls.
   a. True
   b. False
2. The lines in the preliminary sketch show the centers of the inside walls.
   a. True
   b. False
3. The walls shown in these sketches are approximately
   a. 2″ thick
   b. 5″ thick
   c. 8″ thick
   d. 10″ thick
   e. 12″ thick
4. The scale for Exercise 13–1 is
   a. $\frac{1}{16}''$=1′
   b. $\frac{1}{8}''$=1′
   c. $\frac{1}{4}''$=1′
   d. $\frac{1}{2}''$=1′
   e. No scale was used.
5. Which scale is on the same edge as the 1/8 scale?
   a. 1/16
   b. 1/4
   c. 1/2
   d. 3/8
   e. 3/4
6. On a scale of $\frac{1}{8}''$=1′, a 3′ door will actually measure
   a. 3″
   b. $\frac{3}{8}''$
   c. $\frac{3}{4}''$
   d. $1\frac{1}{2}''$
   e. Impossible to tell from the information given

7. On a scale of $\frac{1}{8}''=1'$, a 16' room will actually measure:
   a. 3"
   b. 16"
   c. 2"
   d. 4"
   e. 2½"
8. On a scale of $\frac{1}{8}''=1'$, a 20' room will actually measure:
   a. 3"
   b. 16"
   c. 2"
   d. 4"
   e. 2½"
9. The floor plan can best be described as an orthographic _____ view.
   a. front
   b. top
   c. right-side
   d. left-side
   e. section
10. The inputs from all of the people who have an interest in what the final floor plan looks like requires that the designer must make sure that no one changes the preliminary plan.
   a. True
   b. False

14 Drawing Floor Plans with AutoCAD

OBJECTIVES

After completing this chapter, you will be able to:

☐ Correctly draw floor plans full size using AutoCAD or AutoCAD LT.
☐ Insert predefined blocks of doors, windows, and other items.
☐ Correctly answer questions regarding the following AutoCAD commands:
   Polyline
   Multiline
   Multiline Edit
   Offset
   Trim
   Explode
   Insert
   From

EXERCISE 14–1:
Drawing a Floor Plan Using the Polyline, Offset, Line, Explode, Insert, and Trim Commands

Your final drawing will look similar to the drawing in Figure 14–1 without dimensions.

Step 1. **To begin Exercise 14–1, turn on the computer and start AutoCAD or AutoCAD LT.**

Step 2. **Open drawing EX14-1 supplied on the disk that came with your book.**

Step 3. **Use Zoom-All to view the entire drawing area.**

FIGURE 14–1
Exercise 14–1 Complete

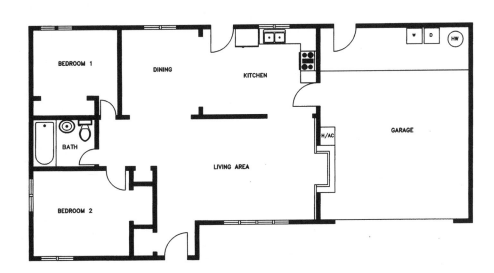

221

Prompt	Response
Command:	Type: **Z <enter>**
Specify corner of window, enter a scale factor (nX or nXP), or [All/ Center/Dynamic/Extents/Previous/ Scale/Window] <real time>:	Type: **A<enter>**

Step 4.   Use the Polyline command to draw the outside edge of the floor plan.

Prompt	Response
Command:	Type: **PL<enter>**
Specify start point:	Type: **8',10'<enter>**
Specify next point or [Arc/Halfwidth/ Length/Undo/Width]:	With ORTHO ON **move the mouse up** and Type: **30'<enter>**
Specify next point or [Arc/Close/ Halfwidth/Length/Undo/Width]:	**Move the mouse to the right** and Type: **58'<enter>**
Specify next point or [Arc/Close/ Halfwidth/Length/Undo/Width]:	**Move the mouse down** and Type: **25'6<enter>**
Specify next point or [Arc/Close/ Halfwidth/Length/Undo/Width]:	**Move the mouse to the left** and Type: **36'<enter>**
Specify next point or [Arc/Close/ Halfwidth/Length/Undo/Width]:	**Move the mouse down** and Type: **4'6<enter>**
Specify next point or [Arc/Close/ Halfwidth/Length/Undo/Width]:	Type: **C<enter>**

Step 5.   Use the Offset command to draw the inside edge of the floor plan (Figure 14–2). Walls are drawn 6″ thick in this exercise so that they lie on convenient snap increments.

Prompt	Response
Command:	Type: **O<enter>**
Specify offset distance or [Through]:	Type: **6<enter>**
Select object to offset or <exit>:	Pick: **the Polyline you just drew**

FIGURE 14–2
Use Polyline and Offset to Draw
the Outside Walls

Specify point on side to offset:	Pick: **any point on the inside of the polyline**
Select object to offset or <exit>:	**<enter>**

Step 6. **On Your Own: Complete the bedroom.**

1. Use the measurements from Figure 14–3 to Offset the interior walls and the closet. All walls on this plan are 6″.

2. Use the Trim command to trim wall intersections and the closet door opening. Do not trim the entry door to the bedroom until after the door has been inserted.

3. Use the Insert command to insert the previously defined blocks, WINDOW and DOOR, as follows:

Prompt	Response
Command:	Type: **I<enter>**
The Insert dialog box appears:	Click: **on WINDOW in the Name: list box**
	Make sure a check appears in the Insertion Point—Specify On-screen box.
	Click: **OK**
Specify insertion point or [Scale/ X/Y/Z/Rotate/PScale/PX/PY/ PZ/PRotate]:	Type: **FRO<enter>**
Base point:	Click: **the intersection of the upper left corner of bedroom 1.**
<Offset>:	Type: **@3′6<0<enter>**
Command:	**<enter>**
The Insert dialog box appears:	Click: **on DOOR in the Name: list box**
	Make sure a check appears in the Insertion Point—Specify On-screen box.
	Click: **OK**
Specify insertion point or [Scale/ X/Y/Z/Rotate/PScale/PX/PY/ PZ/PRotate]:	Type: **MID<enter>**
Of	Click: **the upper line crossing the entry to the bedroom**

FIGURE 14–3
Offset Inside Walls and the
Closet in Bedroom 1

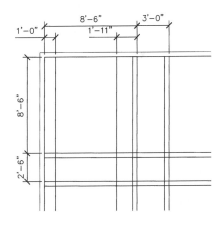

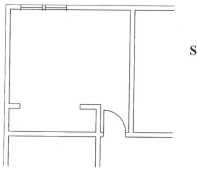

FIGURE 14–4
Use the Trim and Insert Commands to Complete Bedroom 1

4. Explode the DOOR block and trim the door opening as shown in Figure 14–4.

Step 7. **On Your Own: Complete the floor plan.**

1. Use the measurements from Figure 14–5 to Offset the interior walls and the closets. All walls on this plan are 6″. Measurements are to the center of inside walls, so make sure to subtract 3″ from each dimension so that the 6″ offset for the walls gives you the correct distance.

2. Use the Trim command to trim wall intersections and the closet door openings.

3. Use the Insert command to insert the previously defined blocks: Bath Tub, Sink-Oval top, and Toilet-top in the bathroom.

4. Use the Insert command to insert the previously defined blocks: Range-Oven, Refrigerator, and Sink-double in the kitchen. The kitchen counter is 2′ deep, and you can approximate the length.

5. Insert windows, doors, and the FIREPLACE block in their approximate locations shown in Figure 14–1.

6. Insert Washer, Dryer, Water Heater, and Heat-AC blocks in the approximate locations shown in Figure 14–1.

7. Use the Hatch command to fill in all walls with the SOLID hatch pattern.

8. Use the Dtext command to add room labels as shown in Figure 14–1.

9. Click: **Layout1** at the bottom of your screen and complete the title block using the Dtext command. Title the drawing **FLOOR PLAN NO. 1**

10. Use the SAVEAS command to save your drawing as **EX14-1**(your initials) on a floppy disk and again on the hard drive of your computer.

11. Plot or print your drawing at a scale of 1=1, landscape, limits, center the plot, on an 11″ × 8½″ sheet.

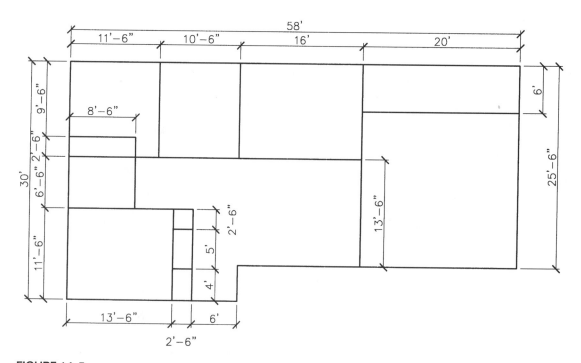

FIGURE 14–5
Dimensions for Exercise 14–1

EXERCISE 14-2:
Drawing a Floor Plan Using the Polyline, Offset, Line, Explode, Insert, and Trim Commands

Your final drawing will look similar to the drawing in Figure 14–6. This floor plan shows the main living level only. The carport and utilities are beneath the level shown, so you will have no heating equipment, water heater, washer, or dryer shown on this plan.

Step 1. **To begin Exercise 14–2, turn on the computer and start AutoCAD or AutoCAD LT.**

Step 2. **Open drawing EX14-2 supplied on the disk that came with your book.**
Because there are several ways to open a drawing, the laboratory instructor must tell you how to do that on your version of AutoCAD.

Step 3. **Use Zoom-All to view the entire drawing area.**

Prompt	Response
Command:	Type: **Z <enter>**
Specify corner of window, enter a scale factor (nX or nXP), or [All/Center/Dynamic/Extents/Previous/Scale/Window] <real time>:	Type: **A<enter>**

Step 4. **Use the Polyline command to draw the outside edge of the floor plan.**

Prompt	Response
Command:	Type: **PL<enter>**
Specify start point:	Type: **8′,10′<enter>**
Specify next point or [Arc/Halfwidth/Length/Undo/Width]:	With ORTHO ON **move the mouse up** and Type: **35′6′<enter>**

FIGURE 14–6
Exercise 14–2 Complete

Specify next point or [Arc/Close/ Halfwidth/Length/Undo/Width]:	**Move the mouse to the right** and Type: **14'<enter>**
Specify next point or [Arc/Close/ Halfwidth/Length/Undo/Width]:	**Move the mouse up** and Type: **4'<enter>**
Specify next point or [Arc/Close/ Halfwidth/Length/Undo/Width]:	**Move the mouse to the right** and Type: **24'<enter>**
Specify next point or [Arc/Close/ Halfwidth/Length/Undo/Width]:	**Move the mouse down** and Type: **4'<enter>**
Specify next point or [Arc/Close/ Halfwidth/Length/Undo/Width]:	**Move the mouse to the right** and Type: **14'<enter>**
Specify next point or [Arc/Close/ Halfwidth/Length/Undo/Width]:	**Move the mouse down** and Type: **35'6<enter>**
Specify next point or [Arc/Close/ Halfwidth/Length/Undo/Width]:	**Move the mouse to the left** and Type: **14'<enter>**
Specify next point or [Arc/Close/ Halfwidth/Length/Undo/Width]:	**Move the mouse down** and Type: **3'<enter>**
Specify next point or [Arc/Close/ Halfwidth/Length/Undo/Width]:	**Move the mouse to the left** and Type: **24'<enter>**
Specify next point or [Arc/Close/ Halfwidth/Length/Undo/Width]:	**Move the mouse up** and Type: **3'<enter>**
Specify next point or [Arc/Close/ Halfwidth/Length/Undo/Width]:	Type: **C<enter>**

Step 5. **Use the Offset command to draw the inside edge of the floor plan (Figure 14–7). Walls are drawn 5″ thick in this exercise.**

Prompt	Response
Command:	Type: **O<enter>**
Specify offset distance or [Through]:	Type: **5<enter>**
Select object to offset or <exit>:	Pick: **the Polyline you just drew**
Specify point on side to offset:	Pick: **any point on the inside of the polyline**
Select object to offset or <exit>:	**<enter>**

Step 6. **On Your Own: Complete the floor plan.**

1. **Use the measurements from Figure 14–8 to Offset the interior walls and the closets. All walls on this plan are 5″. Measurements are to the center of inside walls, so make sure to subtract 2½″ from each dimension so that the 5″ offset for the walls gives you the correct distance.**

2. **Use the Trim command to trim wall intersections and the closet door openings.**

3. **Use the Insert command to insert the previously defined blocks: Bath Tub, Sink-Oval top, and Toilet-top in the bathroom.**

FIGURE 14–7
Draw Outside Walls

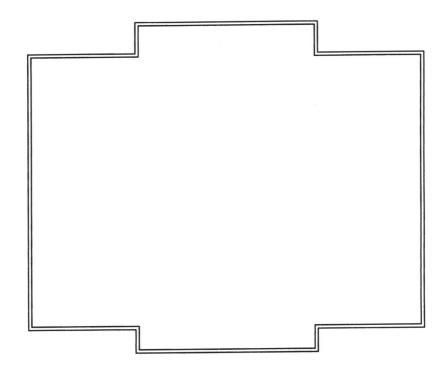

FIGURE 14–8
Dimensions for Exercise 14–2

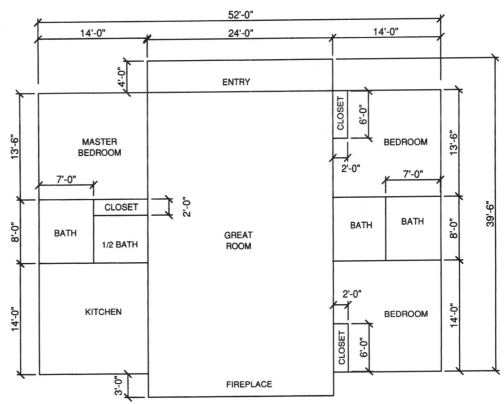

4. Use the Insert command to insert the previously defined blocks: **Range-Oven, Refrigerator,** and **Sink-double** in the kitchen. The kitchen counter is 2′ deep, and you can approximate the length.

5. Insert windows, doors, and the **FIREPLACE** block in their approximate locations shown in Figure 14–6.

6. Use the Hatch command to fill in all walls with the SOLID hatch pattern.

7. Use the Dtext command to add room labels as shown in Figure 14–6.

8. Click: **Layout1 at the bottom of your screen and complete the title block using the Dtext command. Title the drawing FLOOR PLAN NO. 2**

9. Use the **SAVEAS command to save your drawing as EX14-2(your initials) on a floppy disk and again on the hard drive of your computer.**

10. **Plot or print your drawing at a scale of 1=1, landscape, limits, center the plot, on an 11″ x 8½″ sheet.**

EXERCISE14–3:
Drawing a Floor Plan Using the Multiline, Multiline Edit, Explode, Insert, Extend, and Trim Commands

Your final drawing will look similar to the drawing in Figure 14–9 without dimensions. The Multiline Style command has been used to create three multiline styles that you will use in this exercise. The Multiline command allows you to draw up to 16 lines at the same time. In this exercise you will draw three lines at the same time, and you will use the justification option, which allows you to draw from the bottom of the three lines, from the top of the three lines, or from the middle of the three lines. You will also use a different multiline style to draw two lines at the same time when you draw the interior walls. In addition, you will use the Multiline Edit command to trim multiline intersections. You will not use the Multiline Style command in this exercise.

Step 1. **To begin Exercise 14–3, turn on the computer and start AutoCAD or AutoCAD LT.**

Step 2. **Open drawing EX14-3 supplied on the disk that came with your book.**

Step 3. **Use Zoom-All to view the entire drawing area.**

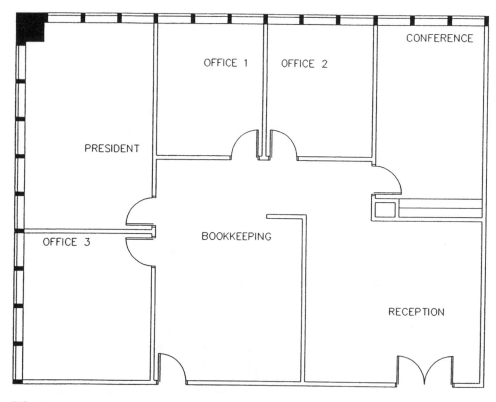

FIGURE 14–9
Exercise 14–3 Complete

Prompt	Response
Command:	Type: **Z** **<enter>**
Specify corner of window, enter a scale factor (nX or nXP), or [All/ Center/Dynamic/Extents/Previous/ Scale/Window] <real time>:	Type: **A<enter>**

Step 4. **Use the Multiline command to draw the north exterior wall of the tenant space floor plan.**

Prompt	Response
Command:	Type: **ML<enter>**
Current settings: Justification = Bottom, Scale = 1.00, Style = THREE	
Specify start point or [Justification/ Scale/STyle]:	Type: **st<enter>** (just to be sure the correct style is current)
Enter mline style name or [?]:	Type: **THREE<enter>**
Specify start point or [Justification/ Scale/STyle]:	Type: **J<enter>**
Enter justification type [Top/Zero/ Bottom] <bottom>:	Type: **T<enter>** (You will now be drawing with the top line, and the other two lines will follow.)
Specify start point or [Justification/ Scale/STyle]:	Type: **INT<enter>**
of	Click: **D1 (Figure 14–10)**
Specify next point:	**Move your mouse to the right** and Type: **48′<enter>**
Specify next point:	**<enter>**

Step 5. **Use the Multiline command to draw the west exterior wall of the tenant space floor plan.**

Prompt	Response
Command:	**<enter>**
Current settings: Justification = Bottom, Scale = 1.00, Style = THREE	
Specify start point or [Justification/ Scale/STyle]:	Type: **st<enter>** (to make the THREE-WEST style current)
Enter mline style name or [?]:	Type: **THREE-WEST<enter>**
Specify start point or [Justification/ Scale/STyle]:	Type: **J<enter>**
Enter justification type [Top/Zero/ Bottom] <bottom>:	Type: **B<enter>** (You will now be drawing with the bottom line, and the other two lines will follow.)
Specify start point or [Justification/ Scale/STyle]:	Type: **INT<enter>**
of	Click: **D2 (Figure 14–10)**

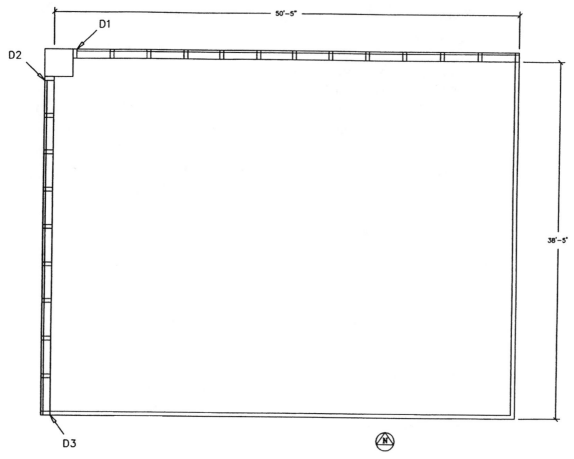

FIGURE 14–10
Draw Outside Walls with Multiline

| Specify next point: | **Move your mouse down** and Type: **36'<enter>** |
| Specify next point: | **<enter>** |

Step 6.   Use the Multiline command to draw the south and east exterior walls.

Prompt	**Response**
Command:	**<enter>**
Current settings: Justification = Bottom, Scale = 1.00, Style = THREE-WEST	
Specify start point or [Justification/Scale/STyle]:	Type: **ST<enter>** (to make the TWO style current)
Enter mline style name or [?]:	Type: **TWO<enter>**
Specify start point or [Justification/Scale/STyle]:	Type: **J<enter>**
Enter justification type [Top/Zero/Bottom] <bottom>:	Type: **B<enter>** (You will now be drawing with the bottom line, and the other two lines will follow.)
Specify start point or [Justification/Scale/STyle]:	Type: **INT<enter>**
of	Click: **D3 (Figure 14–10)**

Prompt	Response
Specify next point:	**Move your mouse to the right** and Type: **50'5<enter>**
Specify next point or [Undo]:	**Move your mouse up** and Type: **38'5<enter>**
Specify next point or [Undo]:	**<enter>**

Step 7. **Use the Multiline command to draw the interior walls for the PRESIDENT's office and OFFICE 3 (Figure 14–11).**

Prompt	Response
Command:	<enter>
Specify start point or [Justification/Scale/STyle]:	Type: **INT<enter>**
of	Click: **D1 (Figure 14–11)**
Specify next point or [Undo]:	Type: **PER<enter>**
to	Click: **D2**
Specify next point:	**<enter>**
Command:	**<enter>**
Specify start point or [Justification/Scale/STyle]:	Type: **INT<enter>**
of	Click: **D3 (Figure 14–11)**
Specify next point:	Type: **PER<enter>**
to	Click: **D4**
Specify next point or [Undo]:	**<enter>**

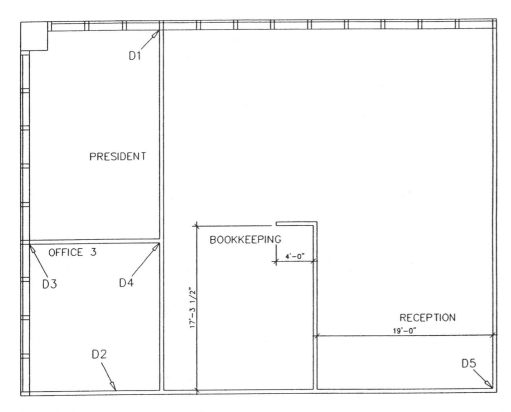

FIGURE 14–11
Draw Interior Walls

Drawing Floor Plans with AutoCAD

Multiline also allows you to create a multiline style that has an Endcap on the end of a line that does not touch another line. This style, TWO-CAP, has already been defined in the drawing and is ready for you to use.

Step 8. **Use the Multiline command and Osnap-From to draw the wall that separates the reception and bookkeeping areas (Figure 14–11).**

Prompt	Response
Command:	<enter>
Current settings: Justification = Bottom, Scale = 1.00, Style = TWO	
Specify start point or [Justification/ Scale/STyle]:	Type: **ST<enter>** (to make the TWO-CAP style current)
Enter mline style name or [?]:	Type: **TWO-CAP-END<enter>**
Specify start point or [Justification/ Scale/STyle]:	Type: **FRO<enter>**
Base point:	Type: **END<enter>**
of	Click: **D5 (Figure 14–11)**
<Offset>:	Type: **@19′5<180<enter>**
Specify next point:	With ORTHO ON **move your mouse up** and Type: **17′3-1/2<enter>**
Specify next point or [Undo]:	**Move your mouse to the left** and Type: **4′<enter>**
Specify next point or [Close/Undo]:	**<enter>**

The Edit Multiline command allows you to change the intersections of multilines in a variety of ways. Just Click: the change you want and then Click: the two multilines whose intersection you want to change.

Step 9. **Use Multiline Edit to trim the intersections of the multilines forming the interior walls to an Open Tee (Figure 14–11).**

Prompt	Response
Command:	Type: **MLEDIT<enter>**
The Multiline Edit Tools dialog box appears:	Click: **Open Tee** (the middle icon in the second column)
	Click: **OK**
Select first mline:	Click: **the vertical wall separating the reception and bookkeeping areas**
Select second mline:	Click: **the south horizontal exterior wall**
Select first mline(or Undo):	Click: **the interior vertical wall of OFFICE 3**
Select second mline:	Click: **the south horizontal exterior wall**
Select first mline (or Undo):	Click: **the interior horizontal wall of the PRESIDENT's office**
Select second mline	Click: **the interior vertical wall of the PRESIDENT's office**
Select first mline (or Undo):	**<enter>**

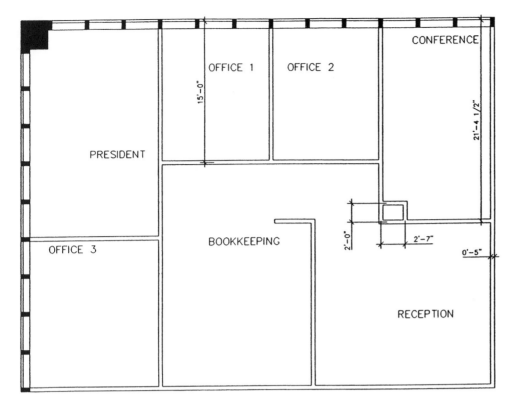

FIGURE 14–12
Draw Remaining Interior Walls

Step 10.   Use Multiline with the correct Multiline Style current to finish drawing the interior walls of the tenant space. Use the dimensions shown in Figure 14–12. Remember that you can use the Modify commands (Extend, Trim, Edit Multiline, and so on) to fix the multilines. You will have to explode multilines before you can use Trim and Extend.

Step 11.   The doors to be inserted are shown in Figure 14–13. Use the dimensions shown in Figure 14–14 to draw the door openings. The 3′4″ opening is for the single door block (DOOR), and the 6′4″ opening is for the double door block (DOORD)

Use the Line command and Osnap-From (Type: FRO<enter>) to draw the first door opening line, and then use Offset to draw the second door opening line.

Explode the multilines, and use the Trim command to complete the openings.

Step 12.   Set Layer A-DOOR current. Use the Insert command to insert the block named DOOR into OFFICE 2 (Figure 14–15).

FIGURE 14–13
The Two Doors Used in This
Exercise

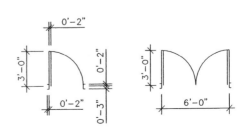

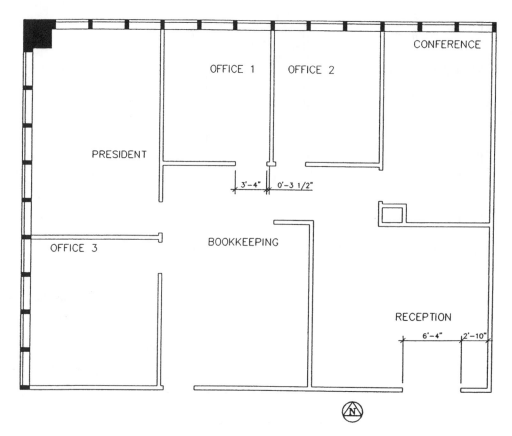

FIGURE 14–14
Make Door Openings

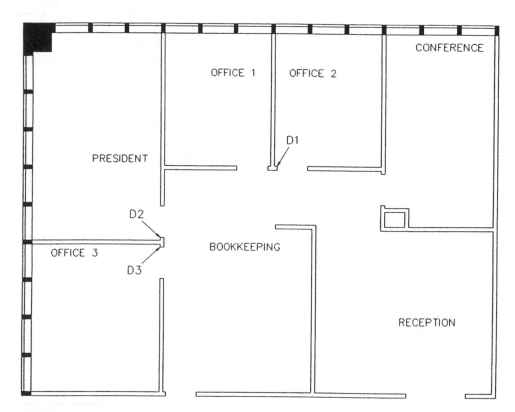

FIGURE 14–15
Insert the DOOR Block

Prompt	Response
Command:	Type: **I<enter>**
The Insert dialog box appears:	Click: **on DOOR in the Name: list box.** (Make sure a check appears in the Insertion Point—Specify On-screen box.)
	Click: **OK**
Specify insertion point or [Scale/X/Y/Z/ Rotate/PScale/PX/PY/PZ/PRotate]:	Type: **INT<enter>**
of	Click: **D1 (Figure 14–15)**

Step 13. **Use the Insert command to insert the block named DOOR into the PRESIDENT's office.**

Prompt	Response
Command:	**<enter>**
The Insert dialog box appears:	Click: **on DOOR in the Name: list box.** (Make sure a check appears in the Insertion Point—Specify On-screen box.)
	Type: **90** (in the Rotation Angle: input box)
	Click: **OK**
Specify insertion point or [Scale/X/Y/Z/ Rotate/PScale/PX/PY/PZ/PRotate]:	Type: **INT<enter>**
of	Click: **D2 (Figure 14–15)**

Step 14. **Use the Insert command and a negative X scale factor (to insert a mirror image of the block), and rotate the block to insert the DOOR into OFFICE 3 (Figure 14–15).**

Prompt	Response
Command:	**<enter>**
The Insert dialog box appears:	Click: **on DOOR in the Name: list box**
	Type: **-1** (in the X scale input box)
	Type: **90** (in the Rotation Angle: input box)
	Click: **OK**
Specify insertion point or [Scale/X/Y/Z/ Rotate/PScale/PX/PY/PZ/PRotate]:	Type: **INT<enter>**
of	Click: **D3 (Figure 14–15)**

Step 15. **On Your Own:**

1. **Use the Insert-Block… command to complete the insertion of all doors in the tenant space.**

2. **Set Layer A-flor-wdwk current. Draw two lines to show the cabinets in the conference room. The upper cabinets are 12″ deep.**

3. **Set Layer A-flor-iden current. Use Dtext, height 9″, to type the identifying name in each room. Use the approximate locations shown in Figure 14–16.**

4. Click: **Layout1 at the bottom of your screen, and complete the title block using the Dtext command. Title the drawing FLOOR PLAN NO. 3**

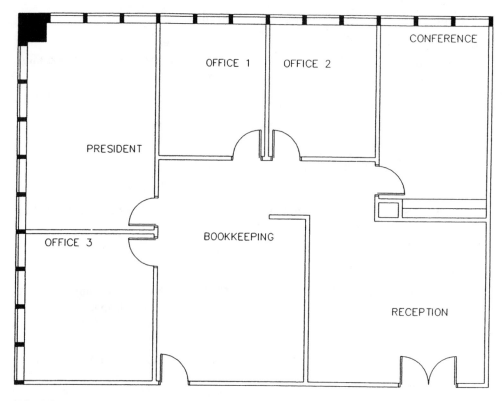

FIGURE 14–16
Exercise 14–3 Complete

5. Use the SAVEAS command to save your drawing as EX14-3(your initials) on a floppy disk and again on the hard drive of your computer.

6. Plot or print your drawing at a scale of 1=1, landscape, limits, center the plot, on an 11″ x 8½″ sheet.

EXERCISES

EXERCISE 14–1. Complete Exercise 14–1 using steps 1 through 8 described in this chapter.
EXERCISE 14–2. Complete Exercise 14–2 using steps 1 through 8 described in this chapter.
EXERCISE 14–3. Complete Exercise 14–3 using steps 1 through 8 described in this chapter.
EXERCISE 14–4. Complete Exercise 14–4 using the specifications described in Figure 14–17.
Use drawing EX14-4 supplied on the disk that came with your book.
Blocks have been defined for the windows, inside doors, and outside doors; and the current multiline style allows you to draw the outside walls using the dimensions shown in Figure 14–17.
Label spaces with 6″-high letters.
After the drawing is complete, Click: **Layout1,** and complete the title block. Title the drawing SMALL OFFICE PLAN.

REVIEW QUESTIONS

Circle the best answer.
1. The lines in the preliminary sketch (Figure 14–1) show the inside of the outside walls.
   a. True
   b. False
2. The lines in the preliminary sketch show the centers of the inside walls.
   a. True
   b. False

FIGURE 14–17
Specifications for Exercise 14–4

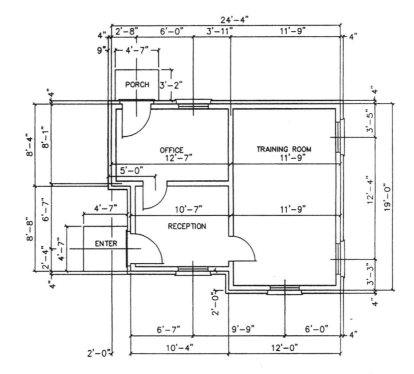

3. The walls shown in the first two exercises are approximately
   a. 2″ thick
   b. 5″ thick
   c. 8″ thick
   d. 10″ thick
   e. 12″ thick
4. The scale for Exercise 14–1 is
   a. $1/16″=1′$
   b. $1/8″=1′$
   c. FULL
   d. $1/2″=1′$
   e. No scale was used.
5. The Multiline command allows you to draw with only the middle line justification.
   a. True
   b. False
6. On a full-scale drawing that has been plotted at a scale of 1/8″=1′, a 3′ door on the plotted drawing will actually measure
   a. 3″
   b. $3/8″$
   c. $3/4″$
   d. $1\frac{1}{2}″$
   e. It is impossible to tell from the information given.
7. On a full-scale drawing that has been plotted at a scale of $1/8″=1′$, a 16′ room width on the plotted drawing will actually measure
   a. 3″
   b. 16″
   c. 2″
   d. 4″
   e. $2\frac{1}{2}″$
8. What is the maximum number of lines that can be drawn at the same time with the Multiline command?
   a. 2
   b. 3
   c. 10
   d. 16
   e. 18

9. The floor plan can be best described as an orthographic _____ view.
   a. Front
   b. Top
   c. Right-side
   d. Left-side
   e. Section
10. You must first explode a multiline before the Multiline Edit command can be used.
   a. True
   b. False

15

Sketching Dimensions

OBJECTIVES

After completing this chapter, you will be able to:

- Correctly sketch dimension lines, extension lines, center lines, architectural ticks, arrowheads, and leaders.
- Correctly dimension rectangles, angles, circles, and arcs.
- Correctly dimension doors, windows, and interior and exterior walls.
- Use the unidirectional and aligned systems for dimensioning.
- Correctly select and place dimensions.
- Use current symbols for diameter and radius.

INTRODUCTION

Most architectural drawings are used for assembling an architectural detail or constructing a building. The person who builds or assembles the product must know not only the shape of the object but also its exact size, the location of features, and the materials and finishes to be used.

Although the CADD operator should know basic construction techniques in order to issue correct instructions to contractors through dimensions and notes, most of the problems of basic dimensioning are covered by a few simple rules. You will have little difficulty if you follow these rules carefully and apply them knowing that someone must actually build the object from your drawing or sketch.

STANDARD DIMENSIONING PRACTICES

Each part of the dimensioning process is governed by specific rules. These parts include:

Lines, symbols, and abbreviations
Size and location dimensions
Drawing to scale
Placement of dimensions
Aligned and unidirectional systems of dimensioning
Dimensioning features
Notes
Tabular dimensioning

Lines, Symbols, and Abbreviations

The four types of lines used in dimensioning are the extension line, dimension line, center line, and the leader. All four lines are drawn thin and dark.

The symbols for diameter and radius are also described in this chapter.

FIGURE 15–1
Extension and Dimension Lines
and Their Spacing

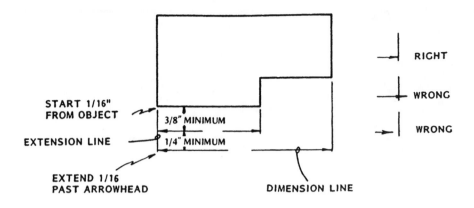

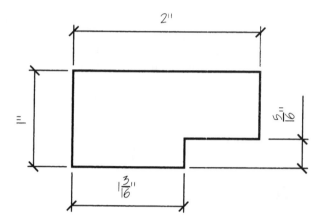

Extension Line

The *extension line* (Figure 15–1) starts about $\frac{1}{16}''$ away from the object and extends to about $\frac{1}{16}''$ beyond the arrowhead. Leave a gap where extension lines cross other extension lines or dimension lines.

Dimension Line

The *dimension line* (Figure 15–1) has an arrowhead or other symbol such as a slash called a *tick mark* at each end to show where the measurement is made. The arrowhead just touches the extension line. The arrowhead is approximately three times as long as it is wide. The wings of the arrowhead are straight and very close to the shaft. A gap is often left near the middle for the dimension text. In architectural drawings the dimension line is often unbroken, and the text is placed above a horizontal dimension or to the left of a vertical one. The arrowhead may also be a different shape, such as the one shown in Figure 15–3. The dimension line may also extend beyond the extension line a short distance if the architect chooses. On small drawings such as the ones in this chapter, dimension lines are spaced $\frac{1}{2}''$ from the object and $\frac{3}{8}''$ apart. The minimums of $\frac{3}{8}''$ and $\frac{1}{4}''$ shown in Figure 15–1 are used where space is very limited. On larger drawings the spacing can be greater, but the first dimension is always placed farther from the object lines of the drawing than the spacing between dimensions.

Center Line

Center lines (Figure 15–2) are used to show the centers of symmetrical features and are used in place of extension lines for locating holes and other round features. End center lines about $\frac{1}{16}''$ to $\frac{1}{8}''$ outside the hole or feature.

Leader

A *leader* (Figure 15–3) is a thin solid line that leads from a note or dimension and ends with an arrowhead touching the part.

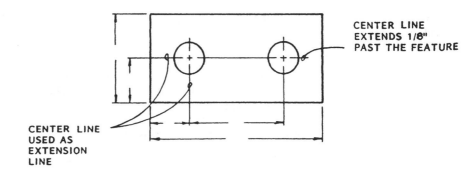

FIGURE 15–2
Center Lines

CENTER LINE
EXTENDS 1/8"
PAST THE FEATURE

CENTER LINE
USED AS
EXTENSION
LINE

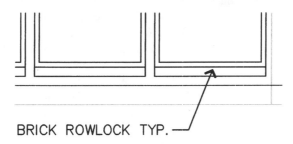

FIGURE 15–3
Leaders

BRICK ROWLOCK TYP.

Leaders are often straight, inclined lines (never vertical or horizontal) that are usually drawn at 45°, 60°, or 30° angles but may be drawn at any convenient angle. A short horizontal shoulder may be extended out from midheight of the lettering of the note accompanying the leader. Leaders may extend from either the center of the beginning line or the ending line of the note, but *not* from the inside lines. Leaders may also be curved to add character to the drawing if the architect chooses.

Symbols and Abbreviations

The following standard symbols and abbreviations are used in this chapter:

Diameter: ∅
Radius: **R**
Places: **PL** (as in the "dimension occurs in 4 places")
Typical: **TYP** (as in "this thickness is the same or typical throughout the part")

Size and Location Dimensions

There are two types of dimensions: those that show the size of a feature and those that show the location of the feature (Figure 15–4).

FIGURE 15–4
Size and Location Dimensions

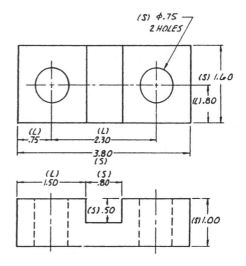

Drawing to a Scale

Drawings and sketches are often made to a scale. This scale is shown on the drawing, usually in the title block. If a minor change is to be made in one of the dimensions, a wavy line may be placed under the dimension to show that the dimension is not to scale. Regardless of the scale used, dimensions are always those of the feature to be built, not the size of that feature on the drawing.

Placement of Dimensions

Examples of correct and incorrect placement of dimension lines are shown in Figure 15–5. The shortest dimensions are closest to the object outline.

Dimension lines should not cross extension lines, which results from placing the shorter dimensions outside. (This is sometimes unavoidable, however.) Be aware that it is acceptable for extension lines to cross each other.

A dimension line should never coincide with or form a continuation of any line of the drawing.

Avoid crossing dimension lines with other dimension lines whenever possible.

In general, avoid dimensioning to hidden lines (Figure 15–6). Place dimensions where the feature is seen as a solid line. (A section drawing may be necessary.)

If possible, place dimensions in close relationship to the feature shown (Figure 15–7). Place as many of the dimensions as possible between the views and on the view that shows the shape of the feature best (Figure 15–8).

If the drawing contains fractional dimensions that run into each other, stagger the dimensions to place one above the other so that both are easily read.

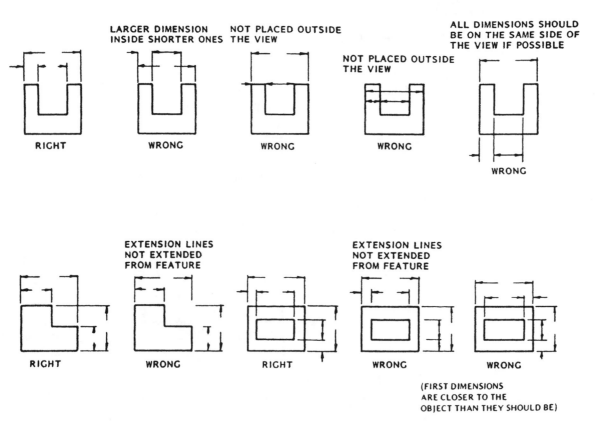

FIGURE 15–5
Correct and Incorrect Placement of Dimensions

FIGURE 15–6
Avoid Dimensioning to Hidden Lines

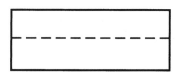

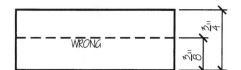

WRONG

RIGHT

FIGURE 15–7
Place Dimensions Close to the Feature

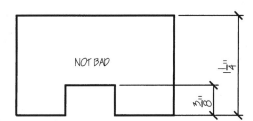

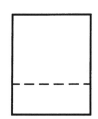

NOT BAD

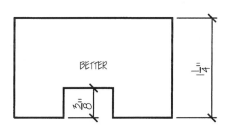

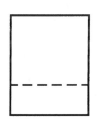

BETTER

FIGURE 15–8
Place Dimensions between Views Where Possible

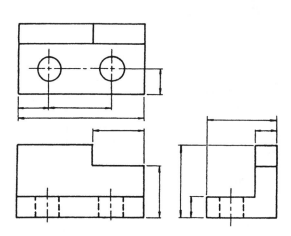

Unidirectional and Aligned Systems of Dimensioning

Both the aligned and the unidirectional systems of dimensioning are widely used. Each system has advantages and disadvantages.

Unidirectional System

In the unidirectional system (Figure 15–9) the dimensions are placed to read from the bottom of the drawing, and fraction bars (if any) are parallel with the bottom of the drawing.

Aligned System

In the aligned system of dimensioning (Figure 15–10) the dimensions are placed parallel to the lines of the drawing, and they are read from the bottom or right side of the drawing.

Dimensions and notes with leaders are aligned with the bottom of the drawing (placed in a horizontal position) in both systems.

Dimensioning Features

Angles

Angles are dimensioned in degrees (Figure 15–11). All the methods of dimensioning angles shown in the figure are acceptable. You will find occasion to use all of them if you dimension many angles.

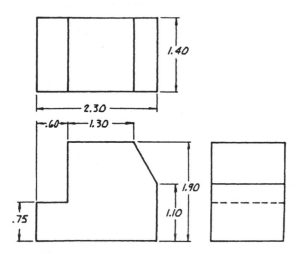

FIGURE 15–9
Unidirectional System of Dimensioning

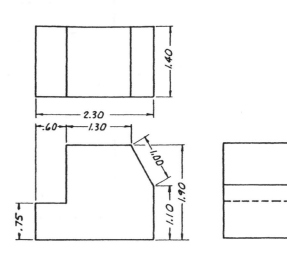

FIGURE 15–10
Aligned System of Dimensioning

FIGURE 15–11
Dimensioning Angles

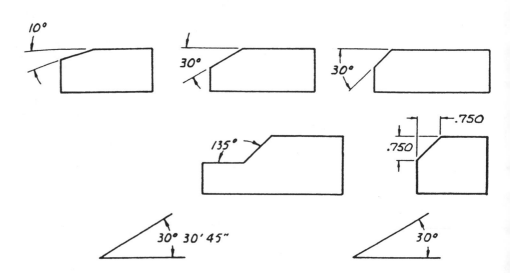

FIGURE 15–12
Dimensioning Holes and Cylinders

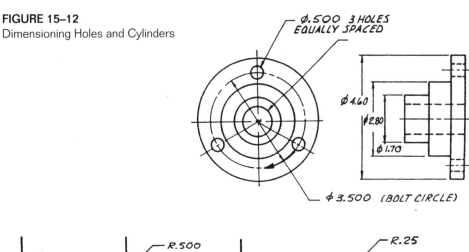

FIGURE 15–13
Dimensioning Radii

Circles

There are two common types of circular features: holes and cylinders (Figure 15–12). Holes are dimensioned on the view in which the hole is seen as a circle. Cylinders are dimensioned on the view where the cylinder is seen as a rectangle.

A circular center line (called a *bolt circle*) is used to locate holes from the center of a cylindrical piece.

Radius

A radius is dimensioned in the view in which its true shape is seen (Figure 15–13). The abbreviation R is used for radius. If a large radius cannot be located because of space, a false center can be located.

Notes

Two types of notes are shown on drawings: general and specific. General notes pertain to the whole drawing, and specific notes apply to one feature on the drawing. These notes are usually located on the drawing in a specific place that is preprinted with the drawing format. If these is no specific place for notes, they can be placed anywhere on the field of the drawing where they will be uncrowded and can be read easily.

Tabular Dimensioning

Some drawings can be used for several sizes of an object that have the same appearance. Figure 15–14 is an example of tabular dimensioning.

Dimensioning to Windows, Doors, and Exterior and Interior Walls

The sizes of windows and doors are not shown on the floor plan. Instead, the windows are identified with a letter inside a polygon, and the doors are identified with a number inside a circle. The specifications for both windows and doors are shown on a window and door *schedule* (a table) elsewhere in the set of plans. Windows and doors are located, however, by showing the measurement from a wall to the center of the window or door. Measurements are often shown from the outside of an exterior wall to the center of an inside wall, from the outside to outside of exterior walls, and from the center of an inside wall to the

FIGURE 15–14
Tabular Dimensioning

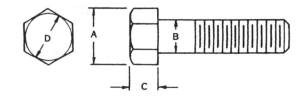

SIZE	A	B	C	D
1/2	0.866	0.515	11/32	3/4
3/4	1.299	0.768	1/2	1-1/8
1	1.732	1.022	43/64	1-1/2
1 1/4	2.165	1.277	27/32	1-7/8

FIGURE 15–15
Dimensioning Walls and Windows

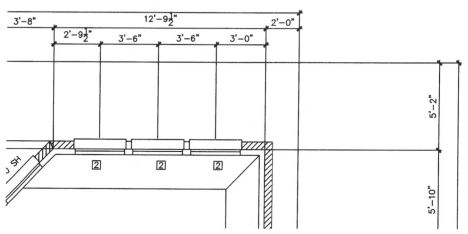

center of another inside wall. There are exceptions to these guidelines, however, which you will see in the dimensioning examples. These variations are a result of construction methods and the architect's individual preference. Figures 15–15 through 15–19 show the placement of these dimensions.

EXERCISES

EXERCISE 15–1.   Remove the sheet labeled EXERCISE 15–1 from your book and sketch the dimensions on it. Refer to Figures 16–2 and 16–5 if necessary to determine what dimensions are necessary and where they should be placed.

> Use three-place decimal dimensions.
> Leave $\frac{1}{2}''$ between the drawing and the first dimension.
> Leave $\frac{3}{8}''$ between dimension lines.
> Use good line weights and be consistent with letter size, arrowheads, and extension line offset from the part, and extension line extension past the arrowhead.

Complete the title block with your best lettering, and name the drawing DIMENSIONING SKETCH 1.

EXERCISE 15–2.   Remove the sheet labeled EXERCISE 15–2 from your book. Measure the drawing using a scale of $\frac{3}{16}''=1'-0''$, and place dimensions showing the following:

> The measurement from the outside of outside walls to the center of inside walls.
> The measurement from the center of inside walls to the center of inside walls.
> Measurements to the centers of all windows and doors.
> Refer to Figure 15–16 for ideas about how to dimension this floor plan.

FIGURE 15–16
Dimensioning Example

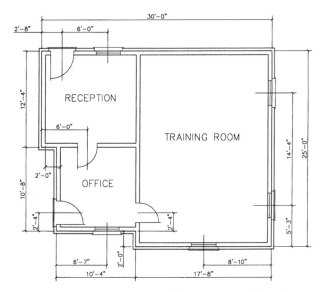

Match the existing method of dimensioning using the same spacing, line weight, and letter height as shown on the exercise sheet.

Leave a greater space between the drawing and the first line of dimensions than between the first and second line of dimensions.

Use good line weights and be consistent with letter size, ticks, and extension line offset from the part, and extension line extension past the tick mark.

Complete the title block with your best lettering, and name the drawing FLOOR PLAN 1.

EXERCISE 15–3.   Remove the sheet labeled EXERCISE 15–3 from your book. Measure the drawing using half scale ($\frac{1}{2}''=1''$), and place dimensions as shown in Figure 15–17.

Match the existing method of dimensioning using the same spacing, line weight, and letter height as shown on the exercise sheet.

Leave a greater space between the drawing and the first line of dimensions than between the first and second line of dimensions.

Use good line weights and be consistent with letter size, ticks, and extension line offset from the part, and extension line extension past the tick mark.

Complete the title block with your best lettering, and name the drawing DOOR JAMB DETAIL.

EXERCISE 15–4.   Remove the sheet labeled EXERCISE 15–4 from your book. Measure the drawing using a scale of $\frac{1}{4}''=1'\text{-}0''$, and place dimensions showing the following:

FIGURE 15–17
Dimensioning Example

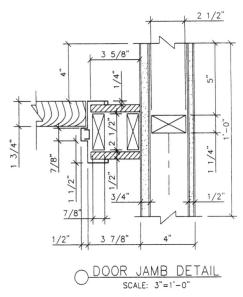

DOOR JAMB DETAIL
SCALE: 3"=1'-0"

The measurement from the outside of outside walls to the outside of other outside walls.

Measurements to the centers of all windows and doors.

Match the method of dimensioning from Exercise 15–2 using the same spacing, line weight, and letter height as shown in that exercise.

Leave a greater space between the drawing and the first line of dimensions than between the first and second line of dimensions.

Use good line weights and be consistent with letter size, ticks, and extension line offset from the part, and extension line extension past the tick mark.

Complete the title block with your best lettering, and name the drawing FLOOR PLAN 2.

EXERCISE 15–5. Remove the sheet labeled EXERCISE 15–5 from your book. Measure the drawing using a scale of $\frac{1}{8}''$ 1'-0'', and place dimensions showing the following:

The measurement from the outside of outside walls to the center of inside walls.

The measurement from the center of inside walls to the center of inside walls.

Measurements to the centers of all windows and doors.

Refer to Figure 15–15, 15–18, 15–19, and 15–20 for ideas about how to dimension this floor plan.

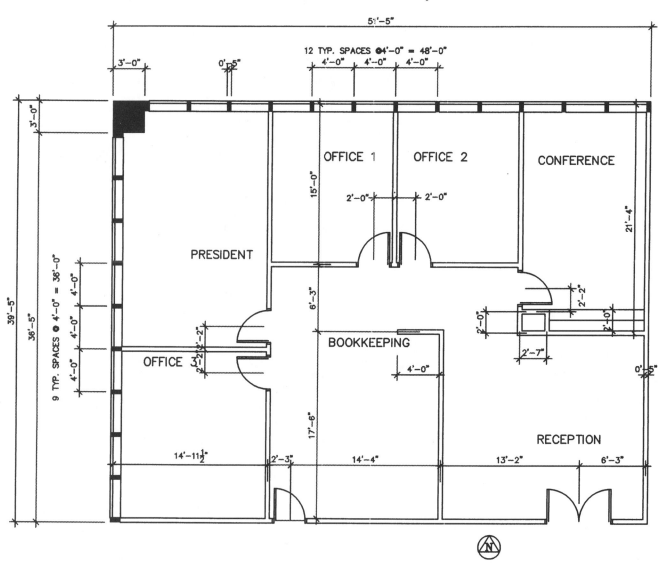

FIGURE 15–18
Dimensioning Example

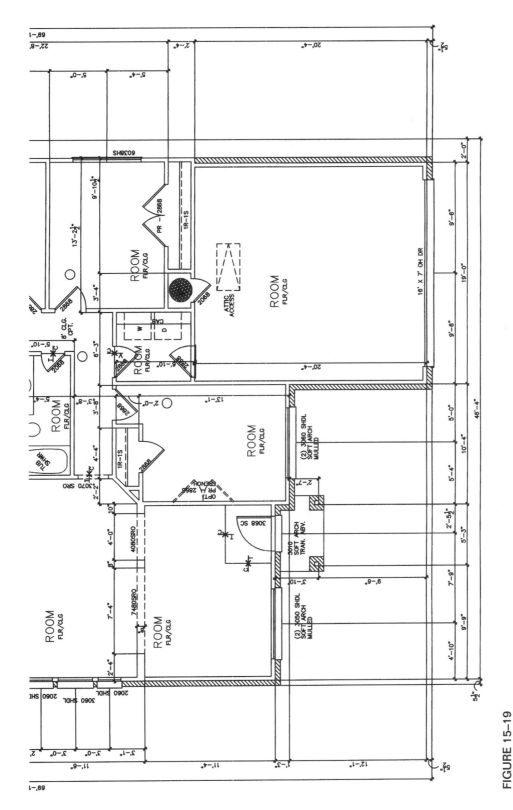

FIGURE 15–19
Dimensioning Example (Courtesy J M Designs Architects, Gary Beavers)

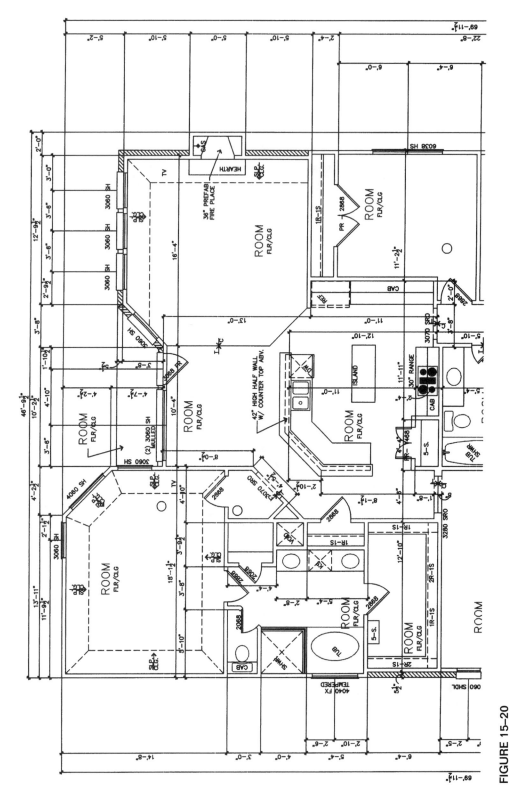

FIGURE 15–20
Dimensioning Example (Courtesy J M Designs Architects, Gary Beavers)

Match the method of dimensioning Exercise 15–2 using the same spacing, line weight, and letter height as shown in that exercise.

Leave a greater space between the drawing and the first line of dimensions than between the first and second line of dimensions.

Use good line weights and be consistent with letter size, ticks, and extension line offset from the part and extension line extension past the tick mark.

Complete the title block with your best lettering, and name the drawing FLOOR PLAN 3.

REVIEW QUESTIONS

Circle the best answer.

1. How much space should be left between the dimension line arrowhead and the extension line to which it points?
   a. $\frac{1}{2}''$
   b. $\frac{3}{8}''$
   c. $\frac{1}{32}''$
   d. $\frac{1}{16}''$
   e. None

2. How much space should be left between the object and the first dimension line on the small drawings in the exercises in this chapter?
   a. $\frac{1}{4}''$
   b. $\frac{3}{8}''$
   c. $\frac{1}{2}''$
   d. $\frac{3}{4}''$
   e. Any spacing is OK.

3. Is it permissible for dimension lines to cross extension lines or other dimension lines?
   a. Yes in all cases
   b. Never
   c. Avoid if possible
   d. No, leave off the crossing dimension
   e. This will never happen if the dimensioning is carefully planned.

4. The dimension line can extend beyond the extension line if the architect chooses to select that method of dimensioning.
   a. True
   b. False

5. If more than one dimension containing a fraction is given on one side of a view, what should be done to make the fractions more legible?
   a. Make the fractions twice the normal size.
   b. Stagger the numbers containing the fractions.
   c. Line up the numbers containing the fractions.
   d. Make the fractions half the normal size.
   e. None of the above

6. Cylindrical objects are dimensioned in the rectangular view with
   a. Extension lines and dimension lines
   b. A leader and a note
   c. Dimension lines only
   d. A leader and a center line
   e. Cylindrical objects are not dimensioned in the rectangular view.

7. Which of these angles would be best for drawing a leader?
   a. 0°
   b. 45°
   c. 90°
   d. 180°
   e. All are equally good.

8. Small holes are dimensioned in the circular view with
   a. Extension lines and dimension lines
   b. A leader and a note
   c. Dimension lines only
   d. A leader and a center line
   e. Holes are not dimensioned in the circular view.
9. Floor plans do not show the sizes of windows and doors.
   a. True
   b. False
10. Dimensions should be made from the outside of the outside wall to the center of the window.
    a. True
    b. False

Dimensioning with AutoCAD

OBJECTIVES

After completing this chapter, you will be able to

☐ Use the dimensioning commands to dimension full-scale drawings of architectural floor plans and architectural details
☐ Correctly answer questions regarding dimensioning commands.

DIMENSIONING

Up to this point you have made several different types of drawings. For construction drawings to be used to construct a building, dimensions must be added. Adding dimensions to a drawing manually is a very time consuming process, but AutoCAD makes adding dimensions much easier. In addition, the AutoCAD dimensioning process verifies the accuracy of the drawing. The associative dimensioning feature of AutoCAD also allows a part size to be changed or corrected, automatically changing the dimension with it.

In this chapter you will dimension some drawings full size, so the dimensioning procedure is relatively simple. Pay particular attention to where you place the dimension lines in relation to the drawing and other dimension lines. Although AutoCAD dimensioning has many settings and other features, this chapter does not cover those. This chapter will give you a good idea of how dimensioning is done when all the settings have been made.

EXERCISE 16–1:
Dimensioning a Mechanical Part

Step 1. To begin Exercise 16–1, turn on the computer and start AutoCAD or AutoCAD LT.
Step 2. Open drawing EX16-1 supplied on the disk that came with your book.
Step 3. Use Zoom-All to view the entire drawing area.

Prompt	Response
Command:	Type: **Z <enter>**
Specify corner of window, enter a scale factor (nX or nXP),or[All/Center/ Dynamic/Extents/Previous/Scale/ Window] <real time>:	Type: **A<enter>**

Step 4. Use the Dimensioning Mode to draw center lines in the circle in the front view.
Be sure SNAP is ON and ORTHO is OFF before you start.

Note: The dimensioning prompts between versions of AutoCAD are slightly different. You may need to experiment with dimensioning commands a little if the prompts are not quite the same as shown in this chapter.

Prompt	Response
Command:	Type: **DIM<enter>**
Dim: Type: **CEN<enter>**	
Select arc or circle:	Pick: **any point on the circumference of the circle in the front view**

Step 5. Continue using the Dimensioning Mode to draw all horizontal dimensions.
Be sure SNAP is ON and ORTHO is OFF before you start.

Prompt	Response
Dim:	Type: **HOR<enter>**
Specify first extension line origin or <select object>:	Pick: **D1 (Figure 16–1)**
Specify second extension line origin:	Pick: **D2**
Specify dimension line location or [Mtext/Text/Angle]:	
Enter dimension text <1.500>:	Pick: **D3** (½″ from the top line of the part) **<enter>**
Dim:	**<enter>**
Specify first extension line origin or <select object>:	Pick: **D4 (Figure 16–1)**
Specify second extension line origin:	Pick: **D5**
Specify dimension line location or [Mtext/Text/Angle]:	
Enter dimension text <2.500>:	Pick: **D6** (⅜″ from the first dimension line) **<enter>**
Dim:	**<enter>**
Specify first extension line origin or <select object>:	Pick: **D7**
Specify second extension line origin:	Pick: **D8**
Specify dimension line location or [Mtext/Text/Angle]:	
Enter dimension text <3.500>:	Pick: **D9 <enter>**
Dim:	**<enter>**

FIGURE 16–1
Horizontal Dimensioning of Exercise 16–1

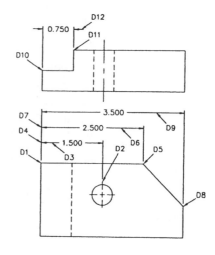

Prompt	Response
Specify first extension line origin or <select object>:	Pick: **D10**
Specify second extension line origin:	Pick: **D11**
Specify dimension line location or [Mtext/Text/Angle]:	
Enter dimension text <0.750>:	Pick: **D12<enter>**

Step 6. Use the Dimensioning Mode to draw all vertical dimensions.

Prompt	Response
Dim:	Type: **VER<enter>**
Specify first extension line origin or <select object>:	**<enter>**
Select object to dimension:	Pick: **D1 (Figure 16–2)**
Specify dimension line location or [Mtext/Text/Angle]:	
Enter dimension text <0.750>:	Pick: **D2** ($\frac{1}{2}''$ from the right side of the part) **<enter>**
Dim:	**<enter>**
Specify first extension line origin or <select object>:	Pick: **D3 (Figure 16–2)**
Specify second extension line origin:	Pick: **D4**
Specify dimension line location or [Mtext/Text/Angle]:	
Enter dimension text <1.000>:	Pick: **D5** ($\frac{3}{8}''$ from the first vertical dimension line) **<enter>**
Dim:	**<enter>**
Specify first extension line origin or <select object>:	Pick: **D6**
Specify second extension line origin:	Pick: **D7**
Specify dimension line location or [Mtext/Text/Angle]:	

FIGURE 16–2
Vertical Dimensioning of Exercise 16–1

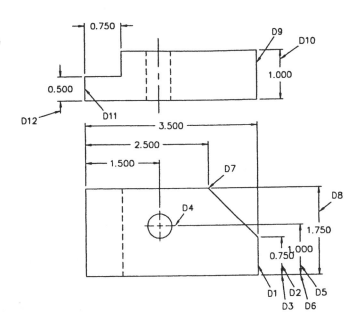

Enter dimension text <1.750>:	Pick: **D8 <enter>**
Dim:	**<enter>**
Specify first extension line origin or <select object>:	**<enter>**
Select object to dimension:	Pick: **D9**
Specify dimension line location or [Mtext/Text/Angle]:	
Enter dimension text <1.000>:	Pick: **D10 <enter>**
Dim:	**<enter>**
Specify first extension line origin or <select object>:	**<enter>**
Select object to dimension:	Pick: **D11**
Specify dimension line location or [Mtext/Text/Angle]:	
Enter dimension text <0.500>:	Pick: **D12 <enter>**

Note: You can use grips to move text as well as using Dimtedit. To do this: Press: **Esc twice** to exit from a command and the dimensioning mode. Also, turn SNAP, ORTHO, and OSNAP OFF. Click: **any point on the dimension**, and small blue squares will appear. Click: **the blue square on or near the text to be moved.** The square will turn red, making it active. Move the text to where you want it to be. Press: **Esc twice** to exit from grips. Turn SNAP, and ORTHO back ON and proceed to dimension the drawing.

Step 7. **Use the Dimtedit command from the Dim: prompt to move some vertical dimension text so it does not overlap.**

Prompt	Response
Dim:	Type: **TEDIT<enter>**
Select dimension:	Pick: **the 1.000 vertical dimension in the front view**
Specify new location for dimension text or [Left/Right/Center/Home/Angle]:	Pick: **a new position for the 1.000 text as shown in Figure 16–3**

Step 8. **Use the Dimensioning Mode to dimension the circle diameter.**

Prompt	Response
Dim:	Type: **DIA<enter>**
Select arc or circle:	Pick: **any point on the circumference of the circle in the front view**
Enter dimension text <0.500>:	**<enter>**
Specify dimension line location or [Mtext/Text/Angle]:	Pick: **a point so the diameter is shown in the approximate position shown in Figure 16–4**

Step 9. **Use the Tedit command from the Dim: prompt to move the diameter text off the object to a new location.**

FIGURE 16–3
Use Dimtedit to Move Text

FIGURE 16–4
Dimension the Diameter

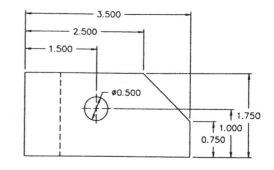

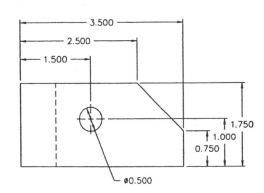

FIGURE 16–5
Move the Diameter Dimension

Prompt	Response
Dim:	Type: **TEDIT<enter>**
Select dimension:	Pick: **the 0.500 diameter dimension in the front view**
Specify new location for dimension text or[Left/Right/Center/Home/Angle]:	Pick: **a new position for the 0.500 diameter text as shown in Figure 16–5**

Step 10. Use the Dtext command to complete the title block as you did for previous exercises. Name the drawing DIMENSIONING.

Step 11. Use the SAVEAS command to save your drawing as EX16-1(your initials) on a floppy disk and again on the hard drive of your computer.

Step 12. Plot or print your drawing full size on an 11″ x 8½″ sheet.

EXERCISE 16–2:
Dimensioning Your First Floor Plan

Step 1. To begin Exercise 16–2, turn on the computer and start AutoCAD or AutoCAD LT.

Step 2. Open drawing EX16-2 supplied on the disk that came with your book.

Step 3. Use Zoom-All to view the entire drawing area.

Prompt	Response
Command:	Type: **Z <enter>**
Specify corner of window, enter a scale factor (nX or nXP),or[All/Center/ Dynamic/Extents/Previous/Scale/ Window] <real time>:	Type: **A<enter>**

Important: Be sure SNAP is ON when you pick points.

Step 4. Use the Dimensioning Mode to draw all horizontal dimensions on the top of the floor plan.

Prompt	Response
Command:	Type: **DIM<enter>**
Dim:	Type: **HOR<enter>**
Specify first extension line origin or <select object>:	Pick: **D1 (Figure 16–6)**
Specify second extension line origin:	Pick: **D2**
Specify dimension line location or [Mtext/Text/Angle]:	
Enter dimension text <5′-6″>:	Pick: **D3** (two grid marks from the top line of the floor plan) **<enter>**

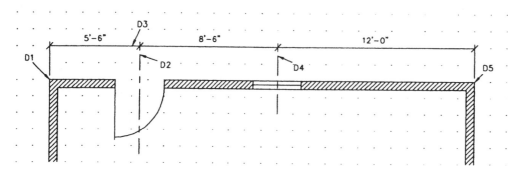

FIGURE 16–6
Dimension the Upper Part of the Floor Plan

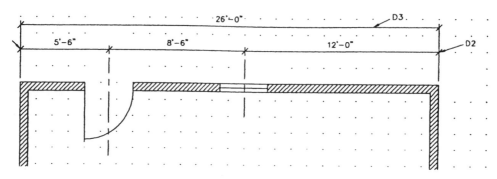

FIGURE 16–7
Show the Overall Dimension

Prompt	Response
Dim:	Type: **CON<enter>** (for continue dimension)
Specify a second extension line origin or [Undo/Select] <Select>:	Pick: **D4**
Dimension text = 8'-6"	**<enter>**
Dim:	**<enter>**
Specify a second extension line origin or [Undo/Select] <Select>:	Pick: **D5**
Dimension text = 12'-0"	**<enter>**
Dim:	Type: **HOR<enter>**
Specify first extension line origin or <select object>:	Pick: **D1 (Figure 16–7)**
Specify second extension line origin:	Pick: **D2**
Specify dimension line location or [Mtext/Text/Angle]:	
Enter dimension text 26'-0"	Pick: **D3** (1½ grid marks from the first dimension line) **<enter>**

Step 5.   On Your Own:
Draw the 11'-0" dimension at the bottom of the floor plan as shown in Figure 16–8.

Step 6.   Use the Dimensioning Mode to draw all vertical dimensions.

Prompt	Response
Dim:	Type: **VER<enter>**
Specify first extension line origin or <select object>:	Pick: **D1 (Figure 16–9)**

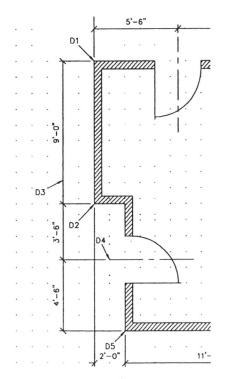

FIGURE 16–9
Vertical Dimensions on the Left Side

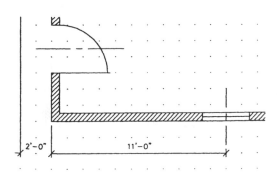

FIGURE 16–8
Draw Horizontal Dimensions on the
Lower Part of the Floor Plan

Specify second extension line origin:	Pick: **D2**
Specify dimension line location or [Mtext/Text/Angle]:	
Enter dimension text = 9'-0"	Pick: **D3<enter>**
Dim:	Type: **CON<enter>**
Specify a second extension line origin or [Undo/Select] <Select>:	Pick: **D4**
Dimension text = 3'-6"	**<enter>**
Dim:	**<enter>**
Specify a second extension line origin or [Undo/Select] <Select>:	Pick: **D5**
Dimension text = 4'-6"	**<enter>**
Dim:	**<enter>**

Step 7. **On Your Own:**
Draw dimensions on the right side of the floor plan as shown in Figure 16–10. Your final floor plan should appear as shown in Figure 16–11.

Step 8. Use the Dtext command to complete the title block as you did for previous exercises. Name the drawing FLOOR PLAN WITH DIMENSIONS.

Step 9. Use the SAVEAS command to save your drawing as EX16-2(your initials) on a floppy disk and again on the hard drive of your computer.

Step 10. Plot or print your drawing at a scale of 1 plotted inch = 48 drawing units (¼"=1') on an 11" x 8½" sheet. Use Landscape for the Drawing Orientation.

Dimensioning with AutoCAD

259

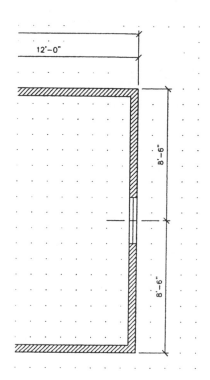

FIGURE 16–10
Vertical Dimensions on the Right Side

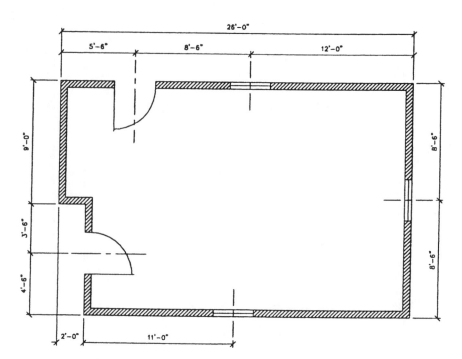

FIGURE 16–11
Exercise 16–2 Complete

EXERCISE 16–3:
Dimensioning the Second Floor Plan

Step 1. To begin Exercise 16–3, turn on the computer and start AutoCAD or AutoCAD LT.

Step 2. Open drawing EX16-3 supplied on the disk that came with your book.

Step 3. Use Zoom-All to view the entire drawing area.

Prompt	Response
Command:	Type: **Z <enter>**
Specify corner of window, enter a scale factor (nX or nXP),or[All/Center/ Dynamic/Extents/Previous/Scale/ Window] <real time>:	Type: **A<enter>**

Step 4. **On Your Own:**
Use Figure 16–12 as a reference and make all the dimensions as shown in that figure.
When you have completed the drawing, Click: the Floor Plan #2 Layout tab at the bottom of your screen.

Step 5. Use the Dtext command to complete the title block as you did for previous exercises. Name the drawing FLOOR PLAN No. 2.

Step 6. Use the SAVEAS command to save your drawing as EX16-3(your initials) on a floppy disk and again on the hard drive of your computer.

Step 7. Plot or print your drawing at a scale of 1 plotted inch = 1 drawing unit (1=1) on an 11″ x 8½″ sheet. Use Landscape for the Drawing Orientation, and Extents or Limits for the Plot Area. This layout has been scaled at ¼″=1′-0″.

FIGURE 16-12
Dimensions for Exercise 16-3

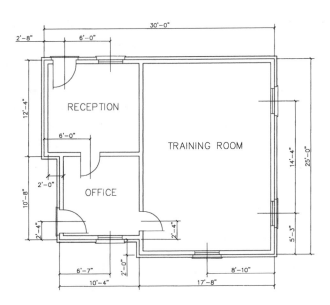

EXERCISE 16-4:
Dimensioning the Door Jamb Detail

Step 1. To begin Exercise 16-4, turn on the computer and start AutoCAD or AutoCAD LT.

Step 2. Open drawing EX16-4 supplied on the disk that came with your book.

Step 3. Use Zoom-All to view the entire drawing area.

Prompt	Response
Command:	Type: **Z** <enter>
Specify corner of window, enter a scale factor (nX or nXP),or[All/Center/ Dynamic/Extents/Previous/Scale/ Window] <real time>:	Type: **A**<enter>

Step 4. **On Your Own:**
Use Figure 16-13 as a reference and make all the dimensions as shown in that figure.
When you have completed the drawing, Click: **the Door Jamb Detail Layout tab at the bottom of your screen.**

FIGURE 16-13
Dimensions for Exercise 16-4

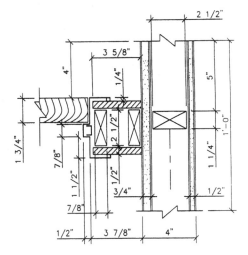

Step 5. Use the Dtext command to complete the title block as you did for previous exercises. Name the drawing DOOR JAMB DETAIL.

Step 6. Use the SAVEAS command to save your drawing as EX16-4(your initials) on a floppy disk and again on the hard drive of your computer.

Step 7. Plot or print your drawing at a scale of 1 plotted inch = 1 drawing unit (1=1) on an 11″ x 8½″ sheet. Use Landscape for the Drawing Orientation, and Extents or Limits for the Plot Area. This layout has been scaled at 1″=1′-0″.

EXERCISE 16–5:
Dimensioning the Third Floor Plan

Step 1. To begin Exercise 16–5, turn on the computer and start AutoCAD or AutoCAD LT.

Step 2. Open drawing EX16-5 supplied on the disk that came with your book.

Step 3. Use Zoom-All to view the entire drawing area.

Prompt	Response
Command:	Type: **Z <enter>**
Specify corner of window, enter a scale factor (nX or nXP),or[All/Center/ Dynamic/Extents/Previous/Scale/	
Window] <real time>:	Type: **A<enter>**

Step 4. **On Your Own:**
Use Figure 16–14 as a reference and make all the dimensions as shown in that figure.

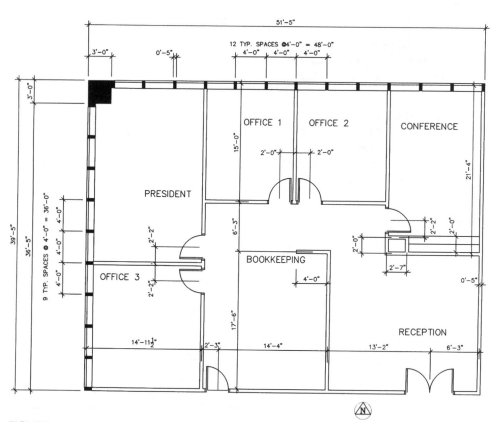

FIGURE 16–14

Dimensions for Exercise 16–5

When you have completed the drawing, Click: the Floor Plan 3# Layout tab at the bottom of your screen.

Step 5.   Use the Dtext command to complete the title block as you did for previous exercises. Name the drawing FLOOR PLAN No. 3.

Step 6.   Use the SAVEAS command to save your drawing as EX16-5(your initials) on a floppy disk and again on the hard drive of your computer.

Step 7.   Plot or print your drawing at a scale of 1 plotted inch = 1 drawing unit (1=1) on an 11″ x 8½″ sheet. Use Landscape for the Drawing Orientation, and Extents or Limits for the Plot Area. This layout has been scaled at ¼″=1′-0″.

EXERCISES

EXERCISE 16–1.   Complete Exercise 16–1 using steps 1 through 12 described in this chapter.
EXERCISE 16–2.   Complete Exercise 16–2 using steps 1 through 10 described in this chapter.
EXERCISE 16–3.   Complete Exercise 16–3 using steps 1 through 7 described in this chapter.
EXERCISE 16–4.   Complete Exercise 16–4 using steps 1 through 7 described in this chapter.
EXERCISE 16–5.   Complete Exercise 16–5 using steps 1 through 7 described in this chapter.

REVIEW QUESTIONS

1. What three letters must be typed to draw a horizontal dimension from the Dim: prompt?

_____

2. What three letters must be typed to draw a vertical dimension from the Dim: prompt?

_____

3. In what position does the CONTINUE dimensioning command place dimensions?

_____

4. What three letters must be typed from the Dim: prompt to draw a diameter dimension for a circle?

_____

5. For what purpose was the Tedit command used in this chapter?

_____

17 Sketching Elevations

OBJECTIVES

After completing this chapter, you will be able to:

☐ Correctly sketch elevations to scale from floor plans and other specifications.

INTRODUCTION

Elevation drawings are used to show the buyer, lender, and city officials how the building will look from the front, rear, and right and left sides when it is completed. These are two-dimensional drawings that do not show depth, as found in perspective drawings. Elevations show exterior details such as:

the style and sizes of windows and doors
the type of siding or brick
gutters
roof style and pitch
porches and decks
chimneys
molded concrete features
finished floor level
finished ceiling level
wood trim

Steps in Sketching the Front Elevation

All elevations must show all features in the same location and the same size as they appear on the floor plan. Therefore, the first step in drawing the elevation is to locate the floor plan and any other specifications that show sizes and shapes of windows, doors, roofs, and any other features that are needed to show the complete exterior details of the building.

Step 1. **Collect the information needed to complete the drawing.**
Figure 17–1 is the floor plan that shows the location of all windows, doors, and other features. Figure 17–2 is a scaled drawing showing the front elevation of a house similar to the one you will be drawing. All windows and doors, and the roof, chimney, and brick quoins are the same as on your drawing. The location of doors and windows and the chimney has been changed, so you will have to make sure that you locate features as shown on the floor plan.

Step 2. **Sketch the outside limits of the elevation as shown in Figure 17–3.** Also show center lines to locate windows and doors.

Step 3. **Sketch the the roof as shown in Figure 17–4.** Notice the numbers shown above the diagonal lines of the roof (Figure 17–2). These represent run and rise dimensions. Run is the horizontal dimension (in this case, 12), and rise is the vertical dimension (6). This means that for each 12 feet in the horizontal direction the roof will rise 6 feet. Be sure your run/rise is 12/6.

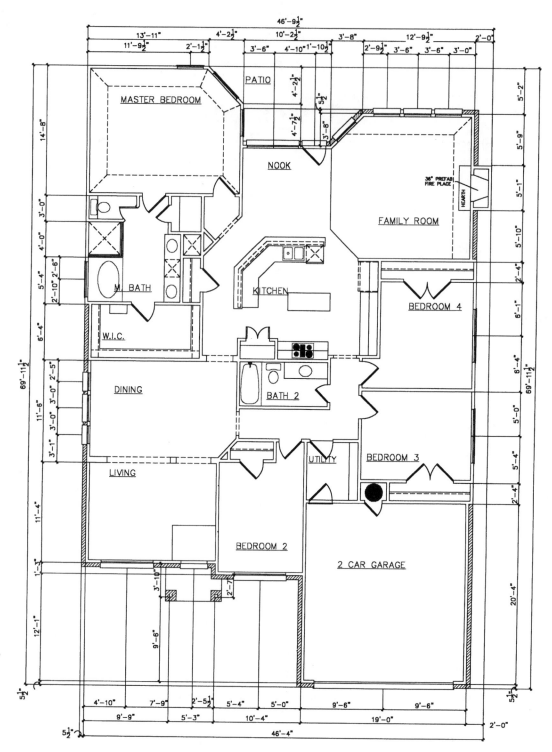

FIGURE 17–1
Floor Plan
(Courtesy J M Designs Architects, Gary Beavers)

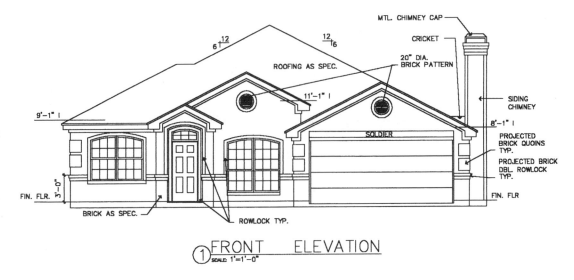

FIGURE 17–2
Front Elevation
(Courtesy J M Designs Architects, Gary Beavers)

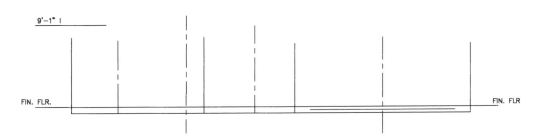

FIGURE 17–3
Sketch Outside Dimensions

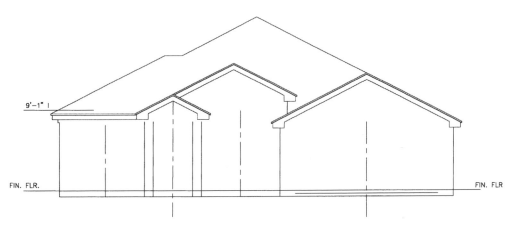

FIGURE 17–4
Sketch Roof

Step 4. **Locate windows and doors and sketch them in place as shown in Figure 17–5, and add details under the eves of the roof.** Dimensions from the floor plan must be used to place windows and doors in their correct locations.

Step 5. **Sketch the chimney and other details as shown in Figure 17–5.**

Step 6. **Add leaders and notes showing the finished floor height, finished ceiling heights, and other construction notes for siding, brick, and other details, and complete the title block as shown in Figure 17–6.**

FIGURE 17–5
Sketch Chimney and Other
Details

FIGURE 17–6
Exercise 17–1 Complete

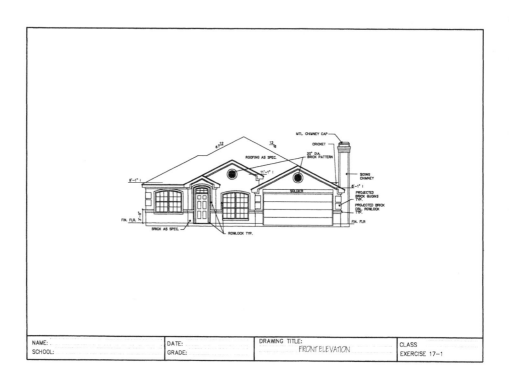

| NAME: | DATE: | DRAWING TITLE: | CLASS |
| SCHOOL: | GRADE: | FRONT ELEVATION | EXERCISE 17–1 |

EXERCISES

EXERCISE 17–1.   Remove the sheet labeled EXERCISE 17–1 from your book, and sketch the front elevation of the floor plan shown in Figure 17–7 to a scale of $\frac{1}{8}''$=1'-0''. Refer to Figure 17–8 for the sizes of all details. Be sure to notice that the floor plan is drawn to a different scale from the elevations and that you will have to measure details to one scale and draw them to another.

Complete the title block with your best lettering, and name the drawing FRONT ELEVATION.

EXERCISE 17–2.   Remove the sheet labeled EXERCISE 17–2 from your book, and sketch the rear elevation of the floor plan shown in Figure 17–7 to a scale of $\frac{1}{8}''$=1'-0''. Refer to Figure 17–8 for the sizes of all details. Be sure to notice that the floor plan is drawn to a different scale from the elevations and that you will have to measure details to one scale and draw them to another.

Complete the title block with your best lettering, and name the drawing REAR ELEVATION.

EXERCISE 17–3.   Remove the sheet labeled EXERCISE 17–3 from your book, and sketch the left elevation of the floor plan shown in Figure 17–7 to a scale of $\frac{1}{8}''$=1'-0''. Refer to Figure 17–9 for the sizes of all details. Be sure to notice that the

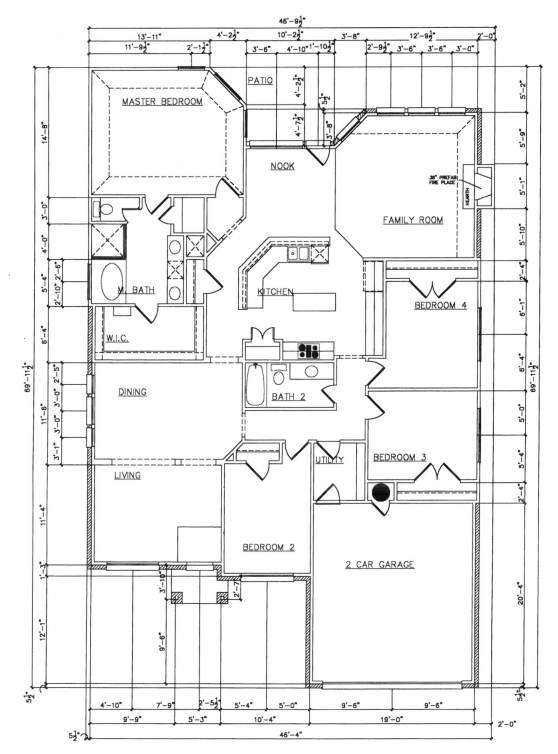

FIGURE 17–7
Floor Plan for Exercises 17–1 through 17–4
(Courtesy J M Designs Architects, Gary Beavers)

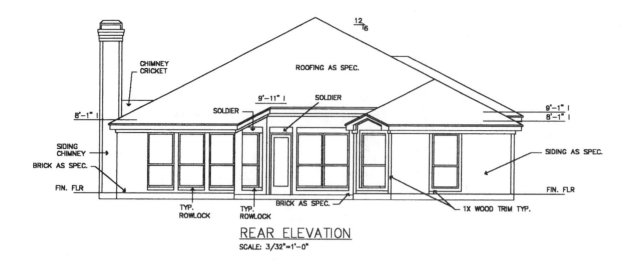

REAR ELEVATION
SCALE: 3/32"=1'-0"

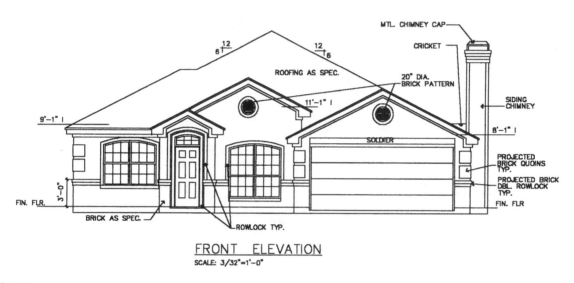

FRONT ELEVATION
SCALE: 3/32"=1'-0"

FIGURE 17–8
Specifications for Exercises 17–1 and 17–2
(Courtesy J M Designs Architects, Gary Beavers)

floor plan is drawn to a different scale from the elevations and that you will have to measure details to one scale and draw them to another.

Complete the title block with your best lettering, and name the drawing LEFT ELEVATION.

EXERCISE 17–4. Remove the sheet labeled EXERCISE 17–4 from your book, and sketch the right elevation of the floor plan shown in Figure 17–7 to a scale of $\frac{1}{8}''=1'-0''$. Refer to Figure 17–9 for the sizes of all details. Be sure to notice that the floor plan is drawn to a different scale from the elevations and that you will have to measure details to one scale and draw them to another.

Complete the title block with your best lettering, and name the drawing RIGHT ELEVATION.

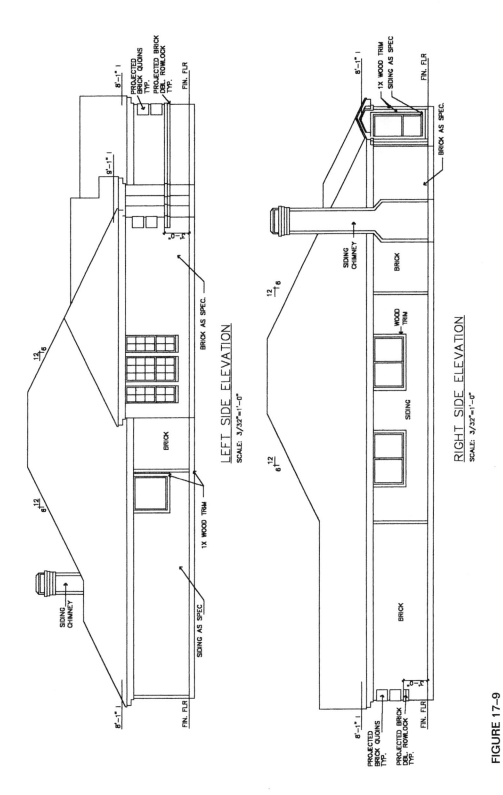

LEFT SIDE ELEVATION
SCALE: 3/32"=1'-0"

RIGHT SIDE ELEVATION
SCALE: 3/32"=1'-0"

FIGURE 17-9

Specifications for Exercises 17–3 and 17–4
(Courtesy J M Designs Architects, Gary Beavers)

REVIEW QUESTIONS

Circle the best answer.

1. It is not necessary to make sure that the locations of windows and doors on the elevation are the same as on the floor plan.
   a. True
   b. False

2. Which of the following that is on the floor plan will not appear on the front elevation?
   a. Chimney
   b. Front door
   c. Roof style
   d. Kitchen cabinet
   e. Finished floor level

3. Which of the following appears on all four elevations of the house shown in Figure 17–1?
   a. Front door
   b. Back door
   c. Garage door
   d. Chimney
   e. Chimney cricket

4. Run and rise refers to which of the following?
   a. Roof
   b. Finished floor height
   c. Finished ceiling height
   d. Siding
   e. Windows and doors

5. Which of the following will provide an incline of 45°?
   a. Run 6 rise 12
   b. Run 12 rise 6
   c. Run 6 rise 6
   d. Run 6 rise 9
   e. Run 9 rise 6

6. The distance from the left corner of the front of the house in Figure 17–1 (inside surface of the brick) to the center of the front door is
   a. $4'\text{-}10''$
   b. $12'\text{-}7''$
   c. $9'\text{-}9''$
   d. $15'\text{-}0''$
   e. $17'\text{-}3''$

7. The living room measures approximately
   a. $15'\text{-}0'' \times 11'\text{-}4''$
   b. $22'\text{-}10'' \times 15'\text{-}0''$
   c. $11'\text{-}4'' \times 12'\text{-}1''$
   d. $14'\text{-}4'' \times 12'\text{-}1''$
   e. $12'\text{-}1'' \times 15'\text{-}0''$

8. The chimney measures approximately
   a. $1'\text{-}0'' \times 5'\text{-}1''$
   b. $2'\text{-}6\frac{1}{2}'' \times 6'\text{-}0''$
   c. $1'6'' \times 5'\text{-}1''$
   d. $1'\text{-}6'' \times 6'\text{-}4''$
   e. $3'\text{-}0'' \times 5'\text{-}1''$

9. How many windows are there in the family room?
   a. One
   b. Two
   c. Three
   d. Four
   e. Five

10. The 1/8 scale is found on the same edge of the architect's scale as the _____ scale.
    a. 1/4
    b. 1/2
    c. 3/16
    d. 1
    e. 1/16

18

Drawing Elevations with AutoCAD

OBJECTIVES

After completing this chapter, you will be able to:

☐ Correctly draw elevations full size from floor plans and other specifications using AutoCAD.
☐ Print or plot elevations to scale from paper space.

INTRODUCTION

Elevations are drawn more easily using AutoCAD by using full scale and plotting at the desired scale. Because you have already used all the commands necessary to make the drawings in this chapter, the prompt–response format will not be used. Steps in drawing these elevations will be described in detail; however, it will be up to you to execute the commands on your own. The use of paper space to document and plot or print your drawings will also be described in detail.

Steps in Drawing the Front Elevation Using AutoCAD

All elevations must show all features in the same location and the same size as they appear on the floor plan; therefore, the first step in drawing the elevation is to locate the floor plan and any other specifications that show sizes and shapes of windows, doors, roofs, and any other features needed to show the complete exterior details of the building. In this case, blocks of the roof, doors, windows, and other details have been included in the drawings that you will open from the disk supplied with the book. The floor plan itself is also included as a block, so you may use it as a reference to locate many items.

EXERCISE 18–1:
Drawing the Front Elevation

Your final drawing will look similar to the drawing in Figure 18–2.

Step 1. **To begin Exercise 18–1, turn on the computer and start AutoCAD or AutoCAD LT.**

Step 2. **Open drawing EX18-1 supplied on the disk that came with your book.**
Figure 18–1 is the floor plan that shows the location of all windows, doors, and other features and the lines that presently exist on drawing EX18-1. Notice that the center lines of all windows and doors and the lines showing the outside walls are taken from the floor plan. Figure 18–2 is a scaled drawing showing the completed Exercise 18–1, the front elevation. All windows and doors, and the roof, chimney, and brick quoins are the same as on your drawing.

Step 3. **Use Zoom-All to view the entire drawing area.**

273

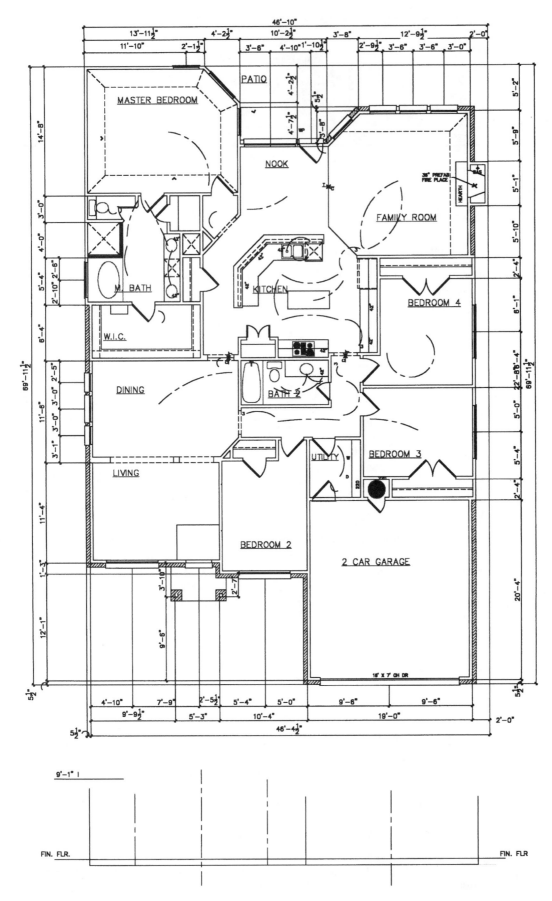

FIGURE 18–1
Using the Floor Plan to Draw the Front Elevation

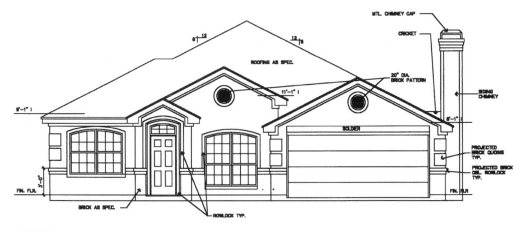

FIGURE 18-2
Exercise 18–1 Complete
(Courtesy J M Designs Architects, Gary Beavers)

Step 4. **On Your Own: Complete the front elevation.**

1. **Insert window blocks (Figure 18–3). Zoom a window close around the existing lines. Use the Insert command** (Type: **I<enter>**) **to insert:**

   WINDOW-1 block using the insertion point D1 (use Osnap-INTersection)

   WINDOW-2 block using the insertion point D2 (use Osnap-INTersection)

   WINDOW-3 block using the insertion point D3 (use Osnap-INTersection)

   You will have to scroll to the bottom of the list of blocks in the drawing to find the three windows.

2. **Insert front- and garage-door blocks (Figure 18–4). Use the Insert command to insert:**

   Front-door block using the insertion point D1 (use Osnap-INTersection)

   Garage-door block using the insertion point D2 (use Osnap-INTersection)

FIGURE 18-3
Insert Windows

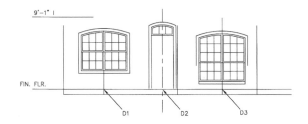

FIGURE 18–4
Insert Front and Garage Doors

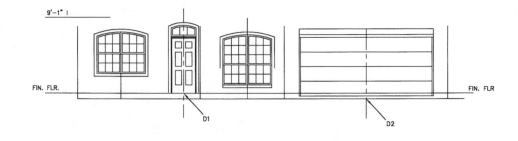

FIGURE 18–5
Insert Roof

3. **Insert the roof block (Figure 18–5). Use the Insert command to insert:**

   **Roof block using the insertion point D1
   (use Osnap-ENDpoint)**

4. **Insert right and left rowlocks and offset the outside wall (Figure 18–6). Use the Insert command to insert:**

   Double-rowlock-left: Type: **I<enter>** Select:
   Double-rowlock-left from the blocks list
   Click: **OK**
   Type: **FRO<enter>**
   Click: **D1 as the base point**
   Type: **@3'<90 as the offset distance and direction**

   Repeat for the insertion point D2.

FIGURE 18–6
Insert Right and Left Rowlocks
and Offset Outside Wall

FIGURE 18–7
Insert Right and Left Rowlocks
on the Offset Walls

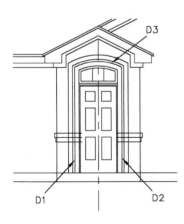

Double-rowlock-right: Type: **I<enter>** Select:

Double-rowlock-right from the blocks list

Click: **OK**

Type: **FRO<enter>** Click: **D3 as the base point**

Type: **@3′<90 as the offset distance and direction**

Use the Offset command to copy the left outside wall to the area surrounding the front door.

Type: **O<enter>** Type: **10′ for the offset distance** Click: **D4 as the object to offset**

Click: **any point to the right as the point on the side to offset**

Offset the new line 6′2″ to the right.

5. **Insert right and left rowlocks on the walls you just offset (Figure 18–7). Use the Insert command to insert:**

Double-rowlock-left: Type: **I<enter>** Select:

Double-rowlock-left from the blocks list

Click: **OK**

Type: **FRO<enter>** Click: **D1 as the base point**

Type: **@3′<90 as the offset distance and direction**

Double-rowlock-right: Type: **I<enter>** Select:

Double-rowlock-right from the blocks list

Click: **OK**

Type: **FRO<enter>**

Click: **D2 as the base point**

Type: **@3′<90 as the offset distance and direction**

6. **Explode the block WINDOW 2 (above the front door), join lines into a polyline, and offset the polyline twice (Figure 18–8).**

Type: **X<enter>** Click: **any point on the window above the door** Press: **<enter>**

Type: **PE<enter>** Click: **D1 (you do want to make it a polyline)** Press: **<enter>** Type: **J<enter> (to join lines)** Click: **D2, D3** Press: **<enter>**

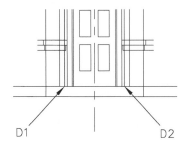

FIGURE 18–9
Explode Existing Rowlocks, Erase
Horizontal Lines, and Insert
Opposite Rowlocks

Type: **O<enter>** Type: **2<enter> as the distance to offset** Click: **the joined line as the object to offset** Click: **any point on the outside of the line as the point on side to offset**

Offset the new line 4″ to the outside.

7. **Explode existing rowlocks, erase horizontal lines, and insert opposite rowlocks (Figure 18–9).**

    Type: **X<enter>** Click: **any point on two existing rowlocks shown in Figure 18–9**

    Press: **<enter>**

    Type: **E<enter> and erase the horizontal lines on the existing rowlocks**

Use the Insert command to insert:

   Double-rowlock-right: Type: **I<enter>** Select:
   Double-rowlock-right from the blocks list
   Click: **OK**
   Type: **FRO<enter>** Click: **D1 as the base point**
   Type: **@3′<90 as the offset distance and direction**

   Double-rowlock-left: Type: **I<enter>** Select:
   Double-rowlock-left from the blocks list
   Click: **OK**
   Type: **FRO<enter>** Click: **D2 as the base point**
   Type: **@3′<90 as the offset distance and direction**

8. **Explode the new rowlock blocks and trim all lines so they appear as shown in Figure 18–10.**

    Type: **X<enter> and** Click: **the two rowlocks**

    Type: **TR<enter>** Type: **All to select cutting edges** Press: **<enter>** Click: **Lines to be trimmed**

9. **Explode the Window blocks and extend rowlocks to the edges of the windows (Figure 18–11).**

    Type: **X<enter> and** Click: **the WINDOW-1 and WINDOW-3 blocks** Press: **<enter>**

    Type: **EX<enter>** Click: **the edge of the windows as the boundary edge** Press: **<enter>** Click: **the ends of the horizontal lines of the rowlocks to extend them to the window edges**

Repeat for the rowlock on the left side of the garage door. Remember to explode the block before you try to extend.

10. **Insert the chimney (Figure 18–12).**

    Use the Insert command to insert:

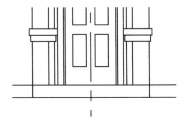

FIGURE 18–10
Explode Blocks and Trim
Rowlocks

FIGURE 18–11
Extend Rowlocks to Windows

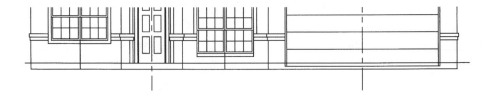

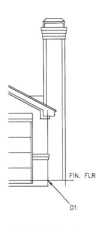

FIGURE 18–12
Insert Chimney

FIGURE 18–13
Insert Left and Right Quoins

Chimney-front block using the insertion point D1 (use Osnap-INTersection).

11.   Insert left and right quoins (Figure 18–13).

BEFORE YOU START BE SURE TO TRIM ALL WALL LINES THAT INTERSECT THE ROWLOCKS AND THE ROOF. YOU WILL USE THE MIDPOINT OF THE TRIMMED LINES TO INSERT LEFT AND RIGHT QUOINS.

Use the Insert command to insert:

Quoins-left block using the midpoint point of D1 (use Osnap-MIDpoint)

Quoins-left block using the midpoint point of D2 (use Osnap-MIDpoint)

Quoins-right block using the midpoint point of D3 (use Osnap-MIDpoint)

12.   Insert brick patterns (Figure 18–14).

Use the Insert command to insert:

Brick-pattern block: Type: **I\<enter\>** Select:
Brick-pattern from the blocks list Click: **OK**

FIGURE 18–14
Insert Brick Patterns

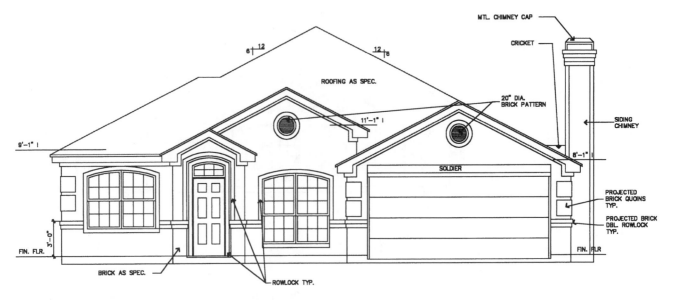

FIGURE 18–15
Exercise 18–1 Complete
(Courtesy J M Designs Architects, Gary Beavers)

Type: **FRO<enter>** Click: **D1 as the base point**

Type: **@2′<270 as the offset distance and direction**

Repeat for D2.

13. **Trim any unnecessary lines and add any lines not already on the drawing. Add callouts as shown on Figure 18–15.**

14. **Click: the layout labeled Front Elevation at the bottom of your screen and complete the title block using the Dtext command. Title the drawing FRONT ELEVATION.**

15. **Use the SAVEAS command to save your drawing as EX18-1(your initials) on a floppy disk and again on the hard drive of your computer.**

16. **Plot or print your drawing at a scale of 1=1, using Landscape, Limits, Center the plot, on an 11″ x 8½″ sheet.**

EXERCISES

EXERCISE 18–1.   Complete Exercise 18–1 using steps 1 through 16 described in this chapter.

EXERCISE 18–2.   Draw the rear elevation of the floor plan shown in Figure 18–16. Open drawing EX18-2 on the disk that came with your book. Use a similar method to the one used to draw Exercise 18–1. Insert the following blocks as needed:

Window-4

(Use absolute coordinates—the current UCS is located at the lower left corner of the elevation. (*Note:* If the UCSICON is in your way, turn it off by typing **UCSICON<enter>,** then type: **OFF<enter>.**)

(*Example:* After Selecting the Window-4 block from the Insert dialog box and clicking **OK,** Type: **3′5,1′<enter>** to insert the first Window-4 block.)

Insert Window-4 at the following locations:

X = 3′-5″	Y = 1′-0″
X = 6′-11″	Y = 1′-0″
X = 10′-5″	Y = 1′-0″
X = 20′-7½″	Y = 1′-0″
X = 23′-7½″	Y = 1′-0″
X = 35′	Y = 1′-0″

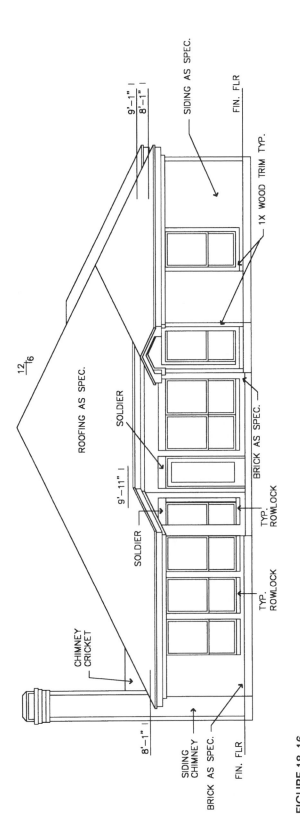

FIGURE 18-16
Exercise 18-2 Complete
(Courtesy J M Designs Architects, Gary Beavers)

Window-5

X = 14′-4½″   Y = 1′-0″

Window-6

X = 27′-10″   Y = 0

Back-door

X = 17′-6″   Y = 6½″

Roof-rear

Insertion point: Type: **0,0**

Chimney-rear

Insertion point: Type: **0,0**

After inserting the blocks, clean up the drawing so it looks like Figure 18–16. You may need to explode blocks to do that. Use a scale of ⅛″=1′0″ to make any measurements from the drawing in the book.

Click: **the layout labeled Front Elevation at the bottom of your screen and complete the title block using the Dtext command. Title the drawing REAR ELEVATION**

Use the **SAVEAS command to save your drawing as EX18-2(your initials) on a floppy disk and again on the hard drive of your computer.**

Plot or print your drawing at a scale of **1=1, using Landscape, Limits, Center the plot, on an 11″ × 8½″ sheet.**

EXERCISE 18–3. Draw the left elevation of the floor plan shown in Figure 18–17. Open drawing EX18-3 on the disk that came with your book. Use a similar method to the one used to draw Exercise 18–1. Insert the following blocks as needed: Window-9 (Use absolute coordinates—the current UCS is located at the lower left corner of the elevation. (**Note:** If the UCSICON is in your way, turn it off by typing **UCSICON<enter>,** then Type: **OFF<enter>.**)
(*Example:* After selecting the Window-9 block from the Insert dialog box and clicking **OK,** Type: **21′10,3′<enter>** to insert the Window-9 block.)
IMPORTANT: Before you use the Insert command, be sure to click: **Model** at the bottom of your display (next to Left Elevation) so you are sure you are in Model space.

Window-9

X = 21′-10″   Y = 3′-0″

Window-10

X = 34′-9″   Y = 2′-4″
X = 40′-9″   Y = 2′-4″

Window-11

X = 37′-3″   Y = 2′-4″

Roof-left

X = 0   Y = 0

Double-rowlock-right

X = 69′-11 1/2″   Y = 3′-8″
X = 60′-5 1/2″   Y = 3′-8″
X = 57′-11 1/2″   Y = 3′-8″
X = 56′-11 1/2″   Y = 3′-8″

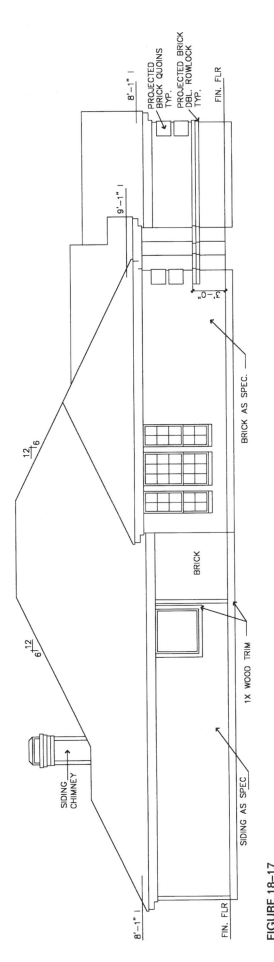

FIGURE 18–17
Exercise 18–3 Complete
(Courtesy J M Designs Architects, Gary Beavers)

8'-1"

9'-1"

PROJECTED
BRICK QUOINS
TYP.

PROJECTED BRICK
DBL. ROWLOCK
TYP.

FIN. FLR

3'-0"

BRICK AS SPEC.

12
6

6
12

BRICK

1X WOOD TRIM

SIDING
CHIMNEY

SIDING AS SPEC

FIN. FLR

8'-1"

Chimney-left

X = 12'-3"	Y = 13'-4 3/8"

Right-quoins

X = 56'-7 1/2"	Y = 6'-0"
X = 69'-11 1/2"	Y = 5'-6"

After inserting the blocks, clean up the drawing so it looks like Figure 18–17. You may need to explode blocks to do that. Use a scale of $\frac{1}{8}$"=1'0" to make any measurements from the drawing in the book.

Click: **the layout labeled Left Elevation at the bottom of your screen and complete the title block using the Dtext command. Title the drawing LEFT ELEVATION**

Use the SAVEAS command to save your drawing as EX18-3(your initials) on a floppy disk and again on the hard drive of your computer.

Plot or print your drawing at a scale of 1=1, using Landscape, Limits, Center the plot, on an 11" × 8½" sheet.

EXERCISE 18–4.

Draw the right elevation of the floor plan shown in Figure 18–18. Open drawing EX18-4 on the disk that came with your book. Use a similar method to the one used to draw Exercise 18–1. Insert the following blocks as needed:

Window-7 (Use absolute coordinates—the current UCS is located at the lower left corner of the elevation. (*Note:* If the UCSICON is in your way, turn it off by typing **UCSICON<enter>,** then type: **OFF<enter>.**)

(*Example:* After Selecting the Window-7 block from the Insert dialog box and clicking **OK**, Type: **25'6,3'8<enter>** to insert the first Window-7 block.)

Window-7

X = 25'-6"	Y = 3'-8"
X = 37'	Y = 3'-8"

Window-8

X = 66'-5"	Y = 1'-4"

Roof-right

X = 0	Y = 7'-4"

Double-rowlock-left

X = 0	Y = 3'-8"

Chimney-right

X = 54'-3½"	Y = 8"

Left-quoins

X = 0	Y = 5'-6"

After inserting the blocks, clean up the drawing so it looks like Figure 18–18. You may need to explode blocks to do that. Use a scale of $\frac{1}{8}$"=1'0" to make any measurements from the drawing in the book.

Click: **The layout labeled Right Elevation at the bottom of your screen and complete the title block using the Dtext command. Title the drawing RIGHT ELEVATION**

Use the SAVEAS command to save your drawing as EX18-4(your initials) on a floppy disk and again on the hard drive of your computer.

Plot or print your drawing at a scale of 1=1, using Landscape, Limits, Center the plot, on an 11" × 8½" sheet.

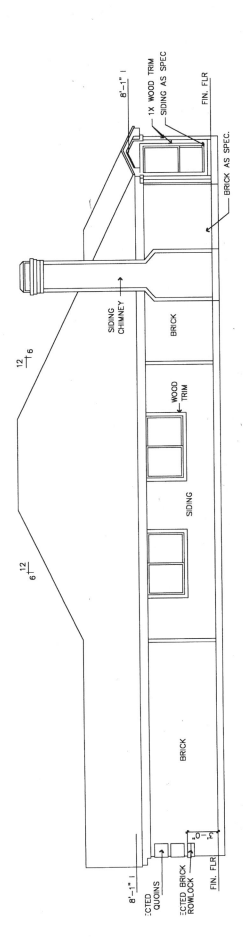

FIGURE 18–18

Exercise 18–4 Complete

(Courtesy J M Designs Architects, Gary Beavers)

REVIEW QUESTIONS

Circle the best answer.

1. Placing the floor plan above the front elevation is a good way to make sure window, doors, and other features are located properly.
   a. True
   b. False

2. Inserting a block with an insertion point of 27'5,3'8 is an example of using
   a. Absolute coordinates
   b. Polar coordinates
   c. Relative coordinates
   d. Direct distance entry
   e. Filters

3. Inserting a block with an insertion point of @3'6,8'3 is an example of using
   a. Absolute coordinates
   b. Polar coordinates
   c. Relative coordinates
   d. Direct distance entry
   e. Filters

4. To make the UCSICON disappear you must activate the command by typing
   a. UCS<enter>
   b. WORLD UCS<enter>
   c. UCSICON<enter>
   d. MOVEUSE<enter>
   e. DELETE<enter>

5. If you insert a block using "FROM" and Type: @3'<90<enter>, for the offset you are using
   a. Absolute coordinates
   b. Polar coordinates
   c. Relative coordinates
   d. Direct distance entry
   f. Filters

6. If you insert a block using "FROM" and Type: @3'<90<enter>, the block is inserted _____ from the base point.
   a. 3' to the right
   b. 3' up
   c. 3' down
   d. 3' to the left
   e. 3' in the direction of the mouse movement

7. To erase the horizontal lines of only the left and right rowlocks you must first use which command?
   a. Trim
   b. Explode
   c. UCS
   d. Block
   e. Delete

8. To join two lines touching an arc into a single polyline, Type:
   a. JOINLINE<enter>
   b. EXPLODE<enter>
   c. PL<enter>
   d. PE<enter>
   e. MERGE<enter>

9. The insertion point for the left and right quoins is
   a. At the bottom of the lower quoin
   b. At the top of the lower quoin
   c. At the top of the upper quoin
   d. At the bottom of the upper quoin
   e. Midway between the upper and lower quoins

10. Which of the following appear(s) in all four elevations?
    a. Chimney
    b. Left-quoins
    c. Left-double-rowlocks
    d. WINDOW-1
    e. WINDOW-2

19

Sketching Electrical Plans

OBJECTIVES

After completing this chapter, you will be able to:

☐ Correctly sketch reflected ceiling, power, lighting, and outlet plans on floor plans using the correct electrical symbols.
☐ Correctly sketch an electrical legend for each type of plan.

INTRODUCTION

Electrical information is often shown on floor plans or on separate sheets where only the floor plan is shown with many of the details deleted. With AutoCAD the electrical information can be shown on separate layers that can be turned on or off as needed. In this chapter you will locate the electrical components for both a commercial and a residential building and show how they connect to switches. You will also sketch legends that label each symbol that is used on the plan.

Steps in Sketching the Reflected Ceiling Plan (Figure 19–1)

In this exercise you will use two sheets to complete this figure. On the first sheet you will sketch the legend that shows all the symbols that are used on sheet 2, where you will draw the reflected ceiling plan.

Step 1. **Draw the lighting legend to a scale of $\frac{1}{4}''=1'-0''$.**
Figure 19–2 is the legend that you will sketch on the sheet labeled EXERCISE 19–1 Sheet 1 of 2. Draw the fluorescent and incandescent fixtures to scale, and draw the exit sign and switch to the approximate size shown on Figure 19–2.

Step 2. **Sketch the symbols in place as shown in Figure 19–1.**
Sketch symbols in place on the sheet labeled EXERCISE 19–1 Sheet 2 of 2. Be sure to use three-way switches in every place where two switches turn on the same light.

Step 3. **Use hidden lines to show the electrical connection between switches and lighting components.**
Use hidden lines to show how switches and lighting components are connected. All lines should be dark and the same thickness throughout.

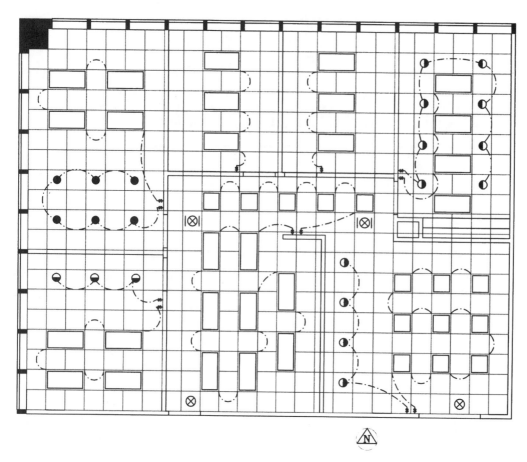

FIGURE 19–1
Reflected Ceiling Plan (Scale: 1/8″=1′0″)

EXERCISES

EXERCISE 19–1. REFLECTED CEILING PLAN
EXERCISE 19–1 Sheet 1 of 2
Remove the sheet labeled EXERCISE 19–1 Sheet 1 of 2 from your book, and sketch the legend for the reflected ceiling plan to a scale of $\frac{1}{4}''=1'$-0″. Refer to Figure 19–2 for the correct sizes. Be sure to label all symbols as shown in Figure 19–2.

EXERCISE 19–1 Sheet 2 of 2
Remove the sheet labeled EXERCISE 19–1 Sheet 2 of 2 from your book, and sketch the reflected ceiling plan to a scale of $\frac{1}{8}''=1'$-0″. Sketch symbols in place. You will be drawing the symbols half the size shown on the legend. Refer to Figure 19–1 for the approximate locations.

Use hidden lines to show how switches and lighting components are connected. All lines should be dark and the same thickness throughout.

Complete the title block with your best lettering, and name both sheets of the drawing REFLECTED CEILING PLAN.

EXERCISE 19–2. POWER PLAN
EXERCISE 19–2 Sheet 1 of 2
Remove the sheet labeled EXERCISE 19–2 Sheet 1 of 2 from your book, and sketch the legend for the power plan to a scale of $\frac{1}{4}''=1'$-0″. Refer to Figure 19–3 for the correct sizes. Be sure to label all symbols as shown in Figure 19–3.

EXERCISE 19–2 Sheet 2 of 2
Remove the sheet labeled EXERCISE 19–2 Sheet 2 of 2 from your book, and sketch the power plan to a scale of $\frac{1}{8}''=1'$-0″. Sketch symbols in place.

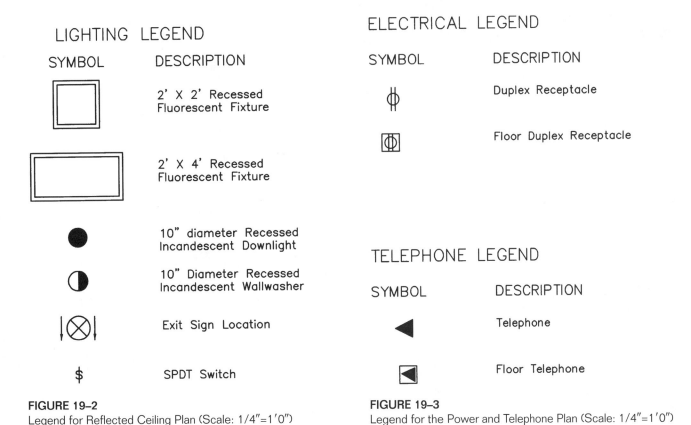

LIGHTING LEGEND

SYMBOL — DESCRIPTION

2' X 2' Recessed
Fluorescent Fixture

2' X 4' Recessed
Fluorescent Fixture

10" diameter Recessed
Incandescent Downlight

10" Diameter Recessed
Incandescent Wallwasher

Exit Sign Location

$ SPDT Switch

FIGURE 19–2
Legend for Reflected Ceiling Plan (Scale: 1/4"=1'0")

ELECTRICAL LEGEND

SYMBOL — DESCRIPTION

Duplex Receptacle

Floor Duplex Receptacle

TELEPHONE LEGEND

SYMBOL — DESCRIPTION

Telephone

Floor Telephone

FIGURE 19–3
Legend for the Power and Telephone Plan (Scale: 1/4"=1'0")

You will be drawing the symbols half the size shown on the legend. Refer to Figure 19–4 for the approximate locations.

Complete the title block with your best lettering, and name both sheets of the drawing POWER PLAN.

EXERCISE 19–3. HOUSE LIGHTING AND OUTLET PLAN
EXERCISE 19–3 Sheet 1 of 2
Remove the sheet labeled EXERCISE 19–3 Sheet 1 of 2 from your book, and sketch the legends for the house lighting and outlet plan to a scale of $\frac{1}{4}''=1'-0''$. Refer to Figure 19–5 for the correct sizes. Be sure to label all symbols as shown in Figure 19–5. This exercise shows grounded receptacles in several locations. These receptacles must be used in every location where there is the possibility that water may be present.

EXERCISE 19–3 Sheet 2 of 2
Remove the sheet labeled EXERCISE 19–3 Sheet 2 of 2 from your book, and sketch the house lighting and outlet plan to a scale of $\frac{1}{8}''=1'-0''$. Sketch symbols in place. You will be drawing the symbols half the size shown on the legend. Refer to Figure 19–6 for the approximate locations.

Complete the title block with your best lettering, and name both sheets of the drawing ELECTRICAL PLAN.

EXERCISE 19–4. HOUSE LIGHTING AND OUTLET PLAN
Design your own electrical plan. Refer to the electrical plan of Figure 19–6 to determine the spacing of outlets and lighting fixtures. Remove the sheet labeled EXERCISE 19–4 from your book, and sketch the house lighting and outlet plan to a scale of $\frac{1}{8}''=1'-0''$. Sketch symbols from Figure 19–5 in place. You will be drawing the symbols half the size shown on the legend.

Complete the title block with your best lettering, and name the drawing ELECTRICAL PLAN.

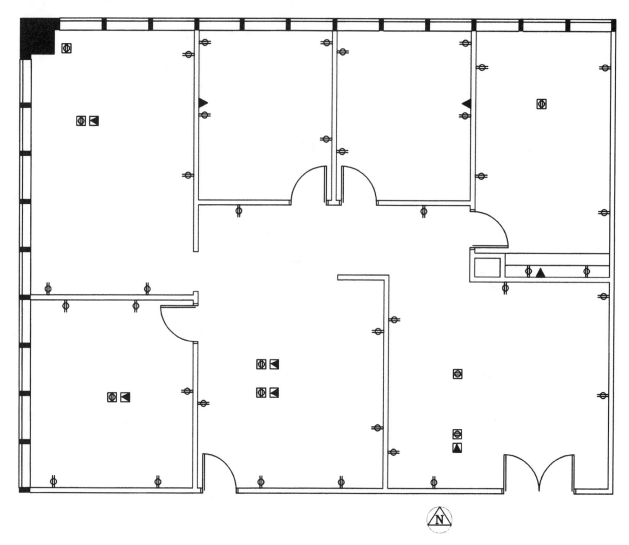

FIGURE 19–4
Power and Telephone Plan (Scale: 1/8″=1′0″)

ELECTRICAL LEGEND

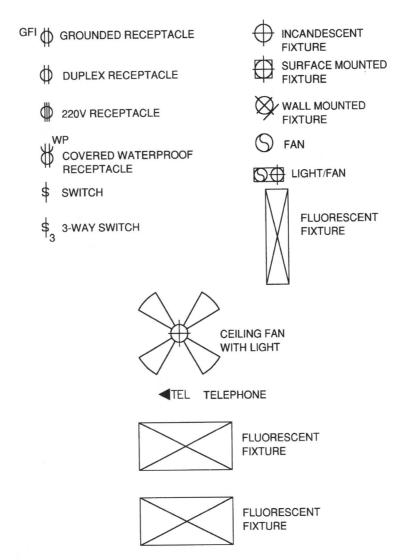

GFI ⏀ GROUNDED RECEPTACLE

⏀ DUPLEX RECEPTACLE

⏀ 220V RECEPTACLE

WP
⏀ COVERED WATERPROOF
RECEPTACLE

$ SWITCH

$₃ 3-WAY SWITCH

⊕ INCANDESCENT
FIXTURE

⊕ SURFACE MOUNTED
FIXTURE

⊗ WALL MOUNTED
FIXTURE

◯ FAN

◯⊕ LIGHT/FAN

FLUORESCENT
FIXTURE

CEILING FAN
WITH LIGHT

◀TEL   TELEPHONE

FLUORESCENT
FIXTURE

FLUORESCENT
FIXTURE

FIGURE 19–5
Legend for the House Lighting and Outlet Plan (Scale: 1/4″=1′0″)

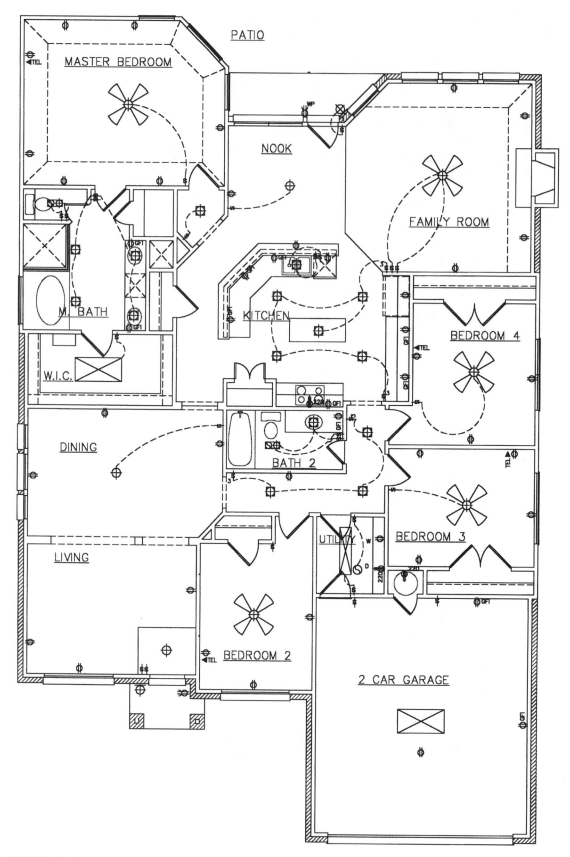

FIGURE 19-6
House Lighting and Outlet Plan (Scale: 1/8"=1'0")
(Courtesy J M Designs Architects, Gary Beavers)

REVIEW QUESTIONS

FIGURE 19–7

FIGURE 19–8

FIGURE 19–9

FIGURE 19–10

FIGURE 19–11

FIGURE 19–12

FIGURE 19–13

Circle the best answer.

1. The symbol shown in Figure 19–7 is a
   a. Switch
   b. Duplex receptacle
   c. Telephone
   d. Floor duplex receptacle
   e. Grounded receptacle
2. The symbol shown in Figure 19–8 is a
   a. Switch
   b. Duplex receptacle
   c. Telephone
   d. Floor duplex receptacle
   e. Grounded receptacle
3. The symbol shown in Figure 19–9 is a
   a. Switch
   b. Duplex receptacle
   c. Telephone
   d. Floor duplex receptacle
   e. Grounded receptacle
4. The symbol shown in Figure 19–10 is a(n)
   a. Ceiling fan
   b. Fan
   c. Fluorescent Fixture
   d. Incandescent Fixture
   e. Exit sign
5. The symbol shown in Figure 19–11 is a(n)
   a. Ceiling fan
   b. Fan
   c. Fluorescent Fixture
   d. Incandescent Fixture
   e. Exit sign
6. The symbol shown in Figure 19–12 is a(n)
   a. Ceiling fan
   b. Fan
   c. Fluorescent Fixture
   d. Incandescent Fixture
   e. Exit sign
7. The symbol shown in Figure 19–13 is a(n)
   a. Ceiling fan
   b. Fan
   c. Fluorescent Fixture
   d. Incandescent Fixture
   e. Exit sign

FIGURE 19–14

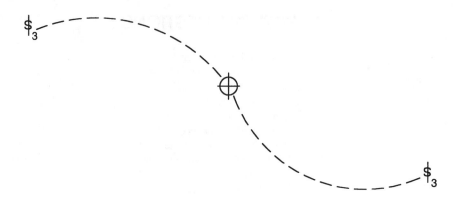

8. Switches shown in the diagram of Figure 19–14 are
   a. Single-pole switches
   b. Three-way switches
   c. Grounded receptacles
   d. Duplex receptacles
   e. 220V switches
9. Three-way switches are used when two switches must be capable of turning on the same light.
   a. True
   b. False
10. Grounded receptacles are used in areas where there is the possibility that water may be present.
    a. True
    b. False

20 Drawing Electrical Plans Using AutoCAD

OBJECTIVES

After completing this chapter, you will be able to:

□ Use AutoCAD to make blocks of electrical symbols that can be used on any electrical plan.
□ Use AutoCAD to draw reflected ceiling, power, lighting, and outlet plans using the correct electrical symbols and linetypes.

INTRODUCTION

In this chapter you will make the same drawings as you did in Chapter 19, except that now you will draw them with the AutoCAD program. In addition, you will make blocks of symbols that can be used on any drawing. You can now draw the lighting legend on the same sheet as the electrical plan because the drawing can be plotted at a smaller scale and still be read easily.

EXERCISE 20–1:
Drawing the Lighting Legend Full Scale

Step 1. To begin Exercise 20–1, turn on the computer and start AutoCAD or AutoCAD LT.
Step 2. Open drawing EX20-1 supplied on the disk that came with your book. Click: **Model** to make sure you are in model space.
Step 3. Use Zoom-All to view the entire drawing area, then Undo to go back to the legend area.
Step 4. Use the Rectangle command to draw the 2′ × 2′ Recessed Fluorescent Fixture symbol.

Prompt	Response
Command:	Type: **REC\<enter>**
Specify first corner point or [Chamfer/Elevation/Fillet/Thickness/Width]:	Pick: **a point for the lower left corner in the approximate location shown in Figure 20–1**
Specify other corner point or [Dimensions]:	Type: **@2′,2′\<enter>**
Command:	Type: **O\<enter>**
Specify offset distance or [Through] \<Through>:	Type: **2\<enter>**
Select object to offset or \<exit>:	Pick: **any point on the rectangle**

295

FIGURE 20–1
Legend for Reflected Ceiling Plan

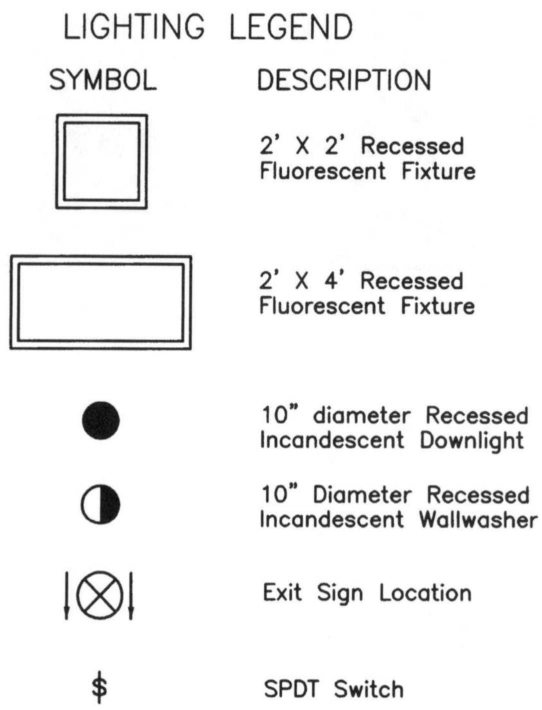

LIGHTING LEGEND

SYMBOL	DESCRIPTION
☐	2' X 2' Recessed Fluorescent Fixture
▭	2' X 4' Recessed Fluorescent Fixture
●	10" diameter Recessed Incandescent Downlight
◑	10" Diameter Recessed Incandescent Wallwasher
|⊗|	Exit Sign Location
$	SPDT Switch

Specify point on side to offset:	Pick: **any point inside the rectangle**
Select object to offset or <exit>:	**<enter>**

Step 5. **On Your Own:**
Use the **Rectangle** and **Offset** commands to draw the **2' × 4' Recessed Fluorescent Fixture** symbol in the approximate location shown in Figure 20–1.

Step 6. Use the **Donut** command to draw the **10″-diameter Recessed Incandescent Downlight** symbol.

Prompt	Response
Command:	Type: **DO<enter>**
Specify inside diameter of donut <0'-0 1/2">:	Type: **0<enter>**
Specify outside diameter of donut <0'-1">:	Type: **10<enter>**
Specify center of donut or <exit>:	Pick: **a point to center the donut in the approximate location shown in Figure 20–1,<enter>**
Specify center of donut or <exit>:	**<enter>**

Step 7. Use the **Line, Donut, Trim,** and **Circle** commands to draw the **10″-diameter Recessed Incandescent Wallwasher** symbol.

Prompt	Response
Command:	Type: **L<enter>**
Specify first point:	Pick: **a point about 10″ below the donut aligned with the donut center**
Specify next point or [Undo]:	With ORTHO ON **move your mouse down and** Type: **20<enter>**
Specify next point or [Undo]:	**<enter>**

Prompt	Response
Command:	Type: **DO<enter>**
Specify inside diameter of donut <0'-0">:	**<enter>**
Specify outside diameter of donut <0'-10">:	**<enter>**
Specify center of donut or <exit>:	Type: **MID<enter>**
Of	Pick: **any point on the line you just drew**
Specify center of donut or <exit>:	**<enter>**
Command:	Type: **TR<enter>**
Select cutting edges ...	
Select objects:	Pick: **any point on the line (D1, Figure 20–2)**
Select objects:	**<enter>**
Select object to trim or shift-select to extend or [Project/Edge/Undo]:	Pick: **D2 (on the outside edge of the donut)**
Select object to trim or shift-select to extend or [Project/Edge/Undo]:	**<enter>**
Command:	Type: **E<enter>**
Select objects:	Pick: **the line**
Select objects:	**<enter>**
Command:	Type: **C<enter>**
Specify center point for circle or [3P/2P/Ttr (tan tan radius)]:	Type: **CEN<enter>**
of	Pick: **D1 (Figure 20–3)**
Specify radius of circle or [Diameter]:	Type: **5<enter>**

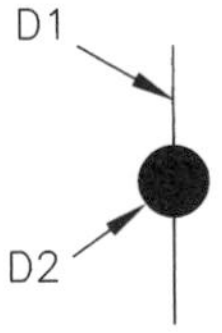

FIGURE 20–2
Draw and Trim a 10"-Diameter Donut

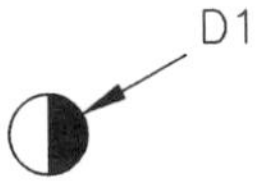

FIGURE 20–3
Draw a Circle around the Trimmed Donut

Step 8. **Use the Circle, Line, Rotate, and Leader commands to draw the Exit Sign Location symbol.**

Prompt	Response
Command:	Type: **L<enter>**
LINE Specify first point:	Pick: **a point about 20" below the Wall washer symbol center (SNAP ON)**
Specify next point or [Undo]:	**Move the mouse down** and Type: **12<enter>**
Specify next point or [Undo]:	**<enter>**
Command:	**<enter>**
Specify first point:	Type: **FRO<enter>**
Base point:	Type: **MID<enter>**
of	Pick: **any point on the line just drawn**
<Offset>:	Type: **@6<0<enter>**
Specify next point or [Undo]:	**Move your mouse to the left** and Type: **12<enter>**
Specify next point or [Undo]:	**<enter>**
Command:	Type: **C<enter>**
CIRCLE Specify center point for circle or [3P/2P/Ttr (tan tan radius)]:	Pick: **the intersection of the two lines**

Prompt	Response
Specify radius of circle or [Diameter] <0' -5" >:	Type: **6<enter>**
Command:	Type: **RO<enter>**
Select objects:	Select: **the two lines and the circle**
Select objects:	**<enter>**
Specify base point:	Pick: **the intersection of the two lines**
Specify rotation angle or [Reference]:	Type: **45<enter>**
Command:	Type: **dim<enter>**
Dim:	Type: **L<enter>**
Leader start:	With **SNAP ON** Click: **the endpoint of the arrowhead one snap to the left of the symbol**
To point:	**Move the mouse up** and Click: **a point 12" directly above the first point**
To point:	Press: **the Esc key**

Step 9. **On Your Own:**

Repeat the Leader sequence for the right side of the symbol. Press: Esc to exit from the Dim mode.

Step 10. Use Wblock command to make a separate drawing file for the 2' × 2' **Recessed Fluorescent Fixture symbol.** You can then use these symbols on any drawing. (You can also use the Design Center to access any block on any drawing.)

Prompt	Response
Command:	Type: **WBLOCK<enter>** (or W<enter>)
The Write Block dialog box appears:	In the File name: box, Type: **2X2RFF**
	Insert a floppy disk in the A: drive and make sure the Location: box reads **A:**
	Select: **Objects in the Source area**
	Click: **Pick point** (in the Base point area)
Specify insertion base point:	With OSNAP ON Pick: **the Endpoint of the lower left corner of the symbol**
	In the Objects: area Click: **Retain** (so a dot appears in the radio button)
The Write Block dialog box appears:	Click: **Select objects**
Select objects:	**Use a window to select the entire symbol**.
Select objects:	**<enter>**
The Write Block dialog box appears:	Click: **OK**

You now have a drawing file of the 2' × 2' Recessed Fluorescent Fixture symbol on a floppy disk in your A: drive.

Step 11. **On Your Own:**

Use the Wblock command to make separate drawing files for the remaining symbols using the following names and insertion points. Place all symbols on the same floppy, Zip, or compact disk.

Symbol	Wblock Name	Insertion Point
2' × 4' Recessed Fluorescent Fixture	2X4RFF	Lower left corner of the symbol
10" diameter Recessed Incandescent Downlight	10RID	The center of the symbol

10″ diameter Recessed Incandescent Wallwasher	10RIW	The center of the symbol
Exit Sign Location	EXIT	The center of the symbol
SPDT Switch	SW	The top endpoint of the symbol

Step 12. Click: the layout labeled Reflected Ceiling Legend at the bottom of your screen and complete the title block using the Dtext command with $^3/_{32}$″-high letters. Title the drawing REFLECTED CEILING LEGEND.

Step 13. Use the SAVEAS command to save your drawing as EX20-1(your initials) on a floppy disk and again on the hard drive of your computer.

Step 14. Plot or print your drawing at a scale of 1=1, using Portrait, Window (Click: a window around the legend), Center the plot, on an 11″ × 8½″ sheet.

EXERCISE 20–2:
Drawing the Reflected Ceiling Plan Full Scale

Step 1. To begin Exercise 20–1, turn on the computer and start AutoCAD or AutoCAD LT.

Step 2. Open drawing EX20-2 supplied on the disk that came with your book.

Step 3. Use Zoom-All to view the entire drawing area.

Step 4. Use the Insert command to draw the 2′ × 2′ Recessed Fluorescent Fixture symbol.

Prompt	Response
Command:	Type: **I<enter>**

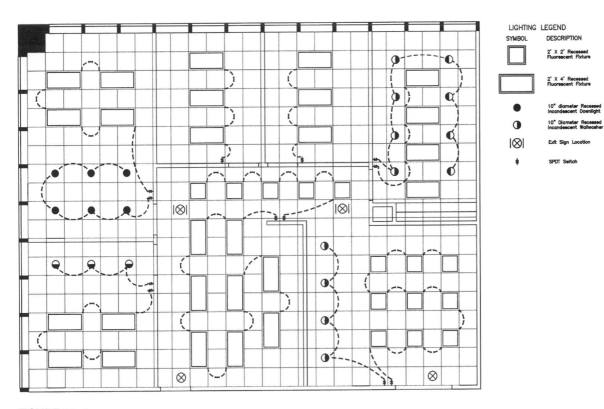

FIGURE 20–4
Exercise 20–2 Complete

Drawing Electrical Plans Using AutoCAD

The Insert dialog box appears:	Click: **Browse (with the floppy disk containing the 2X2RFF symbol drawing in the A: drive)**
The Select Drawing File dialog Box appears:	Click: **3½ Floppy (A:)in the Look in: list box.**
	Pick: **2X2RFF**
	Click: **Open**
The Insert dialog box appears:	Click: **OK**
Specify insertion point or [Scale/ X/Y/Z/Rotate/PScale/PX/PY/PZ/ PRotate]:	With SNAP ON Click: **a point to place the symbol on the grid as shown in Figure 20–5**

Step 5. **Use the Array command to copy the 2′ × 2′ Recessed Fluorescent Fixture symbol five times (Figure 20–6).**

Prompt	Response
Command:	Type: **-AR<enter>** (if you leave off the minus you get a dialog box that allows you to make the same array pattern.)
Select objects:	Pick: the **2X2RFF** symbol
Select objects:	**<enter>**
Enter the type of array [Rectangular/ Polar] <R>:	Type: **R<enter>**
Enter the number of rows (---) <1>:	Type: **3<enter>**
Enter the number of columns (‖‖) <1>	Type: **3<enter>**
Enter the distance between rows or specify unit cell (---):	Type: **4′<enter>**
Specify the distance between columns (‖‖):	Type: **−4′<enter>**(be sure to include the minus symbol so the array will be to the left

Step 6. **Insert and copy all remaining symbols.**

On Your Own

1. **Insert SW, EXIT, 10RIW symbols in the area as shown in Figure 20–7.**

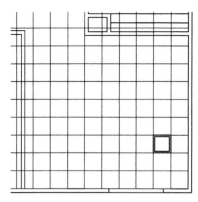

FIGURE 20–5
Insert the 2X2RFF Symbol

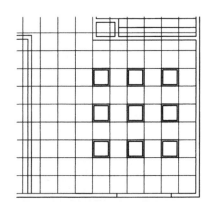

FIGURE 20–6
Array the 2X2RFF Symbol

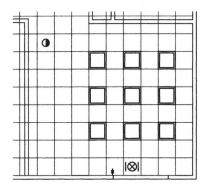

FIGURE 20–7
Insert EXIT, SW, and 10RIW Symbols

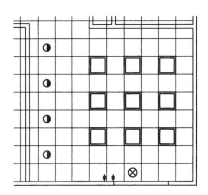

FIGURE 20–8
Use the Insert, Copy, Array, Explode, and Erase Commands to Finish Symbols in This Area

2. **Explode the EXIT symbol and erase the two arrows on each side of the symbol.**

3. **Copy the SW symbol as shown in Figure 20–8.**

4. **Array the 10RIW symbol as shown in Figure 20–8.**

Step 7. **Use Polyline to draw lines showing electrical connections.**
Set Layer E-LITE-W current.

Prompt	Response
Command:	Type: **PL\<enter>**
Specify start point:	Pick: **the top end of the SW symbol Figure 20–9**
Current line-width is 0'-0"	
Specify next point or [Arc/Close/ Halfwidth/Length/Undo/Width]:	Type: **W\<enter>**
Specify starting width <0'-0">:	Type: **1-1/2\<enter>**
Specify ending width <0'-1 1/2">:	**\<enter>**
Specify next point or [Arc/Close/ Halfwidth/Length/Undo/Width]:	Type: **A\<enter>**
Specify endpoint of arc or[Angle/ CEnter/CLose/Direction/Halfwidth/ Line/Radius/Second pt/Undo/Width]:	Type: **D\<enter>**
Specify the tangent direction for the start of arc:	Pick: **D1 (in the approximate location shown in Figure 20–9)**

FIGURE 20–9
Drawing Electrical Connecting Lines

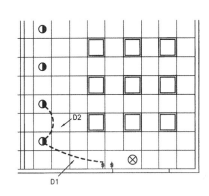

Specify endpoint of the arc:	Pick: **the edge of the 10RIW symbol (Figure 20–9)**
Specify endpoint of arc or [Angle/ CEnter/CLose/Direction/Halfwidth/ Line/Radius/Second pt/Undo/Width]:	**<enter>**
Command:	**<enter>**
Specify start point:	Pick: **the top edge of the lowest 10RIW symbol (Figure 20–9)**
Current line-width is 0'-1 1/2"	
Specify next point or [Arc/Close/ Halfwidth/Length/Undo/Width]:	Type: **A<enter>**
Specify endpoint of arc or[Angle/ CEnter/CLose/Direction/Halfwidth/ Line/Radius/Second pt/Undo/Width]:	Type: **D<enter>**
Specify the tangent direction for the start point of arc:	Pick: **D2 (in the approximate location shown in Figure 20–9)**
Specify endpoint of the arc:	Pick: **the edge of the next 10RIW symbol (Figure 20–9)**
Specify endpoint of arc or [Angle/ CEnter/CLose/Direction/Halfwidth/ Line/Radius/Second pt/Undo/Width]:	**<enter>**

Step 8. **Use Array to copy lines showing electrical connections (Figure 20–10).**

Prompt	Response
Command:	Type: **-AR<enter>**
Select objects:	Pick: **the polyline just drawn**
Select objects:	**<enter>**
Enter the type of array [Rectangular/ Polar] <R>:	**<enter>**
Enter the number of rows (---) <1>:	Type: **3<enter>**
Enter the number of columns (|||) <1>	**<enter>**
Enter the distance between rows or specify unit cell (---):	Type: **4'<enter>**

Step 9. **Use Polyline, Copy, Rotate, and Mirror to draw remaining connections in this area (Figure 20–11).**

FIGURE 20–10
Copy Connections Using Array

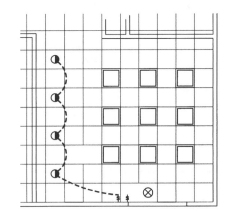

FIGURE 20–11
Draw Remaining Connections

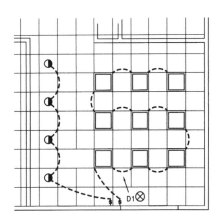

Chapter 20

On Your Own

1. Use Polyline (Type: **PL<enter>**) to draw the polyline arc from the top of the SW symbol on the right to the lower left corner of the lower left 2X2RFF symbol.

2. Use Polyline to draw the polyline arc from the 2X2RFF symbol on the lower left to the one next to it. You will have to Pick: **D1 (the approximate point)** after you Type: **D<enter>** to indicate the direction the arc should take.

3. Use the Copy command to copy the polyline just drawn to the right connecting the second and third symbols. Copy this same polyline to the upper right corner of the third symbol.

4. Use the Rotate command to rotate the copied polyline so it connects the lower right symbol to the one above it.

5. Use the Mirror command to copy the rotated polyline so it connects the left side of the first and second rows of symbols, then move it so it connects the second and third rows.

6. Use the Mirror command to copy the two bottom connecting lines to the middle row of symbols.

7. Use the Copy command to copy the connecting lines on the middle row to the top row.

Step 10. On Your Own:

1. Insert the remaining symbols and draw the connecting lines using procedures similar to the ones described in steps 1 through 9 so the drawing appears as shown in Figure 20–4.

2. Insert EX20-1 (the legend for this drawing) and place it in the approximate location shown in Figure 20–4.

3. Click: the layout labeled Reflected Ceiling Legend at the bottom of your screen and complete the title block using the Dtext command with $^3/_{32}$"-high letters. Title the drawing REFLECTED CEILING PLAN.

4. Use the SAVEAS command to save your drawing as EX20-2(your initials) on a floppy disk and again on the hard drive of your computer.

5. Plot or print your drawing at a scale of 1=1, using Portrait, Window (Click: a window around the legend), Center the plot, on the 11" × 8½" sheet.

EXERCISES

EXERCISE 20–1.   REFLECTED CEILING PLAN LEGEND
Draw the legend for the reflected ceiling plan using steps 1 through 14 described in this chapter.

EXERCISE 20–2.   REFLECTED CEILING PLAN
Draw the reflected ceiling plan using steps 1 through 10 described in this chapter.

EXERCISE 20–3.   POWER PLAN LEGEND
Draw the legend for the power plan shown in Figure 20–12 full scale (you will have to measure Figure 20–12 using a scale of $\frac{1}{4}''=1'-0''$). Open drawing EX20-3 on the disk that came with your book. Use a method similar to the one used to draw Exercise 20–1. Click: Model to be sure you are in Model space. Be sure to Wblock all symbols so they can be used on the Power Plan, Exercise 20–4.

Click: the layout labeled Power Plan Legend at the bottom of your screen and complete the title block using the Dtext command. Title the drawing POWER LEGEND.

Use the SAVEAS command to save your drawing as EX20-3(your initials) on a floppy disk and again on the hard drive of your computer.

Plot or print your drawing at a scale of 1=1, using Landscape, Limits, Center the plot, on an $11'' \times 8\frac{1}{2}''$ sheet.

EXERCISE 20–4.   POWER PLAN
Draw the power plan shown in Figure 20–13. Open drawing EX20-4 on the disk that came with your book. Use a method similar to the one used to draw Exercise 20–2. Be sure to insert the legend from EX20-3.

Click: the layout labeled Power Plan at the bottom of your screen and complete the title block using the Dtext command. Title the drawing POWER PLAN.

Use the SAVEAS command to save your drawing as EX20-4(your initials) on a floppy disk and again on the hard drive of your computer.

Plot or print your drawing at a scale of 1=1, using Landscape, Limits, Center the plot, on an $11'' \times 8\frac{1}{2}''$ sheet.

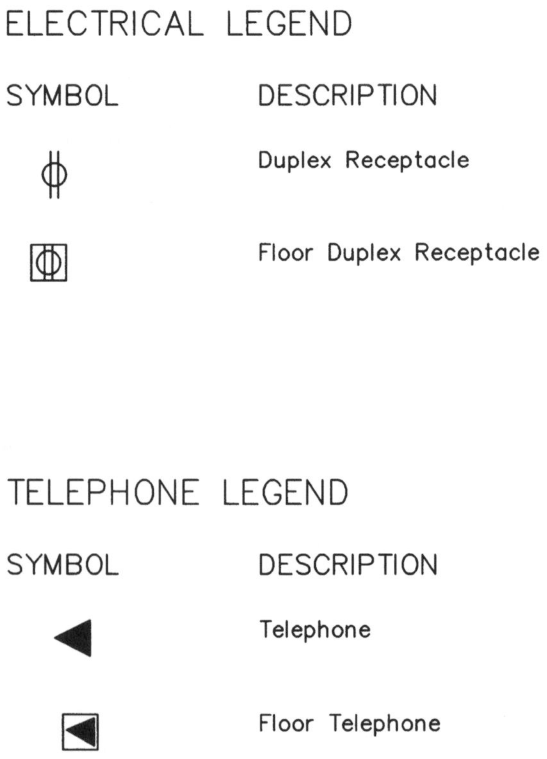

FIGURE 20–12
Power Plan Legend Complete
(Scale 1/4″=1′0″)

ELECTRICAL LEGEND

SYMBOL   DESCRIPTION

                          Duplex Receptacle

                          Floor Duplex Receptacle

TELEPHONE LEGEND

SYMBOL   DESCRIPTION

                Telephone

                Floor Telephone

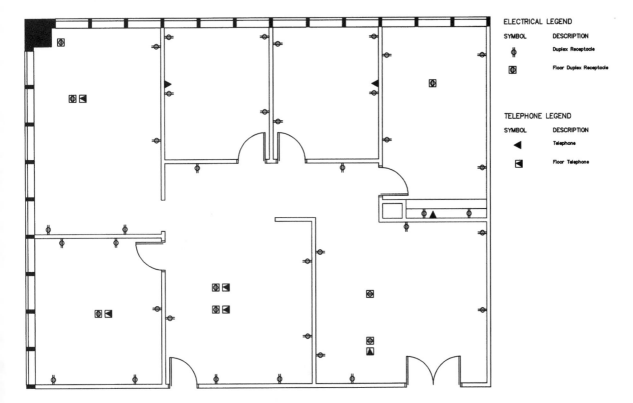

ELECTRICAL LEGEND

SYMBOL   DESCRIPTION

                Duplex Receptacle

                Floor Duplex Receptacle

TELEPHONE LEGEND

SYMBOL   DESCRIPTION

                Telephone

                Floor Telephone

FIGURE 20–13
Exercise 20–4 Complete

EXERCISE 20–5.   HOUSE LIGHTING AND OUTLET PLAN LEGEND

Draw the legend for the house lighting and outlet plan shown in Figure 20–14 full scale (you will have to measure Figure 20–14 using a scale of $\frac{1}{4}''=1'-0''$). Open drawing EX20-5 on the disk that came with your book. Use a method similar to the one used to draw Exercise 20–1. Be sure to Wblock all symbols so they can be used on the House Lighting and Outlet Plan, Exercise 20–6. Check to be sure you are in Model space before you start to draw.

Click: the layout labeled House Lighting Legend at the bottom of your screen and complete the title block using the Dtext command. Title the drawing HOUSE LIGHTING AND OUTLET LEGEND.

Use the SAVEAS command to save your drawing as EX20-5(your initials) on a floppy disk and again on the hard drive of your computer.

Plot or print your drawing at a scale of 1=1, using Landscape, Limits, Center the plot, on an $11'' \times 8\frac{1}{2}''$ sheet.

EXERCISE 20–6.   HOUSE LIGHTING AND OUTLET PLAN

Draw the house lighting and outlet plan shown in Figure 20–15. Open drawing EX20-6 on the disk that came with your book. Use a method similar to the one used to draw Exercise 20–2. Be sure to insert the legend from EX20-5.

Click: the layout labeled Lighting and Outlet Plan at the bottom of your screen and complete the title block using the Dtext command. Title the drawing LIGHTING AND OUTLET PLAN.

Use the SAVEAS command to save your drawing as EX20-6(your initials) on a floppy disk and again on the hard drive of your computer.

FIGURE 20–14
House Lighting and Outlet Legend (Scale 1/4"=1'0")

ELECTRICAL LEGEND

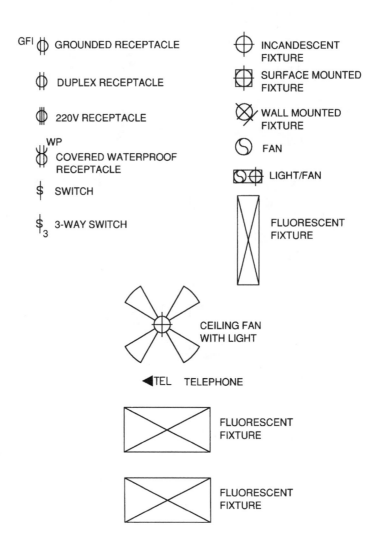

EXERCISE 20–7.   HOUSE LIGHTING AND OUTLET PLAN

Design your own house lighting and outlet plan for the floor plan shown in Figure 20–16. Open drawing EX20-7 on the disk that came with your book. Refer to the electrical plan of Figure 20–15 to determine the spacing of outlets and lighting fixtures. Use a method similar to the one used to draw Exercise 20–2. You can use the same legend as you used for EX20-6, so, be sure to insert the legend from EX20-5.

Click: the layout labeled Lighting and Outlet Plan at the bottom of your screen and complete the title block using the Dtext command. Title the drawing LIGHTING AND OUTLET PLAN.

Use the SAVEAS command to save your drawing as EX20-7(your initials) on a floppy disk and again on the hard drive of your computer.

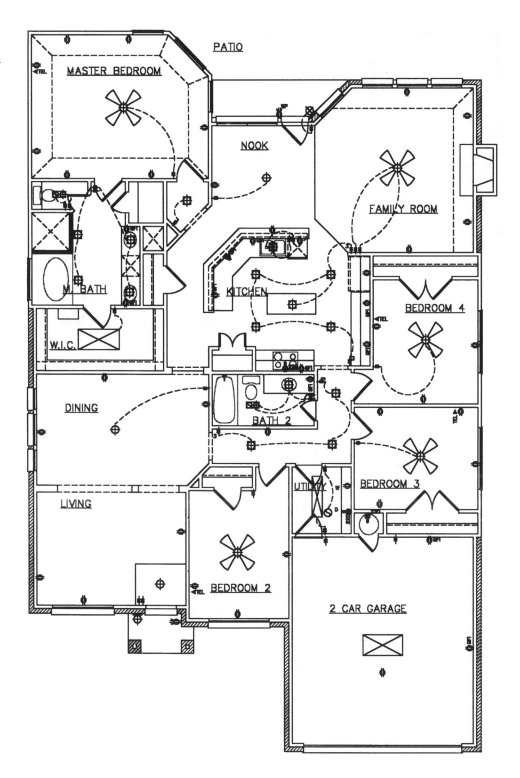

PATIO

MASTER BEDROOM

NOOK

FAMILY ROOM

M. BATH

KITCHEN

BEDROOM 4

W.I.C.

DINING

BATH 2

LIVING

UTILITY

BEDROOM 3

BEDROOM 2

2 CAR GARAGE

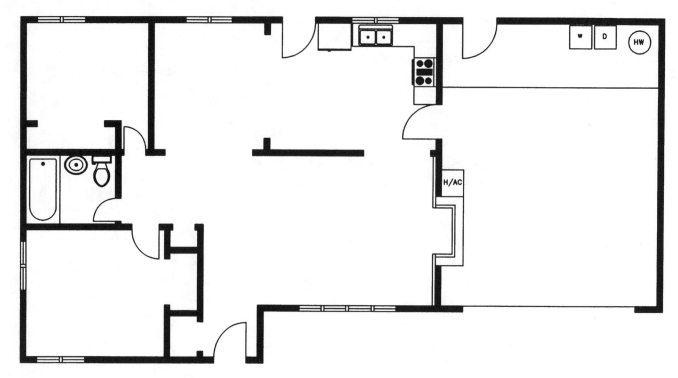

FIGURE 20–16
Floor Plan for Exercise 20–7

REVIEW QUESTIONS

Circle the best answer.

1. In the legend exercises you drew all symbols
   a. Full scale
   b. Half scale
   c. $\frac{1}{4}$ scale
   d. $\frac{1}{8}'' = 1'$ scale
   e. $\frac{1}{4}'' = 1'$ scale

2. Which command will draw a solid 10″-diameter symbol?
   a. Donut—Inside diameter, 10″—Outside diameter 0″
   b. Donut—Inside diameter, 0″—Outside diameter 10″
   c. Donut—Inside diameter, 10″—Outside diameter 10″
   d. Circle—10″ diameter—Fill
   e. Circle—0″ inside diameter, 10″ Outside diameter

3. A solid 10″ dot cannot be trimmed.
   a. True
   b. False

4. Which of the following commands was used to draw the $2' \times 4'$ Recessed Fluorescent Fixture symbol in this chapter?
   a. Line
   b. Leader
   c. Trim
   d. Rectangle
   e. Donut

5. Which of the following commands was used to draw the directional arrows on the right and left sides of the EXIT symbol?
   a. Line
   b. Leader
   c. Trim
   d. Rectangle
   e. Donut

6. When you are drawing with a command in progress and you Type: FRO<enter>, what is the first thing AutoCAD asks you for?
   a. Offset
   b. Intersection
   c. Midpoint
   d. Base point
   e. First point
7. When you are using the Rotate command, a positive-number response to the "Specify rotation angle" prompt will rotate the selected object
   a. Clockwise
   b. Counterclockwise
8. The Wblock command creates which type of file?
   a. Drawing file
   b. Backup file
   c. Template file
   d. Bitmap file
   e. This command does not create any file.
9. What must you first do to an inserted EXIT symbol before you can erase the directional arrows?
   a. Separate it
   b. Explode it
   c. Save it
   d. Wblock it
   e. Trim it
10. The D<enter> response to the polyline arc prompt tells AutoCAD you are specifying a
    a. Destination
    b. Dtext
    c. Distance
    d. Direction
    e. Diameter

Exercises to Chapters

Exercises to Chapters

— START ALL LINES FROM THIS VERTICAL GRID

ARCHITECT'S SCALE

4'-3"   @3/4"=1'
6'-2"   @3/4"=1'
1.5'-6"   @1/8"=1'
7'-10"   @1/2"=1'
5-3/4"   @3/4"=1"
6-3/4"   @3/4"=1"
20-1/2"   @1/8"=1'
8-1/4"   @1/2"=1"

CIVIL ENGINEER'S SCALE

84'   @1"=20'
68'   @1"=20'
1650'   @1"=400'
214 MILES   @1"=50 MILES
5.5"   @1/2"=1"
6.2"   @1/2"=1"
17.5"   @1/4"=1"
11.4"   @1/4"=1"

| NAME: | DATE: | DRAWING TITLE: | CLASS |
| SCHOOL: | GRADE: | | EXERCISE 2-1 |

CLASS

EXERCISE 2-2

DRAWNG TITLE:

DATE:

GRADE:

NAME:

SCHOOL:

CLASS

EXERCISE 2-3

DRAWING TITLE:

DATE:

GRADE:

NAME:

SCHOOL:

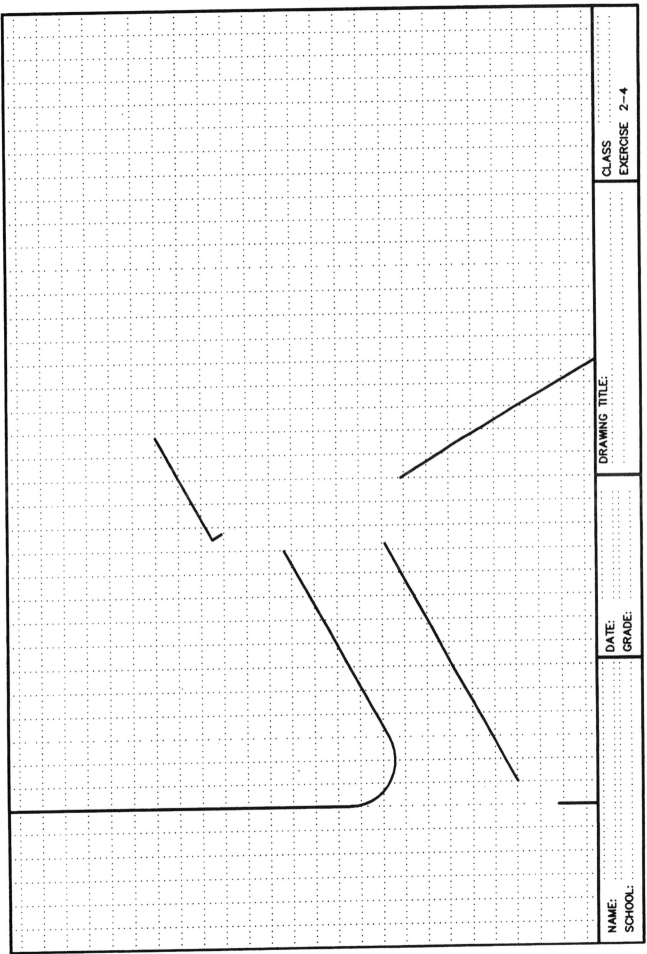

CLASS

EXERCISE 2-4

DRAWING TITLE:

DATE:

GRADE:

NAME:

SCHOOL:

DRAW LETTERS AND NUMBERS 7 TIMES

A	B
C	D
E	F
G	H
I	J
K	L
M	N
O	P
Q	R
S	T
U	V
W	X
Y	Z
I	2
3	4
5	6
7	8
9	O

$1\frac{1}{2}$"

5 TIMES

$2\frac{3}{4}$"

5 TIMES

GOOD LETTERING MAKES A GOOD SKETCH BETTER

G
G
G
G

5 TIMES

NAME	DATE	DRAWING TITLE:	CLASS
SCHOOL	GRADE		EXERCISE 4-1

Kirkpatrick, *Architectural Drawing Using Pencil Sketches and AutoCAD*, © 2002 by Pearson Education, Inc.

DRAW LETTERS AND NUMBERS 7 TIMES

A   B
C   D
E   F
G   H
I   J
K   L
M   N
O   P
Q   R
S   T
U   V
W   X
Y   Z
1   2
3   4
5   6
7   8
9   0

$1\frac{1}{2}''$ $2\frac{3}{4}''$

5 TIMES   5 TIMES

GOOD LETTERING MAKES A GOOD SKETCH BETTER

G
G
G
G

5 TIMES

NAME	DATE	DRAWING TITLE:	CLASS
SCHOOL	GRADE		EXERCISE 4-2

Kirkpatrick, *Architectural Drawing Using Pencil Sketches and AutoCAD*, © 2002 by Pearson Education, Inc.

NAME:

SCHOOL:

DATE:

GRADE:

DRAWING TITLE:

CLASS

EXERCISE 5-1

NAME:

SCHOOL:

DATE:

GRADE:

DRAWING TITLE:

CLASS

EXERCISE 5-2

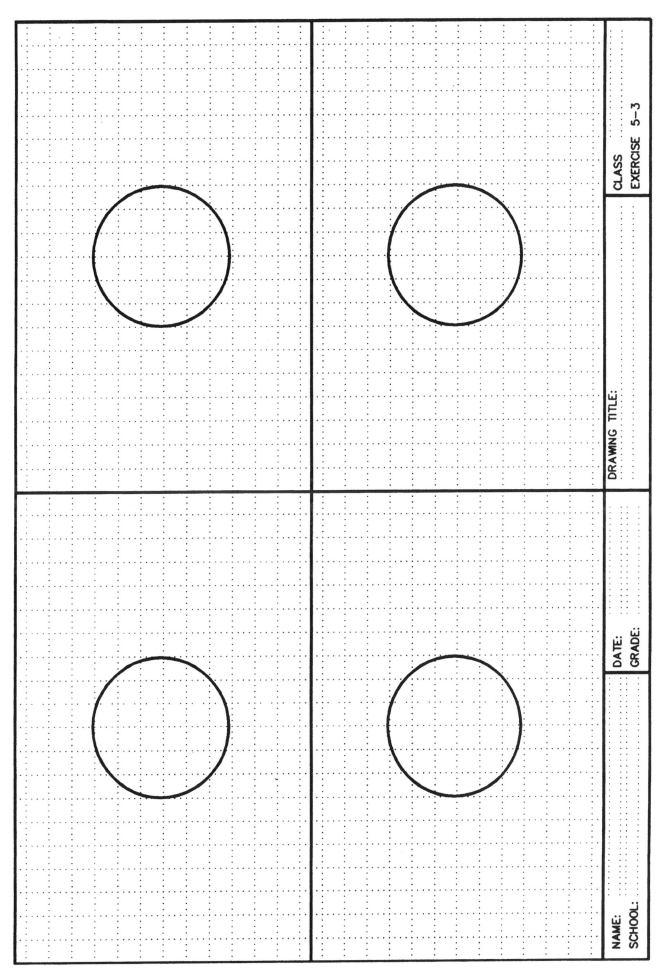

Kirkpatrick, *Architectural Drawing Using Pencil Sketches and AutoCAD*, © 2002 by Pearson Education, Inc.

NAME:

SCHOOL:

DATE:

GRADE:

DRAWING TITLE:

CLASS

EXERCISE 5—4

NAME:

SCHOOL:

DATE:

GRADE:

DRAWING TITLE:

CLASS

EXERCISE 5-5

NAME:

SCHOOL:

DATE:

GRADE:

DRAWING TITLE:

CLASS

EXERCISE 5—6

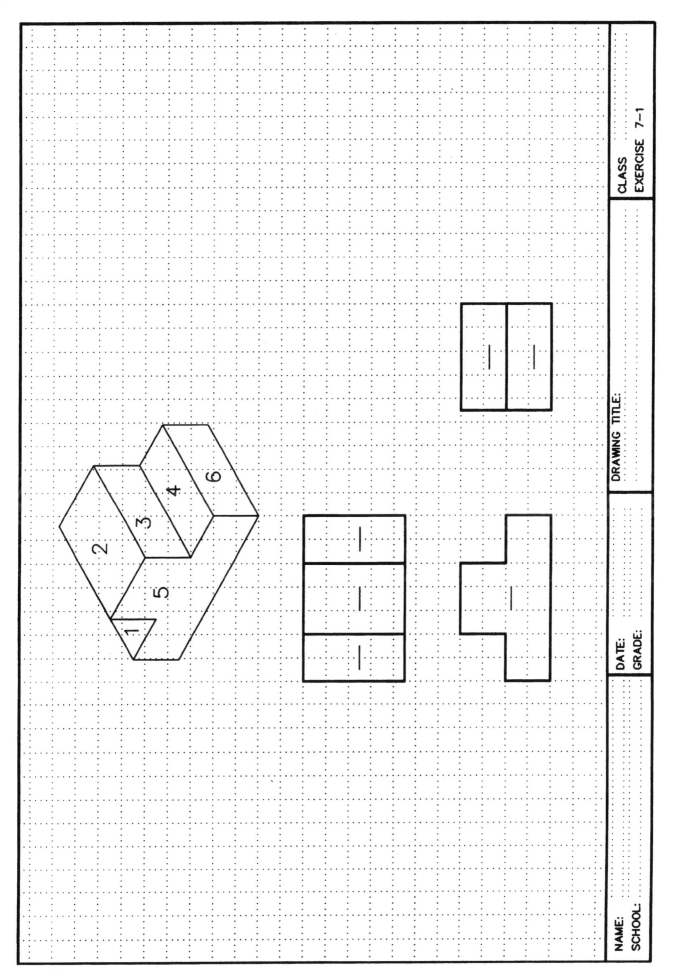

CLASS

EXERCISE 7–1

DRAWING TITLE:

DATE:

GRADE:

NAME:

SCHOOL:

1
2
3
4
5
6

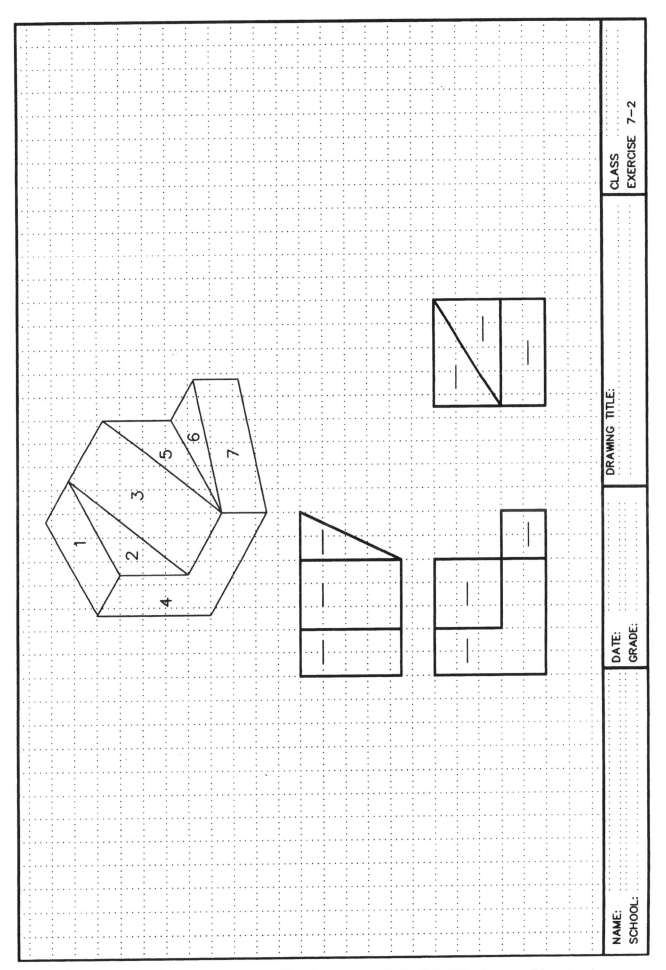

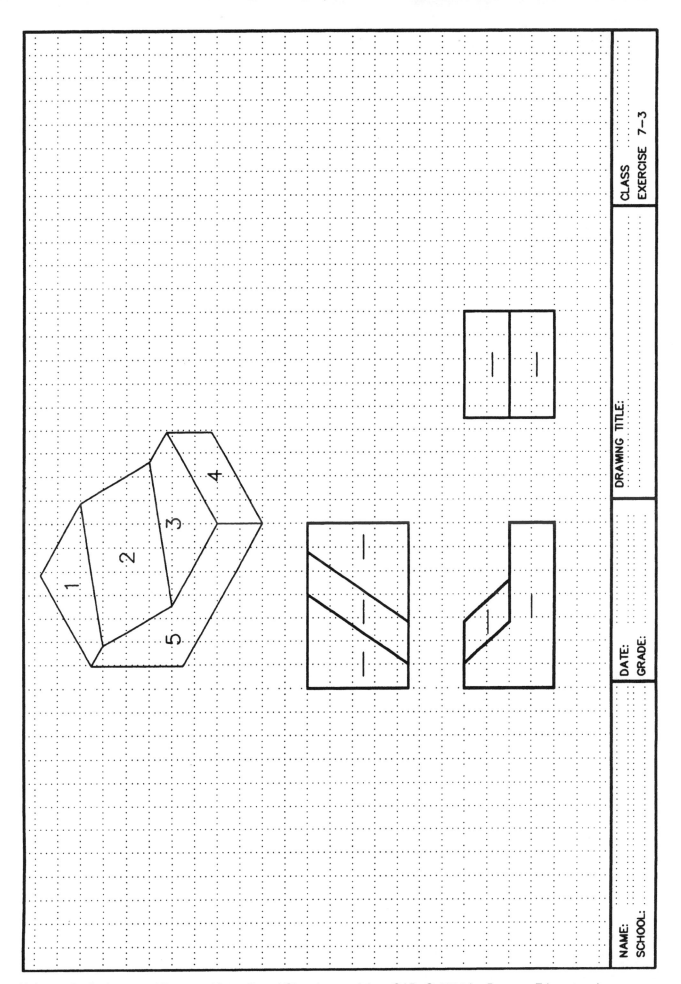

CLASS

EXERCISE 7-3

DRAWING TITLE:

DATE:

GRADE:

NAME:

SCHOOL:

Kirkpatrick, *Architectural Drawing Using Pencil Sketches and AutoCAD*, © 2002 by Pearson Education, Inc.

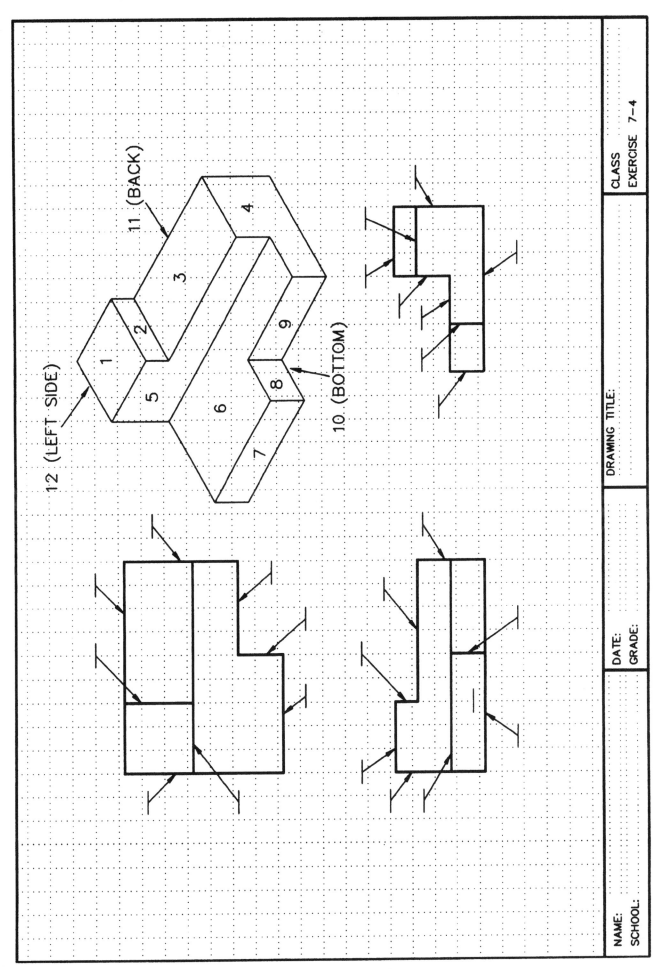

12 (LEFT SIDE)

11 (BACK)

10 (BOTTOM)

CLASS

EXERCISE 7-4

DRAWING TITLE:

DATE:

GRADE:

NAME:

SCHOOL:

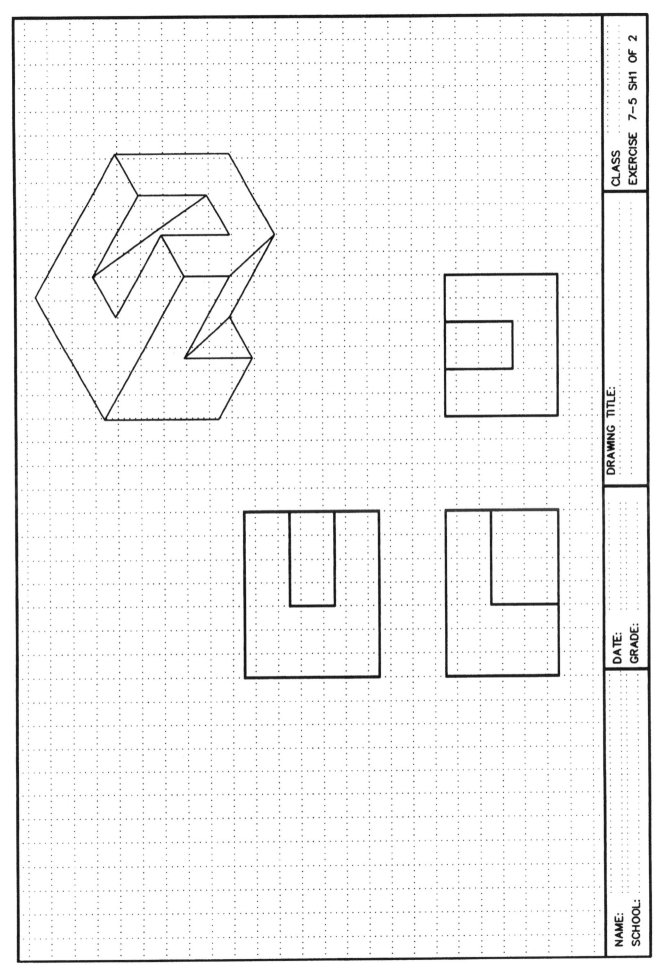

DRAWING TITLE:

DATE:

GRADE:

NAME:

SCHOOL:

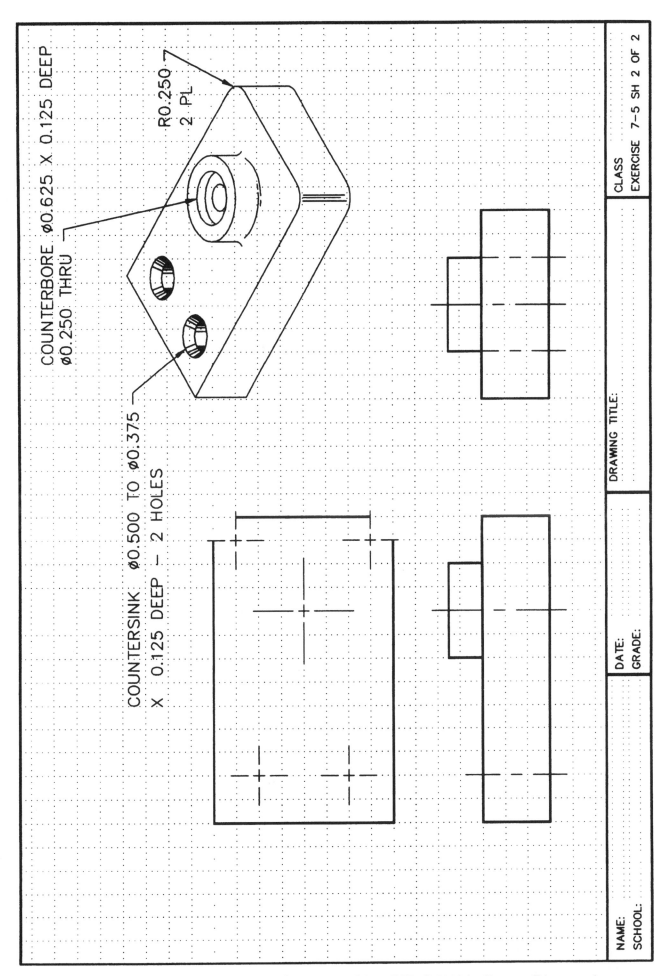

COUNTERBORE ∅0.625 X 0.125 DEEP
∅0.250 THRU

R0.250
2 PL

COUNTERSINK ∅0.500 TO ∅0.375
X 0.125 DEEP – 2 HOLES

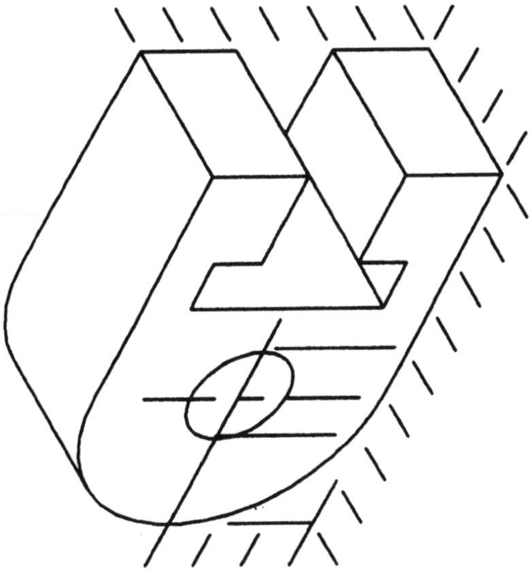

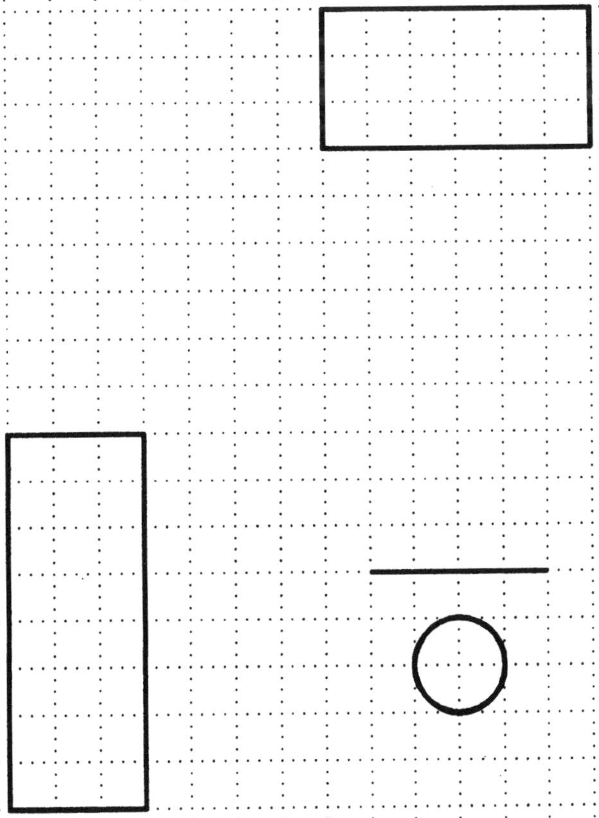

NAME:
SCHOOL:
DATE:
GRADE:
DRAWING TITLE:
CLASS
EXERCISE 7–6

DRAWING TITLE:

DATE:

GRADE:

NAME:

SCHOOL:

Kirkpatrick, *Architectural Drawing Using Pencil Sketches and AutoCAD*, © 2002 by Pearson Education, Inc.

NAME:

SCHOOL:

DATE:

GRADE:

DRAWING TITLE:

CLASS

EXERCISE 7-9

NAME:

SCHOOL:

DATE:

GRADE:

DRAWING TITLE:

CLASS

EXERCISE 7–10

NAME:

SCHOOL:

DATE:

GRADE:

DRAWING TITLE:

CLASS

EXERCISE 7–11

CLASS

EXERCISE 7–12

DRAWING TITLE:

DATE:

GRADE:

NAME:

SCHOOL:

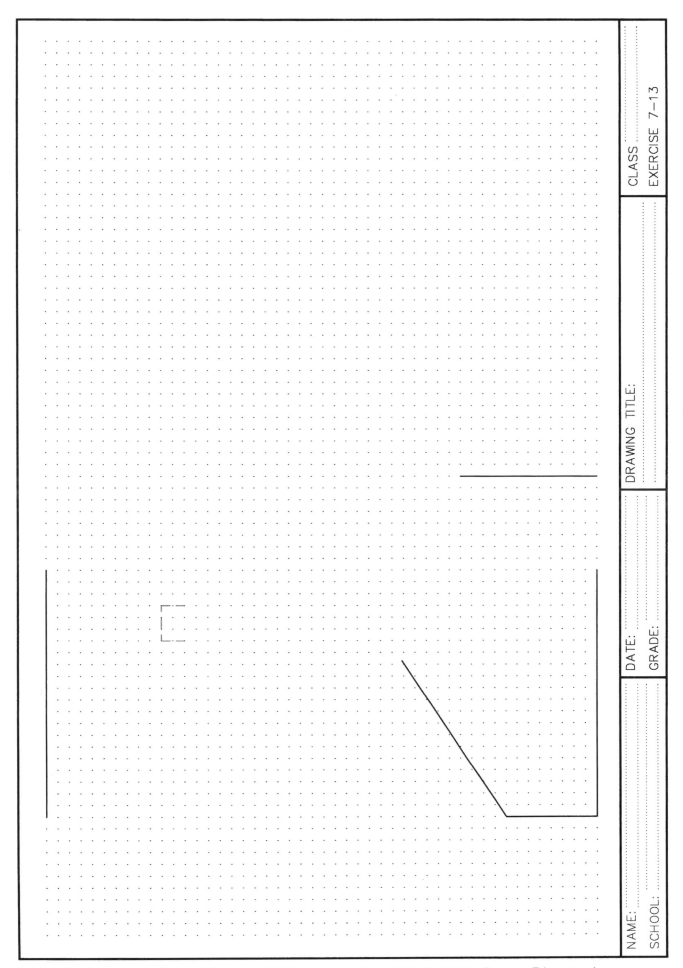

Kirkpatrick, *Architectural Drawing Using Pencil Sketches and AutoCAD*, © 2002 by Pearson Education, Inc.

CLASS

EXERCISE 7–13

DRAWING TITLE:

DATE:

GRADE:

NAME:

SCHOOL:

COMPLETE THIS VIEW

COMPLETE THIS VIEW

COMPLETE THIS VIEW

COMPLETE THIS VIEW

COMPLETE THIS VIEW

COMPLETE THIS VIEW

COMPLETE THIS VIEW

COMPLETE THIS VIEW

COMPLETE THIS VIEW

COMPLETE THIS VIEW

NAME:	DATE:	DRAWING TITLE:	CLASS.
SCHOOL:	GRADE:		EXERCISE 7-14

Kirkpatrick, *Architectural Drawing Using Pencil Sketches and AutoCAD*, © 2002 by Pearson Education, Inc.

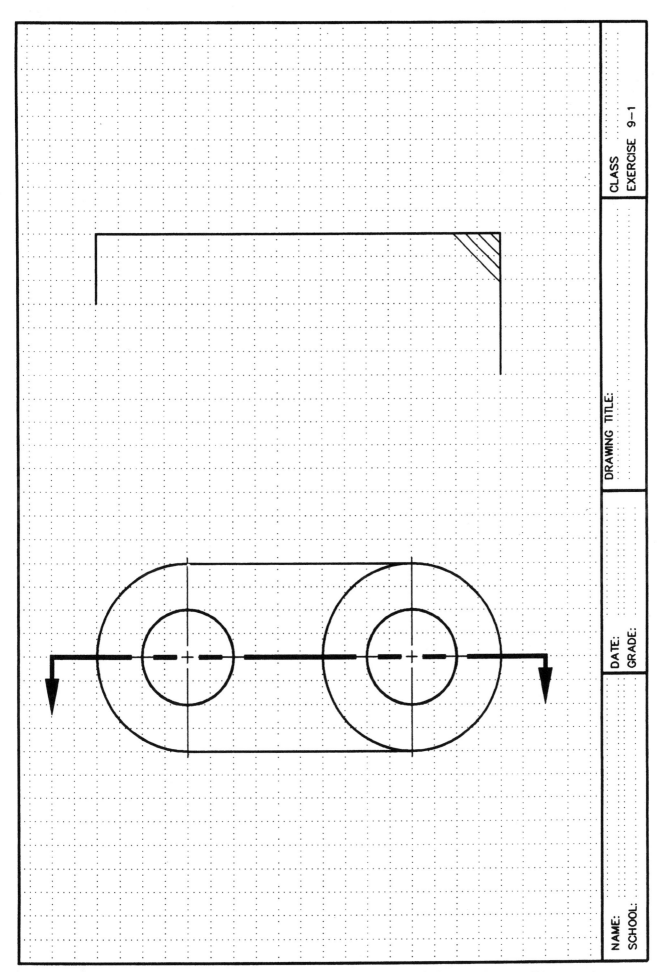

CLASS

EXERCISE 9-1

DRAWING TITLE:

DATE:

GRADE:

NAME:

SCHOOL:

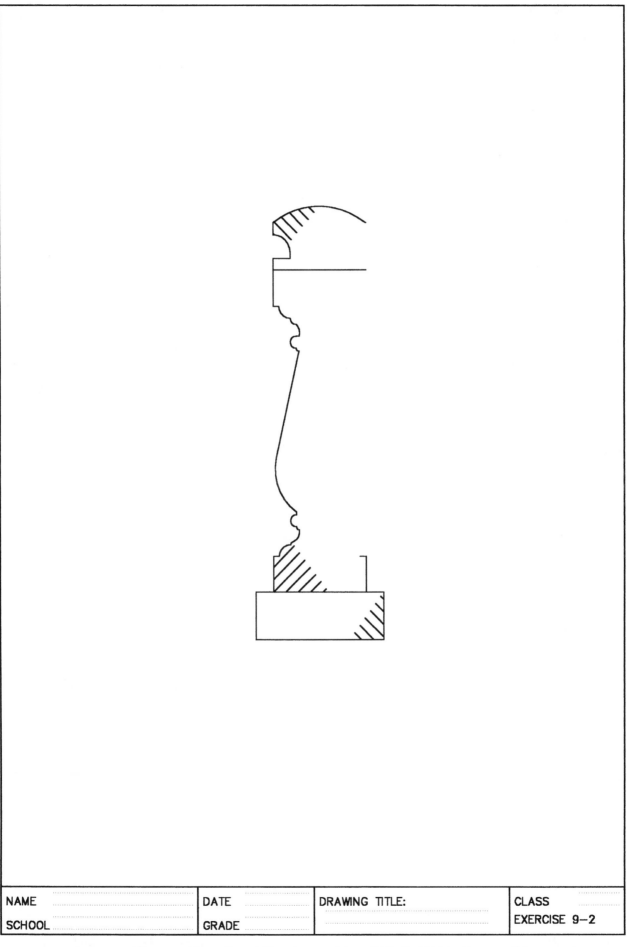

Kirkpatrick, *Architectural Drawing Using Pencil Sketches and AutoCAD*, © 2002 by Pearson Education, Inc.

Kirkpatrick, *Architectural Drawing Using Pencil Sketches and AutoCAD*, © 2002 by Pearson Education, Inc.

Kirkpatrick, *Architectural Drawing Using Pencil Sketches and AutoCAD*, © 2002 by Pearson Education, Inc.

DRAWING TITLE:

DATE:

GRADE:

NAME:

SCHOOL:

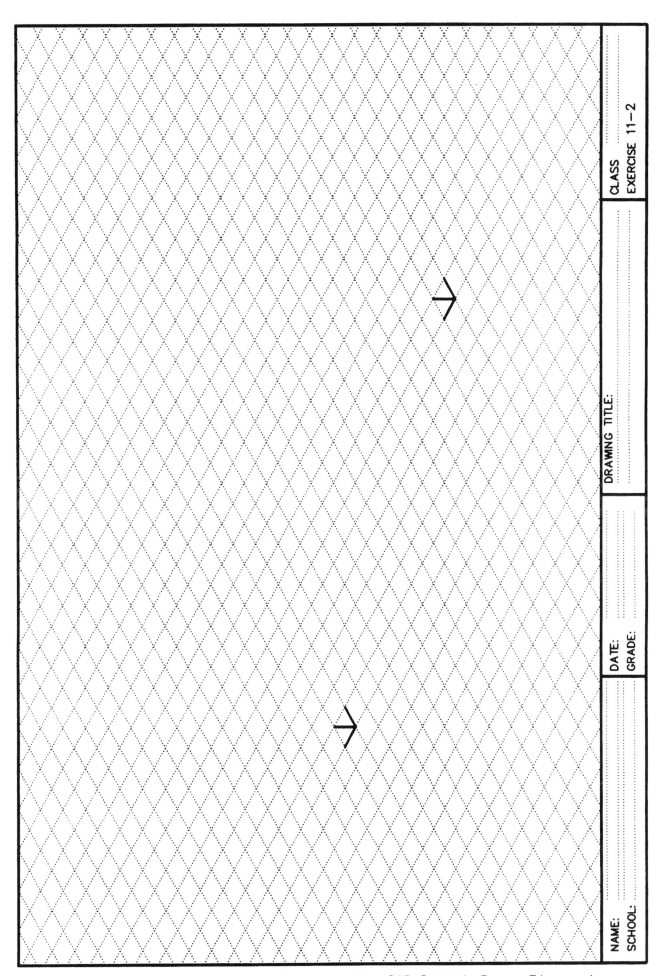

NAME:

SCHOOL:

DATE:

GRADE:

DRAWING TITLE:

CLASS

EXERCISE 11–2

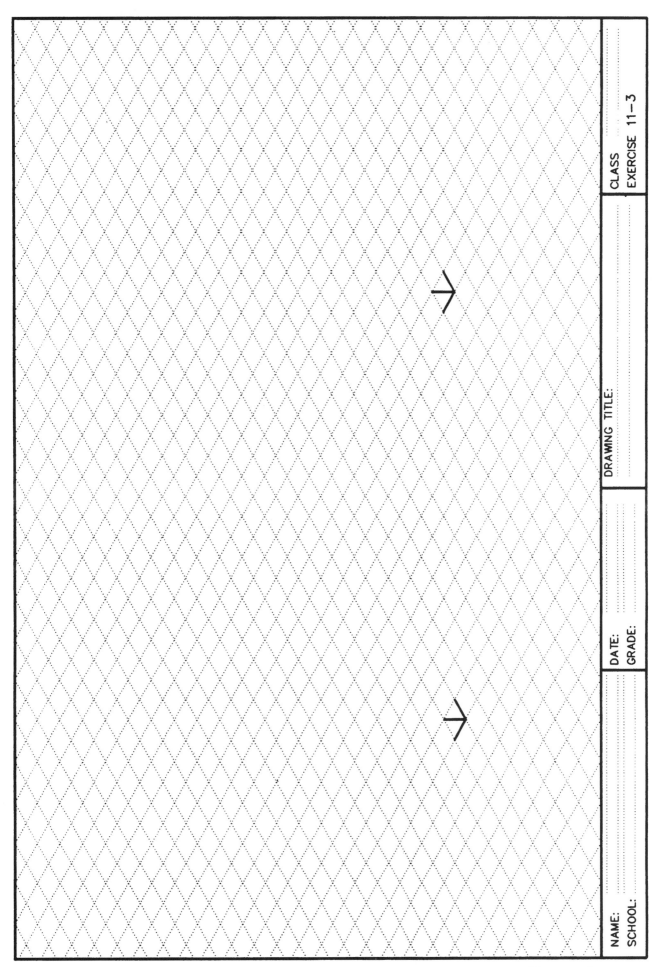

DRAWING TITLE:

CLASS

EXERCISE 11—3

DATE:

GRADE:

NAME:

SCHOOL:

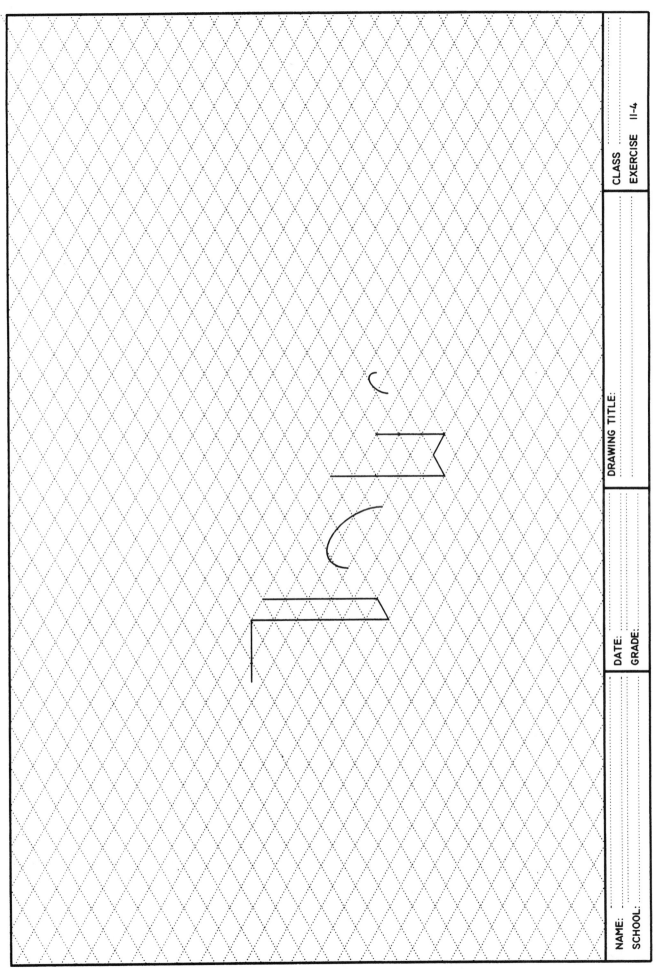

NAME:
SCHOOL:
DATE:
GRADE.
DRAWING TITLE:
CLASS
EXERCISE II-4

NAME:
SCHOOL:
DATE:
GRADE:
DRAWING TITLE:
CLASS
EXERCISE   II-5

NAME:

SCHOOL:

DATE:

GRADE:

DRAWING TITLE:

CLASS

EXERCISE 11—6

CLASS

EXERCISE 11–7

DRAWING TITLE:

DATE:

GRADE:

NAME:

SCHOOL:

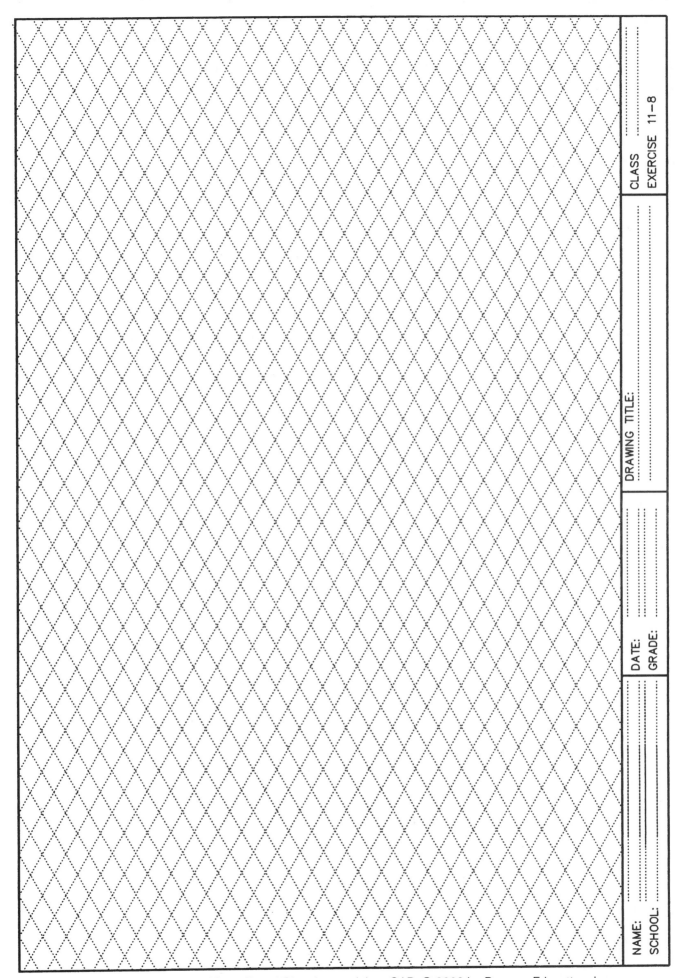

CLASS

EXERCISE 11-8

DRAWING TITLE:

DATE:

GRADE:

NAME:

SCHOOL:

Kirkpatrick, *Architectural Drawing Using Pencil Sketches and AutoCAD*, © 2002 by Pearson Education, Inc.

NAME: ....

SCHOOL: ....

DATE: ....

GRADE: ....

DRAWING TITLE: ....

CLASS ....

EXERCISE 11—9

Kirkpatrick, *Architectural Drawing Using Pencil Sketches and AutoCAD*, © 2002 by Pearson Education, Inc.

NAME:

SCHOOL:

DATE:

GRADE:

DRAWING TITLE:

CLASS

EXERCISE 13—2

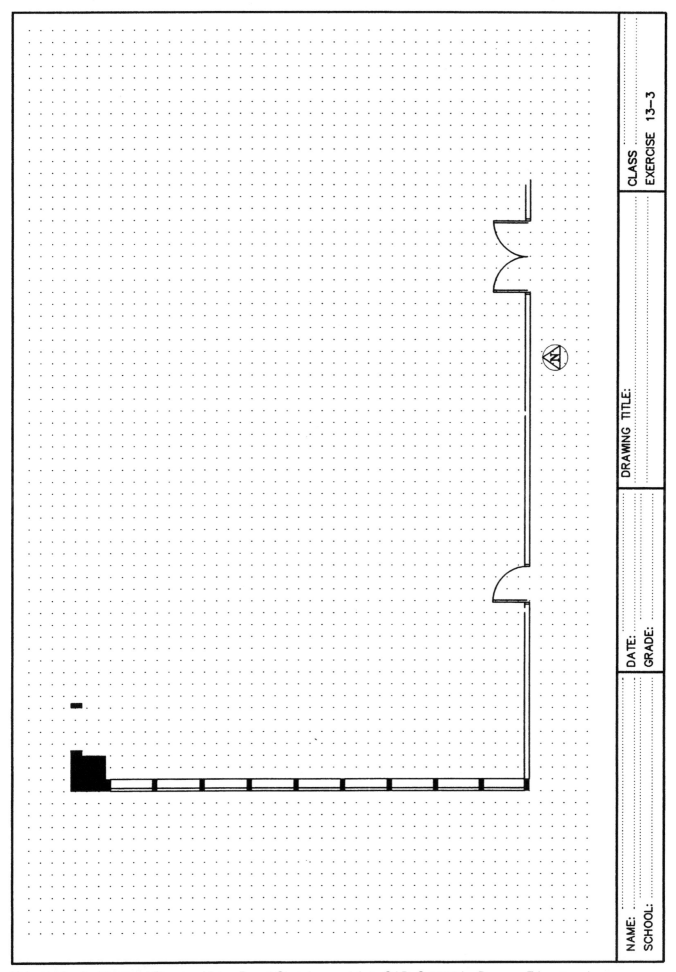

CLASS

EXERCISE 13—3

DRAWING TITLE:

DATE:

GRADE:

NAME:

SCHOOL:

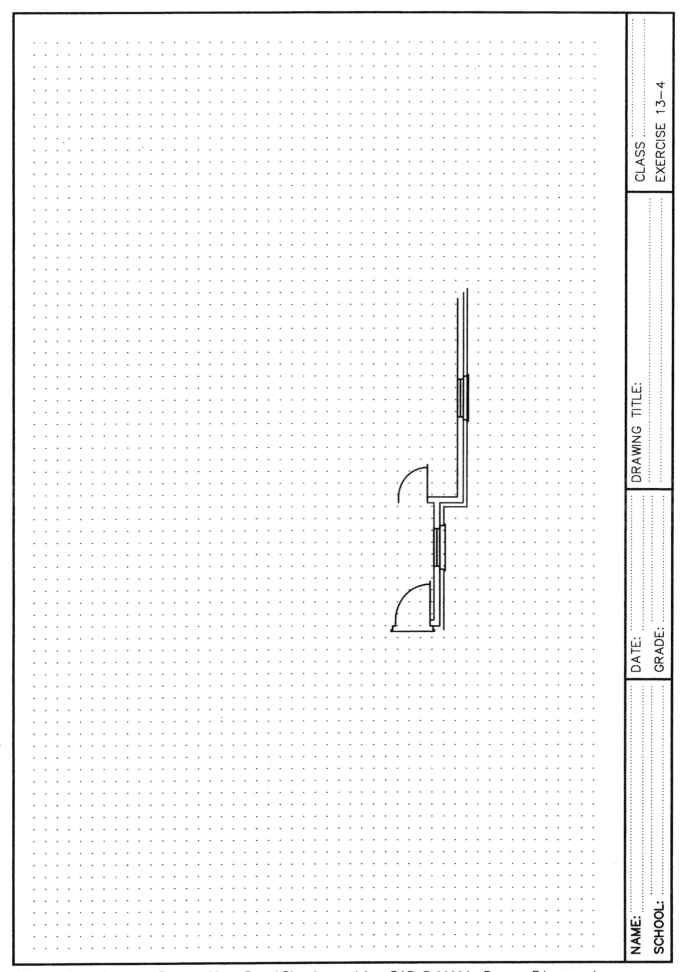

NAME:

SCHOOL:

DATE:

GRADE:

DRAWNG TITLE:

CLASS

EXERCISE 15−1

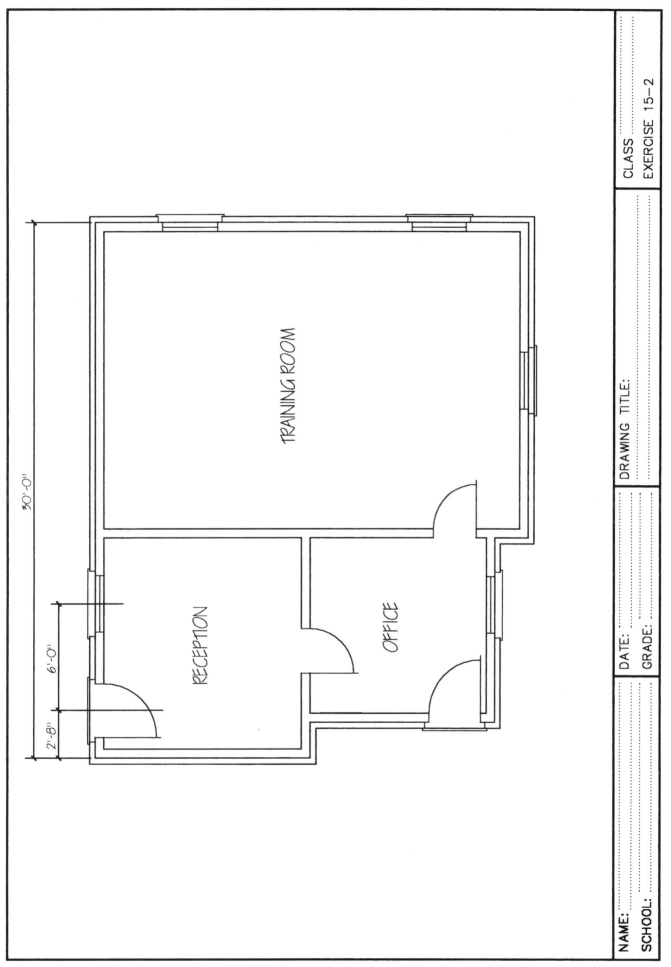

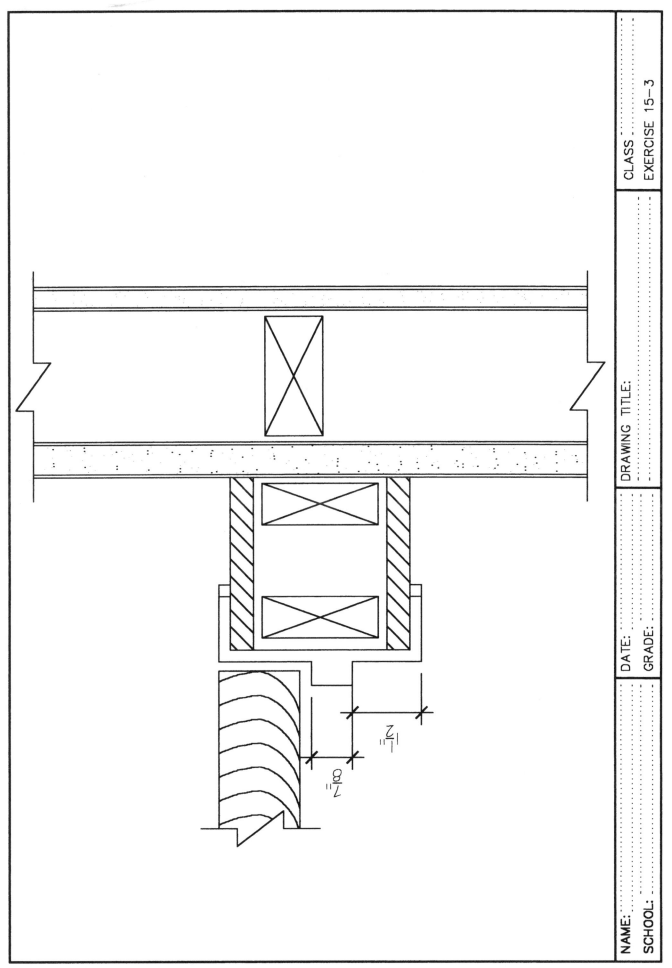

$\frac{1}{2}$"

$\frac{7}{8}$"

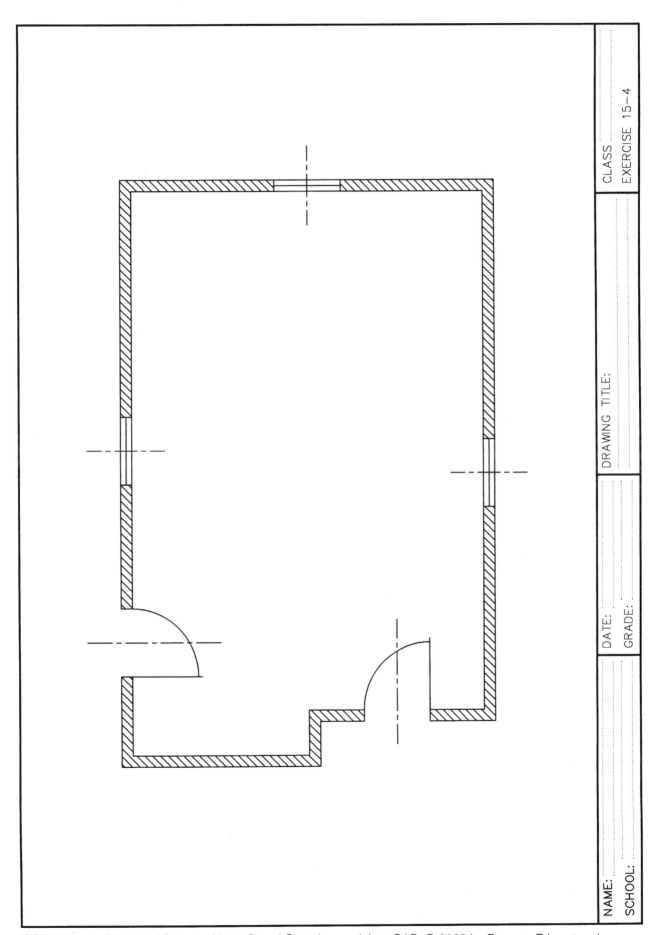

CLASS

EXERCISE 15—4

DRAWING TITLE:

DATE:

GRADE:

NAME:

SCHOOL:

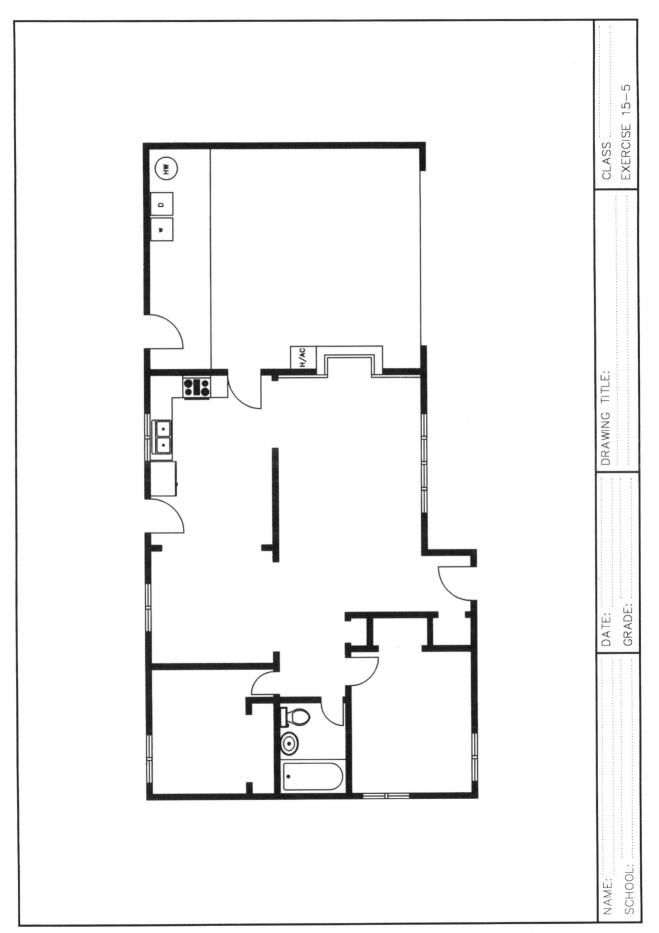

HW

W   D

H/AC

CLASS
EXERCISE 15–5

DRAWING TITLE:

DATE:
GRADE:

NAME:
SCHOOL:

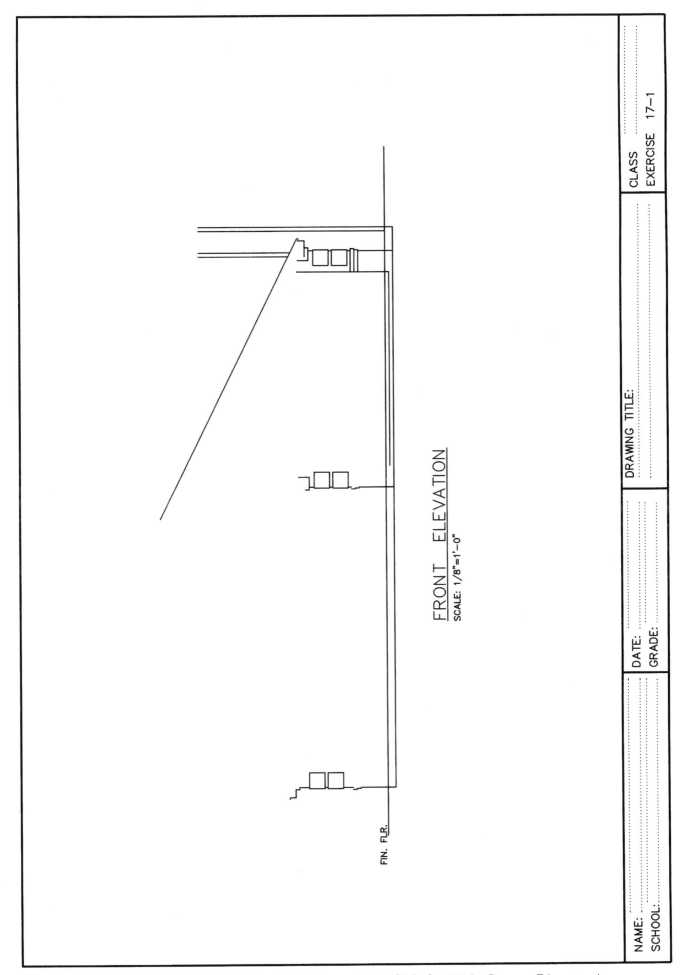

FRONT ELEVATION
SCALE: 1/8"=1'-0"

FIN. FLR.

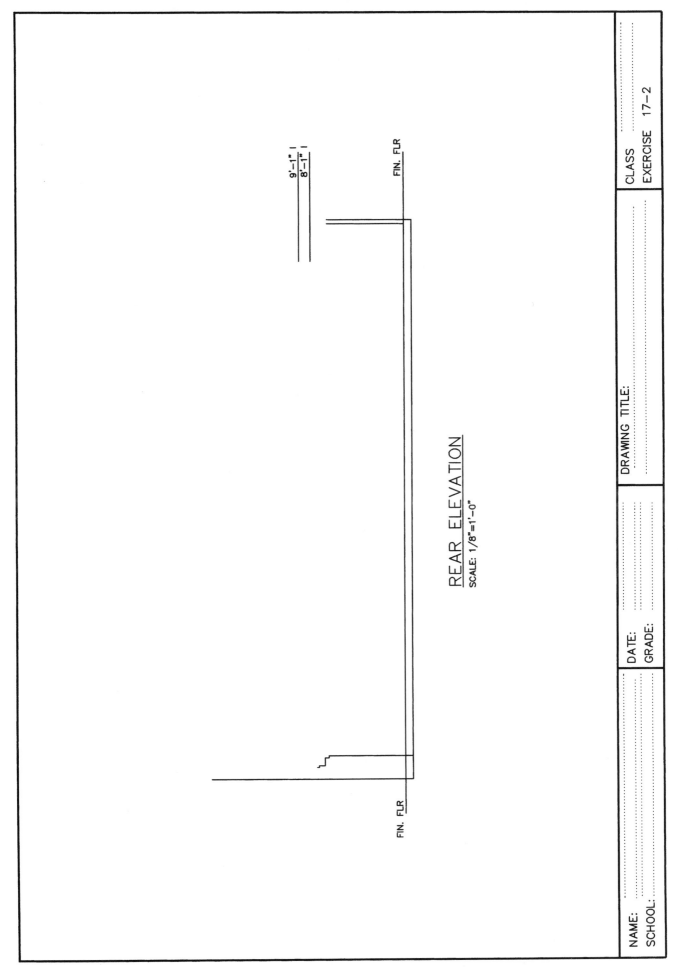

REAR ELEVATION
SCALE: 1/8"=1'-0"

9'-1"
8'-1"

FIN. FLR

FIN. FLR

NAME:
SCHOOL:

DATE:
GRADE:

DRAWING TITLE:

CLASS
EXERCISE 17–2

LEFT SIDE ELEVATION

SCALE: 1/8"=1'-0"

FIN. FLR

FIN. FLR

8'-1"

FIN. FLR

Kirkpatrick, *Architectural Drawing Using Pencil Sketches and AutoCAD*, © 2002 by Pearson Education, Inc.

RIGHT SIDE ELEVATION

SCALE: 1/8"=1'-0"

FIN. FLR

FIN. FLR

LIGHTING LEGEND

SYMBOL   DESCRIPTION

                2' X 2' Recessed
                Fluorescent Fixture

                2' X 4' Recessed
                Fluorescent Fixture

  ○   10" diameter Recessed
                Incandescent Downlight

  ○   10" Diameter Recessed
                Incandescent Wallwasher

  ○   Exit Sign Location

  S   SPDT Switch

NAME:	DATE:	DRAWING TITLE:	CLASS
SCHOOL:	GRADE:		EXERCISE 19—1 Sheet 1 of 2

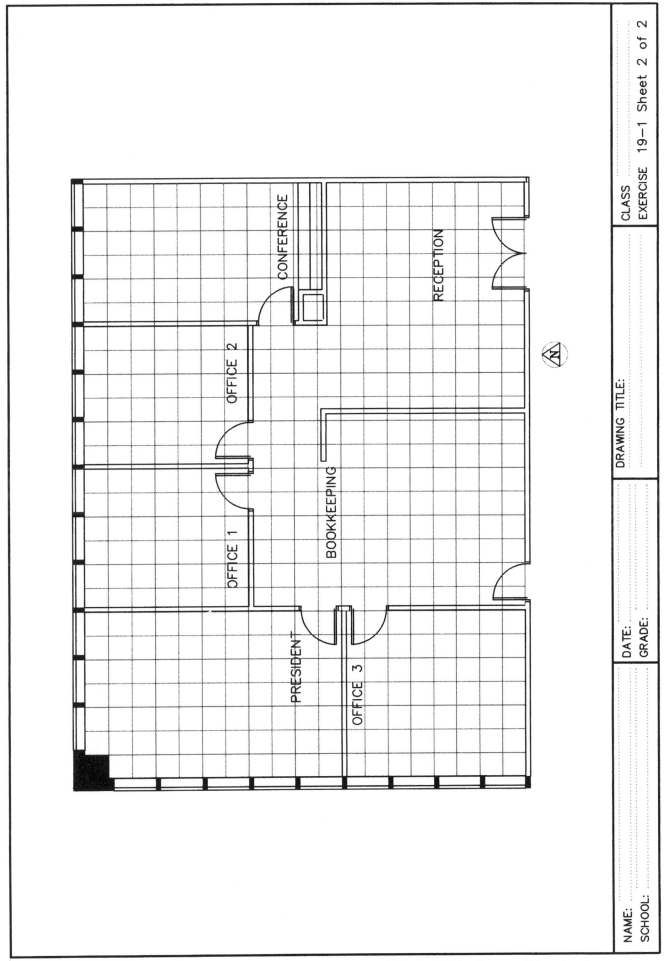

CONFERENCE

OFFICE 2

RECEPTION

OFFICE 1

BOOKKEEPING

PRESIDENT

OFFICE 3

DRAWING TITLE:

DATE:

GRADE:

NAME:

SCHOOL:

ELECTRICAL LEGEND

SYMBOL   DESCRIPTION

                Duplex Receptacle

                Floor Duplex Receptacle

TELEPHONE LEGEND

SYMBOL   DESCRIPTION

                Telephone

                Floor Telephone

NAME:	DATE:	DRAWING TITLE:	CLASS
SCHOOL:	GRADE:		EXERCISE 19−2 Sheet 1 of 2

Kirkpatrick, *Architectural Drawing Using Pencil Sketches and AutoCAD*, © 2002 by Pearson Education, Inc.

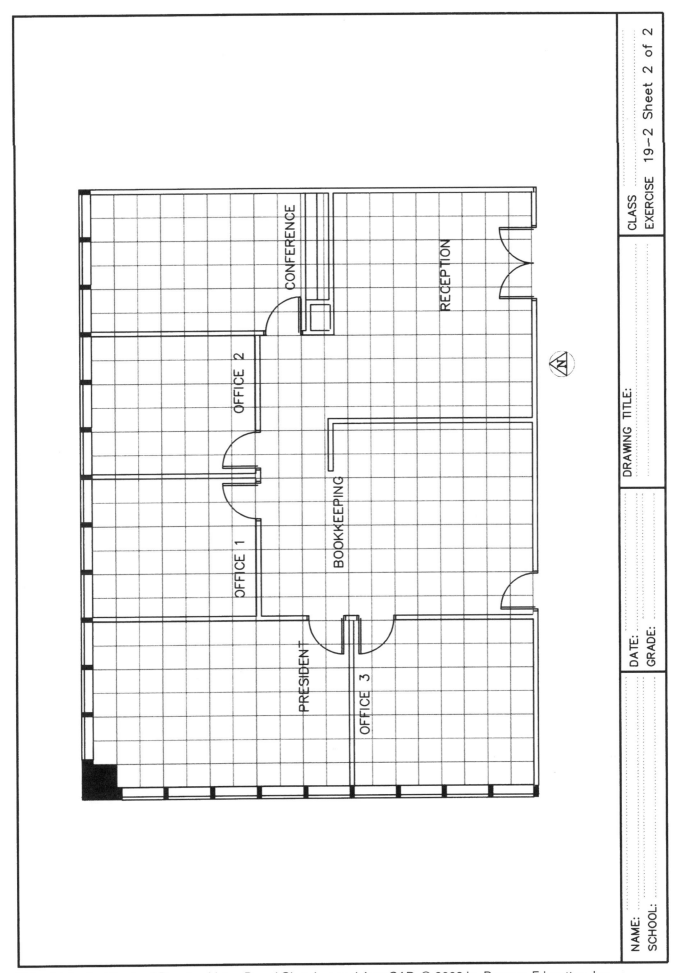

ELECTRICAL LEGEND

○ GROUNDED RECEPTACLE

○ DUPLEX RECEPTACLE

○ 220V RECEPTACLE

○ COVERED WATERPROOF
   RECEPTACLE

S SWITCH

S 3-WAY SWITCH

○ INCANDESCENT
   FIXTURE

○ SURFACE MOUNTED
   FIXTURE

○ WALL MOUNTED
   FIXTURE

○ FAN

☐ LIGHT/FAN

FLUORESCENT
FIXTURE

○ CEILING FAN
   WITH LIGHT

◄ TELEPHONE

FLUORESCENT
FIXTURE

FLUORESCENT
FIXTURE

NAME:	DATE:	DRAWING TITLE:	CLASS
SCHOOL:	GRADE:		EXERCISE 19—3 Sheet 1 of 2

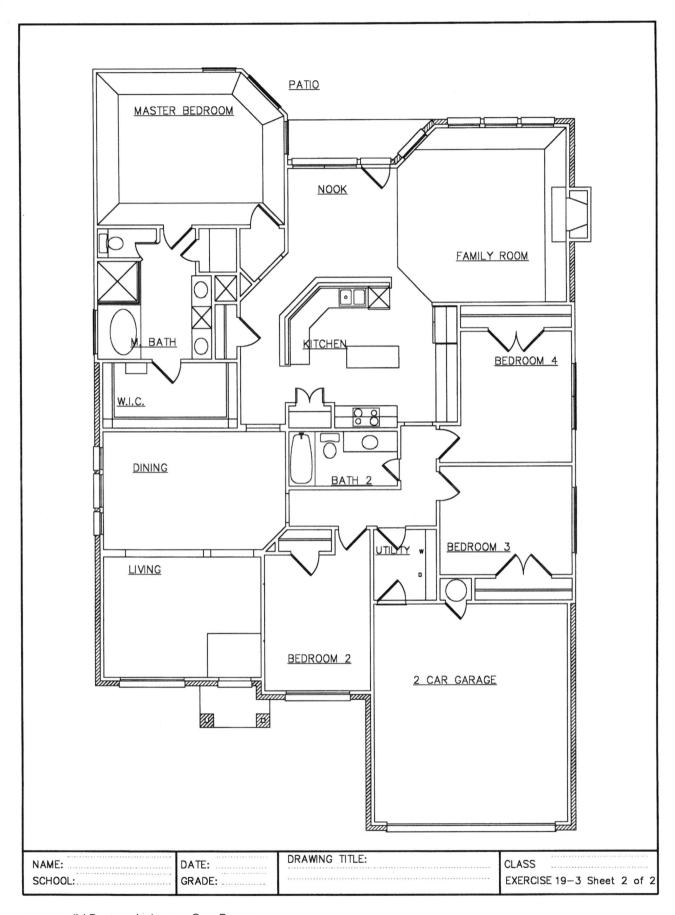

PATIO

MASTER BEDROOM

NOOK

FAMILY ROOM

M. BATH

KITCHEN

BEDROOM 4

W.I.C.

DINING

BATH 2

LIVING

UTILITY

W

D

BEDROOM 3

BEDROOM 2

2 CAR GARAGE

NAME:	DATE:	DRAWING TITLE:	CLASS
SCHOOL:	GRADE:		EXERCISE 19−3 Sheet 2 of 2

courtesy JM Designs Architects, Gary Beavers

Kirkpatrick, *Architectural Drawing Using Pencil Sketches and AutoCAD*, © 2002 by Pearson Education, Inc.

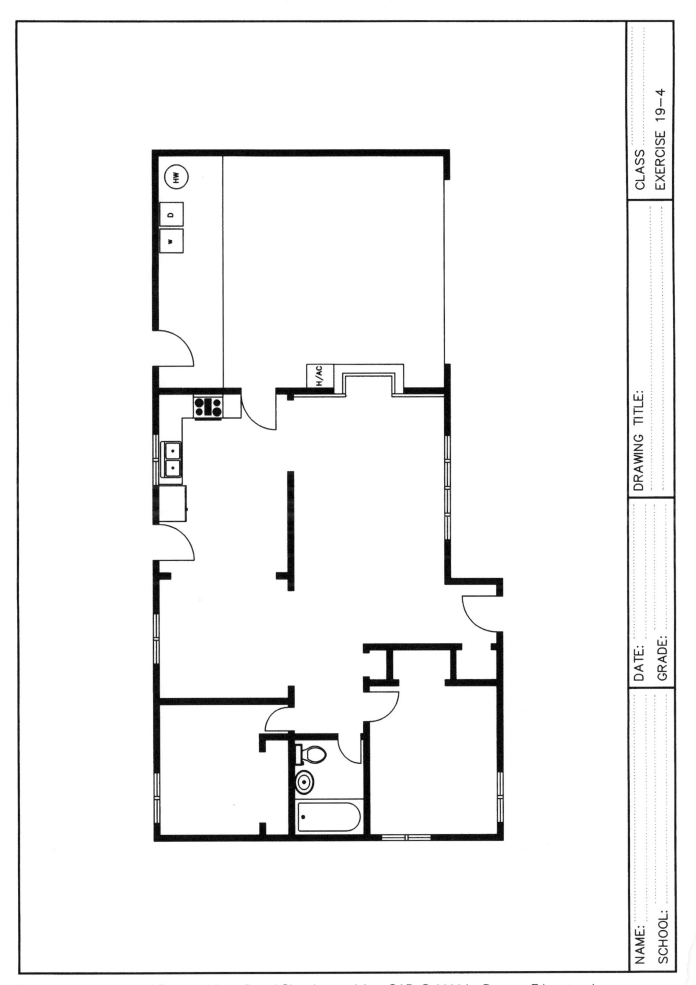

Kirkpatrick, *Architectural Drawing Using Pencil Sketches and AutoCAD*, © 2002 by Pearson Education, Inc.

CLASS

EXERCISE 19—4

DRAWING TITLE:

DATE:

GRADE:

NAME:

SCHOOL:

HW

D

W

H/AC

Index

E

F

G

H

I

K

L

Sketching perpendicular lines, 47
Sketching polygons, 56
Sketching tangents, 47-53
Sketching tools, 13
Snap, 27
Snap, isometric, 189
Software, 11
Spheres in isometric sketching, 175, 199
Surfaces, 90-92
Switches, three-way, 287

T

Tabular dimensioning, 245
Tangent, 43
Tangents, sketching, 47-53
TEDIT, 256, 257
Template, circle, 15
Third-angle orthographic projection, 88
Three-way switch, 287
Tips for AutoCAD users, 32
Toggling to isoplanes, 191
Tools, sketching, 13-15
Triangles, 14, 15
Trim command, 65, 115
Types of drawings, 4-7

U

Undo, 32
Unidirectional dimensioning, 224
Units, 26

V

Vertical dimensions, 255
Video monitor, 8
Views for orthographic projection, 87-104
Views, aligning, 98
Views, pictorial, 171, 207
Views, sectional, 149, 150
Views, selecting, 98-101

W

Wall section, 166, 168
Wblock, 298
Wood pencil, using, 42

Z

Zip disk, 7
Zoom command, 65
Zoom, window, 66